DESIGN BEYOND THE HUMAN

DESIGN BEYOND THE HUMAN

Transdisciplinary Conversations about the Planet

EDITED BY
ELIO CACCAVALE AND
GORDON HUSH

BLOOMSBURY VISUAL ARTS
LONDON • NEW YORK • OXFORD • NEW DELHI • SYDNEY

BLOOMSBURY VISUAL ARTS
Bloomsbury Publishing Plc, 50 Bedford Square, London, WC1B 3DP, UK
Bloomsbury Publishing Inc, 1385 Broadway, New York, NY 10018, USA
Bloomsbury Publishing Ireland, 29 Earlsfort Terrace, Dublin 2, D02 AY28, Ireland

BLOOMSBURY, BLOOMSBURY VISUAL ARTS and the Diana logo are trademarks of Bloomsbury Publishing Plc

First published in Great Britain 2026

Cover design: Matteo Morelli
Cover image © Apollo 11 Mission-Roll-Frame AS11-36-5339.
Image courtesy of the Earth Science and Remote Sensing Unit, NASA Johnson Space Center; https://eol.jsc.nasa.gov/

A catalogue record for this book is available from the British Library.

Library of Congress Cataloging-in-Publication Data
Names: Caccavale, Elio, editor. | Hush, Gordon, editor.
Title: Design beyond the human : transdisciplinary conversations about the planet / edited by Elio Caccavale and Gordon Hush.
Description: London ; New York : Bloomsbury Visual Arts, 2025. | Includes bibliographical references and index.
Identifiers: LCCN 2025011420 | ISBN 9781350338074 (hardback) | ISBN 9781350338067 (paperback) | ISBN 9781350338081 (epub) | ISBN 9781350338098 (pdf)
Subjects: LCSH: Architecture–Environmental aspects. | Architectural design–Philosophy. | Sustainable development. | Human ecology.
Classification: LCC NA2542.35 .D4585 2025 | DDC 720.1/03--dc23/eng/20250510
LC record available at https://lccn.loc.gov/2025011420.

ISBN: HB: 978-1-3503-3807-4
PB: 978-1-3503-3806-7
ePDF: 978-1-3503-3809-8
eBook: 978-1-3503-3808-1

Typeset by Deanta Global Publishing Services, Chennai, India
Printed and bound in India

For product safety related questions contact productsafety@bloomsbury.com.

To find out more about our authors and books visit www.bloomsbury.com and sign up for our newsletters.

CONTENTS

FIGURES

FOREWORD

Erin O'Donnell

Water is life. Rivers breathe, in and out, ebb and flow, to their own rhythms. The pulse of life carried by floodwaters connects vast landscapes, bringing species together and triggering new life as fish spawn, birds nest and frogs clasp each other excitedly in "amplexus". Rivers are carried far out to sea in the bodies of eels and migratory fish as they travel to distant breeding grounds. Slender, glasslike elvers reconnect the ocean to the river as they return upstream once more. Rivers are umbilical cords, connecting all of us to Mother Earth. Water is alive. Rivers are living waters, spiritual entities, ancient serpents and ancestral beings. First Law, the laws of the First Peoples (Indigenous Peoples), has always known rivers as living entities. Humans have lived with rivers in mutual obligation and reciprocity relationships for tens of thousands of years. As Bawaka Country et al. explain, First Peoples not only 'Care *for* Country, but Care *as* Country' (2013, 185).

Water has rights. Western law is finally catching on. Rivers around the world are being recognized in (Western or settler state) law as legal persons, legal subjects and living entities. In doing so, the law creates an opportunity for all of us to renew, reset and rebuild our relationships with rivers. These profound legal changes are the foundation of this new relationship, but their transformative potential cuts both ways. When rivers become legal persons, we can become trapped in an adversarial relationship, defined by an individualist conflict between competing rights. Alternatively, the new river persons can inspire us to understand and value our mutual interdependence and a relationship defined by an ethic of care.

Rivers are not alone in gaining new legal rights and status. Natural entities in many countries, including mountains, national parks, lakes, wetlands, glaciers and all of nature, have become legal subjects. As these new legal powers require us to begin to reset our relationships with more-than-human nature, during an era defined by the climate crisis and unprecedented biodiversity loss, so much is at stake. How do we choose the right path and create the relationship that best supports our joyfully entangled interdependence? Can we set aside the modern ideology that 'has worked to divide and erode deep relationalities, producing unsustainable and unjust worlds' (Akama, Light and Kamihira 2020, 1)? By stepping beyond the human-centred design approach that dominates our lives, design informed by an appreciation of what lies *beyond the human* can offer us a set of tools that elucidates and supports the interconnected nature of being.

We tend to think of design as quintessentially human, in that we use it to craft and create the world *we* envision, but the desire and capacity to design is also something we share with many other species. Mushrooms design and construct 'wood wide webs' of mycelia, responsive to the needs and desires of both the fungi and the trees they connect (Rhodes 2017, 331). Tiny tropical fish create extraordinary, mathematically precise, circular patterns in the sand to attract a mate, relying on their design's perfection. Bowerbirds collect and display jewel-like objects; weaverbirds knit grass stems into elegant nests that combine function with beautiful form; termites design large citadels precisely oriented to the sun and the wind; and spiders weave silken snares. Viruses are little more than living, weaponized blueprints, imprinting their design into the intracellular workings of their hosts.

Every species experiences the world differently, depending on the senses we have and how we use them. Even when we share the same space, the unique experience of each species and the meaning we assign to the sensory inputs ensure that our *Umwelten* are distinct, even as they may overlap. These 'lively entanglements of humans and other creatures' (Schroer 2021, 133) mean that our designs are also entangled. As biologist von Uexküll described it, '[e]very subject spins out, like the spider's threads, its relations to certain qualities of things and weaves them into a solid web, which carries its existence' (2010, 53). Design is an embodiment of these relations, imprinted onto the specific world we each experience.

When we change our own *Umwelt*, we also affect the *Umwelten* of other species. From this perspective, design has always been a more-than-human endeavour, although mostly unintentionally. Human cities redesign entire landscapes, paving over floodplains, channelling rivers and replacing woodlands with towering glass and steel constructs. In our urban spaces, it is easy to believe that human design has swept away the *Umwelten* of all who previously shared this space, but even here, the more-than-human persists. Peregrines nest at the apex of skyscrapers, rock pigeons cluster under bridges, possums invade the interstitial spaces of our homes and foxes slink down alleyways after dark. Our designs remain entangled with other lives even when we create a space solely for human benefit. Of course, the persistence of more-than-human life in anthropocentric designs should not obscure the dark side of design. Human design is a way to control the world, to remake it in an image of our choosing. Unsurprisingly, design is also a key feature of colonialism. Invaders and colonists established their identity in the colonized Country by re-creating the designs of buildings, towns, industries, technology and food production of their country of origin. Design has a normative function in these settings: the displacement of the designs and technology of Indigenous Peoples is underpinned by the (erroneous) belief that colonial designs are more advanced, more efficient, more effective, *better*. Too late, colonial societies learn the limits of their ability to impose their will on the world they have stolen. As the planet warms, species vanish and human societies are increasingly experiencing natural disasters wrought by the systems of capitalism, imperialism and white supremacy, we are all at risk of failed design.

But design offers hope too. In this book, diverse authors from many countries, disciplines and lived experiences engage in a transdisciplinary, transcultural conversation on the possibility of design to transform humanity's relationship(s) with the living world. Design that reaches beyond the human helps us chart a path out of the quagmire of the Capitalocene/Anthropocene (Moore 2017) and can restore our relations with the world around us. The collection begins by acknowledging that humans are not alone. Despite a history of industrialized, anthropocentric design processes, we remain symbiotically entangled with the world around us. We remain Country, and acknowledging this enables us to restore joy, wonder and connection as central design themes. Part II sets out an agenda for design beyond the human and beyond the Anthropocene. From deep time to deep space, this collection explores new life-centred, relational design frameworks. Finally, in Part III, authors showcase ideas for how design can help to mediate human and non-human relationships, with the potential to bring us back into 'good relations'.

As a process, design connects thinking and doing. It is reflexive: even as we shape and create our designs, they shape us in turn. When we turn our (human) minds to the more-than-human world, we can begin to identify and fix the problems of our own making. From the smallest of scales (installing nest boxes in trees for birds and possums) to the engineering marvels of landscaped wildlife highway crossings and fish ladders that traverse large dams, design can empower us to reconnect with ourselves and the world. In returning to rivers, which in many countries have been hammered into straight lines, the soft, dynamic riverscape replaced by concrete channels, design that goes beyond the human is starting to shape a re-wilding of rivers. This is partly achieved through engineered re-meandering but also through co-design with more-than-human collaborators through the re-introduction of beavers. This collection of essays goes beyond seeking solutions to the problems confronting us today. Instead, *Design Beyond the Human* brings many voices together from across the world to showcase the power of design to reconnect people and Place, as well as to restore our relationships with the more-than-human world.

References

Akama, Yoko, Ann Light and Takahito Kamihira. 'Expanding Participation to Design with More-Than-Human Concerns'. In *Proceedings of the 16th Participatory Design Conference 2020 – Participation(s) Otherwise Volume 1 (PDC '20)*. New York: Association for Computing Machinery, 2020, 1–11. https://doi.org/10.1145/3385010.3385016

Bawaka Country, et al. 'Caring as Country: Towards an Ontology of Co-Becoming in Natural Resource Management'. *Asia Pacific Viewpoint* 54, no. 2 (2013): 185–97. https://doi.org/10.1111/apv.12018

Moore, Jason W. 'The Capitalocene, Part I: On the Nature and Origins of Our Ecological Crisis'. *The Journal of Peasant Studies* 44, no. 3 (2017): 594–630. https://doi.org/10.1080/03066150.2016.1235036

Rhodes, Cristopher. 'The Whispering World of Plants: The Wood Wide Web'. *Science Progress* 100, no. 3 (2017): 331–7. https://doi.org/10.3184/003685017X14968299580423

Schroer, Sara Asu. 'Jakob von Uexküll: The Concept of Umwelt and its Potentials for an Anthropology beyond the Human'.' *Ethnos* 86, no. 1 (2021): 132–52 Doi.org/10.1080/00141844.2019.1606841.

von Uexküll, Jakob. A For*ay into the Worlds of Animals and Humans with a Theory of Meaning*, translated by Joseph D. O'Neil. Minneapolis: University of Minnesota Press, 2010.

ACKNOWLEDGEMENTS

First and foremost, this book would not have been possible without the support of all contributors. The arguments you find in this edited volume owe everything to them. So, our debt of gratitude goes to (in alphabetical order): Samer Akkach, Rachel Armstrong, Priyanka Bista, Joanna Boehnert, Danielle Celermajer, Domitilla Dardi, Matthew Darmour-Paul, Kate Fletcher, Helen Hollyman, Desiree Hernandez Ibinarriaga, Noboru Ishikawa, Steve McMullen, J. Paul Neeley, François-Xavier Nzi iyo Nsenga, Erinma Ochu, Erin O'Donnell, John Powell, James Skeet, Xinlin Song, Kris Spiros, Peter Sutoris, Alice Twemlow, Felipe Viveros, Naiyi Wang and Caroline Ward. Our conversations with them and their work have enriched the ability to put this volume together in inspiring ways. We are deeply thankful for their willingness to engage with us in this transdisciplinary and planetary project that spills across borders both earthly and conceptually. A thank you also to Matteo Morelli for the cover design and to the Earth Science and Remote Sensing Unit, NASA Johnson Space Center, for letting us use the Apollo 11 Mission-Roll-Frame AS11-36-5339 image for the book cover. We would like to thank Bloomsbury, and Publisher and Commissioning Editor, Louise Baird-Smith for her unwavering support and believing in our initial proposal. We want to thank our editorial assistant Joseph Skingsley for helping us turn these pages from manuscript proposal to book. We want to thank our families, especially Tareena, Mylo (EC) and Pamela (GH). We are forever grateful for their limitless support. Last but not least, we want to thank The Glasgow School of Art for the opportunity to author this volume and our colleagues and students for their greatest inspiration.

INTRODUCTION

Elio Caccavale and Gordon Hush

National Aeronautics and Space Administration (NASA) astronauts Michael Collins, Neil Armstrong and Buzz Aldrin carried out a mission to the Moon and back again from 16 July to 24 July 1969. They viewed the Earth from afar on their way to the Moon and saw it from a novel perspective. This view of the Earth from space triggered what space philosopher Frank White called an 'overview effect' (1988), which transformed the crew's perception of both our planet and their own existence. Mission documentation of the conversations between Apollo 11 astronauts and NASA Mission Control gives a unique insight into what it was like to see the Earth from space. Neil Armstrong spoke about feeling very small, while during an interview for the online radio show *Pulse of the Planet* to celebrate the fiftieth anniversary of Apollo 11 landing on the Moon, Michael Collins described the Earth using the following words:

> It is hard to see life on Earth from the lunar distance, which is roughly a quarter of a million miles. But you do see a beautiful object. One very small – about the size of your thumbnail if you hold your arm out at length in front of you. It is primarily a blue and white Earth. It is predominantly the white of the clouds and the blue of the ocean that you see. And it gleams; it glistens in the sunlight. It is a very beautiful small little globe, and above all, it conveys a feeling of fragility. I used to think that the Earth was a rugged place. Having seen it from a great distance, I don't have that feeling of ruggedness or strength. I have the feeling it is very small; it is interconnected. I have the feeling that we go about our business without really caring for the fragility of the Earth. (Collins 2019)

In 1827, the mathematician and physicist Joseph Fourier published an article titled *On the Temperature of the Earth and Planetary Spaces*, arguing that the Earth should be colder and that solar radiation from the Sun did not solely drive the temperature of the planet but that it was also kept warm by having an atmosphere. His finding was the first understanding of the concept of a *greenhouse effect* – though he never used the term (Fleming 1999). Fast-forward to 2026: global temperatures are rising at an unprecedented rate, and countries are continuing to debate how to fight climate change and its consequences. These negotiations have produced many international environmental agreements, reports and declarations, including the Montreal Protocol 'to protect the ozone layer' (1987), the *Our Common Future Report* (also known as the Brundtland Report) 'aimed at redefining economic development in terms of sustainable development' (1987), the Rio Declaration on Environment and Development 'to guide countries in future sustainable development' (1992), the Kyoto Protocol 'to reduce greenhouse gas emissions' (1997), the United Nations (UN) seventeen Sustainable Development Goals (SDGs) 'to balance the economic, social and ecological dimensions of sustainable development' (2015), the Paris Agreement 'for climate change mitigation, adaptation and finance' (2015), the many

State of the Global Climate Reports published by the World Meteorological Organization that show 'the planetary scale changes on land, in the ocean and in the atmosphere caused by greenhouse gases' and *Assessment Reports* produced by the UN Intergovernmental Panel on Climate Change 'to document the latest scientific and socio-economic knowledge on climate change, its impacts and future risks, and strategies for reducing the rate at which climate change is taking place', the Glasgow Climate Pact Agreement 'to curb greenhouse gas emissions' (2021), the Declaration on Forests and Land Use developed during the Glasgow UN Climate Change Conference (COP26) 'to stop, and reverse, forest loss and land degradation' (2021) and the most recent United Arab Emirates COP28 Climate and Health Declaration 'to transition away from fossil fuels' (2023). However, despite intensified diplomacy and discussions, our planet is still facing devastating consequences caused by the impact of human activities.

We are officially in the *Holocene* epoch (from the Greek for 'completely new'), which started 11,700 years ago, marking the end of the Ice Age (Cookson 2023). Nevertheless, in 2000, atmospheric chemist Paul Crutzen and limnologist Eugene F. Stoermer published an article in the Newsletter of the International Geosphere-Biosphere Programme, proposing that human activities had so profoundly altered the planet as to push it into a new geological epoch – the *Anthropocene* (after the Greek 'anthropos', for 'human', and 'cene', meaning 'recent' or 'new'). According to researchers from the Anthropocene Working Group, we now live in a new geological era distinguished by human activity and evident in the accumulation of greenhouse gases acting upon global climate, loss of biodiversity and the irreversible damage caused by the over-consumption of natural resources (Zalasiewicz et al. 2017). For the time being, the Anthropocene remains a theory without official scientific recognition (Fremaux 2019). However, acknowledging the many years scientists have spent discussing when and how Humanity began altering the Earth, the scientific community has recently chosen Crawford Lake in Canada to represent the Anthropocene with an official declaration starting in August 2024 (McCarthy et al. 2023). As reported in an online article published by the journal *Nature*, the lake contains sediments, such as 'chemical traces of the fallout from nuclear bombs and other forms of environmental degradation'. The article also explains, 'Lake Crawford's Anthropocene marker would join similar sites designating other geological time boundaries. A spot in the Greenland ice sheet, for example, designates the beginning of the Holocene epoch, 11,700 years ago' (Witze 2023).

Crucially, the consequences for the planetary climate and ecosystem, can be seen to have been exacerbated by the predominance of capitalism and the emergence of a truly global economy over the last 200 years, as many planetary citizens have improved their 'quality of life'. The condition of human life-support systems has long been of great concern to many scientists. They believe that, with present aggregate consumption levels, Humanity cannot be supported indefinitely on our single, finite planet. The potential consequences were emphasized in the 1992 'World Scientists' Warning to Humanity' letter published by The Union of Concerned Scientists, which was endorsed by over 1,700 leading scientists, including more than half of the living Nobel laureates in science. It stated in part:

> Human beings and the natural world are on a collision course. Human activities inflict harsh and often irreversible damage to the environment and critical resources. If not checked, many of our current practices put at serious risk the future that we wish for human society, the planet and animal kingdoms, and many so alter the living world that it will be unable to sustain life in the manner that we know. Fundamental changes are urgent to avoid the collision our present course will bring about. (Kendall 1992, 1)

Anthropocentrism refers to an approach to existence that places humans at the centre of everything and makes 'us' the most important measure of all things. The inherent assumption of human superiority and centrality has resulted in environmental degradation, species extinction and the abusive treatment of non-humans. Environmental anthropologist Georgette Leah Burns explains, 'Humans have been comfortable and largely unchallenged in these superior roles for too long. The state of the planet is now challenging our sense of mastery over nature, causing us to question its effect and search for alternative paths to a sustainable future' (2014, 12). While the idea that humans have become one of the dominant factors in shaping planet Earth is not new, the Anthropocene concept is one of the latest and most influential constructs attempting to convey this insight. Previous concepts range from geologist Antonio Stoppani's Anthropozoic Era (1873), biochemist Vladimir Vernadsky, philosopher and mathematician Édouard Le Roy and philosopher and palaeontologist Pierre Teilhard de Chardin's Noosphere (1922), sociologist William Catton's Homo Colossus (1980), science and environmental writer Andrew Revkin's Anthrocene (1992), and conservationist Michael Samways's Homogenocene (1999), to the more recent Great Acceleration (Schimel et al. 2007).

Many scholars would argue that discussing the Anthropocene as a challenge to all humankind avoids a conversation about *who* is historically responsible for the 'state shifts' in planetary natures and, most importantly, what processes drive these shifts (Barnosky et al. 2012). It can be argued that the Anthropocene is a historical moment that denies/reduces/erases difference, the substantive expression of the human (gender/class, etc.) – a perverse reduction of the concept of 'species being' (Marx) to *homo economicus*. Environmental philosopher Anne Fremaux and Professor of Green Political Economy John Barry argue that the concept of the Anthropocene 'erases issues of class, gender, race and geographical position, as an undifferentiated Humanity faces the planet' (2019, 2). Thus, global warming, over-consumption, biodiversity loss, deforestation and desertification may not be attributed to an abstract concept of Humanity, the *Anthropos* (Moore 2017). Indeed, these ecological blights are predominantly the negative consequences of the capitalist mode of production and ideology; therefore, they are not just geological and, thus, *Anthropogenic*, but specifically *Capitalogenic* (Moore 2016; Haraway 2016). As philosopher, anthropologist and sociologist Bruno Latour (2014, 139) points out:

> The 'Anthropos' of the Anthropocene is not exactly anybody, it is made of highly localised networks of some individual bodies whose responsibility is staggering . . .
>
> This dispersion of the 'Anthropos' into specific historical and local networks, actually gives a lot of weight to the other candidate for naming the same period of geohistory, that of 'capitalocene', a swift way to ascribe this responsibility to whom and to where it belongs.

Many scholars have critiqued both the human-centredness and the economic and geographical specificity of the term 'Anthropocene'. For instance, Professor in the History of Consciousness Donna Haraway uses the term 'Chthulucene' (2015) to describe our epoch as one which is defined precisely by not being able to think of humans as removed from the rest of life on Earth or dominant over it. Regarding those with whom humans share the planet, conservation biologist Kieran Suckling uses the term 'Homogenocene' (2015) to emphasize that our era is characterized by increasing homogenization caused by a strong human impact on the environment. Postcolonial studies scholar Dipesh Chakrabarty also supports this argument by suggesting, 'The contingent history of our falling into the Anthropocene cannot be defined by recourse to the idea of species, for the Anthropocene would not have been possible, even as a theory, without the history of industrialisation' (2009, 219). There is also the term 'Plantationocene' (Haraway et al. 2016), which has gained traction in the environmental humanities, and which, according to Haraway, refers to 'The devastating transformation of diverse kinds of human-tended farms, pastures, and forests into extractive and enclosed plantations, relying on slave labour and other forms of exploited, alienated, and usually spatially transported labour' (2015, 162). Furthermore, biologist and naturalist Edward O. Wilson suggests that we should name our era the Eremocene (2016), the age of loneliness, acknowledging biodiversity extinctions and loss (Martin 2014). The range of terms and definitions that parallel or echo the Anthropocene tell their own story, such as Anthrobscene (Parikka 2014), Manthropocene (Raworth 2014), Carbonocene (LeCain 2015), Necrocene (McBrien 2016), Neganthropocene (Stiegler 2018), Technocene (Martins 2018) and Anthropo-Not-Seen (de la Cadena 2019), to mention but a few. It is little surprise that Latour points out in the essay 'Telling Friends from Foes at the Time of the Anthropocene' that 'the very notion of the Anthropocene is indeed an enormous source of confusion' (2014, 13).

The scholarly tendency to categorize and compartmentalize itself betrays a problem, with the aspiration towards a seemingly universal terminological framework contradicting the richness of existence and our experience(s) of the world. The inherent homogeneity at the heart of such a linguistic and scientific project sits at odds with the ambitions of this volume: the stimulation of a 'planetary conversation' is born of the heterogeneous differences in discourse and method contained within the transdisciplinary engagement. *Design Beyond the Human* wishes to consider precisely who has benefitted from this putative mastery, and who – both human and non-human – has suffered under the rhetorics of evolution, development and progress, understood as the material enrichment of 'Humanity'. The centrality of the human/nature antinomy to capitalist and neoliberal self-understanding is exposed by historian and geographer Jason W. Moore:

> Our reality is one in which humans live in a peculiar kind of civilisation, capitalism. Capitalism is absurd in all sorts of ways. In terms of this discussion, one absurdity is especially powerful: capitalism is premised on the separation of Humanity and Nature. The whole thrust of capitalist civilisation develops the premise that we inhabit something called Society, and act upon something called Nature. (2017, 600)

The nineteenth century's industrialization has exponentially advanced Humanity, technologically and materially. However, for obvious reasons linked to imperialism and colonialism, the attendant benefits and consequences are most evident in distinct parts of the world. Historian and philosopher Yuval Noah Harari writes in *Sapiens: A Brief History of Humankind*:

> The Industrial Revolution opened new ways to convert energy and produce goods, liberating humankind from its dependence on the surrounding ecosystem. Humans cut down forests, drained swamps, dammed rivers, flooded plains, laid down hundreds of thousands of railroad tracks, and built skyscrapers and metropolises. As the world was moulded to fit the need of *Homo sapiens*, habitats were destroyed, and species went extinct. Our once again green and blue planet is becoming a concrete and plastic shopping centre. (2015, 392)

Correspondingly, as design theorist and philosopher Tony Fry points out, 'Claims that modernity brought us universal progress are purely Eurocentric and blind to its ambiguities and contradictions. Modernity did not merely unsettle the world and many of its people, but in many ways devastated it' (2017, 6). As such, it may be argued that a specific group of humans is responsible for many irreparable environmental disasters (and their reparation). Take, for example, the devastating consequence for the environment and local communities of the 60,000 tonnes of fast-fashion used clothing dumped from Europe, America, and Asia in the Atacama Desert in Northern Chile (Bartlett 2024), or the Chernobyl (1986) and Fukushima (2011) nuclear disasters or the Great Pacific Garbage Patch (also known as the Pacific Trash Vortex), which is a floating island consisting of microplastic waste and debris located somewhere in the ocean between California and the Hawaiian Islands. While many different types of trash enter the ocean, most of the debris forming the patch comes from consumer products, commercial by-products and industrial fishing used in the 'Global North' – for example, plastic bags, nylon fishing nets, bottle caps and water bottles. Once in the water, single-use plastic breaks down into tiny particles that impact wildlife health – and the ocean's ability to store carbon.

According to a study published in the science and medicine open-access mega journal *PLoS One*, there are over 170 trillion plastic particles afloat in the world's oceans – scientists refer to this 'plasticized' marine environment as the Plastisphere (Zettler 2013), which is home to plastic-colonizing organisms such as bacteria, fungi, crabs and jellyfish, capable of breaking down polyethylene terephthalate and thriving in this unique disastrous human-made oceanic environment (Eriksen et al. 2023). Unsurprisingly, microplastics have also been detected in the human body (Amato-Lourenço et al. 2021; Ragusa et al. 2021; Leslie et al. 2022) and most recently, as reported by a paper published in *Environmental Chemistry Letters*, even in clouds around Japan's Mount Fuji and Mount Oyama (Wang et al. 2023). These examples are a clear indication that since the rise of the plastic industry in the early decades of the twentieth century, human impact on the environment has caused unimaginable damage, destroying habitats, harming wildlife and contaminating the food chain with plastic pollution, not to mention that most plastic is made from fossil fuels such as crude oil, itself a significant driver of the climate crisis. As stated in the *Plastic Waste Makers Index: Revealing the Source of the Single-Use Plastics Crisis Report* produced by the Minderoo Foundation, 'Of approximately three hundred single-use polymer producers operating globally, just twenty account for more than half of all single-use plastic waste generated globally and the top hundred account for over 90 per cent, this small fraction holds the fate of the world's plastic crisis in their hands' (Charles et al. 2021, 31).

Even when we leave our planet for distant explorations, we irresponsibly damage the outer space environment or other planets. Scientists caution that the environmental impact of human activities is extending beyond Earth, prompting calls for the recognition of a 'Lunar Anthropocene' (Holcomb et al. 2023). As documented by the European Space Agency, millions of debris objects are floating in space along with trash left behind by astronauts during Moon explorations, from food packaging, flags, golf balls, used wet wipes and packets of human urine to tools and lunar vehicles. Imagine if everyone disposed of garbage on the streets, and no one cleaned it up. After a while, no one would be able to walk anywhere anymore. This is what is happening in the ocean, in outer space, on the Moon and on Mars. Nevertheless, one might argue that it is all worth it, if only for the pleasure of using handheld cordless vacuums, wireless headsets and camera phones, which were technologies initially developed for space exploration, or paving the way for Richard Branson's Virgin Galactic, Jeff Bezos' Blue Origin and Elon Musk's SpaceX commercialization and exploitation of planetary outer space.

In 1955, the American industrial designer Henry Dreyfuss wrote the seminal book *Designing for People*, in which he illustrated a collection of ergonomic reference charts providing precise specifications for design. The book paved the way for the discipline of Human Factors, which has contributed to the rise of many research approaches popularized during the 1980s, 1990s and 2000s, including User-Centred Design (UCD) and Human-Centred Design (HCD). It is important to acknowledge that HCD has improved many people's lives, especially when engaging with user or human experience, efficiency, usability, productivity or even delight. However, considering its provenance, it is sufficient to say that

HCD's conceptualization reflects an Anglophone and Eurocentric way of thinking about life, which has for many years neglected the idea that a plurality of peoples inhabits our planet with different ways of inhabiting, knowing, learning and understanding, which as explained by Professor of Social Anthropology and contributor to this collection Noboru Ishikawa, 'have their own paths of endogenous development, rather than the growth of per capita income or population' (Haraway et al. 2015, 543).

Equally, the aspirations of UCD or HCD are not inherently bad, and they were not formulated as ways of duping design students, practitioners or consumers – they were part of a reaction against the Modernist canon; they were about saying that other forms of value, experiential and interactive, were as important as form and function. However, their philosophical ambition has been captured and converted into consumer demand, need and even pleasure, all too often. Furthermore, as we continue to gain a deeper understanding of the human impact on global health, it has become clear that the HCD celebrated in the Western world has challenged our planet's ability to support life as it used to do. HCD has been focused at the level of consumer behaviours rather than the human species, leading Don Norman to revise the concept to *Humanity*-Centred Design (2021). Arguably, Humanity has been sub-divided, even as it has built global organizations, such as the UN (1945), the UN Educational, Scientific and Cultural Organization (1945), the World Health Organization (1948) or the World Trade Organization (1995). This sub-division is predicated upon who is permitted the utilization of resources, as well as who has to move, surrender ancestral lands and ways of life and witness the global systems of resource extraction annihilate what formed over geological epochs and had previously sustained civilizations and ways of living for millennia.

Those who are dispossessed are with us still. In shifting the exotic, the primitive or the 'other' from the realm of culture (civilization) into the realm of Nature, they can be de-legitimated, removed from law and rights and re-positioned (geographically) to a less inconvenient location – the link between land and life, people and place can be re-drawn in seemingly arbitrary fashion. The safari parks of Africa and the reservations 'granted' to Indigenous peoples in America and Australia serve to remind us – as do items on display in museums – of how we, and others, used to live (Appadurai 2020). In re-positioning these 'other' people, we can appear to be distinct, distinguished or even alone, and the separation of production from consumption through global supply chains merely supports this pretence, as it serves to outsource the environmental consequences of our way of living.

Design Beyond the Human argues that if design is to be relevant to the way we relate to and sustain our planet now and in the future, it must keep in mind not only a selected group of humans, who share and benefit from the current economic and cultural model, but Humanity as a whole, and also other species and ecosystems. You may be asking, why the diverse voices of this collection are gathered in response to *design*. It is precisely design's historical centrality to the logic and language of the 'Global North's' techno-industrial culture and its mechanistic and binary (human/non-human) worldview, which positions nature within the realm of production, capital investment and 'value extraction' (Mazzucato 2019). As such, Professor of Environmental Biology and Member of the Citizen Potawatomi Nation Robin Wall Kimmerer reminds us, 'One must just think about how we speak of the land as "natural resources" or "ecosystem services" as if the lives of other beings were our property' (2013, 383). This is most evident in the way our planet has been geologically classified, as Professor of Inhumane Geography Kathryn Yusoff explains in *A Billion Black Anthropocenes or None*, 'Geological classification enabled the transformation of territory into a readable map of resources and organised the apprehension of extraction and the designation of extractable territories' (2018, 89). Another source of insight is philosopher Hannah Arendt's seminal book *The Human Condition*, an exploration of political philosophy on the various manifestations of human activity that relate humans to one another and to the material world. Arendt suggests that humans' being-in-the-world had been disrupted in the modern age, resulting in alienation from the common, artefactual human world and from nature (1958).

Take, for example, smartphones; they represent the perfect techno-utopian artefact. They allow us to make our life easier – we can watch movies, send emails, play games, check bank statements, take pictures, order food or even choose a dating partner – all in one device. But at what cost? According to an online article published by the World Economic Forum (WEF), 'There are more mobile phones than people in the world, with a life expectancy of up to five–ten years; however, most consumers in the 'Global North' use them for an average of only twelve months' (Richter 2023). In most cases, electronic devices originate in remote mines in Africa, India, Brazil or China, with the extraction of minerals causing devastating environmental consequences or human rights abuses, and they end up in landfills, such as the Baogang Tailings Dam in Inner Mongolia, or Agbogbloshie in Ghana, one of the world's largest e-waste dumping sites. This is also the case for solar panels or lithium-ion batteries used to power electric vehicles, build wind farms and store grid-scale electricity. The urgency in extracting lithium, nickel, copper, manganese, cobalt and other metals has produced an extensive sourcing and mining industry, including deep-sea mining, causing irreversible environmental damage. If using electric cars means an enormous amount of mining, refining and the various polluting activities that come with it, naturally, one might ask whether they are environmentally sound or not, regardless that much of the power used to charge car batteries still comes from fossil fuels (Riofrancos 2021). The devastating environmental impact of electronic devices has been documented by Geography Professor Josh Lepawsky with the Reassembling Rubbish research project at Memorial University of Newfoundland:

> By the 2030–40s, if the rates continue, consumers will discard in excess of 100 million tonnes of electronic devices globally per year . . .
>
> Of course, one of the most pressing concerns is the way in which devices like mobile phones, laptops, desktops, tablets, and the networks that they run on contribute to climate breakdown. Apple's environmental sustainability reports are particularly illuminating here. The company is sure to emphasise its progress towards sustainability – but its own data in these reports show, for example, that over eighty per cent of the carbon footprint of the latest iPhone comes from manufacturing it while only fourteen per cent arises from its use. (2018, 19–21)

The idea that design requires a *planetary perspective*, rather than a disciplinary or industrial viewpoint, is gaining traction (Escobar 2018; Fry 2020). Only an acknowledgement of the interconnected, historical processes that have built global capitalism will reveal the structural causes of 'unsustainment' (Fry 2003, *passim*) and its threat to the very concept of 'the future', for multiple species, including, perhaps, our own, while obliging specific human populations to experience climate changes, desertification and sea-level rise. *Design Beyond the Human* endeavours to generate a transdisciplinary debate capable of charting the critical and conceptual territory required to respond to this emerging eventuality, its intellectual scale and its looming consequences:

> These massive defuturing effects amount to a civilisational crisis. Everywhere one looks, we see instances of life being destroyed, the planet being wounded, its people being exploited and damaged. Confronted with this dramatic situation, only strategies aiming to recreate and strengthen local and regional capabilities to heal and sustain the web of life seems to make any sense. It is

> imperative that humans regain their ability to see and make otherwise, so as to make plural futures again possible. As a form of agency, design/ing is central to this historical conjuncture. (Escobar 2020, 24–5)

Only by facilitating a transdisciplinary conversation can design, as an academic pursuit or a material practice, disassociate itself from its disciplinary past and its implication in capitalist extraction, imperial projects and ecological catastrophe. In assembling voices from around the globe, from within and beyond the academy, across a multitude of disciplines, practices, professions and lived experiences, we seek to engender just such a vital discussion:

> [Design] has been squarely situated within that world – hetero-patriarchal, modern, capitalist, racist – that is today in crisis; it has also been a paramount agency of that crisis. If one accepts that today's conjuncture is one of the modern problems for which modernity is unable to provide effective solutions, this means that design is itself deeply in crisis (Fry and Nocek 2021). This double historicity-being itself in crisis, and being located within a world in crisis-confers upon design a particularly problematic, but potentially significant, role. The question arises: Is a significant onto-epistemic reorientation of design possible? (Escobar 2020, 24–5)

In navigating or un-picking this 'double conjuncture' in search of the 'onto-epistemic reorientation of design', those of us working within design, with designers or practising as designers will be required to build intellectual alliances, seek new conceptual frameworks and collaborate across disciplines, continents and complex phenomena. The raw materials of such a response can be found in the pages of this book, in the transdisciplinary critique, the interplay between the examples discussed and the voices invited into that discussion, and, crucially, in sketching out what a transformed approach to design and designing might look like – what might be required for its existence, its practice and its transmission to future generations. *Design Beyond the Human* is located on the faultline of anthropologist Arturo Escobar's *double conjuncture*; it is a moment of fracture, where we seek to forge a break with the past born of critique, while assembling the intellectual voices and resources required to create a radically distinct and different future. In recognizing our 'defutured' moment (Fry), the contributors here seek to identify examples of what will be necessary and may be possible if we wish our fragile planet to continue to sustain Humanity and not simply some human populations.

To acknowledge the distinction between Humanity and (some) human beings is to acknowledge the relational participation in the processes of production and consumption, to accept the winners and losers in a historical process that has ravaged the biosphere, to allow inequality to appear natural and deny the kinship of all other living things on Earth. The acquiescence to such anthropocentric thinking is a failure of the imagination and the intellect; it is a failure to comprehend the ecological complexity of existence and create a conceptual approach capable of responding to this. Any perpetuation of the disciplinary segregation of knowledge will undermine the onto-epistemic reorientation of design sought by Escobar. Design and designers must not only accept and acknowledge the ecological consequences of contemporary life, such as global warming, over-consumption, overpopulation, biodiversity loss, deforestation and desertification but also reflect upon the unequal access to designed goods or services and how these shape both life experience and life chances.

Expanding on *An Essay on the Principle of Population*, written by economist Thomas Robert Malthus in 1798, biologists Paul and Anne Ehrlich, who also wrote about unsustainable global human population growth in the book *The Population Bomb* published in 1968 (for reference, when they wrote the book, there were three and a half billion people on Earth; there are now eight billion), write in their more recent volume, *The Dominant Animal: Human Evolution and the Environment*:

> Human beings live in a world of constant changes and always have. But in recent decades, the world has been changing faster than ever before, largely because of human modification of our planet, and the pace is accelerating. Those modifications have, at least temporarily, enabled the power and consumption patterns of a billion or so people to be enormously enhanced and allowed a couple of billion to be doing all right, while leaving a few billion others living in poverty and, often, hopelessness . . .
>
> The remarkable technological accomplishments of modern human beings have had unfortunate, if unintended, consequences. They have not been matched by comparable advances in how wisely we treat one another and our environment. (2009, 3)

Questioning anthropocentrism and 'capitalcentrism' (Gibson-Graham 2006) in design is far more than just an intellectual exercise. Design must cease to be a discourse and discipline of the 'Global North', capable of accommodating its critics and opponents – incorporating, even embracing, feminist, ecological or ideological critique – without substantively altering its relationship to the capitalist mode of production and the ecological consequences it is wreaking upon the globe. In rejecting the existing asymmetry of health, wealth and opportunity in which the inhabitants of our planet are located, we are also rejecting the capitalist rhetoric of a HCD that promises more goods, more services (depending upon your ability to pay) and that passes itself off as *progress*.

This is just as true of emerging technologies and the developing digital economy. The overall carbon emissions from digital services and experiences are vast, and growing: the most obvious evidence for this is that twenty-eight years ago, the internet used 0 per cent of human energy consumption. Today, our digitally mediated interactions use 10 per cent of the world's total electricity, or the same amount that was used to light the entire planet in 1985 (Coupland, Obrist and Basar 2015). Consequently, it is no surprise that Iceland was the first country to use more electricity for mining cryptocurrencies than powering its households (Hern 2018). Likewise, this demand is also driven by the so-called Internet of Things (IoT): the increasing array of everyday devices – from TVs, through domestic security devices, to lighting systems and countless modes of transport – that constantly emit and receive data. The environmental implications of digital technology and its networked infrastructure have been the subject of many studies, primarily related to the extraction of raw materials, chemical use and waste handling. When we think of helping the environment, driving electric vehicles, turning off the light and recycling our electrical appliances all spring to mind long before the idea of taking a selfie, swiping a few profiles on Tinder and Bumble, creating a video on TikTok, spending time in the Metaverse, trading in Cryptocurrency, investing in NFT Art or training Artificial Intelligence (AI) networks. To put this into perspective, an online article published in 2019 by the *MIT Technology Review* reported, 'Researchers at the University of Massachusetts performed a life cycle assessment for training several common large AI models. They found that the process can emit more than 626,000 pounds of carbon dioxide (CO2) equivalent – nearly five times the lifetime emissions of an average car' (Hao 2019).

Every day, people watch more than a billion hours of video online. As claimed by YouTube, the children's video *Baby Shark Dance* has set an internet record with well over thirteen billion views (2025). *Baby Shark Dance* also reached a less celebrated milestone in the process: it consumed as much energy as many 'Global South' countries combined do in an entire year. We are all (in)directly implicated in damaging ecosystems each time we send an email, tweet, post a like, google, watch a video on YouTube, watch a movie or a TV show on Netflix or use digital banking. The BBC online article 'Why Your Internet Habits Are Not as Clean as You Think', affirms that the internet and the systems supporting it account for about 3.7 per cent of global greenhouse emissions (Griffiths 2020). To provide a tangible example, the Amazon Sustainability 2020 Report *Further and Faster Together* states that the online shopping giant alone emitted nearly 61 million metric tons of carbon dioxide in 2020, with an increase of 69 per cent in fossil fuel emissions from the previous year, mainly due to the increased usage of digital services during the Covid-19 pandemic 'lockdowns'. If the internet was a country, there is no doubt that it would be included in the top ten list of countries that emit the most CO2. However, there are significant differences between the 'Global South' and 'Global North' regarding access to and use of digital technologies. As mentioned by the UN Report *Road Map for Digital Cooperation*, 'In 2019, close to 87 per cent of individuals in developed countries used the Internet, compared with only 19 per cent in the least developed countries [. . .] only 53.6 per cent of the world's population now use the Internet, leaving an estimated 3.6 billion without access' (2020, 5).

So, what do all these examples have in common? Most likely, they were developed using the same human-centred value-driven extraction pattern of decision-making. Unsurprisingly, many Fortune 500 companies, 'Global North' design consulting firms and design schools promote, use and teach HCD approaches. Evidence of this can be found on the websites of many organizations. For example (at the time of writing), leading design consultancy IDEO's 'about us' page proclaims, 'As early leaders of Human-Centred Design, we keep people at the centre of our work. It is a key tenet of design thinking, and even as our methods evolve in response to new, complex challenges, we are always designing solutions for people first.' Furthermore, IDEO's co-chair Tim Brown explains, 'Design Thinking is a human-centred approach to innovation that draws from the designer's toolkit to integrate the needs of people, the possibilities of technology, and the requirements for business success.' Another example can be found at Stanford d.school with its Human-Centred Design Philosophy used by 'social sector organisations seeking to bring a meaningful and creative change in the world', or at the Royal College of Art with its Executive Education Programme, which promotes 'a people-focused and user-centric approach to innovation', or in the latest UK Design Council Strategy Report 2020–2024 *Using Design as a Force for Change*, which describes the role and value of design through 'problem-solving, humanity-centred and practical skills' (2020, 6). These examples are a reminder that the concept of human(ity) has become a proxy for inhabitants of a consumer society based in the 'Global North' and engaged in energy-rich behaviours and consumption patterns. In essence, 'a relatively small and wealthy group is responsible for most resource claims and ecological damage and hence for the existential threats faced most severely by impoverished populations' (Rammelt et al. 2022, 214).

Despite the pervasive use of HCD, some hopeful examples indicate that some institutions, design scholars and practitioners are reevaluating a design approach that elevates the needs of humans in the 'Global North' above all else. A growing body of design research and practices is attempting to address the climate crisis and challenge Western human-centrism, variously termed as Autonomous Design (Escobar 2018), Bio-Design (Myers 2012), Bioinclusive Design (Pierre 2017), Biophilic Design (Kellert and Calabrese 2015), Cosmopolitical Design (Yaneva and Zaera-Polo 2017), Cradle to Cradle Design (McDonough and Braungart 2002), Design Activism (Faud-Luke 2009), Ecospheric Design (García-Acosta and Romeva 2010), Geo Design (Chan 2022), Planet-Oriented Design (Tironi et al. 2022), Redirective Design (Fry and Dilnot 2003), Regenerative Design (Lyle 1994), Symbiotic Design (Sánchez Ruano 2016), Systemic Design (Sevaldson 2019) and Transition Design (Irwin et al. 2015). There are also the Decolonising Design Group (2019) and the Design Justice Network (2016), challenging Anglocentric and Eurocentric design ontologies and epistemologies or the Copenhagen Interaction Design Institute, advocating for a Life-Centred Design approach, which aims to address not only human needs but also the increasingly complex interdependencies that exist across all life (Ciid 2022). Another example is the Swiss Design Network Research Summit *Counterparts: Exploring Design Beyond the Human*, organized by the Zurich University of the Arts, which investigated 'human exceptionalism in design, more-than-human ecologies and post-anthropocentric design practices' (2022), and the exhibition *More Than Human* (2025), organized by the Design Museum in London, showcasing projects by designers whose work focuses on the belief that human progress can only thrive in harmony with other species and ecosystems. Similarly, the *Systems-Shifting Design Report* (2021), published by the UK Design Council and the Point People, documenting the work of designers who are exploring new systems of planetary health and wellbeing, and the *Design for Planet Festival*, aiming at 'galvanising and supporting the UK's 1.97 million strong design community to address the climate emergency' (Design Council 2022). Furthermore, the European Union's *Bauhaus of the Sea* initiative (2021), intended to promote an ethical relationship with our coastal regions and oceans, and the Earthshot Prize, inspired by the seventeen UN SDGs, created to incentivize environmental change, or the German museum BIOTOPIA Naturkundemuseum Bayern, which asserts, 'BIOTOPIA's mission is to explore, question and reconfigure the relationships between humans and other living beings. The museum allows visitors to forge a deeper and more caring connection to the place they call home and the species they share it with' (2024). Also in Germany, the Kunstgewerbemuseum (Museum of Decorative Arts) in Berlin has introduced the initiative *More than Human: Design after the Anthropocene* (2024), aiming to explore the complex, multidimensional concept of the more-than-human through pop-up exhibitions, lectures, workshops and discussion panels.

Ironically, even Distinguished Professor Emeritus of Cognitive Science and Psychology and founding director of the Design Lab at the University of California, Don Norman, who is considered the 'godfather' of HCD, argues in his latest book, *Design for a Better World: Meaningful, Sustainable, Humanity Centred* (2023), that designers need to consider Humanity as a whole and how design decisions might affect planetary issues of sustainability, inclusivity, accessibility and representation. Additionally, the frameworks developed by international institutions to ascertain what we think matters most in our lives, such as the Human Development Index (Ul Haq; United Nations Development Programme 1990), the Happy Planet Index (New Economics Foundation 2006), the Thriving Places Index (Centre for Thriving Places 2010), the Better Life Index (Organisation for Economic Co-operation and Development 2011), the Inclusive Wealth Index (United Nations Environment Programme 2012) and the Social Life Index (Social Progress Imperative 2013), are now resources for designers. These approaches and frameworks are perhaps more relevant to the twenty-first century than Gross Domestic Product (GDP) because they relate to sustainable development's social and environmental pillars.

Some governments are also starting to recognize the need to shift from traditional economic indicators, acknowledging concepts like the 'planetary wellbeing' explored in this volume. A growing number of economists, policymakers, businesses, activists, social entrepreneurs and other changemakers have been developing new conversational frameworks for organizing economies, measuring societal progress and protecting the environment. They may have used different approaches and different languages, but all share a common goal. This expanded conception of economic thought has brought us concepts like the Caring Economy, the Sharing Economy, the Circular Economy, the Blue Economy and the Wellbeing Economy. It has incorporated ecological economics, feminist economics and 'doughnut economics' (Raworth 2012), along with other new ways of looking at what creates and sustains prosperity while protecting the planet.

In 2019, the Prime Minister of New Zealand, Jacinda Ardern, published the country's first 'Wellbeing Budget' – a budget that moved beyond GDP. Ardern collaborated with Iceland's Prime Minister, Katrín Jakobsdóttir, and former First Minister of Scotland, Nicola Sturgeon, to put social and ecological wellbeing at the heart of their economic policies and adhering to a Net Zero strategy. These countries, along with Canada, have formed a new loose partnership: the Wellbeing Economy Alliance. A Wellbeing Economy Governments Parentship (WEGo) was first officially discussed at an institutional conference in Scotland in 2017 and formally launched in November 2018 at the Organisation for Economic Co-operation and Development World Forum in Incheon, South Korea. The partnership includes New Zealand, Scotland, Iceland, Wales and Finland, but it is expected to grow, with many other governments in both the 'Global North' and 'Global South' showing interest in participating. The main objective is to enable cross-government engagement, learning and collaboration and to utilize the advice of experts and deepen understanding of how to deliver a Wellbeing Economy for citizens and the environment.

Members of WEGo aim at advancing three key principles: live within planetary ecological boundaries, ensure equitable distribution of wealth and opportunity and efficiently allocate resources (including environmental and social public goods), bringing wellbeing to the heart of policymaking and, in particular, economic policymaking. This approach is exemplified through *environmental personhood*, which has been formulated to protect nature and advocated by the Global Alliance for the Rights of Nature, a global network of institutions and individuals fighting for universal implementation of legal systems that recognize, value and enforce the 'Rights of Nature'. The Whanganui River and the Te Urewera National Park in New Zealand are the most well-known examples of natural phenomena being recognized as legal entities. These initiatives have their roots in sustainability and *deep ecology*, specifically, in the conviction that nature, ecosystems and human and non-human species all possess fundamental and irreplaceable intrinsic value (Strand et al. 2022). However, there is nothing new about these ideas if we think of Bhutan's Gross National Happiness Index introduced in 1972 by King Jigme Singye Wangchuck, which gives equal importance to non-economic aspects of wellbeing, such as ecological diversity, environmental conservation and preservation. Equally the Latin-American concept of *buen vivir*, which loosely means 'living well', in harmony with each other and with nature, the Southern African philosophy *ubuntu*, which celebrates the common good of society and nature, rather than divisions within it, or the *Quechua* (a language family broadly spoken in the Andes) word *ayllu*, which is used to refer to a network in which humans and other-than-humans are connected by kinship ties (the list can go on), are all examples of *ways of being* which promote 'enoughness' (Hickel 2017; Jungell-Michelsson and Heikkurinen 2022) and harmony with each other and nature (Kothari et al. 2019).

In *Braiding Sweetgrass: Indigenous Wisdom, Scientific Knowledge and the Teaching of Plants*, Kimmerer explains:

> This is the vision of the economy of the commons, wherein resources fundamental to our wellbeing, like water and land and forests, are commonly held rather than commodified. Properly managed, the commons approach maintains abundance, not scarcity. These contemporary economic alternatives strongly echo the indigenous worldview in which the Earth exists not as a private property, but as a commons, to be tended with respect and reciprocity for the benefit of all. (2013, 376)

Paradoxically, according to a report by the WEF titled *Nature Risk Rising: Why the Crisis Engulfing Nature Matters for Business and the Economy*, more than half of the world's GDP depends on nature, with species and ecosystems collaborating to provide humans with water, clean air, food, raw materials for medicine and animal products (Herweijer et al. 2020). Not to mention that globally, nature creates billions of jobs; therefore, it must be restored and protected for its own wellbeing and for the many people who depend on it. This paradox is eloquently discussed in the documentary film *Our Planet: Too Big to Fail* produced by the World Wide Fund for Nature and Silverback Films:

> Our economy is fundamentally underpinned by the stability and resilience of the natural world, and yet our financial system has been oriented to focus on very short-term profits on tracking indexes and more passive investment, all at the expense of our long-term future. Our economic and financial system prioritises GDP and ignores, to a large degree, environmental and social externalities, causing immense damage to our planet. (Huertas 2023, 0:8:45)

In 1972, researchers from the Massachusetts Institute of Technology published a report commissioned by the global 'think tank' The Club of Rome, which considered the way that humans live on our planet, entitled *The Limits to Growth*. The report concluded:

> If the present growth trends in the world population, industrialisation, pollution, food production, and resource depletion continue unchanged, the limits to growth on this planet will be reached sometime within the next one hundred years. The most probable result will be a rather sudden and uncontrollable decline in both population and industrial capacity. (Meadows et al. 1974, 23)

Recent updates of the original study based on empirical data gathered from government and non-government agencies, including the UN and the World Bank, confirm that our planet is following the risky path predicted by the original report. Sustainability analyst Gaya Herrington suggests in the *Update to Limits to Growth: Comparing the World3 Model with Empirical Data Report*, published by the *Yale Journal of Industrial Ecology*, that the planetary tipping point could come around 2040. However, she also argues that there is still time to change Humanity's impact on ecosystems if we adopt an 'agrowth' position (2020). Professor of Environmental and Climate Economics Jeroen C. J. M. van den Bergh, who first introduced the concept of 'agrowth' suggests:

> We should become agnostic and indifferent about GDP growth, i.e. adopt an agrowth position. One reason is that the GDP is not a good indicator of happiness or social welfare . . .
>
> Modern economies and lifestyles are highly dependent on burning fossil fuels, generating CO2 emissions responsible for global warming . . . under serious climate policy the rate of economic growth is thus likely to drop for some time, possibly until we have reached a zero-carbon economy. Such a consequence will induce fear for and opposition to associated climate policies in many advocates of green growth. An agrowth strategy, on the other hand, will facilitate the acceptance of these policies as it will free us from the unnecessary, welfare-obstructing growth paradigm. This will result in removing false trade-offs between GDP growth and other goals arising from the constraint of always, at any time and under any conditions, having to achieve GDP growth. (2018, 54–5)

Herrington and van den Bergh remind us that design-led consumerism has fuelled an anthropocentric economy in lieu of an ecological approach. Supporting this view, Professor of Practice in Contemporary Design at Aalto University Julia Lohmann argued during an online exchange with the PhD-Design List members that:

> It is precisely the 'human-centredness' of design that has led to many unintended consequences, impacting negatively on the ecosystems and non-human beings that sustain us. Consequently, the

> future of our own species has become uncertain. This is because we still largely lack the inclusion of the needs of non-human stakeholders in our decision-making processes. If we were to constructively change our decision-making processes towards building the regenerative capacities needed to address the multiple crises we face, we need to expand our remit beyond addressing immediate human needs. Already in 1979, the German philosopher Hans Jonas described in the book *The Imperative for Responsibility: In Search of an Ethics for the Technological Age* the need to expand our consideration of ethics beyond our species' needs. He argued that a technological society whose impact on the planet is all-encompassing needs to match this transformative power with an equally all-encompassing ethical awareness and responsibility. (2021)

The myopia of twenty-first-century design has excluded from its conception of the world, and an aligned design practice, the lives, experiences and voices of all that fall outside its definition of 'human'. This volume explores how design enquiry might reimagine our relationship with other species and ecosystems. These complex issues offer a transdisciplinary opportunity for design and designers to engage in reconceptualizing the capitalist conception of creative disciplines. Considering this, *Design Beyond the Human* seeks to present a critical perspective and exceed the current anthropocentric and 'capitalocentric' view of the partnership between humans, non-humans, ecosystems and design. This collection of essays identifies an opportunity for a fundamental shift in how design and designers relate to our planet and its inhabitants. The contributors demonstrate how the partnership between design and other disciplines can provide a framework for pursuing material and immaterial conversations about the conditions, methodologies and interventions, of inclusion and exclusion, that impact all life on our planet.

So, what is *Design Beyond the Human* for? This volume does not pretend to 'solve' the planet's predicament – but it does generate ways of thinking about how the human and non-human branch out, entangle and crisscross. We do not claim that the essays in *Design Beyond the Human* provide a manual for global solutions or liberate the intellectual orientation of design from its origins in the Industrial Revolution. However, each essay is an opportunity to question if design (in a *more than human way*) will continue its relationship to capitalism and contemporary lifestyle practices, effectively re-producing an ecologically aware version of today. Or, in going *beyond the human*, how design might develop a transdisciplinary perspective capable of envisioning an alternative vision of life on Earth – to negate the negation (Fry 2020) – and what examples of such an ambition and exploration might look like. So, instead of searching for 'design solutions' to the *problems* of today and their *consequences* for tomorrow, or 'sustaining the unsustainable' (Fry 2009)), authors here offer multiple and diverse perspectives that rethink the sustainability of the relationship between our planetary present and its ecological future. Ultimately, we hope each essay provides a reflective space to challenge the normative, HCD-derived model established and exported by Anglo-American society and move towards articulating design practices that respond more appropriately to planetary conditions and the interrelationship of living beings. As Adam Nocek and Tony Fry write in the introduction of the edited volume *Design in Crisis: New Worlds, Philosophies and Practices*:

> One thing is clear however: the various calls to design for social, ecological, and political change, using pre-packaged innovation toolkits and other *dispositifs* of the knowledge economy, are largely window dressing when it comes to a deep and sustained engagement with design's implication in and possible transformation of planetary crises. While there are now countless books, articles,

> conferences, symposia, and festivals all championing some form of design for social good – which extends to areas as diverse as refugees, waste, fast fashion, urban farming, infostructure, geology, biotechnology, and so on – the modern metaphysics of design remains unchanged . . .
>
> Design can't limit itself to changing the patterns of human consumption, to altering supply chains, or to sourcing biodegradable materials. It must envision the possibility of designing *new conditions of being human*. (2021, 2–3)

Endings have occurred before. Over the past 450 million years, life on Earth has been devastated by at least five extinctions (Ordovician-Silurian, Late Devonian, Permian, Triassic-Jurassic and the Cretaceous-Tertiary), so from an evolutionary perspective, there is no reason to assume that design will help Humanity to be eternal. After all, 'We are creatures of Darwinism evolution, a transient species with a limited lifespan as were all our numerous distant ancestors' (Lovelock 2010, 6). Geological records demonstrate that species evolve with their context or become extinct sooner or later. Yuval Noah Harari explains:

> Sixty-five million years ago, an asteroid wiped out the dinosaurs, opening the way forward to mammals. Today, humankind is driving many species into extinction and might even annihilate itself. But other organisms are doing quite well. Rats and cockroaches, for example, are in their heyday. These tenacious creatures would probably creep out from beneath the smoking rubble of a nuclear Armageddon, ready and able to spread their DNA. Perhaps 65 million years from now, intelligent rats will look back gratefully on the decimation wrought by humankind, just as we today can thank that dinosaur-busting asteroid. (2019, 393)

As discussed by many scientists and reported in an article published in *Biological Reviews*, the sixth extinction of the planet's biodiversity might be already underway (Ripple et al. 2017). This extinction is more advanced on land than in the oceans, though many marine species are also in danger due to human activities (Cowie et al. 2022). Moreover, according to a recent article published in *Science Advances*, 'Planetary Boundaries Framework update finds that six of the nine boundaries are transgressed, suggesting that Earth is now well outside of the safe operating space for Humanity' (Richardson et al. 2023, 1) – these six boundaries include climate change, biosphere integrity, land system change, freshwater change, biogeochemical flows and novel entities such as synthetic chemicals and nuclear waste. The possible journey to human extinction, however, should not necessarily be exponentially damaging for the other elements of the ecosystem, to the point where the metabolism of the planet is transformed irreversibly (Haraway 2017); there are other ways to become extinct as a species, while attempting remediation and leaving some sort of legacy (Rull 2009), or as explained by design academic and author Ezio Manzini's analogy offered during the *Bauhaus of the Sea* conference in 2021, 'We can look at our planet in two different ways. We can consider it as a spaceship, a machine that must be repaired by reducing complexity or as a living organism that requires healing.' However, social theorist, political philosopher, and founder of the Social Ecology Movement, Murray Bookchin, challenged the spaceship analogy as techno-utopian during a lecture at the Toward Tomorrow Fair held in Amherst, Massachusetts:

> I do not believe that the Earth is a spaceship. I am asking you to think about what it means to think of the Earth as a spaceship. It does not have valves. It does not have all kinds of radar equipment to guide it. It is not moved by rockets. It hasn't got any plumbing. We may have plumbing. But it is not 'a

> spaceship'. It is an organic, living thing, to a very great extent, at least on its surface, built of inorganic material. It is in the process of growth and it is in the process of development. It is not 'a spaceship'. (1978, 0:10:28)

In this sense, one of the tasks of design, as explored in this volume, might be to support Humanity towards a replenishment and partial healing trajectory and explore a possible transition beyond the capitalist human/nature binary by moving into a 'relational design' (Hernandez Ibinarriaga 2025) understanding of life based on 'interdependence' and a 'poetics of relating' (Avila 2022) and a 'lively cohabitation' (Celermajer & Darnour-Paul 2024); or, to borrow the thought-provoking and ironic words of the Museum of Modern Art Design and Architecture Senior Curator Paola Antonelli, 'to help us to imagine a beautiful ending' (2019).

While contemplating these options, we should also take responsibility for and question the desirability of possible present and future societies, as well as question the directionality of the change we will inevitably inherit. We must explore how traditions of the 'Global North', hitherto heavily dependent on the duality between nature and society, can confront their internal limits and intellectual tipping points. The conceptual flexibility of these inherited academic traditions needs to be enhanced and adapted to the experience of the putative Anthropocene era – indeed, the meaning of being human and caring for the planet are truly significant challenges for design, as well as other disciplines and forms of practice. As Aboriginal scholar Tyson Yunkaporta argues in *Sand Talk: How Indigenous Thinking Can Save the World*:

> When it comes to global environmental catastrophe, the jury is done deliberating and the case is closed. It requires no more debate. This apocalypse is real. On the upside, apocalypses have proven to be survivable in the past, although on the downside it usually means that your culture and society will never be the same again . . .
>
> You can live with it, but you need to adapt and change every aspect of your society and culture when transitioning from one era to the next . . .
>
> Considering that the catastrophes we are experiencing may take decades or even centuries to play out, then another century for us to recover after that, it may be advisable for us to get ahead of the game and begin creating cultures and societies of transition, to lessen the impacts of this calamity on our communities and potentially avoid post-apocalyptic stress altogether. (2022, 78–81)

Design Beyond the Human does not claim to be exhaustive, definitive or to provide a singular solution and a moral case for action: far from it. It is the first step of a journey born of a cluster of ideas and conversations regarding 'matters of concern' (Latour 2004) and 'matters of care' (Puig de la Bellacasa 2017). Feminist economic geographers Julie Graham and Katherine Gibson similarly suggest that an 'ethics of care' is needed, treating planet Earth like a family. Can we extend our solidarity, they ask, to the more-than-human and other life forms? If we can, they conclude, 'That would certainly usher in a new mode of Humanity and a new form of belonging' (2011, 17).

The supra-disciplinary nature of this collection provides an opportunity to evidence the multiple perspectives offered across disciplines and lived experiences. Despite the specific expertise, knowledge, methodologies or language used by each contributor, it is evident that there is a fertile opportunity born of shared concerns, driven by planetary events. Global challenges, such as climate change and ecological degradation, prove that a singular disciplinary approach is an inadequate response to complex issues or discursive 'hyperobjects' (Morton 2013), where societal behaviours, individual choices, political decisions and economic, technological and scientific development intersect. In no field is this so evident as in design, which recognizes the need for interaction with other knowledge areas and lived experiences. As such, *Design Beyond the Human* is a collection of essays that gathers scholars, designers and engaged citizens from the 'Global South' and 'Global North', encompassing activism, anthropology, design practice, design theory, economics, environmental humanities, ethics, history, law, philosophy, politics, science, sociology and technology. Rather than attempting to be a comprehensive illustration of a singular field of expertise or voice, this book is a conversational cross-section of ideas which overlap, intersect and reflect upon each other, even as they cater to specific or different enquires.

Design Beyond the Human collects and connects ideas that are regarded as belonging to separate disciplinary discourses. The text is organized in three sections, containing thematically grouped essays that scaffold a transdisciplinary conversation capable of thinking about life on planet Earth: challenging the Anglo-European anthropocentric conceptualization of design that dominates practice, education and academic discourse. Each section is unique and distinct – *We Are Not Alone*, *Design Beyond the Human* and *Mediating Human-Non-Human Relations through Design* – while contributing to a polyvocal and post-disciplinary critique of design and its relationship to our ecological circumstances, to capitalism and its anthropomorphic economics. What emerges is an *assemblage* of design discourses, practices and projects that are attempting to reconcile Humanity's relationship with the planet, its ecosystems and inhabitants. In this sense, the design activities discussed in *Design Beyond the Human* address subjects such as animal ethics, biodiversity, biotechnology, cellular agriculture, chemistry, climate change, community-based conservation, computing, digital technology, eco-tourism, ecology, human activism, human-animal relations, Indigenous design, Indigenous knowledge, living architecture, multispecies justice, new materialism, physics, poetry, regenerative agriculture, relational design, space debris and transition design. Furthermore, *Design Beyond the Human* allows the reader to engage with divergent expertise, knowledge, methodologies, lived experiences and languages, offered across disciplines, cultures and belief systems, shaped by shared concerns, motivations and challenges.

Indeed, we are entering uncharted territory for Humanity, just as those astronauts who first glimpsed Earth from space did. Each chapter here both offers and forces us to consider new perspectives and realize that we require to learn and unlearn. Ideas are the cogs that drive design onwards, for good and ill; the descriptions, stories and worlds that emerge from the conversations that these pages create will help shape the world we will live within and will narrate the possibilities for our planet. The transdisciplinary perspective assembled here allows an understanding of the complexity of the task at hand, and it is an essential part of the equipment needed by engaged designers to make better sense of the world. Therefore, each contributor wishes to open up topics, rather than narrow them down. Thus, a broader view is desirable, combining the emergent ideas that constitute the framework of a larger conversation about design and its interrelationship with other ways of thinking, doing, learning and knowing. While the transition from a stable planet to an unstable planet is happening on our watch, we hope that bringing together these authors and ideas will provide pathways to better understanding and respecting life on our planet. We call this *Design Beyond the Human: Transdisciplinary Conversations about the Planet*.

Note **–** Throughout the book, we refer to 'Global South' and 'Global North' in quotation marks. During the last decade, scholars, activists and commentators have begun to use the terms 'Global North' and 'Global South' to describe the world's development or standard of living between 'rich' and 'poor' countries. We are conscious that the two terms do not represent much evolution from the 'West' and 'Third World' descriptions previously used, as well as the still-used 'developed' and 'developing' worlds. We have used these terms in this book but have constantly reminded ourselves that our planet cannot meaningfully, fairly and accurately be classified under two concepts. We tried to look for a substitute description that is less deterministic and more relational, where North and South refer not just to privilege and marginalization, but failed to do so. We are sorry for this shortcoming, hoping that we will be ready to overcome these considerable dividing global classifications in a revisited version of this book.

References

Amato-Lourenço, Luis Fernando, et al. 'Presence of Airborne Microplastics in Human Lung Tissue'. *Journal of Hazardous Materials* 416 (2021): 126124. https://doi.org/10.1016/j.jhazmat.2021.126124

Antonelli, Paola. *Broken Nature*. Milan: Rizzoli International Publications, 2019.

Ansoff, H. Igor. 'Managing Strategic Surprise by Response to Weak Signals'. *California Management Review* 18, no. 2 (1975): 21–33. https://doi.org/10.2307/41164635

Appadurai, Arjun. 'Tournament of Value - In Conversation with Beatrice Von Bismark and Benjamin Meyer-Krahmer'. In *Curatorial Things*, edited by Beatrice Von Bismark and Benjamin Meyer-Krahmer. London: Sternberg Press, 2020.

Arendt, Hannah. *The Human Condition*. Chicago: University of Chicago Press, 1958.

Avila, Martin. *Design for Interdependence: A Poetics of Relating*. London: Bloomsbury, 2022.

Augusta, Pownall. 'We Don't Have the Power to Stop Our Extinction'. *Dezeen*, December, 2022. https://www.dezeen.com/2019/02/22/paola-antonelli-extinction-milan-triennale-broken-nature-exhibition/

Barad, Karen. 'TransMaterialities: Trans/Matter/Realities and Queer Political Imaginings'. In *More-Than-Hu-an*, edited by Penny Harvey, Marina Otero Verzier and Lucia Pietroiusti. Rotterdam: Het Nieuwe Instituut, 2021.

Barners-Lee, Mike. *How Bad Are Bananas? The Carbon Footprint of Everything*. London: Profile Books, 2020.

Barnosky, Anthony D., et al. 'Approaching A State Shift in Earth's Biosphere'. *Nature*, 486, no. 7401 (2012): 52–8. https://doi.org/10.1038/nature11018

Bartlett, John. 'Chile's Atacama Desert Has Become a Fast Fashion Dumping Ground'. *National Geographic*, 5 March 2024. https://www.nationalgeographic.com/environment/article/chile-fashion-pollution

Basar, Shumon, Douglas Coupland and Hans Ulrich Obrist. *The Age of Earthquakes: A Guide to The Extreme Present*, London: Penguin, 2015, 5.

Bauhaus of The Seas. 'Bauhaus of The Seas'. Accessed 10 August 2022. https://bauhaus-seas.eu

Benson, Melinda Harm and Robin Kundis Craig. 'The End of Sustainability'. *Society & Natural Resources* 27, no. 7 (2017): 777–82. https://doi.org/10.1080/08941920.2014.901467

Berkes, Fikret. *Sacred Ecology: Traditional Ecological Knowledge and Resource Management*. New York: Routledge, 2008.

BIOTOPIA. 'Mission and Values'. Naturkundemuseum Bayern, 2024. https://www.biotopia.net/en/vision/mission-values.

Blake, Charlie, Molloy, Claire and Steven Shakespeare. *Beyond Human: From Animality to Transhumanism*. London: Bloomsbury, 2012.

Bookchin, Murray. 'Ecology Versus Environmentalism and Human Attitudes Toward Nature; Evolution of Human Ideas About Nature'. Lecture, Toward Tomorrow Fair, Amherst, 24 August 1978. https://credo.library.umass.edu/view/full/mums741-b237-i005

Boehnert, Joanna. *Design Ecology Politics: Towards the Ecocene*. London: Bloomsbury Academic, 2018.

Burns, Georgette Leah. *Engaging with Animals: Interpretations of a Shared Existence*. Sidney: Sidney University Press, 2014, 12–3.

Chan, T. F. 'Formafantasma on Their GEO-Design Master's Programme, and Designers Thinking Big'. *Wallpaper*, 7 October 2022. https://www.wallpaper.com/design/formafantasma-interview-2021

Chakrabarty, Dipesh. 'The Climate of History: Four Theses'. *Critical Inquiry* 35, no. 2 (2009): 197–222. https://doi.org/10.1086/596640

Charles, Dominic, Laurent, Kimman and Nakul Saran. *Review of Plastic Waste Makers Index: Revealing the Source of the Single-Use Plastics Crisis*, edited by Shanta Barley. Australia: Minderoo Foundation, 2021, 31. https://cdn.minderoo.org/content/uploads/2021/05/27094234/20211105-Plastic-Waste-Makers-Index.pdf

Ciid. 'Copenhagen Institute of Interaction Design Curriculum'. Accessed 10 July 2022. https://www.ciid.dk/idpcurriculum

Cole, Nicki Lisa. 'Theories of Ideology: The Concept and Its Relationship to Marxist Theory'. *ThoughtCo*, Accessed 5 October 2022. 2019. https://www.thoughtco.com/ideology-definition-3026356

Collins, Michael. 'Pulse of the Planet. "Apollo 11 – The Fragile Earth"'. *Pulse of the Planet*, 7 July 2019.

Cookson, Clive. 'Year in a Word: Anthropocene'. *Financial Times*, 28 December 2023.

Costanza, Robert, et al. 'Evolution of the Human-Environment Relationship'. *The Encyclopedia of Earth*, 2 May 2007. http://www.eoearth.org/article/Evolution_of_the_human environment_relationship

Cowie, Robert H., Bouchet Philippe and Benoît Fontaine. 'The Sixth Mass Extinction: Fact, Fiction or Speculation?' *Biological Reviews*, 97, no. 2 (2002): 640–63. https://doi.org/10.1111/brv.12816

Crutzen, Paul J. 'Geology of Mankind'. *Nature*, 415, no. 6867 (2002): 23–3. https://doi.org/10.1038/415023a

Crutzen, Paul J. and Eugene F. Stoermer. 'The Anthropocene'. *Global Change Newsletter*, 41 (2004): 17–8. http://www.igbp.net/download/18.316f18321323470177580001401/1376383088452/NL41.pdf

Davies, Jeremy. *The Birth of the Anthropocene*. Berkley: University of California Press, 2018.

Decolonising Design Collective. Decolonising Design. Accessed 13 May 2025. https://www.decolonisingdesign.com

de la Cadena, Marisol. 'About Mariano's Archive' Ecologies of Stories'. In *More-Than-Human*, edited by Penny Harvey, Marina Otero Verzier and Lucia Pietroiusti. Rotterdam: Het Nieuwe Instituut, 2019.

de La Bellacasa, María Puig. *Matters of Care: Speculative Ethics in More than Human Worlds*. Minneapolis: University of Minnesota Press, 2017.

de La Bellacasa, María Puig. 'Soil Times: The Pace of Ecological Care'. In *More-Than-Human*, edited by Penny Harvey, Marina Otero Verzier and Lucia Pietroiusti. Rotterdam: Het Nieuwe Instituut, 2021, 396–429.

Descola, Philippe. *Beyond Nature and Culture*. Chicago: University of Chicago Press, 2013.

Design Council. 'Design for Planet'. Last modified 13 May 2025. https://www.designcouncil.org.uk/our-mission/

Design Council. 'Using Design as a Force for Change'. Strategy 6. London: Design Council. 2020. https://www.designcouncil.org.uk/sites/default/files/asset/document/Design%20Council%202020-24%20Strategy.pdf

Design Justice Network. 'Design Justice Network Principles'. Design Justice Network. Accessed 13 May 2025. https://designjustice.org/read-the-principles

Design Museum. 'More Than Human'. , Accessed 16 November 2024. https://designmuseum.org/exhibitions/more-than-human

Dixson-Declève, Sandrine, et al. *Earth for All: A Survival Guide for Humanity: A Report to the Club of Rome, Fifty Years after the Limits of Growth (1972).* Gabriola Island, British Columbia, Canada: New Society Publishers, 2022.

Douglas, Sarah. 'Terra Carta Design Lab Announced by Jony Ive and HRH Prince Charles'. *Wallpaper*, 11 October 2022. https://www.wallpaper.com/design/prince-charles-jony-ive-terra-carta-design-lab.

Earle, Steven. *A Brief History of the Earth's Climate: Everyone's Guide to Science of Climate Change*. Gabriola, BC: New Society Publishers, 2021.

Ehrlich, Paul R. and Anne H. Ehrlich. *The Dominant Animal: Human Evolution and the Environment*. Washington: Island Press, 2008.

Eriksen, Marcus, et al. 2023. 'A Growing Plastic Smog, Now Estimated to Be over 170 Trillion Plastic Particles Afloat in the World's Oceans—Urgent Solutions Required'. *PLoS One* 18, no. 3 (2023): e0281596.

Escobar, Arturo. 'Designing As a Futural Praxis for The Healing of The Web of Life'. In *Design in Crisis: New Worlds, Philosophies and Practices*, edited by Tony Fry and Adam Nocek. London: Routledge, 2020, 25–42.

Escobar, Arturo. *Designs for the Pluriverse: Radical Interdependence, Autonomy, and the Making of Worlds (New Ecologies for the Twenty-First Century)*. Durham: Duke University Press, 2018.

Escobar, Arturo. 'Latin America at a Crossroads'. *Cultural Studies* 24, no. 1 (2010): 1–65. https://doi.org/10.1080/09502380903424208

European Space Agency. 'Space Debris by The Numbers'. Accessed 3 April, 2022. https://www.esa.int/Safety_Security/Space_Debris/Space_debris_by_the_numbers.

Fuad-Luke, Alastair. *Design Activism: Beautiful Strangeness for a Sustainable World*. London: Earthscan, 2009.

Federici, Silvia. 'Feminism and the Politics of the Commons in an Era of Primitive Accumulation'. In *More-Than-Human*, edited by Penny Harvey, Marina Otero Verzier and Lucia Pietroiusti. Rotterdam: Het Nieuwe Instituut, 2021.

Fleming, James R. 'Joseph Fourier's Theory of Terrestrial Temperatures'. *Historical Perspectives on Climate Change.* New York: Oxford Academic, 1998.

Fleming, James R. 'Joseph Fourier, the Greenhouse Effect, and the Quest for a Universal Theory of Terrestrial Temperatures'. *Endeavour* 23, no. 2 (1999): 72–5

Fletcher, Kate, Tham Mathilda and Pierre Louise St. *Design and Nature: A Partnership*. London: Routledge, 2019.

Freire, Paulo. *Education For Critical Consciousness*. London: Bloomsbury Academic, 2021.

Fremaux, Anne. *After the Anthropocene: Green Republicanism in a Post-Capitalist World.* London: Palgrave Macmillan, 2019.

Fremaux, Anne and John Barry. 'The Good Anthropocene and Green Political Theory: Rethinking Environmentalism, Resisting Eco-Modernism'. In *Anthropocene Encounters: New Directions in Green Political Thinking*, edited by Frank Biermann and Eva Lövbrand. Cambridge (Massachusetts): Cambridge University Press, 2019, 171–90. https://doi.org/10.1017/9781108646673.009

Fry, Tony. 'Design For/By the Global South'. *Design Philosophy Papers* 15, no. 1 (2017): 3–37. https://doi.org/10.1080/14487136.2017.1303242

Fry, Tony. *Design Futuring: Sustainability, Ethics and New Practices*. Oxford: Berg, 2009.

Fry, Tony. 'The Dialectic of Sustainment'. *Design Philosophy Papers* 1, no. 5 (2003): 289–297.

Fry, Tony and Adam Nocek. *Design in Crisis: New Worlds, Philosophies and Practices*. London: Routledge, 2021.

Fry, Tony, and Clive Dilnot. 'Manifesto for Redirective Design: Hot Debate'. *Design Philosophy Papers* 1, no. 2 (2003): 95–103. https://doi.org/10.2752/144871303X13965299301795

Future of Education. 'Future of Design Education'. Accessed 5 December 2022. https://www.futureofdesigneducation.org/

García-Acosta, Gabriel, and Carles Riba Romeva. 'From Anthropocentric Design to Ecospheric Design: Questioning Design Epicentre'. In *Proceedings of DESIGN 2010, the 11th International Design Conference, Dubrovnik, Croatia, 17–20 May 2010,* 29–37. Farnham: The Design Society, 2010.

Ghosh, Amitav. *The Great Derangement: Climate Change and The Unthinkable*. Chicago: University of Chicago Press, 2016.

Gibson-Graham, J. K. 'A Feminist Project of Belonging for The Anthropocene'. *Gender, Place and Culture*, 18, no. 1 (2011): 1–21. https://doi.org/10.1080/0966369x.2011.535295

Gibson-Graham, J. K. *End of Capitalism (As We Knew It): A Feminist Critique of Political Economy*. Minneapolis: University of Minnesota Press, 2006.

Gilbert, Scott F. 'Holobiont by Birth: Multilineage Individuals as the Cocreation of Cooperative Processes'. In *More-Than-Human*, edited by Penny Harvey, Marina Otero Verzier and Lucia Pietroiusti. Rotterdam: Het Nieuwe Instituut, 2021.

Godee, Kelvin and Simon Wijrdeman. 'Non-Human Centred Design Methods'. *Nonhumandesign.Com*. https://www.nonhumandesign.com

Goldman, Emma and Max Baginski. 'Mother Earth'. *Mother Earth* 1 (1906): 1–3.

Goldman, Emma and Candace Falk. *Emma Goldman, Vol. 2: A Documentary History of the American Years, Volume 2: Making Speech Free, 1902–1909*. Champaign: University of Illinois Press, 2008, 175. https://doi.org/org/10.5406/j.ctt1cx3vqw

Grattan-Guinness, Ivor and Jerome R. Ravetz. Joseph Fourier, *1768-1830: A Survey of His Life and Work*. Cambridge, MA: MIT Press, 2003.

Griffiths, Sarah. 'Why Your Internet Habits Are Not as Clean as You Think'. *BBC*, 6 March 2020. https://www.bbc.com/future/article/20200305-why-your-internet-habits-are-not-as-clean-as-you-think

Gudynas, Eduardo. 'Buen Vivir: Today's Tomorrow'. *Development* 54, no. 4 (2011): 441–7. https://doi.org/10.1057/dev.2011.86

Gutiérrez, Luis. 'Fjord 2020 Trends – Life-Centred Design Will Change Financial Services Offerings'. *Financial Services Accenture*. Accessed 22 October 2021. https://financialservicesblog.accenture.com/fjord-2020-trends-life-centred-design-will-change-financial-services-offerings.

Hansen, James. *Storms of My Grandchildren: The Truth About the Coming Climate Catastrophe and Our Last Chance to Save Humanity*. New York: Bloomsbury, 2011.

Hao, Karen. 'Training a Single AI Model Can Emit as Much Carbon as Five Cars in Their Lifetimes'. *MIT Technology Review*, 6 June 2019.

Harari, Yuval Noah. *Sapiens: A Brief History of Humankind.* London: Vintage, 2015.

Haraway, Donna 'Anthropocene, Capitalocene, Plantationocene, Chthulucene: Making Kin'. *Environmental Humanities* 6, no. 1 (2015): 159–65. https://doi.org/10.1215/22011919-3615934

Haraway, Donna. 'Awash in Urine: DES and Premarin in Multispecies Response-ability'. In *More-Than-Human*, edited by Penny Harvey, Marina Otero Verzier and Lucia Pietroiusti. Rotterdam: Het Nieuwe Instituut, 2021.

Haraway, Donna. *Donna Haraway – Staying with the Trouble: Making Kin in The Chthulucene*. YouTube, uploaded by San Francisco Art Institute, 25 April 2017. https://www.youtube.com/watch?v=GrYA7sMQaBQ&t=1720s

Haraway, Donna. *Staying with the Trouble: Making Kin in the Chthulucene*. Durham: Duke University Press, 2016.

Haraway, Donna. 'Staying With the Trouble'. In *Anthropocene Or Capitalocene?* edited by Jason W. Moore, Oakland: PM Press, 2016, 34–76.

Haraway, Donna, et al. 'Anthropologists Are Talking - About the Anthropocene'. *Ethnos* 81, no. 3 (2015): 535–64. https://doi.org/10.1080/00141844.2015.1105838.

Heikkurinen, Pasi, et al. 'The Anthropocene Exit: Reconciling Discursive Tensions on the New Geological Epoch'. *Ecological Economics* 164 (2019): 106369.

Helmore, Edward. 'Yep, It Is Bleak, Says Expert Who Tested 1970S End-Of-The-World Prediction'. *The Guardian*, 25 July 2021. https://www.theguardian.com/environment/2021/jul/25/gaya-herrington-mit-study-the-limits-to-growth

Hernandez Ibinarriaga, Desiree. *Decolonising and Indigenising Design: Theory, Methodologies, Storytelling, and Creative Practice*. London: Routledge, 2025.

Hern, Alex. 'How Iceland Became the Bitcoin Miners' Paradise'. *The Guardian*, 13 February 2018. https://www.theguardian.com/world/2018/feb/13/how-iceland-became-the-bitcoin-miners-paradise

Herrington, Gaya. 'Update to Limits to Growth: Comparing The World3 Model With Empirical Data'. *Journal of Industrial Ecology* 25, no. 3 (2021): 614–26. https://doi.org/10.1111/jiec.13084

Herweijer, Celine, et al. *Nature Risk Rising: Why the Crisis Engulfing Nature Matters for Business and the Economy*. Geneva: World Economic Forum, 2020.

Hickel, Jason. 'Human Flourishing Doesn't Require Perpetual Growth; It Requires Sufficiency'. 2017. Accessed 12 October 2023. https://www.jasonhickel.org/blog/2017/12/23/martin-ravallion-is-wrong-endless-growth-is-notnecessary-for-human-well-being

Holcomb, Justin A., Rolfe D. Mandel and Karl Wegmann. 2023. 'The Case for a Lunar Anthropocene'. *Nature Geoscience* 17 (2024): 2–4. https://doi./org/10.1038/s41561-023-01347-4

Huertas, Daniel. *Our Planet: Too Big to Fail*. Netflix and Silverback Films, 2023. https://www.ourplanet.com/en/video/our-planet-too-big-to-fail/

Ideo. 'About IDEO: Our Story, Who We Are, How We Work'. Accessed 4 April 2022. https://www.ideo.com/about

Ideo. Design Thinking. Accessed 13 May 2025. https://designthinking.ideo.com

IDEO. *Design Thinking*. Palo Alto, CA: IDEO, n.d.IDEO. *Design Thinking Defined*. Palo Alto, CA: IDEO., n.d.Intergovernmental Panel on Climate Change (IPCC). 2023. *Climate Change 2023: Synthesis Report. Contribution of Working Groups I, II and III to the Sixth Assessment Report of the Intergovernmental Panel on Climate Change*. Summary for Policymakers. Geneva: IPCC.

Ivakhiv, Adrian J. 'Against the Anthropocene'. *Immanence: Ecoculture, Geophilosophy, Mediapolitics,* Accessed 7 July 2022. https://blog.uvm.edu/aivakhiv/2014/07/07/against-the-anthropocene/.

Jackson, Chris. 'What Is Planet-Centric Design?' *We Create Futures*. Accessed 11 January 2022. https://www.wecreatefutures.com/blog/what-is-planet-centric-design

Jacque, André, Marina Otero Verzier, Lucia Pietrolusti and Lisa Mazza. *More-Than-Human*. Rotterdam: Het Nieuwe Instituut, 2020.

Jungell-Michelsson, Jessica, and Pasi Heikkurinen. 'Sufficiency: A Systematic Literature Review'. Ecological Economics 195 (2022): 107380. https://doi.org/10.1016/j.ecolecon.2022.107380

Kellert, Stephen R., and Elizabeth F. Calabrese. The Practice of Biophilic Design. 2015. https://www.biophilic-design.com/

Kendall, Henry. *World Scientists' Warning to Humanity*. Cambridge, MA: Union of Concerned Scientists, 1992.

Kimmerer, Robin Wall. *Braiding Sweetgrass: Indigenous Wisdom, Scientific Knowledge and the Teachings of Plants*. Minneapolis: Milkweed Editions, 2013.

Klein, Naomi. *This Changes Everything: Capitalism vs Climate Change*. London: Allen Lane, 2014.

Kohn, Eduardo. *How Forests Think: Toward an Anthropology beyond the Human*. Oakland: University of California Press, 2013.

Kolbert, Elizabeth. *The Sixth Extinction: An Unnatural History*. New York: Henry Holt and Company, 2014.

Kothari, Ashish, et al. *Pluriverse: A Post-Development Dictionary*. New Delhi: Tulika Books, 2019.

Kunstgewerbemuseum. 'More than Human: Design after the Anthropocene'. Accessed 16 November 2024. https://www.museumsportal-berlin.de/en/exhibitions/more-than-human/ coincidentally

Latour, Bruno. 'Agency at the Time of the Anthropocene'. *New Literary History* 45, no. 1 (2014): 1–18. https://doi.org/10.1353/nlh.2014.0003

Latour, Bruno. 'Anthropology at the Time of the Anthropocene: A Personal View of What Is to Be Studied'. In *The Anthropology of Sustainability*, edited by March Brightman and Jerome Lewis. Palgrave Macmillan, 2017, 35–49.

Latour, Bruno. 2014. 'Telling Friends from Foes in the Time of the Anthropocene'. *The Anthropocene Review* 1 (1): 62–75. https://doi.org/10.1177/2053019613516291.

Latour, Bruno. *Why Has Critique Run out of Steam? From Matters of Fact to Matters of Concern*. Chicago: University of Chicago Press, 2004.

LeCain, T.J. 2015. 'Against the Anthropocene: A Neo-Materialist Perspective'. *International Journal for History, Culture and Modernity* 3, no. 1 (2015): 1–28. https://doi.org/10.18352/hcm.474.

Lepawsky, Josh. 'E-Waste as a Challenge for Design and Society'. In *Waste Age: What Can Design Do?* edited by Justin McGuirk, London: Design Museum, 2022, 19–21.

Lepawsky, Josh. *Reassembling Rubbish: Worlding Electronic Waste*. Cambridge , MA: MIT Press, 2018.

Leslie, Heather A., et al. 'Discovery and Quantification of Plastic Particle Pollution in Human Blood'. *Environment International* 163 (2022): 107199. https://doi.org/10.1016/j.envint.2022.107199

Lewis, Simon and Mark A. Maslin. 'Defining the Anthropocene'. *Nature* 519, no. 7542 (2015): 171–80. https://doi.org/10.1038/nature14258

Lohmann, Julia. 'Re: Future of Design Education: More Than Human-Centred Design?' *Message to [PhD-Design]*. Accessed 29 April 2021. https://www.jiscmail.ac.uk/cgi-bin/wa-jisc.exe?A2=ind2104&L=PHD-DESIGN&P=R407>

Lovelock, James. *Gaia: A New Look at Life on Earth*. Oxford University Press, 2016.

Lovelock, James. *The Vanishing Face of Gaia: A Final Warning*. London: Penguin, 2010.

Luciano, Eugenio, and Elena Zanoni. 'Antonio Stoppani's "Anthropozoic" in the Context of the Anthropocene'. *The British Journal for the History of Science* 56, no. 1 (2023): 103–14. https://doi.org/10.1017/S0007087422000590

Lutz, Damien. 'A Holistic Design Toolkit for Life-Centred Design'. *Uxdesign*, Accessed 14 December 2022. https://uxdesign.cc/a-holistic-design-toolkit-for-life-centred-design-cc229faefa28

Lyle, John Tillman. *Regenerative Design for Sustainable Development*. New York: John Wiley & Sons, 1994.

Lyons, Kristina. 'Emergent Forms of Death Warning: Highly Toxic Experiments'. In *More-Than-Human*, edited by Penny Harvey, Marina Otero Verzier and Lucia Pietroiusti. Rotterdam: Het Nieuwe Instituut, 2021, 178–203.

MacCormack, Patricia. 'After Life'. In *More-Than-Human*, edited by Penny Harvey, Marina Otero Verzier and Lucia Pietroiusti. Rotterdam: Het Nieuwe Instituut, 2021, 261–271.

Maher, John T. 'Legal Technology Confronts Speciesism, or We Have Met the Enemy and He is Us'. In *More-Than-Human*, edited by Penny Harvey, Marina Otero Verzier and Lucia Pietroiusti. Rotterdam: Het Nieuwe Instituut, 2021.

Mallonee, Laura. 'Inside The Icelandic Facility Where Bitcoin is Mined'. *Wired*, 3 November 2019. https://www.wired.com/story/iceland-bitcoin-mining-gallery/

Malm, Andreas. *How to Blow Up a Pipeline: Learning to Fight in a World on Fire*. London: Verso Books, 2021.

Mann, Michael. *The New Climate War: The Fight to Take Back Our Planet*. Brunswick: Scribe Publications, 2021.

Manzini, Ezio. *Bauhaus of the Seas*. YouTube, uploaded by the European Union, 20 May 2021.

Manzini, Ezio. *Politics of the Everyday (Designing in Dark Times)*. London: Bloomsbury Visual Arts, 2019. https://www.youtube.com/watch?v=ZSel4B70DMs
Marder, Michael. 'For a Phytocentrism to Come'. In *More-Than-Human*, edited by Penny Harvey, Marina Otero Verzier and Lucia Pietroiusti. Rotterdam: Het Nieuwe Instituut, 2021, 432–443.
Marquardt, Jens. 'Worlds Apart?' In *The Anthropocene Debate and Political Science*, edited by Thomas Hickmann, et al. London: Routledge, 2018, 200–18. https://doi.org/10.4324/9781351174121-12
Martin, Laura Jane. 'Is A Footprint the Right Metaphor for Ecological Impact?' *Scientific American*, 2 April 2014. https://blogs.scientificamerican.com/guest-blog/is-a-footprint-the-right-metaphor-for-ecological-impact/
Martins, Hermínio. *The Technocene: Reflections on Bodies, Minds, and Markets*, edited by S. Ravi Rajan and Danielle Crawford. New York: Anthem Press, 2018.
Mazzucato, Mariana. *The Value of Everything: Making and Taking in the Global Economy*. London: Penguin, 2019.
McBrien, Justin. 'Accumulating Extinction: Planetary Catastrophism in the Necrocene'. In *Anthropocene or Capitalocene? Nature, History, and the Crisis of Capitalism*, edited by Jason W. Moore, 116–137. Oakland, CA: PM Press, 2016.
McCarthy, Francine M. G., et al. 'The Varved Succession of Crawford Lake, Milton, Ontario, Canada as a Candidate Global Boundary Stratotype Section and Point for the Anthropocene Series'. *The Anthropocene Review* 10, no. 1 (2023): 146–76. https://doi.org/10.1177/20530196221149281
McDonough, William, and Michael Braungart. *Cradle to Cradle: Remaking the Way We Make Things*. New York: North Point Press, 2002.
McGuire, Bill. *Hothouse Earth: An Inhabitant's Guide*. London: Icon Books, 2022.
Meadows, Donella, et al. *The Limits to Growth: A Report for the Club of Rome's Project on the Predicament of Mankind*. New York: Universe Books, 1974.
Metzner, Jim. 'Apollo 11 - The Fragile Earth'. *Pulse of The Planet*. Accessed 17 July 2021. https://shows.acast.com/pulseoftheplanet/episodes/apollo11-thefragileearth
Mixed Methods. 'The Future Is Life-Centred'. Accessed 4 April 2021. https://www.mixed-methods.org/episodes/2019/7/24/the-future-is-symbiotic-jane-fulton-suri-ideo
Moore, Jason W. *Anthropocene or Capitalocene? Nature, History, and the Crisis of Capitalism*. Oakland: PM Press/Kairos, 2016.
Moore, Jason W. 'The Capitalocene, Part I: On the Nature and Origins of Our Ecological Crisis'. *The Journal of Peasant Studies* 44, no. 3 (2017): 594–630. https://doi.org/10.1080/03066150.2016.1235036
Moore, Jason W. . 'The Capitalocene, Part II: Accumulation by Appropriation and The Centrality of Unpaid Work/Energy'. *The Journal of Peasant Studies* 45, no. 2 (2017): 237–79. https://doi.org/10.1080/03066150.2016.1272587
Morris, James D. K. and Jacinta Ruru. 'Giving Voice to Rivers: Legal Personality as a Vehicle for Recognising Indigenous Peoples' Relationships to Water?' *Australian Indigenous Law Review* 14, no. 2 (2010): 49–62.
Morton, Timothy. *Humankind: Solidarity with Non-Human People.* New York: Verso Books, 2017.
Morton, Timothy. *Hyperobjects: Philosophy and Ecology After the End of the World.* Minneapolis: University of Minnesota Press, 2013.
Myers, William. *Bio Design: Nature + Science + Creativity*. New York: Museum of Modern Art, 2012.
Nasa. 'Apollo 11 - Technical Air-To-Ground Voice Transcription'.15 Accessed May 2022. https://www.hq.nasa.gov/alsj/a11/a11transcript_tec.html
National Geographic Society. 'Great Pacific Garbage Patch'. Accessed 17 June 2021. https://www.nationalgeographic.org/encyclopedia/great-pacific-garbage-patch/
New European Bauhaus. 'New European Bauhaus: Beautiful, Sustainable, Together'. Accessed 9 March 2021. https://europa.eu/new-european-bauhaus/index_en.
Nixon, Rob. 'The Great Acceleration and the Great Divergence: Vulnerability in the Anthropocene'. *Profession*, March 2014.
Norman, Don. 'Design for a Better World: Meaningful, Sustainable, Humanity Centred', Cambridge, MA: MIT Press, 2024
Norman, Don. 'Humanity-Centred Design'. Interaction Design Foundation – IxDF. 14 June 2021).
Oberthür, Sebastian and Hermann Ott. *The Kyoto Protocol: International Climate Policy for the 21st Century*. Berlin: Springer, 1999.

Olaimy, Leena, et al. 'Planet-Centred Design: Public-Planet Partnerships'. *Udemy*, 2021. https://www.udemy.com/course/public-planet-partnerships-planet-centric-design/

Oliver, Kelly. *Animal Lessons: How They Teach Us to Be Human*. New York: Columbia University Press, 2009.

Owens, Johnathyn. '10 Principles of Life-Centred Design'. *Medium*, 3 June 2022. https://medium.com/the-sentient-files/10-principles-of-life-centred-design-3c5f543414f3

Parikka, Jussi. *The Anthrobscene*. Minneapolis: University of Minnesota Press, 2014.

Paris Agreement to the United Nations Framework Convention on Climate Change, 12 December 2015, TIAS No. 16-1104.

Papanek, Victor. *Design for the Real World: Human Ecology and Social Change*. Chicago: Academy Chicago Publishers, 1985.

Pierre, Louise St. 'Design and Nature A History'. In *Design and Nature: A Partnership*, 2019. doi:10.4324/9781351111515-14

Planet Centric Design. 'Accelerating the Transition'. Accessed 12 November 2022. https://planetcentricdesign.com

Preciado, Paul B. 'Ecosexual Marriage with Annie Sprinkle and Beth Stephens'. In *More-Than-Human*, edited by Penny Harvey, Marina Otero Verzier and Lucia Pietroiusti. Rotterdam: Het Nieuwe Instituut, 2021.

Ragusa, Antonia, et al. 'Plasticenta: First Evidence of Microplastics in Human Placenta'. *Environment International*, 146 (2021): 106274. https://doi.org/10.1016/j.envint.2020.106274

Rammelt, Crelis, et al. 'Impacts of Meeting Minimum Access on Critical Earth Systems Amidst the Great Inequality'. *Nature Sustainability* 6 (2022): 212–21.

Raworth, Kate. A Safe and Just Space for Humanity: Can We Live Within the Doughnut? Oxford: Oxfam International, 2012. https://www-cdn.oxfam.org/s3fs-public/file_attachments/dp-a-safe-and-just-space-for-humanity-130212-en_5.pdf

Raworth, Kate. 'Must the Anthropocene be a Manthropocene?' *The Guardian*, 20 October 2014. https://www.theguardian.com/commentisfree/2014/oct/20/anthropocene-working-group-science-gender-bias

What is Humanity-Centered Design?. Interaction Design Foundation – IxDF. https://www.interaction-design.org/literature/topics/humanity-centered-design

Rodgers, Anna and Doust Roeland, dir. 'Online Habits Killing the Planet: Dispatches Brook Lapping Productions'. *Channel 4*, 2020. https://www.channel4.com/programmes/online-habits-killing-the-planet-dispatches.

Royal College of Art. 'Design Thinking & Innovation in Collaboration with The Design Museum'. Accessed 11 November 2022. https://www.rca.ac.uk/study/programme-finder/design-thinking-innovation-collaboration-design-museum/

Richard, Kevin and Daniele Catalanotto. *Au Delà Du Human Centred Design: Planet Centric Design*. Accessed 9 February2022. https://www.youtube.com/watch?v=kvc8NuflGXQ

Richardson, Katherine, et al. 'Earth beyond Six of Nine Planetary Boundaries'. *Science Advances* 9, no. 2458 (2023): 1–16. https://doi.org/10.1126/sciadv.adh2458

Richter, Felix. 'Charted: There Are More Mobile Phones Than People in the World'. World Economic Forum, 11 April 2023. https://www.weforum.org/stories/2023/04/charted-there-are-more-phones-than-people-in-the-world/

Riofrancos, Thea. 'The Rush to Go Electric Comes with a Hidden Cost: Destructive Lithium Mining'. *The Guardian*, 14 June 2021.

Ripple, William. J., et al.'World Scientists Warning to Humanity: A Second Notice'. *BioScience* 67, no. 12 (2017): 1026–28.

Rosén, Anton Poikolainen, Antti Salovaara, Andrea Botero and Marie Louise. *More-Than-Human Design in Practice*. London: Taylor & Francis, 2024.

Royal College of Art. 'National University of Singapore Business School'. Accessed 13 May 2025. https://www.rca.ac.uk/business/case-studies/national-university-singapore-business-school/

Royal College of Art. *National University of Singapore Business School Executive MBA Design Thinking Workshop*. London: Royal College of Art, n.d.

Rull, Valentí. 'Beyond Us'. *EMBO Reports* 10, no. 11 (2009): 1191–95. https://doi.org/10.1038/embor.2009.225

Sánchez Ruano, David. *Symbiotic Design Practice: Designing with-in Nature*. PhD diss., University of Dundee, 2016. https://doi.org/10.13140/RG.2.2.36192.23046.

Scalar. 'Reassembling Rubbish. *Reassembling Rubbish'*. Accessed 6 February 2022. https://scalar.usc.edu/works/reassembling-rubbish/index

Schimel, D., et al. 'Evolution of the Human-Environment Relationship'. In *The Encyclopedia of Earth*, 2 May 2007. https://editors.eol.org/eoearth/wiki/Evolution_of_the_Human-Environment_Relationship

Sevaldson, Birger. 'What is Systemic Design? Practices Beyond Analyses and Modelling'. Paper presented at the *Relating Systems Thinking and Design (RSD8) Symposium*, Chicago, IL, 13–15 October 2019. https://openresearch.ocadu.ca/id/eprint/3233/

Space 10. 'Beyond Human-Centred Design'. Accessed 9 September 2022. https://space10.com/beyond-human-centred-design/

Stanford d.school. *Human-Centered Design: An Integrative Design Exploration*. Palo Alto, CA: Stanford University, n.d.

Stanford d.school. 'Integrative Design: A Practice to Tackle Complex Challenges'. Accessed 13 May 2025. https://dschool.stanford.edu/stories/integrative-design-a-practice-to-tackle-complex-challenges

Stone, Christopher D. *Should Trees Have Standing? Law, Morality, and the Environment*. New York, Oxford University Press, 2010.

Strand, Roger, et al. 'Exiting the Anthropocene? Exploring Fundamental Change in Our Relationship with Nature'. *European Environment Agency, Briefing* 24 (2022).

Street, Paul. 'How To Stop Capitalism's Deadly War with Nature'. *Truth Dig*, 16 April 2018. https://www.truthdig.com/articles/how-to-stop-capitalisms-deadly-war-with-nature/

Subcommission on Quaternary Stratigraphy. 'Working Group on The Anthropocene'. Accessed 12 October 2021. http://quaternary.stratigraphy.org/working-groups/anthropocene/

Suckling, Kieran. 'Welcome to the Homogenocene: The Mass Extinction of Cultures and Species and How to Reverse the Trend'. Poster presented at the Olajos-Goslow Endowment Speaker Series, Northern Arizona University, 15 April 2015. https://nau.edu/wp-content/uploads/sites/125/2018/05/SucklingPoster.pdf

Sustainable Markets Initiative. 'Terra Carta'. Accessed 1 May 2022. https://www.sustainable-markets.org/terra-carta/

Swiss Design Network. Counterparts: Exploring Design Beyond the Human. Conference held at Zurich University of the Arts, 27–28 October 2022. https://swissdesignnetwork.ch/en/conferences/counterparts-exploring-design-beyond-the-human/

Tassinari, Virginia and Eduardo Staszowski. *Designing in Dark Times: An Arendtian Lexicon*. London: Bloomsbury Visual Arts, 2020.

The Care Collective. *CARE MANIFESTO: The Politics of Compassion*. London: Verso Books, 2020.

Thackara, John. 'Designing For All of Life, Not Just Human Life'. *This is HCD*, 18 October 2018. https://www.thisishcd.com/episode/john-thackara-designing-for-all-of-life-not-just-human-life

Tironi, Martín, et al. *Design for More-Than-Human Futures: Towards Post-Anthropocentric Worlding*. London: Routledge, 2023.

Tironi, Martin, Albornoz Camila and Marcos Chilet. 'Problematizing Human-Centred Design: Notes on Planet-Oriented Design'. *Diid – Disegno Industriale* 77, no.-1 (2022): 38–49. https://doi.org/10.30682/diid7722c

Twemlow, Alice. *Sifting the Trash: A History of Design Criticism*. Cambridge (Massachusetts): MIT Press, 2017.

Tronto, Joan C. 'An Ethic of Care'. *Generations: Journal of the American Society on Aging*, 22, no. 3 (1998): 15–20. http://www.jstor.org/stable/44875693

Tsing, Anna L., Heather Anne Swanson, Elaine Gan and Nils Bubandt. *Arts of Living on a Damaged Planet: Ghosts and Monsters of the Anthropocene*. Minneapolis, University of Minnesota Press, 2017.

Tsing, Anna L. 'When Things We Study Respond to Each Other: Tools for Unpacking 'The Material'. In *More-Than-Human*, edited by Penny Harvey, Marina Otero Verzier and Lucia Pietroiusti. Rotterdam: Het Nieuwe Instituut, 2021, 16–26.

Thunberg, Greta. *The Climate Book*. London: Allen Lane, 2022.

United Nations Environment Programme. 'About Montreal Protocol'. Last modified October 29, 2018. https://www.unep.org/ozonaction/who-we-are/about-montreal-protocol.

United Nation. 'Roadmap For Digital Cooperation'. 2020. Accessed 15 October 2021. https://www.un.org/en/content/digital-cooperation roadmap/assets/pdf/Roadmap_for_Digital_Cooperation_EN.pdf

United Nations. *'Nature's Dangerous Decline Unprecedented; Species Extinction Rates Accelerating*'. Accessed 1 July 2021. https://www.un.org/sustainabledevelopment/blog/2019/05/nature-decline-unprecedented-report/

Van den Bergh, Jeroen. 2018. 'Agrowth Instead of Anti-And Pro-Growth: Less Polarization, More Support For Sustainability/Climate Policies'. *The Journal of Population and Sustainability*, 3, no. 1 (2018): 53–7. https://doi.org/10.3197/jps.2018.3.1.53

Voigt, Jonas. 'Post Social: Towards Design Beyond the Human'. In *NERD – New Experimental Research in Design 2: Positions and Perspectives*, edited by Michelle Christensen, Ralf Michel and Wolfgang Jonas. Berlin: Birkhäuser, 2022, 153–72. https://doi.org/10.1515/9783035623666-012

Wakkary, Ron. *Things We Could Design: For More Than Human-Centered Worlds*. Cambridge, MA: MIT Press, 2021.

Wallace-Wells, David. *The Uninhabitable Earth: A Story of the Future*. London: Allen Lane, 2019.

Wallin, Jason. 'Dark Pedagogy'. In *More-Than-Human*, edited by Penny Harvey, Marina Otero Verzier and Lucia Pietroiusti. Rotterdam: Het Nieuwe Instituut, 2021.

Wang, Yize, et al. 'Airborne Hydrophilic Microplastics in Cloud Water at High Altitudes and Their Role in Cloud Formation'. *Environmental Chemistry Letter* 21 (2023): 3055–62. https://doi.org/10.1007/s10311-023-01626-x

Warkentin, Traci. 'Interspecies Etiquette: An Ethics of Paying Attention to Animals'. *Ethics and The Environment* 15, no. 1 (2010): 101. https://doi.org/10.2979/ete.2010.15.1.101

Waters, N. Colin and Simon D. Turner. 'Defining the onset of the Anthropocene'. *Science* 378, no. 6621 (2015): 706–8. https://doi.org/10.1126/science.ade2310

WEAll. *'Wellbeing Economy Alliance'.* Accessed 24 November 2020. https://weall.org

White, Franke. *The Overview Effect: Space Exploration and Human Evolution*. Reston: American Institute of Aeronautics & Astronautics, 1997.

WHO. 'One Health'. World Health Organization, 2023. Accessed 19 January 2023. (https://www.who.int/health-topics/one-health)

Wikipedia contributors. 'Baby Shark'. Wikipedia, The Free Encyclopedia. Last modified 11 May 2025. https://en.wikipedia.org/wiki/Baby_Shark

Wilson, Edward O. *Half-Earth: Our Planet's Fight for Life*. New York: Liveright Publishing Corporation, 2016.

Witze, Alexandra. 'This Quiet Lake Could Mark the Start of a New Anthropocene Epoch'. *Nature*. 11 July 2023. https://www.nature.com/articles/d41586-023-02234-z

Wood, Chloe. *Our Time on Hearth*. London: Barbican, 2023.

World Economic Forum. *Nature Risk Rising: Why the Crisis Engulfing Nature Matters for Business and the Economy*. Geneva: World Economic Forum, 2020.

World Meteorological Organization. 'State of The Global Climate 2020'. WMO – No. 1264, 2021. https://library.wmo.int/?lvl=notice_display&id=21880#.Yd274i-I1pQ

World Meteorological Organization. *State of the Global Climate in 2021*. Geneva: WMO, 18 May 2022.

World Meteorological Organization. 'State of the Global Climate 2022'. Geneva: WMO, 2023. https://library.wmo.int/records/item/66214-state-of-the-global-climate-2022.

Yaneva, Albena and Alejandro Zaera-Polo. *What is Cosmopolitical Design? Design, Nature and the Built Environment*. London: Routledge, 2017.

Yunkaporta, Tyson. *Sand Talk: How Indigenous Thinking Can Save the World*. Melbourne: Text Publishing, 2020.

Yusoff, Kathryn. *A Billion Black Anthropocenes or None*. Minneapolis: University of Minnesota Press, 2018.

Zalasiewicz, Jan, et al. 'Working Group on the Anthropocene 2016'. *Subcommission on Quaternary Stratigraphy of the International Union of Geological Sciences (IUG.S).*

Zalasiewicz, Jan, et al. 'The Working Group on the Anthropocene: Summary of Evidence and Interim Recommendations'. *Anthropocene* 19, no. 9 (2017): 55–60. https://doi.org/10.1016/j.ancene.2017.09.001

Zettler, Erik R. and Tracy J. Mincer. 'Life in the Plastisphere: Microbial Communities on Plastic Marine Debris'. *Environmental Science and Technology* 47, no. 13 (2013): 7136–46. https://doi.org/10.1021/es401288x

Zylinska, Joanna. 'A Feminist Counterapocalypse'. In *More-Than-Human*, edited by Penny Harvey, Marina Otero Verzier and Lucia Pietroiusti. Rotterdam: Het Nieuwe Instituut, 2021, 55–60.

PREFACE: PARTS I, II AND III

Elio Caccavale and Gordon Hush

Despite the United Nations General Assembly resolution passed on 28 July 2022, recognizing a clean, healthy and sustainable environment as a human right, global challenges such as climate change and ecosystem degradation are demonstrating that a singular disciplinary approach is inadequate to respond to issues where societal behaviours, individual choices, political decisions and economic, technological and scientific developments are so densely entangled – not least in design. But what happens when we turn things around and decentre 'the human' to look at our relationship with the planet, its ecosystems and inhabitants beyond the capitalist human-nature binary worldview?

To use the words of anthropologist and author of the book *How Forests Think: Towards an Anthropology Beyond the Human* Eduardo Kohn, a deeper engagement with other species and ecosystems ultimately opens up 'new kinds of possibilities for relating and understanding even though their existence extends beyond us . . . it can help us understand how we might better live in a world we share with other kinds of lives' (2013, 7, 22). From this perspective, collectively, the essays included in the following three sections generate conversations capable of thinking about life on planet Earth, challenging the Anglo-European anthropocentric conceptualization of design that dominates practice, education and academic discourse. Each section is unique: charting the transdisciplinary cultural perspective and lived experiences that are required to comprehend our predicament, the critique of human-centred design and its interdependence with capitalism and the nascent design practices and projects that are attempting to reconcile humanity's possible relationship with the planet, its ecosystems and inhabitants.

Cumulatively, these contributions offer readers an opportunity to engage with expertise, knowledge and methodologies from across disciplines as well as lived experiences shaped by shared concerns and provide an opportunity to question if design in a more-than-human way might reimagine design's relationship to capitalism and contemporary lifestyles. Will our planetary future be merely an ecologically aware version of today, or, in going *beyond the human*, might we develop a transdisciplinary perspective capable of imagining an alternative vision of life on Earth?

PART I

WE ARE NOT ALONE

INTRODUCTION: WE ARE NOT ALONE

We Are Not Alone explores our relationship with other species and ecosystems from a transdisciplinary perspective across activism, anthropology, artificial intelligence, economics, education, ethics, history, Indigenous knowledge, philosophy, politics, regenerative agriculture, science and sociology. Additionally, it aims to examine and unpick the anthropomorphism/anthropocentrism as a 'driver' that has brought us here, to a crisis point. The historical efforts of some to shape the future and fashion increased wellbeing have left all of us vulnerable to the ecological consequences of the economic system of production that we have developed.

We Are Not Alone highlights the key terms, historical processes and contemporary consequences of our global capitalism, which has delivered planetary consequences. Each contribution looks deep beneath the surface of humanity's lived reality, showing that we are truly interconnected and entangled in a symbiotic relationship with our planet. Biologist Lynn Margulis and chemist and environmentalist James Lovelock called this interconnectedness and entanglement that keeps our planet balanced Gaia – named after the ancient Greek Earth's goddess. The Gaia theory, also known as the Gaia principle or the Gaia hypothesis, proposes that all life on Earth and inorganic environments are linked, forming a single and self-regulating complex system that maintains the conditions for life on our planet (Lovelock 1979). This notion is also exemplified by ideas like Deep Ecology (Næss 1973), Strong Sustainability (Turner 1993), the Chthulucene (Haraway 2015) and the Symbiocene (Albrecht 2015), which offer motivation for reconsidering how people and nature interact, reminding us that we have a symbiotic relationship with other species and ecosystems (Strand et al. 2022).

The diversity of authors, disciplines, lived experiences and examples in this section is a key aspect of the book, taking design into academic and cultural territories far removed from the Anglo-European design tradition, especially design's relationship with other disciplinary practices, cultures and capitalism. In transcending the historical, cultural and disciplinary origins of design and its associated vocabulary, *Design Beyond the Human* re-positions design as a constituent element in a transdisciplinary conversation capable of critiquing the contemporary global present.

In the essay 'A Political Economy of Structural Anthropocentrism', Economics Professor Steven McMullen examines the systematic nature of public and private decision-making in the 'Global North', emphasizing its consistent prioritization of human interests at the expense of neglecting non-human animals. McMullen explores approaches to increase the representation of non-human animals and ecosystems within political and economic institutions, hopefully resulting in downstream practices that are not focused on anthropocentrism and, thus, less destructive.

In their collaborative essay 'Co-creating Multispecies Worlds', Professor of Sociology and Social Policy Danielle Celermajer and architect Matthew Darmour-Paul explore the need to redefine justice, extending it beyond the human realm to encompass the natural world. Their discussion addresses the far-reaching effects of climate change, Indigenous rights, resource depletion and the consequences of industrial farming. In their text, Celermajer and Darmour-Paul not only draw from their personal experiences but also extend beyond the established principles and challenges that scholars in multispecies justice have started to outline. Their essay explores tangible practices involved in shaping spaces such as homes, workplaces and areas for recreation designed to be welcoming and accommodating to multispecies living.

Professor of Social Anthropology Noboru Ishikawa's essay 'Global Trajectories of Oil Palm: From African Communal Groves to Asian Plantation Frontiers' provides a historical account of the transportation of plants from different locations and their subsequent cultivation. Ishikawa argues that the intercontinental movements have homogenized the flora at a rate unprecedented in the Earth's history, leading Haraway and others to call the post-Columbian era the Plantationocene (2015), a geological period of anthropogenic reorganization of the web of lives. More precisely, Ishikawa examines the historical trajectory of oil palm, emphasizing the displacement of both human populations and plants lacking a documented history. He also explores how the pollen of plants transported from their original locations to the frontiers of plantations constitutes a unique geological layer, serving as a significant reference point for future generations.

Journalist and editor Helen Hollyman, whose work focuses on regenerative agriculture, and member of the Navajo Nation and Indigenous farmer James Skeet examine regenerative agricultural methods to reimagine future food systems and land stewardship. Their essay 'The Call of the Cricket' includes Indigenous voices, emphasizing ancient technologies and insights and focusing on utilizing these traditional perspectives to restore degraded land, enhance biodiversity, facilitate carbon drawdown and challenge industrialized lifestyles. Hollyman and Skeet's essay emphasizes the value of Indigenous knowledge and practices in addressing environmental challenges and promoting sustainable approaches to living in harmony with the natural world.

Environmental anthropology scholar and Associate Professor in Climate and Development Peter Sutoris's chapter 'Design, Education and the Moulding of Alternative Futures in the Anthropocene' reflects on the philosophical consequences of the Anthropocene within the realm of design. By drawing parallels with education, a domain significantly impacted by humanity's unparalleled influence on the natural environment, Sutoris's essay explores the dilemma faced by designers. The central question posed is whether design will be relegated to a mere tool for supporting human survival in the Anthropocene or whether it will actively seek to facilitate human flourishing by reshaping our relationship with the planet. Sutoris provides context to this question by incorporating perspectives from activist environmental movements in the 'Global South'. This inclusion serves to illustrate alternative ways of conceptualizing design in the Anthropocene, challenging the prevailing human-centric and Eurocentric paradigm.

1

A POLITICAL ECONOMY OF STRUCTURAL ANTHROPOCENTRISM

Steven McMullen

Starting in the 1980s, biologist Eugene Stoermer started using the term 'Anthropocene' to refer to our present epoch in which human activity is a defining feature of natural planetary processes (Steffen et al. 2011). This term is particularly fitting for an age of climate change, but it is also an apt description of our age in other respects. The last two centuries have been a disaster for the wellbeing of non-human animals and important ecosystems. There are only a few animal species whose populations have exploded in the last 100 years, and they are all domesticated animals farmed and enjoyed by humans. In contrast, the populations of non-domesticated animals, including mammals, fish, birds, reptiles and amphibians, have declined by an astonishing 68 per cent since 1970 (Almond, Grooten and Petersen 2020). It is a defining feature of the world today that the wellbeing of non-human animals and plants is almost entirely determined by the place that they have in the lives of humans.

One way to describe such a world is to say that it is anthropocentric. Human preferences and human institutions are at the centre of the most momentous decisions. Where human interests are in conflict with the interests of non-human life on our planet, human interests prevail. In recent decades, it has become apparent that our anthropocentric society, particularly the wealthiest countries, is so narrowly concerned with the wellbeing of humans that even the longer-term welfare of natural systems that are essential to human life have been sacrificed in order to meet the short-term interests of present-day wealthy humans. We see this most clearly in the extinction crisis and anthropogenic climate change, where action by rich countries has been inadequate to the task of even preserving those things that will be essential for human wellbeing in the next couple of centuries.

In the case of these acute crises, there is no mystery about what could be done to rectify the problems. A more rapid global investment in renewable energy and a consistently high tax on carbon would go a long way towards limiting carbon emissions and slowing climate change. Similarly, a rapid decrease in habitat destruction and over-harvesting of wild species could turn the trend on species extinctions. However, while progress has been made, we have not mustered the political and social will to make these big, and admittedly costly, changes to the way we live. This failure to act raises an important question: what is it about our current mode of social organization that prevents us from taking full account of the interests of non-human life?

Answering this question requires that we think deeply about two different ways in which anthropocentrism manifests itself. First, we can note that people might have anthropocentric beliefs or practices. If someone argues that it is more important to preserve jobs in a logging industry than to preserve the habitat of an endangered bird, for example, that person might be expressing a belief that human interests should generally trump environmental protection. This would be an anthropocentric belief. However, there is a second kind of anthropocentrism that is more important for understanding our society-wide ecological failures. The second kind of anthropocentrism is structural. When institutions are designed to be responsive to human interests and ignore the interests of other species, then even well-meaning individuals might be constrained to act in an anthropocentric manner.

In many wealthy countries, our political and economic systems are structurally anthropocentric. The interests of non-human species have no direct voice in policymaking or law. Instead, they only receive attention when particular individual humans choose to use their power on behalf of non-humans. Similarly, our economic life gives economic power and privilege only to the preferences of individual humans with access to some wealth. This means that our ecological crises are, in some sense, a matter of design. We have designed a system that is responsive only to a subset of interests, and the result is predictable negligence and environmental decline. An analysis of this systemic anthropocentrism is ultimately hopeful, however, because it points to the possibility of an alternative design that is more responsive to the interests of a broader community of species on Earth.

It is worth noting, at the outset, that one can be concerned with the ecological crisis we face, and with the structural anthropocentrism that undergirds it, without adopting a view that all life has an equal value in some ethical sense. That is, one could easily hold that, when in conflict, any one human life is more valuable than the life of an insect or bird, while still believing that the life of the insect or bird warrants far more concern than our current system offers them. There are some true dilemmas in which important interests of humans and other living organisms are in conflict. In these situations, it may be appropriate to consider those interests with a greater weight on the lives of humans. Even in these situations, though, we would do well to design a system that allows us to weigh and consider the interests of non-human life at all times.

Structural anthropocentrism

Structural anthropocentrism is an attribute of a system, not individuals, and it points to the elements of the system that are automatically responsive to the interests of humans over and above the interests of other life. Let me start by sketching, in broad terms, the ways in which anthropocentrism can be structural. First, it is often the case that social institutions create some diffusion of responsibility for decision-making. Each person can lean on the consensus of a larger group (of humans) so that the moral weight of a decision does not fall fully on them. Second, there is often a distance between the decision and the effect on other living beings. This moral distance makes it easier to accept the status quo and ignore the consequences of any given choice. Third, social institutions often operate with an implicit or explicit anthropocentric purpose. Even environmental movements might purport to exist to 'preserve the world for our children and grandchildren' or to 'maintain the conditions for full human flourishing'. Finally, such institutions usually require a high degree of consensus among humans to change the system.

It may not be that all of these elements are obviously present in a social institution, but the combination creates a potent cultural barrier to change and a kind of moral alienation for individuals. A conscientious individual, who thinks and cares deeply about environmental harm, might still find themselves in a position where their job or social role dictates an action that is harmful to non-human life. They are not offered an ecologically respectful path, and so it would take a heroic level of creativity and commitment to live within their moral convictions. In this sense, it is clearly the system that is anthropocentric, not the individual, and any wide-scale change would have to be one of institutional design, not just moral suasion.

Animal agriculture: A case study

There may be no institution in which humans and the natural world collide so directly as in agriculture, and so it is useful to examine animal agriculture in some detail to understand the depth and complexity of anthropocentrism in our economic institutions. On the one hand, it is simple to observe that we slaughter billions of animals to feed humans. This arrangement clearly advances some purported interests of humans and proceeds at the expense of the animals. In that sense, animal agriculture appears, on its face, anthropocentric. On the other hand, in order to really understand the depth and impact of this anthropocentrism, it is useful to consider two important arguments made in defence of animal agriculture.

First, consider a simple defence of animal agriculture: that animals must be well treated and live good lives on a farm, since a neglected or harmed animal would not grow well, would produce less meat/milk/eggs and would ultimately be a loss for the farmer. The heart of this argument is that farmers have an economic incentive to take care of their animals, and the animals benefit from this. This is closely tied to the arguments of free market environmentalism more broadly (Anderson and Leal 2001; Lusk and Norwood 2011). If this response is correct, and animal ownership aligns the interests of animals and humans, then anthropocentrism is unproblematic, since there is no conflict. In some limited ways, moreover, the argument holds up quite well. Farmers do protect their animals from some kinds of harm, and farmed animals are never underfed. However, agricultural economists Bailey Norwood and Jayson Lusk demonstrate that the profit motive will not maximize animal welfare but will always sacrifice animal welfare, even when it hurts animal productivity, if it increases profits (2011). They also show that this conflict is a normal occurrence. The only animal interests that are protected are the ones that are in alignment with those of their human owners.

Second, consider a more formidable defence of animal agriculture: the argument that has come to be named the 'Logic of the Larder'. In simple terms, the argument is that animals are better off as a result of having been farmed. Because existence is a good thing, and many more pigs exist in agriculture than do otherwise, it can be said that agriculture has been a blessing for pigs, overall. There is no doubt that the populations of domesticated farmed animals have exploded. The most numerous mammals on the planet are pigs and cows. The most numerous birds are chickens. The conclusion of the argument is that even institutions that look exploitative can be mutually beneficial, at least at a species-population level.

Scholars have examined the 'logic of the larder' argument in great detail, offering empirical and philosophical critiques (Lamey 2019; Matheny and Chan 2005; McMullen 2016, ch. 3; Norwood and Lusk 2011). A short examination of the arguments will suffice here. The starting place for understanding the problem with the 'logic of the larder' argument, and the earlier argument about farm productivity, is that it ignores any interests that animals might have other than population growth. Even a cursory examination of the welfare of the animals in confined agricultural settings, however, reveals that most of an animal's interests are ignored or suppressed. Farmed animals live much shorter lives than the normal lifespan for their species; they live in barren environments, are subjected to painful procedures, are deprived of normal socialization or familial relationships and often find their bodies failing due to accelerated growth and lack of movement (Halteman 2011; Norwood and Lusk 2011). There may be some utilitarian ethic under which these harms are less important than overall population success, but a more reasonable conclusion is that the arrangement noticeably harms these animals.

The depth of the impact of anthropocentrism on farmed animals, however, is revealed when we examine the ways that human control has changed farmed animals over time. The genetic selection and careful breeding of animals, by humans, has left a mark on the varieties of animals that are commonly farmed. Compared to chickens from 100 years ago, chickens farmed today are specially bred for a purpose: either to produce meat by growing unnaturally large very quickly or to produce eggs far more rapidly in great quantities. These genetic changes have imposed great costs on the birds; broiler chickens often struggle to walk when they are full-grown at only three months old, and the bodies of laying hens are quickly depleted of calcium and nutrients from laying eggs at an unnatural rate. Farmed turkeys face similar challenges. These selected characteristics, which harm the animals, reveal the degree to which anthropocentrism permeates agriculture – the very bodies of animals have been conformed to the specific interests of human consumption at the expense of the animals.

The anthropocentrism of animal agriculture is structural. Part of the reason that the system remains indifferent to the interests of farmed animals is that individual consumers and individual farmers have a difficult time creating the space for alternatives within the system. Consider the situation of a farmer who wants to buck the industry and provide their chickens with a natural environment. In most cases, this would noticeably increase their costs. If the farmer was unable to charge a higher price for their product, they would likely go out of business. In this environment, the farmer could easily say that the consumers, or other farmers, dictate their behaviour. However, the best way to think about it is that we have built a market system in which lowering costs often crowds out other goals (McMullen 2015).

Alternatively, consider the consumer, who is faced with little information about the way their food is produced. Some more expensive products have animal-welfare labels, but many of these labels signal only the weakest commitments to the welfare of animals and can be deceiving. In that environment, the consumer might rightly note that they are not really in a position to make a difference without going outside of the primary food distribution system. In the market system, neither the consumer nor the farmer is able to make changes on their own. This diffuses responsibility across many people who would have to coordinate their behaviour or build different institutions in order to be in a position to change animal agriculture.

Endangered species

While anthropocentrism might be expected in a consumer-driven institution like animal agriculture, it is also the rule in other institutions. Even those institutions that exist to protect non-human life fall into this trap. In the United States., it is common for government-owned parks, which are often a refuge for plants and animals, to be justified solely in terms of the value that is brought to citizens. In this anthropocentric vision, parks exist so that visitors can enjoy their beauty or use the land for recreation.

Similarly, endangered species protections are justified by appealing to the benefits humans might gain, in the future, from the existence of these species.

This anthropocentrism then limits the effectiveness of these institutions as well. Consider the signature legislation that protects endangered species in the United States, the Endangered Species Act. The law prohibits the trade, capture or transport of animals that are designated as endangered and places limitations on the use of land that is determined to be critical habitat of those species. While great progress has been made in protecting endangered species, partly as a result of this law, this legal approach has two main failings. First, by limiting critical habitat, it pits the interests of the animal in this habitat against the interests of the landowners. When the land is identified as critical for an endangered species, the value and usefulness of that land, in economic terms, is greatly diminished. This undermines the incentives that landowners have to cooperate with the law (Adler 2008). Second, the Endangered Species Act is chronically underfunded, so remedial efforts to help an endangered population recover are generally inadequate except for particular charismatic species. That is, the real resources needed to help endangered species recover tend to go to those animals that are well loved by humans.

Some critics of the endangered species framework have argued for a stronger emphasis on property-based approaches to species conservation. They argue that animals are best preserved by giving humans clear ownership of said animals and allowing people to make wise decisions to preserve the value of the things they own. This approach makes some sense when there is a common-resource problem (Hardin 1968), since it limits the incentive to over-hunt or over-harvest from the limited population. Given the discussion of animal agriculture, however, it should be clear that ownership by humans, for the purpose of human consumption, is no panacea for non-human animals, even if the total population effects are positive (McMullen 2015). The difficulties with all of these approaches to species conservation demonstrate that a marginal change, in an anthropocentric system, will immediately conflict with other institutions and have limited effect.

Locating power in a liberal market order

The failure of these institutions, for animals, points to an underlying problem: humans hold all the real power in our economic order, by design, and so there are no economic institutions that really work in the interests of non-human life. In a modern liberal market order, there are two broad ways in which we protect important interests. First, we can protect negative interests (interests against harm by another) by granting certain rights by law. Second, we protect positive interests by granting material support or by creating opportunities for self-sufficient production and consumption.

In order to understand the nature of anthropocentrism, consider the ways in which these two kinds of interest-protection work out for humans and don't work for non-humans. First, the system is designed for humans, and so human interests get well cared for, even if this happens unevenly. In a liberal order, negative interests are protected by laws against assault, enslavement and various kinds of deceit. Positive interests are provided through a framework of participation rights (ability to own property), through provided goods (safety net benefits, healthcare, education) and self-sufficient production and consumption (work and income). None of these same power sources are granted for non-human animals, plants and ecosystems. Negative interests are only rarely granted. Protection from harm is granted only to the select animals that humans value as companions and is rarely offered to other animals outside of endangered species protections. Similarly, material aid is granted to non-humans only in rare circumstances. The best analogue for the ability to produce/consume, for a non-human plant/animal, is to be granted land to live on. As we might note from declining populations of animals worldwide, animals are granted the land necessary to flourish in fewer and fewer circumstances, as human activity crowds out other ecosystems. There is no direct way for the interests of non-human plants and animals to be protected in a market where only humans have the ability to own land, purchase goods and services or otherwise exercise economic power.

The anthropocentrism of our economic order is also undergirded by a political order with the same blind spots. Our political structures are also not designed to recognize the interests of non-human life. Democratic institutions are designed to be responsive to the interests of human constituents (Garner 2022). While humans may have the ability to recognize the good of ecosystems nearby, and vote accordingly, this arrangement makes all non-human interests contingent on human interests for recognition. That is, we only protect the interests of non-human life when it also is deemed to be in the interest of humans.

Even when democratic systems create agencies with a mandate to pursue environmental protection and preservation, these agencies exist in a political environment that is only held accountable to humans. If agencies tasked with environmental protection made decisions that were popular with voters but deeply damaging to the environment, there is no obvious way in which they would be held accountable. In many ways, the anthropocentrism of economic life is downstream from the anthropocentrism in the political sphere. The only actors with the power to limit destructive economic practices are, themselves, stuck in a system where doing so would run counter to their own political incentives and mandate.

The design of a political/economic system that respects all life

The primary problem with an anthropocentric social system is that it creates powerful norms that push against any serious independent consideration of the interests of non-human life. At any point in the system, you could place a person who had the goal of working for the interests of other living things, but that person would almost inevitably find that there was no way to do their job well, as their job is conventionally defined, and pursue their non-anthropocentric goals. Farmers and consumers are constrained by market competition. Concerned citizens have no standing or right to challenge the practices of others unless they own the animals or land. Judges and lawyers who might be sympathetic to animal rights are constrained by current laws that give little space for such considerations. Lawmakers are constrained by the powerful interests protecting the status quo and the lack of enfranchisement for non-humans.

The only solution for this kind of systemic problem is an alternative design. If we are able to create a system that is responsive to the interests of all life at multiple key points of power, the incentives and opportunities for leaders and activists throughout the system could change for the better. In the burgeoning literature in what is sometimes called the 'political turn' in animal studies, this is often discussed as a problem of enfranchisement (Vink 2020). While enfranchisement is often conceived in narrow terms – the right to vote – a broader theory is relevant here. Plants, animals and ecosystems might be said to be 'enfranchised' in two ways: they can be granted legal rights with corresponding duties on the part of humans, and they can be given formal representation and consideration in policymaking. In many countries, both kinds of enfranchisement will be a difficult and significant step, but the long-term consequences could be important.

Several scholars have tried to build a non-anthropocentric democratic theory, and these accounts offer some important lessons (Donaldson and Kymlicka 2013; Garner 2017; Vink 2020). I will focus here on four initial changes that can be made to a political/economic system that would explicitly counter the anthropocentric biases built into the liberal market order. The first two changes would amend what is included in property rights for plants, animals and land. The third change is aimed at opening up the legal system to challenges on behalf of animals, and the last change would create a kind of representation for free-living animals and ecosystems by giving wild spaces some political autonomy.

First, our anthropocentric economic order values non-human life primarily in market terms. Forests have a market value, determined by the amount of money that a human would be willing to pay for ownership of that forest. In contrast, we value other humans in non-market terms, and demonstrate that value by precluding a market valuation. We do not allow humans to be bought and sold, precisely because humans have great value. This slavery prohibition caused the old institutions that treated humans as property to crumble. Environmental philosophers have often noted that the key difference depends on our ability to acknowledge that a living thing has not just a use value but also an intrinsic value. Once we recognize that non-human life can have intrinsic value, we must immediately recognize the need for a set of laws that protects some of the basic interests of that life.

For some scholars, the clear implication is that we need to abolish property relations. Among animal rights scholars, for example, Gary Francione is famous for advocating the strict abolition of animal ownership as a way of recognizing inherent value (1995, 2006). However, we need not start there. Even if human ownership of non-human life remains, we can signal the value of plants, animals and ecosystems by protecting some basic interests in law. These protections could take many forms but will usually weaken the kinds of rights that accompany ownership. To offer one example, consider a law that required justification for killing an animal or cutting down a mature tree. The required justification could include a consideration of the interests of the animal/tree themselves (and thus allow the killing of animals and plants that were sick) and could include consideration of the species' normal lifespan. Such a requirement could become a formality that is ignored, but it could also create a reasonable process in which the animal/plant is presumed to have an interest in existence, even if other concerns can outweigh that interest.

A second way to make our political/economic system less anthropocentric is to acknowledge important non-human relationships. Our legal system and dominant economic thinking tend to abstract and atomize individuals and property. As a result, the assumption is that property can be separated and used for alternative purposes at the owner's whim (McMullen and Molling 2015). In fact, though, living things always exist in a web of relationships that are essential to the functioning of life-sustaining ecosystems. We recognize that the actions of one person can harm another person and have built laws around adjudicating those disputes. In order to truly respect the interests of non-human animals, plants and ecosystems, we must acknowledge these kinds of harm in natural relationships. This principle would force us to rethink the existence of road systems that disrupt migration pathways, farming practices that disrupt waterways and hunting/fishing practices that will undermine important species populations. Third, on a more practical level, our legal system will have to adopt some means for non-human interests to have legal representation. One step in that direction is to appoint some people with the standing to enforce laws on behalf of non-human victims, even against owners. In many countries, this falls to the government to prosecute animal cruelty laws or environmental law. Given the anthropocentric political accountability system, however, the laws, and the enforcement of those laws, is often weak. If more citizens had legal standing to represent animals in legal challenges, there would be more accountability for individuals, firms and governments to respect the interests of non-human animals.

The changes that I suggest here will be politically difficult in most countries and are likely to create real losses for people who have built lives and businesses around the ownership and use of the natural world. One way to make progress with less disruption is to create separate spaces where the anthropocentric logic is officially flipped on its head. Whereas most places create entrenched preferences for the interests of humans, we can create parks, nature preserves and wildlife sanctuaries that operate with a very different logic. If these areas are large enough to support significant populations of animals, and if they are offered some level of political protection, simply designating space is an important step that can be taken quickly. Consider the following difference: in most human-dominated spaces, plants and animals exist and thrive only if doing so is not in conflict with human interests. In contrast, in a nature preserve, ideally, the purpose of the space is explicitly non-anthropocentric, and so any human use of the space should be consistent with the interests of the species and ecosystems protected there. The most ambitious proposal, along these lines, is the effort to preserve 30 per cent of land by 2030, promoted by some international conservation organizations (Thompson 2022).

Conclusion

The best way to understand the nature of the ecological crisis facing Earth today is to recognize that we have built a systemically anthropocentric world. We have designed a set of economic and political institutions that are responsive to the interests of humans but that ignore the interests of non-human life except when human interests coincide. In this environment, human actors, even with the best intentions, are often unable to consistently live in ways that are ecologically intelligent. Our economic institutions only give us the information and latitude to pursue personal interests. Competition within large industries prevents firms from making costly commitments to environmental protection. Our political systems make it difficult to gain power without adopting an anthropocentric worldview. Non-human life is politically, legally and economically disenfranchised in this social environment. Only with systemic change can the game's rules be changed enough for a broader set of ecological interests to be given a hearing. The good news is that with some foundational changes, there can be wide impact.

Millions of human consumer decisions could be altered quickly if the underlying market rules gave some weight to the wellbeing of animals in agriculture. Small changes in legal relationships could open up the law to the challenges of the worst environmental abuses. At only a moderate expense, with some coordination, we could create the space for free-living animals, plants and ecosystems to have real political protection and dedicated space to thrive.

References

Adler, Jonathan. 'Money or Nothing: The Adverse Environmental Consequences of Uncompensated Land Use Control'. *Boston College Law Review* 49, no. 2 (2008): 301.

Almond, R. E. A., Monique Grooten and Tanya Petersen. 'Living Planet Report 2020 – Bending the Curve of Biodiversity Loss'. Gland, Switzerland: World Wildlife Fund International, 2020. https://livingplanet.panda.org/en-us/.

Anderson, Terry H. and Leal R. Donald. *Free Market Environmentalism*. New York: Palgrave Macmillan, 2001.

Donaldson, Sue and Will Kymlicka. *Zoopolis: A Political Theory of Animal Rights*. New York: Oxford University Press, 2013.

Francione, Gary L. *Animals, Property, and the Law*. Philadelphia: Temple University Press, 1995.

Francione, Gary L. 'Animals – Property or Persons?' In *Animal Rights: Current Debates and New Directions*, edited by Cass R. Sunstein and Martha C. Nussbaum. New York: Oxford University Press, 2006, 108–42.

Garner, Robert. 'Animals and Democratic Theory: Beyond an Anthropocentric Account'. *Contemporary Political Theory* 16, no. 4 (2017): 459–77. https://doi.org/10.1057/s41296-016-0072-0

Garner, Robert. 'The Case for an Interspecies Theory of Democracy'. *Journal of Animal Ethics* 12, no. 1 (2022): 96–102. https://doi.org/10.5406/21601267.12.1.10

Halteman, Matthew C. 'Varieties of Harm to Animals in Industrial Farming'. *Journal of Animal Ethics* 1, no. 2 (2011): 122–31. https://doi.org/10.5406/janimalethics.1.2.0122

Hardin, Garrett. 'The Tragedy of the Commons'. *Science* 162, no. 3859 (1968): 1243–8 https://doi.org/10.1126/science.162.3859.1243

Lamey, Andy. 'The Logic of the Larder'. In *Duty and the Beast: Should We Eat Meat in the Name of Animal Rights?* Cambridge: Cambridge University Press, 2019, 177–98. https://doi.org/10.1017/9781316672693.008

Lusk, Jayson L. and F. Bailey Norwood. 'Animal Welfare Economics'. *Applied Economic Perspectives and Policy* 33, no. 4 (November 2011): 463–83. https://doi.org/10.1093/aepp/ppr036

Matheny, Gaverick and Kai M. A. Chan. 'Human Diets and Animal Welfare: The Illogic of the Larder'. *Journal of Agricultural and Environmental Ethics* 18, no. 6 (2005): 579–94. https://doi.org/10.1007/s10806-005-1805-x

McMullen, Steven. *Animals and the Economy*. Palgrave Macmillan Animal Ethics Series. London: Palgrave Macmillan, 2016.

McMullen, Steven. 'Is Capitalism to Blame? Animal Lives in the Marketplace'. *Journal of Animal Ethics* 5, no. 2 (2015): 126–34.

McMullen, Steven. 'Property, Regulation, and Endangered Species Conservation'. In *The Routledge Handbook of Animal Ethics*, edited by Bob Fischer, 1st edn New York, NY: Routledge, 2019, 432–43.

McMullen, Steven and Daniel Molling. 'Environmental Ethics, Economics, and Property Law'. In *Law and Social Economics: Essays in Ethical Values for Theory, Practice, and Policy*, edited by Mark D. White. New York: Palgrave Macmillan, 2015, 21–40 .

Norwood, F. Bailey and Jayson L. Lusk. *Compassion, by the Pound: The Economics of Farm Animal Welfare*. New York: Oxford University Press, 2011.

Steffen, Will, Jacques Grinevald, Paul Crutzen and John McNeill. 'The Anthropocene: Conceptual and Historical Perspectives'. *Philosophical Transactions of the Royal Society A: Mathematical, Physical and Engineering Sciences* 369, no. 1938 (2011): 842–67. https://doi.org/10.1098/rsta.2010.0327

Thompson, Andrea. 'How Conserving 30 Percent of U.S. Land by 2030 Could Work'. *Scientific American*, 22 April 2022. https://www.scientificamerican.com/article/how-conserving-30-percent-of-u-s-land-by-2030-could-work/

Vink, Janneke. *The Open Society and Its Animals*. Cham: Palgrave Macmillan, 2020.

2

CO-CREATING MULTISPECIES WORLDS

Danielle Celermajer and Matthew Darmour-Paul

By the early twenty-first century, human societies across the world had become increasingly caught up in the Western modernist story of human exceptionalism and infinite progress. Implicit in the imagination of boundless development was the parallel fantasy of ever more efficient extraction of the Earth's resources. Held in that thrall, we might once have been able to convince ourselves that the ongoing dispossession of and violence against First Nations peoples, the decimation of biodiversity resulting from human encroachment on wild animals' habitats, the environmental degradation resulting from development and pollution and the intensification and spread of animal diseases resulting from industrial animal agriculture were the unfortunate collateral damage of the 'improvement' of human life (Shiva 1991; Weis 2010; Crook, Short and South 2018; Almiron and Tafalla 2019).

The fallout of the global pandemic is a suitable time to reflect critically on the common sense of human exceptionalism. Indeed, the Covid-19 pandemic has forced a reckoning with the foreclosed truth that the business-as-usual destruction of the more-than-human world that is the correlate of colonial capitalist modernity is unavoidably and intimately bound up with the health and wellbeing of all humans (Barouki et al. 2021; Halabowski et al. 2021; Han et al. 2023). Indeed, as the forms of human organization that have been normalized by colonial capitalist modernity place ever greater strain on the conditions required to support all life on our planet, there is a growing awakening to humans' entanglements and shared predicaments with beings other than humans (Rose 2012).

In recent years, Multispecies Justice (MSJ) has emerged as a normative frame that grows from this realization (Celermajer et al. 2021). Importantly, it is not an additive or extensionist form of liberal justice. It is not the case that humans who claim definitional authority come to include certain non-human others as subjects of justice, now that the latter have been deemed to meet certain moral criteria once considered the preserve of (some) humans. Rather, and following the worldviews articulated by many First Nations peoples (Todd 2014; Winter 2023) and ecofeminists (Plumwood 1991), this is a form of justice that begins with a rejection of the hierarchically organized dualisms that have structured hegemonic Western thought and justified the relegation of beings other than humans and some humans to the status of surplus populations. There is a recognition of the ontological and ethical primacy of the relationships that support all life. Moreover, MSJ calls not simply for recognizing the reality that humans share the Earth and vulnerabilities with the more-than-human, but for changes in praxis at all scales. In this regard, MSJ is concerned not only with the transformations of the social, political, cultural and legal institutions that shape relations but also with the forms of attention and care that humans bring to how they think and feel about, design, organize and practise living with others (van Dooren, Kirksey and Munster 2016).

In this chapter, we reflect on the principles and challenges which scholars of MSJ have begun to articulate when reimagining the material practices of creating spaces – homes, workplaces and places of play and leisure – hospitable to multispecies flourishing. In doing so, we draw on experiments that prefigure and enter speculative imaginings of just multispecies cohabitation. To do this, we take a walk through the intentional multispecies home that one of us (Danielle Celermajer, hereafter Dany) has been co-creating with more-than humans. We write outwards from five encounters we believe embody the possibilities of MSJ.

It is important to highlight that MSJ cannot simply be thought into existence: a seismic restructuring of processes that are centuries in the making requires sustained material engagement. To that end, Dany's home is a site where the principles of MSJ hit the ground in diverse ways. Two important notions we thread throughout the encounters are that of labour and the family, which we return to in the conclusion.

Figure 2.1 Mac eating Kikuyu during a compost circuit. Photograph, 2021. Courtesy of Danielle Celermajer and Matthew Darmour-Paul.

Compost as multidirectional remaking

Time at Dany's is characterized by daily compost circuits. Driving in a mini electric all-terrain vehicle (ATV), we go around the extensive, undulating fields with gloves, shovels and extra-large colourful gorilla tubs, picking up manure that the horses, donkeys and pigs have deposited on the land they walked during the previous night or day. In one version of this circuit, we park the ATV and collect from about 50 square metres of area at a time, handling manure into manure scoops, dumping those scoops into the tubs and dumping those tubs into the back of the ATV. In another version, one person slowly drives towards an ever-growing compost pile while the other walks with a shovel and gloves, adding to the small manure mountain on the back of the ATV on the way to its destination: a large concrete platform that houses a mound of compost and two tarp-covered aerators. We are composting.

Does this way of composting belong to (non-human) nature or (human) culture? It depends on how we conceive those terms, and our composting activity affords an opportunity to recompose them. Composting is of course happening all the time on a healthy forest floor: leaf litter falling, mycelium digesting, microbes breaking down substances and soil being built. But what about when humans 'compost', especially when introducing technologies like pump-driven aerators to keep the compost at a certain temperature? The presence of technology might so dominate our picture that we declare this an example of the genius of human culture acting on nature. Or, we might say that humans are acting within nature's productive cycles but as that dimension of nature called human. From this perspective, humans belong in the realm of nature – there is no outside – but one of the affordances of being a human being is this capacity to observe, abstract and facilitate metabolic processes. The best human role here is to watch what is happening, to understand how it is happening and then to add energy and particular affordances, including design capacities, to facilitate that happening in a way that supports the flourishing of all concerned. That is undoubtedly what this activity *feels* like.

Is this what philosopher Spinoza meant when he insisted that if we believe that freedom springs from a form of pure transcendental agency, disconnected from the complex causal relations in which all beings are embedded, such freedom is illusory? True human freedom involves understanding the way that multispecies relationships work and acting with that understanding. Human freedom in the context of composting is given by greater and greater understanding: showing up, seeing what the land and the animals who live there want and acting upon that understanding.

This turns on its head the anthropocentric worldview: instead of my mind directing my hand to feed the donkeys, my hand retrieving the manure, my hand shovelling the compost, all these actions, including the action of thought, are part of larger lifeways that include the animals, the soil, the land and even the feeling for creation. In this inversion, humans are what the soil is doing. There is both urgency and joy in this understanding. On the one hand, there is much work to be done. On the other hand, as Spinoza also teaches, true understanding is the occasion for joy, and there is little that is more joyous than joining in these life-creating flows.

Composting provides a rich challenge to the myth of individual human autonomy and our inherited notions of cause and effect. The process itself is a portal into an extended metabolism. If extractive agricultural practices sap the Earth of life by simplifying and streamlining biology into saleable units that end at the point of consumption, this process has no clear beginning or end because it is circular (Salleh 2010). Donkeys, horses and pigs eat grass, moving around the land according to their own rhythms, then humans see and smell their traces, and pick up the manure and bring it down to the compost station. At Dany's place, this process is facilitated by a vehicle powered by the sun's energy, gathered by solar panels on the roof of the home into which the horses move when they seek shelter from the rain. All of this happens as a precondition for growing the food that the donkeys, horses and humans will subsequently eat. And when the animals die, they will also join in and make the compost.

Another strand of this metabolic pathway is the carbon required to grow the soil which comes from trimming the edges of the surrounding forest, turning those tree branches into wood chips that mix with the manure's nitrogen. In this way, compost is a multidirectional (re)making process. It expands and contracts based on specific conditions which cannot necessarily be predicted. If the donkeys are not digesting things properly, the forest might expand and choke out other forms of life. The sensation is enlivening when you stick your hand into the covered compost pile. We humans attend to it several times a day while it is cooking to ensure that it sits at the sweet spot of between 50 and 55 degrees Celsius. It is a beautiful temperature to experience. Any hotter and beneficial microbes start to die off. There is much to learn by constantly reaching down towards the earth and picking up animal manure. There is a feeling that the process begins to deeply imbricate human and non-human metabolic pathways or return us to metabolisms that can justly support diverse forms of life.

Figure 2.2 Elevated living space with a view through the zen curtains towards the tree canopy, 2021. Courtesy of Danielle Celermajer and Matthew Darmour-Paul.

Glass as metaphor for multispecies injustice

When humans decide to live and work within spaces of glass, they are not simply making aesthetic choices; their actions are matters of justice – MSJ. How can this be so? The answer is at once simple and complex. Simple because the glass that enables pleasure for some (humans) is deadly for others; complex because the 'glass enclaves' that typify hypermodern life form part of and constitute larger political, social, technical and ethical orders and grids of opportunity and loss.

Humans seduced by Western modernity have simply followed the path that promises a perfect alignment between technological innovation and (their) pleasure or success. If, though, we reflect more clearly on the costs of this path, how it distributes those costs and to whom, quite different decision paths become an ethical imperative.

At Dany's multispecies community, the injustice of glass was no esoteric matter. The humans decided to build a home with large glass windows wrapped around the upper floor so that they could have the experience of being immersed in the forest. Only that aspiration to live even more intimately with the forest and birds with whom they shared this place quickly became a nightmare as they realized that their aesthetic choices spelt death or injury for birds. The humans looked out and saw the forest and felt pleasure. The birds looked in and saw the forest and felt the glass slam into their soft bodies. At one level, the humans were confronted with the carnage their own choice had produced; at another, they were encountering the implicit violence of their normalized ways of being human.

In *The World Interior of Capital*, philosopher Peter Sloterdijk depicted the Crystal Palace, the central feature of the 1851 Great Exhibition in London, as emblematic of a new socio-technical order. Such palaces, he argued, placed their human occupants within an immersive environment separated from the external world, yet where that world appeared as transparent and fully available to their gaze.

Creating and then occupying such spaces becomes an embodied technology for forming a particular kind of human: the modern liberal subject who comes to assume a frictionless interior condition safe from the messiness of the outside. A line can be drawn between the 1851 Crystal Palace designed by the gardener engineer Joseph Paxton and the 2017 Apple headquarters designed by the architecture firm Foster and Partners, a building with the largest panes of ultra-clear glass ever constructed.

The Crystal Palace provided an immersive space for the 'opaque' masses to experience the spectacle of global industry under imperialism, a precursor to the entertainment stadia and shopping centres that provide a common experience for citizens in overdeveloped countries today. A century and a half later, the Apple headquarters assumes an already transparent subject to roam its spaces, fully 'open' to the digital surveillance required of Apple and platform capitalism in general.

Sloterdijk sought to make apparent how spatial arrangements and technologies constitute humans in a specific, non-innocent way. As the humans at Dany's place painfully discovered, humans are not the only ones who experience and are impacted by the worlds fashioned in glass. As technologies of transparency have been 'perfected', the worlds they create for beings other than humans have become lethal.

At one level, that lethality is immediate. Glass panes have developed to become so large and transparent that birds are no longer able to discern their materiality. Whereas the human desire for immersion becomes the occasion for a sensual experience of unimpeded access to 'the world' beheld, birds find themselves involuntarily immersed in a perceptual world where their habitats appear to continue, deceptively without impediment, on the other side of a solid surface. Suppose you too have noticed more birds lying stunned or dead beneath large windows in recent years or heard them hit their soft bodies on hard panes. In that case, it is because what we naively call technological innovation conceals a brutal exchange: their lives for erasing all interference with human desire. Their deaths are no accident.

But this is not the only way in which the technologies of 'transparent life' are lethal. Creating and sustaining 'glass boxes', especially under ever more extreme climate change, requires a constant supply of energy. So long as the production of this energy rests on the extraction of fossil fuels, the 'pleasure' of a transparent life forms part of a complex assemblage destroying human and more-than-human life – in the past, right now and reaching into the future. Those deaths are not only largely beyond the purview of behind the glass but also carefully concealed by the political and semiotic systems of the world it helps to create.

Their commitment to MSJ meant that the humans at Dany's had to do something quickly about the immediate dimension of lethality for the birds, by modifying the glass itself and what surrounds it. Given the impact of the birds' deaths on them, they were shocked by how little public discussion there seemed to be about what we are doing to others when we design an architectural aperture to nature. Nevertheless, they discovered several solutions: decals on the windows, or small mesh netting over them, will save birds' lives. The solution they opted for was to install zen curtains – thick strings about 10 centimetres apart that hang from the top of each window. Today, they look beautiful swinging in the breeze, they save the birds lives and they remind the humans that they are not the only ones looking at the glass. But avenues like these will only be pursued when the impact of the technologies of the built environment on other creatures comes to matter to those with the power to make technological and design decisions.

The good news is that there is precedent for recognizing how technology and the built environment create injustice for some, specifically by disabling humans with different abilities. Normalized development processes have long ignored marginalized human groups, but in recent years building regulations in several jurisdictions have been modified to reduce the safety risks large glass windows and doors pose to children and people who are visually impaired. Of course, these did not arise because those with power become enlightened about the implicit exclusions of their ways of making sense of the world, but because people with disabilities spent decades pressing decision-makers to ensure that their different abilities were not the occasion for injustice.

Given that (at present) Western institutions provide no legal or political avenues for birds to advocate their own interests, such changes will only occur when humans (in the hypermodern West) make sense of the world and develop legal, political and design systems that accord real value to lives of beings other than humans. This may seem a long way off, but a start would be interpreting the sign of dead and stunned birds as a meaningful signal of their interest. We may not call it politics, but there is no opacity to the meaning of the communication.

Addressing the more complex lethality will be – well – more complex. Nevertheless, the metaphor of transparency provides a good starting point. As the impacts of environmental destruction on humans press ever more intensely upon us, both directly and in the form of our experience of loss of the worlds we now realize we treasured all along, so too does the pathological and illusory character of the subjectivity constituted behind glass.

The barrier between humans and the worlds they sought to survey, control and exploit did its job only so long as it appeared impenetrable and invisible, and thus completely natural. As damage permeates that barrier, so too, its constructed and fictional nature comes into view. And as the violence wrought by constructed transparency gets closer, other forms of subjectivity also become available and with

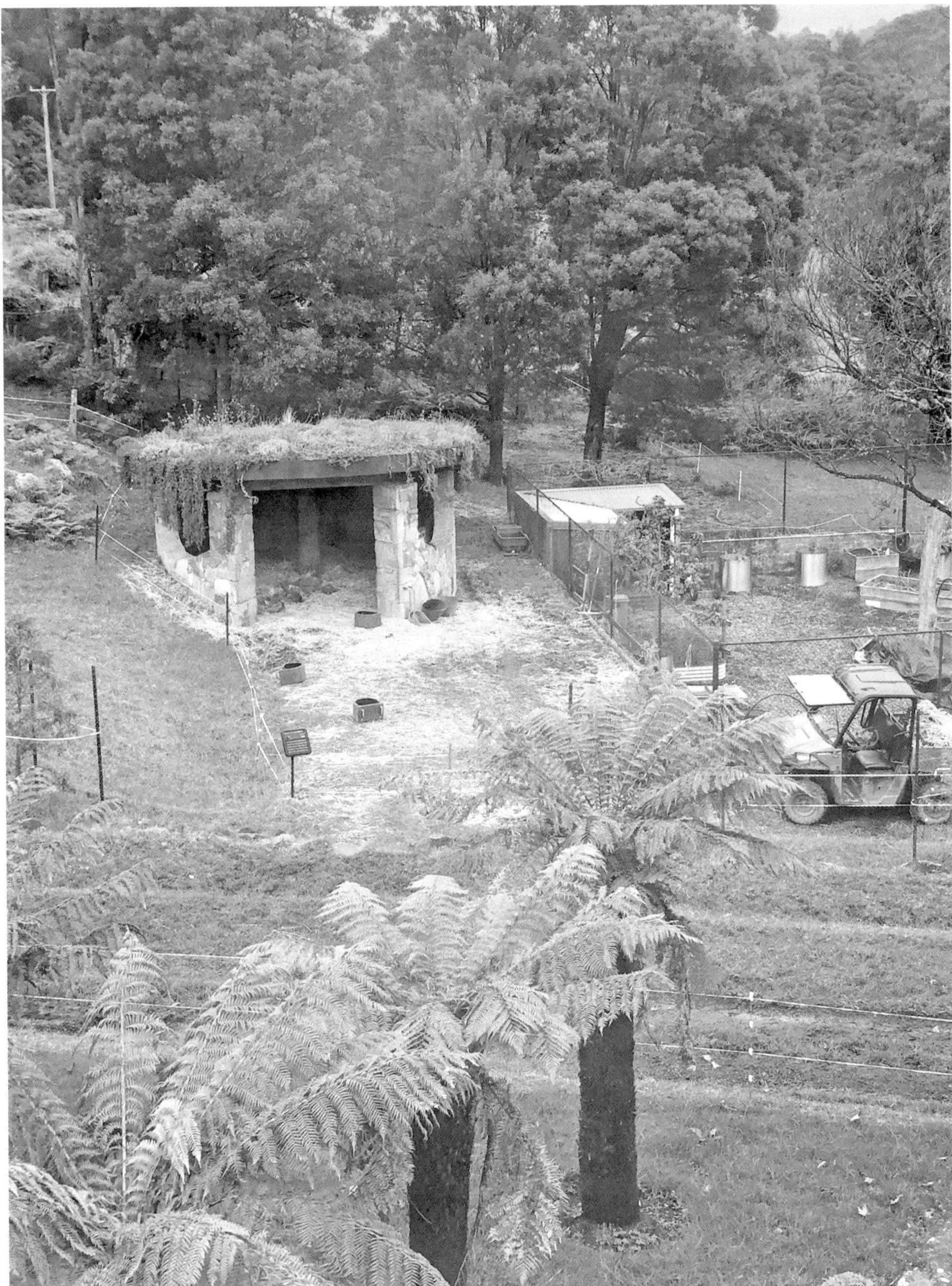

Figure 2.3 View towards the donkey's house with fern forest in the foreground, 2022. Courtesy of Danielle Celermajer and Matthew Darmour-Paul.

them, the realization that we have built worlds in which birds are not the only ones condemned to kill themselves as they hurtle into what they cannot see.

Birds must navigate the environments of today's transparent human subject: one that has gradually grown to be environmentally insensitive, over (air) conditioned and made operational by market forces. Correcting this tendency – unbuilding certain universalizing projects and building others – is a material imperative for MSJ.

Residence as mutual aid

At the end of 2019 and into the first weeks of 2020, devastating fires burned down the east coast of Australia and right up to the edge of the land where Dany and her community live. It is estimated that over three billion native animals were killed during what has become known as the Black Summer fires (which in fact commenced at the end of winter) (Dickman 2021). In the end, it was not human firefighters who stopped the fires but the rain that came in early 2020 and continued, at torrential levels, in the months thereafter. For everyone who lives there, rain at this intensity altered the conditions of life. The rainforest flourished. Some of the trees, overwhelmed by water, turned yellow. The roots of others became so sodden that they could not hold on, and the paths the donkeys took through the forest, or the humans took to visit the river, became impassable, huge trunks lying across them. As new springs opened from within the earth long stabilized by tree roots, the hillsides themselves started to shift, causing huge landslides.

Among the residents of this place are wombats, large low-to-the-ground marsupials who move on all fours and dig underground homes for themselves, including under humans' houses. During the rains, all the wombats were flooded out of their homes. One took up residence outside Dany and her partner's window in a space by the deck where they kept straw for the donkeys; only now the wombat harvested some of the straw to make a soft warm bed. Another took up temporary residence in the horses' stables, although only one of the horses was content to cohabit. Another wombat took up residence in the large donkey shelter made from stones collected on the land. The new constellation of residents did not seem to become friends, but the donkeys made space for the newcomer to burrow into the straw and left him in peace to sleep or watch the rain. The chickens joined as well; they enjoy the safety provided by the donkeys and the donkeys seem to like their company.

When discussing MSJ, there is a familiar retort that multispecies and interspecies space sharing is just too difficult. It is true that when species come together, there will be a proliferation of interests, sometimes competing and thus cause for conflict. Why though does it remain so acceptable to resolve those conflicts in a way that pre-emptively excludes the interests of some? Why, in concrete terms, does throwing some beings out of their homes, either directly through development-driven habitat destruction, or indirectly, through the contamination of lands and waters and the impacts climate change is having on their homes, not occur as a form of injustice that needs to be resolved by attending carefully to conflicting interests?

Over a century ago Peter Kropotkin, the Russian aristocrat turned anarchist, wrote a corrective to the 'survival of the fittest' paradigm that had been (hesitantly) promoted by Charles Darwin and championed by his contemporaries. His careful study of the Siberian Tundra revealed a narrative that was lost in Darwin's reading: collaboration and cooperation within a species community. He describes deer marching together across enormous Siberian rivers, crabs flipping over their upturned kin, birds providing shelter and deflection against agitators and horses forming spokes of a great wheel to protect their oldest and youngest from wolves (Kropotkin 1902). While there is conflict in nature, adversity is not typically members of the same species but the conditions of their environment.

Survival of the fittest is a myth that both legitimates and is perpetuated by the capitalist universe. It works alongside the myth that rational actors invented capitalism through benign forms of barter and trade, rather than by the domination of certain humans and all non-humans through slavery, exploitation and dispossession. The true nature of this history is lost on (liberal) human subjects, who have come to assume that other human beings acting as competitors, fighting for work and/or profits in a fair and open marketplace is natural. In contrast, cooperation is either ideological or can only ever function as a moral superstructure, imposed by commitments that call humans (and others) to act contrary to their nature (Servigne and Chapelle 2021, 29). The habit of performing meaningless human battles inherited from industrial settler colonialism is a tragic (mis)interpretation of 'natural law'.

Kropotkin invented the term 'mutual aid' to describe how the strong and weak alike worked towards the community's welfare to fight back against Social Darwinism. From competition to combination (and compost). From the struggle to the snuggle for existence(!). His views were far from perfect; for instance, he referred to Indigenous peoples as 'savages'. The irony of his racism is that Indigenous peoples have long developed lasting mutual aid networks that have sustained their lives and communities for tens of thousands of years and, more recently, allowed them to survive genocide. What is valuable about Kropotkin's ideas about science, biology and cooperation is increasingly confirmed by modern science pursuing ecological flourishing. As agronomist Pablo Servigne and agricultural engineer Gauthier Chapelle observe, across the living world, we find mutualisms and symbioses, or 'symbiodiversity', interactions that 'have been constantly created, invented, transformed, reinforced, broken down and erased ever since life has existed, in a sort of infinite ballet' (2021, 21). It is not that competition, conflict, predation and parasitism do not exist, but living beings have come to appreciate that 'struggle, mutual aggression, combat, threat or tension' (Servigne and Chapelle 2021, 25) are expensive, and that they all do better if they find ways of living together that create mutual benefit by sharing their respective affordances and accommodating their distinctive needs. Algae, for example, could be prey for fungi, but instead some fungi provide algae with minerals, in turn taking algae's sugars in a mutually beneficial relationship.

Forms of mutualism flourish of their own accord in Dany's community. This, though, is an environment where distinct species and individuals are introduced quickly, thus truncating the time distinct species might need to find a way of accommodating each other. Accordingly, there are myriad soft technologies designed to mediate possible conflicts between species: a loosely slung wire with a low-level electrical current turned on occasionally to remind the donkeys that there is a road with cars on the other side; a tall chain-link fence that once housed a tennis court (now veggie garden) to discourage the wombats from entering to eat those vegetables; thick dry-stacked stone walls from the previous pastoralist owners; sandstone and timber platforms joined (and separated) by tall steps. These are boundaries that support much smaller instruments like buckets, gloves and shovels. There are no barbed wires, blind fences or traps that might be found on a small-scale farm housing the same animals found here. There is a desire to facilitate harmony without asserting dominance. Of course, the design and the material need to be light and responsive to the movements, desires and interactions of everyone who lives there. Sometimes members of distinct species find themselves getting along and a fence needs to come down.

In *Tools for Conviviality*, philosopher, theologian and social critic Ivan Illich suggests an ideal society 'should be designed to allow all its members the most autonomous action by means of tools least controlled by others' (Illich, 1973). Illich was not concerned with interspecies relationships when he reflected on the potential for manipulation and liberation in hand tools, power tools and modern institutions, but his lessons are usefully reworked with an eye towards MSJ. Multispecies coordination is guiding, semi-coercive, semi-affectionate, distant and focused. It is a distributed, loose, non-innocent assemblage of objects, techniques and strategies for harmony. If more-than-human-centred design is an expanded form of mutual aid, then it is 'good' when it enables multispecies autonomy and flourishing and when the myriad tools of coordination are accessible to those ends.

This does not mean a community free of conflict. In some cases, even noticing conflicts requires attention. The free movement of the equines, for example, means the compaction of the soil, detracting from the conditions under which the microbes can flourish. Nor is the resolution simple. Dany is painfully aware of what is happening to the cows on the farm a few kilometres away and would like to offer some of them a home where their children will not be systematically removed, but bringing too many hard-hoofed animals onto the land would have deleterious effects on soil health. There is no formula for living justly in a multispecies community, particularly under the conditions of emergency and widespread violence of our times, and given their continued domination, humans find themselves in the position of having to work out, with others, what the best choices are.

Figure 2.4 View of fern forest towards living space, 2021. Courtesy of Danielle Celermajer and Matthew Darmour-Paul.

Ferns as air conditioners

Dany's community is in a high valley with temperatures generally a few degrees cooler than at lower altitudes, especially in the nearby regional town. Urban development has heated the atmospheric temperature in numerous ways, through its reliance on fossil-fuelled energy at the point of construction (embodied energy) and thereafter (operational energy) and by replacing soil, waterways and forests with hard structures that do not modulate the temperature and in some cases directly increase it. At one time, the southeast coast of Australia was thick with rainforest. Now there are only remnant patches, some quite large as in the area where the land is located, but some small; one can stumble on a rainforest grove sheltered beneath the sandstone cliff faces of the suburbs of Sydney. Accessing the rainforest is a privilege for all creatures learning to live in a warming climate.

Plants like ferns in the rainforest do the 'work' of providing shade and nutrients, taking over fallen trees. Ferns love the rain. They move surprisingly quickly, growing on rocks, trees and alongside streams. On this land, the rainforest around the river is dense and cool, and on a summer day it is the best place to go. Learning from the forest's temperature modulation, Dany planted a grove of ferns next to large, screened openings to their home. The evaporative cooling of the ferns acts as a shared air conditioner. It is not only the humans who benefit, however; the chickens, notoriously sensitive to heat, like to lie underneath them for coolth, and they take their dust baths in the soft humus at the ferns' feet.

Pteridomania was the name given to the explosion of fern growing in Victorian England and later in Australia (primarily Queensland). Once it was understood how these timeless Jurassic plants could propagate asexually, they wound up on wallpaper designs, biscuits and hairstyles across the British Empire. Later in the 1970s, they inspired fractal art, gender fluidity, chaos, complexity theory (and their economic correlates) and more. Their most enduring spatial expression is in the fernery or shade house: large semi-open enclosures that replicate the tree canopy by filtering out light and allowing for moisture to be captured. They are oversized ferns themselves.

Ferneries mark a departure from the glasshouse or conservatory, a space often cited as a conceptual origin point for energy-intensive air conditioning. If the conservatory is like placing a hermetically sealed bell jar over a curated garden, then the fernery merely filters the sun to cut down on direct heat exposure to hardy plants.

In his history of bioclimatic architecture, Professor of Architecture Daniel A. Barber refers to buildings reliant on fully air-conditioned interiors as 'stranded assets' – no longer tenable in a rapidly warming macroclimate (Barber 2020). Fully glazed office tower buildings in the downtowns and business districts of cities like Sydney were designed in the early and mid-twentieth century to accelerate the consumption of (cheap) fossil fuels through their reliance on the power to condition large volumes of air. If air conditioning requires reliable access to electricity and social infrastructure, no longer a given in an era of blackouts and bushfires, then real alternatives to fossil-fuel-powered cooling are urgently needed.

Pandemics and war have brought the costs of energy to the forefront of daily conversation. Meanwhile, large-scale internal cooling powered by fossil fuels is heating up the outside. The ferns at Dany's appear aesthetically beautiful and ethically appropriate to our times: the water necessary to keep ferns happy is repaid in evaporative cooling, carbon sequestration, habitats for insects (and chickens) and visual delight. Ferneries and ferns can propagate in hotter (and wetter) future settlements, so air conditioners can be uninstalled.

Figure 2.5 Penny exploring a heap at the compost station, 2022. Courtesy of Danielle Celermajer and Matthew Darmour-Paul.

Making worlds that fit

Jimmy and Katy were named by the first human who provided them sanctuary after they had been rescued from the factory floor where they had been discarded as 'wastage'. Only days or weeks old, they were tiny and malnourished, and severed from their mother's body, their necessary environment of care, vulnerable to exposure. So, the woman knitted them small sweaters, hoping to create both an immediate and more encompassing world in which they could survive and flourish. When her circumstances changed, and she could no longer sustain a home for all of them, she asked Dany and her partner if Jimmy and Katy could come to live with them. They have both since died, but they left marks in the land and in meaning.

If you walk down from the smaller, barer run where Jimmy and Katy once came up for their food and water, you find yourself in a densely wooded sloped area where the pigs spent their days. It can be difficult to find the pigs, until you discover they are in one of the places they have created. The first one Dany discovered was a carved-out semi-cave-like structure among a fallen tree that Jimmy had engineered to provide a cool space with a soft floor to protect themselves from the hot afternoon sun. Over the following months, it became apparent that this was just one structure Jimmy had designed and built. Others were located where the shade fell at various times, where shelter was afforded against different directional winds or where the muted winter sun provided the most warmth on colder days.

The German biologist Jakob von Uexküll famously theorized that all living organisms live within what he called their distinctive *Umwelt*, whereby they perceive the world in ways that are fitted to their mode of life, with the implication that different organisms experience the world in radically diverse ways (von Uexküll 2013). A vast body of work now exists documenting how, through processes of evolutionary biology, species have come to develop vastly diverse senses and bodily forms that mediate between the external world of others and the environment, on the one hand, and their needs on the other (Yong 2022). Animals other than humans are still represented as the passive products of evolutionary processes that (as distinct from who) develop their forms and capacities as a type of mathematical correlation to the larger world. They are not represented as creative agents who might intervene in the world or themselves in ways that allow them to meet their needs better or fulfil their desires or pleasures.

That they are represented in such a way is consistent with what political scientist John Rodman (1980) called the 'Differential Imperative': a dogma constitutive of hegemonic Western thought, whereby the definition of 'the human' was given not simply by its difference from, but its superiority to other animals (Rodman 1980; Celermajer and Winter 2022). Among the better-known putative differentiating characteristics like reason, language, tool making and the capacity to conceive of one's own death, this hegemonic Western tradition has insisted that humans alone can imagine the world otherwise, creating designs to approximate their imaginings, and then manipulating the material world to realize their designs.

This idea has been challenged in recent years, influenced by both the environmental and biodiversity crises and various posthumanisms (Gordon and Roudavski 2021; Haldrup, Samson and Laurien 2022; Metcalfe 2015; Sheikh, Gonsalves and Foth 2021; Tomitsch et al. 2021). Admittedly, it has long been recognized that some animals manipulate their environment, even to the point of building (think beavers), but such acknowledgements have traditionally remained within functionalist frames, thereby retaining the differential imperative, even as they present an opening to deconstruct it. A commitment to MSJ, by contrast, rejects the constitutive refusal to interpret others' world-making practices as forms of agency or creativity.

However, one of the principles of MSJ is a rejection of assimilative logics, whereby others' 'agency' or moral status is recognized once it can be demonstrated that they possess those capacities that have been thought to confer such status on 'the human'. In the context of thinking about animal designers, this opens the possibility of encountering design otherwise. More specifically, as a designer, engineer and builder Jimmy did not seem to be acting on a passive world, an exteriority that he was manipulating to achieve his independent ends. Rather, he was acting with, feeling with and hence designing with the world. Apart from the wonder that encountering his design practice evokes, what is most exciting is what it suggests as a possibility for humans also.

Conclusion

Both in the way that language is used in Western societies and in the functioning of economic systems, it is commonplace that only humans can labour, or more accurately, that human labour is distinctive and accordingly ought to be afforded a unique status and value. If, however, we understand labour as simply putting energy into a system to make things happen and create things, then everyone in the multispecies community at Dany's is labouring. Their lives are made up of energy, un/rest and movement. They move nutrients through bodies and landscapes and landscapes to nurture their bodies. The theory of justice requires that everybody be rewarded for their labour, yet with dominant conceptions of labour, animals are never seen as workers. If we were to recognize their contribution to the production of wealth, they would need to be appropriately compensated: their work would need to be recognized as work and not just considered 'what animals do'. Acknowledging labour in this way must be removed from the neoliberal pull of 'ecosystem services' and the idea that nature is an enterprise: that their labour can be commodified. Instead, we must acknowledge that non-human labour is work that should be rewarded with flourishing – qualitative, not quantitative valuing.

Which raises the notion of family: the donkeys, Mac, Jimmy, Katy, Penny and Badger are not just machines making the system function; they are part of the family. What could this mean? Problematizing the nuclear family was once a central part of ecological politics. In our era of climate catastrophe, there is a consensus around the imperative to look after one's family, because the state will not be there to protect you (or the state will come but long after the damage is done). If the normative family must replace welfare as we knew it and is 'a method for cheaply arranging the reproduction of the nation's labour-power and securing debt repayments' (Lewis 2022), then huge gains can be made by unsettling its model. In the patriarchal family, reproductive labour (historically performed by women and women of colour) is made invisible and underpaid. In the multispecies community, the donkeys, the microbes, Mac, Penny and Badger perform work that is compensated with care, housing, affection and, most importantly, a say in how life is organized in the otherwise all-too-human drama of life in a settler society. Like most families, members move from utter annoyance to total dependence, based on the time of day and year.

If we had to distil design lessons from these encounters of labouring within a multispecies family, they might read:

- Non-human creatures are our guides, with stories to tell. Build and unbuild together with, and with attention towards them.
- Design in radical solidarity with all living things – do not contribute to the homogenization of the world.
- Refuse to separate food, land, ecology and politics as they are always already entangled.

While the extent of the family is routinely scrutinized – taking on a new member is difficult to achieve – the family is an open gathering of beings that takes aim at the speciest and heteronormative nuclear family, sidestepping its necessary exclusions to remake something better. Noticing, acting upon and coordinating multispecies relationships is the labour of this family: It is not made invisible, and the figures of the family are not patriarchal or normative.

References

Almiron, Nuria and Marta Tafalla. 'Rethinking the Ethical Challenge in the Climate Deadlock: Anthropocentrism, Ideological Denial and Animal Liberation'. *Journal of Agricultural and Environmental Ethics* 32, no. 2 (2019): 255–67.

Barber, Daniel A. *Modern Architecture and Climate: Design Before Air Conditioning*. Princeton: Princeton University Press, 2020.

Barouki, Robert, et al. 'The COVID-19 Pandemic and Global Environmental Change: Emerging Research Needs'. *Environment International* 146 (2021): 106272.

Black, Sophie. *The Exchange*. New York: Graywolf Press, 2013.

Celermajer, Danielle and Christine J. Winter. 'Fables for the Anthropocene: Illuminating Other Stories for Being Human in an Age of Planetary Turmoil'. *Environmental Philosophy* 19, no. 2: (2022): 163–90.

Celermajer, Danielle, et al. 'Multispecies Justice: Theories, Challenges, and a Research Agenda for Environmental Politics.' *Environmental Politics* 30, no. 1–2 (2021): 119–40.

Crook, Martin, Short, Damien, and Nigle South. 'Ecocide, Genocide, Capitalism and Colonialism: Consequences for Indigenous Peoples and Global Ecosystems Environments'. *Theoretical Criminology* 22, no. 3 (2018): 298–317.

de La Bellacasa, Maria Puig. *Matters of Care: Speculative Ethics in More Than Human Worlds*, Minneapolis: University of Minnesota Press, 2017.

Dickman, Christopher R. 'Ecological Consequences of Australia's "Black Summer" Bushfires: Managing for Recovery.' *Integrated Environmental Assessment and Management* 17, no. 6 (2021): 1162–7.

Gatens, Moira. 'Spinoza's Notion of Freedom'. In *A Companion to Spinoza*, edited by Yitzhak Y. Melamed. Hoboken: Wiley Blackwell, 2021, 394–401.

Gordon, Bobbie J. and Stanislav Roudavski. 'More-Than-Human Infrastructure for Just Resilience: Learning from, Working with, and Designing for Bald Cypress Trees (Taxodium Distichum) in the Mississippi River Delta'. *Global Environment* 14, no. 3 (2021): 442–74.

Halabowski, Dariusz and Piotr Rzymski. 'Taking a Lesson from the COVID-19 Pandemic: Preventing the Future Outbreaks of Viral Zoonoses Through a Multi-Faceted Approach'. *Science of the Total Environment* 757 (2021): 43723.

Haldrup, Michael, Samson, Kristine and Thomas Laurien. 'Designing for Multispecies Commons'. Participatory Design Conference, Newcastle, UK, 19 August-1 September, 2022.

Han, Jiatong, et al. 'Environment and COVID-19 Incidence: A Critical Review'. *Journal of Environmental Sciences* 124 (2023): 933–51.

Illich, Ivan. *Tools for Conviviality*. New York: Harper & Row, 1973.

Kropotkin, Petr. *Mutual Aid: A Factor in Evolution*. New York: McClure Phillips & Co, 1902.

Lewis, Sophie. *Abolish the Family: A Manifesto for Care and Liberation*. London: Verso Books, 2022.

Metcalfe, Daniel J. '*Multispecies Design*.' PhD diss. University of the Arts London and Falmouth University, 2015.

Plumwood, Val. 'Nature, Self, and Gender: Feminism, Environmental Philosophy, and the Critique of Rationalism'. *Hypatia* 6, no. 1 (1991): 3–27.

Rodman, John. 'Paradigm Change in Political Science: An Ecological Perspective'. *American Behavioural Scientist* 24, no. 1 (1980): 49–78.

Rose, Deborah Bird. 'Multispecies Knots of Ethical Time'. *Environmental Philosophy* 9, no. 1 (2012): 127–40.

Salleh, Ariel. 'From Metabolic Rift to "Metabolic Value": Reflections on Environmental Sociology and the Alternative Globalization Movement'. *Organisation and Environment* 23, no. 2 (2010): 205–19.

Servigne, Pabolo and Gauthier Chapelle. *Mutual Aid: The Other Law of the Jungle*. London: Polity Press, 2021.

Sheikh, Hira, Gonsalves, Kavita and Marcus Foth. 'Plant(e)tecture: Towards a Multispecies Media Architecture Framework for Amplifying Plant Agencies'. *Media Architecture Biennale 20* (2021): 87–99.

Shiva, Vandana. *The Violence of the Green Revolution: Third World Agriculture, Ecology and Politics*. London: Zed Books, 1991.

Todd, Zoe. 'Fish Pluralities: Human-Animal Relations and Sites of Engagement in Paulatuuq, Arctic Canada.' *Études/Inuit/Studies*, 38, no. 1–2 (2014): 217–38.

Tomitsch, Marti, et al. 'Human Personas: Including Nature in the Participatory Design of Smart Cities'. *Interaction Design and Architecture (s)* 50 (2021).

van Dooren, Thom, Kirksey, Eben and Ursula Munster. 'Multispecies Studies: Cultivating the Arts of Attentiveness'. *Environmental Humanities* 8, no. 1 (2016): 1–21.

von Uexküll, Jakob Johann. *A Foray into the Worlds of Animals and Humans: With a Theory of Meaning*. Translated by Joseph O'Neil. Minneapolis: University of Minnesota Press, 2013.

Weis, Tony. 'The Accelerating Biophysical Contradictions of Industrial Capitalist Agriculture'. *Journal of Agrarian Change* 10, no. 3 (2010): 315–41.

Winter, Christine. 'Unearthing the Time/Space/Matter of Multispecies Justice'. *Cultural Politics* 19, no. 1 (2023): 39–56.

Yong, Ed. *An Immense World: How Animal Senses Reveal the Hidden Realms Around Us*. Toronto: Knopf Canada, 2022.

3
GLOBAL TRAJECTORIES OF OIL PALM

FROM AFRICAN COMMUNAL GROVES TO ASIAN PLANTATION FRONTIERS

Noboru Ishikawa

We have now entered the Anthropocene era, as so many scholars argue. The Holocene epoch is over. In this new geohistorical period, humans are the most powerful agents of change, reshaping the Earth in unprecedented ways. This, in turn, demands new ways of thinking about how humans have become the 'great force of nature' at a planetary scale (Haraway 2015; Ellis 2018, 2; Bauer and Bhan 2018). Even among those who accept the premise of a relatively new Anthropocene era, different theories abound as to when human influence became paramount. Natural scientists search for hints of change in phenomena such as the climate and atmospheric chemistry. Many historians point to the Industrial Revolution and the widespread use of fossil fuels as a crucial inflexion point. Social scientists, for their part, examine changes in social formations, structural relations and forms of governance as well as the intensified movements of people and things at a global scale (Ishikawa 2019).

The long-distance movement of plants from their places of origin to locations of their subsequent cultivation is, without doubt, one of the significant features of the Anthropocene. For future generations, layers of pollen marked in the places of origin and new layers in agricultural frontiers would mark a distinctive geological stratum, providing a point of reference in human history. By paying attention to the movements of plants-cum-commodities, I suggest, we have a better understanding of the dynamics of capitalism, governance and mobilization of labour and utilization of natural resources that have led to profound global transformations. Plant trajectories also uncover the multifaceted entanglements of society, culture, ecology, history and power surrounding the plants at the places of origin as well as subsequent sites of transplantation.

This chapter traces the trajectories of oil palm (*Elaeis guineensis*) from one equatorial zone to another, from West Africa, where it was first domesticated, to Southeast Asia. Descendants of African oil palm have thrived in Southeast Asian frontiers as one of the most prominent and widely cultivated cash crops. In the process, oil palm's nature has been changed from a ubiquitous local plant found in communal groves, deeply rooted in the landscape of West Africa, to an industrial crop in Southeast Asia producing most of the world's palm oil. Following the movement of four original oil palm seedlings, which became the foundation stock of plantation development in Southeast Asia, the episode I recount here sheds light on the transformative changes of plant-human relationships and their impacts on the society and ecology of the tropics.

Uprooted people and crops

After 1492, from the onset of the so-called Columbian Exchange, crops such as sugar cane, rubber, palm and banana were transported, cultivated, harvested and processed by the hands of enslaved and indentured labourers in the Americas and beyond. These plants generated enormous fortunes for a global plantocracy and for capitalist accumulation more generally. Over the course of more than five centuries, the plantation production system massively transformed local ecologies and communities, both human and non-human.

In fact, the voyage of explorer the Christopher Columbus in 1492 triggered a large and diverse spatial rearrangement of the natural landscape across the surface of the Earth. The intercontinental movements and interchanges are said to have homogenized the flora at a rate unprecedented in the Earth's history, leading some to call the post-Columbian era the *Plantationocene*, a geological period of anthropogenic reorganization of the web of lives (cf. Haraway et al. 2016). The Plantationocene is an epoch characterized explicitly by the emergence of a large-scale, monocropping production system. Significantly, each constituent of this production system – plant, land, labour, technology and infrastructure – is mutually dependent and essential to the operation of the whole (cf. Mintz 1959, 44, 1985).

Since the Columbian Exchange, the spatial mobility of people has also accelerated. According to the early work of the notable economist Arthur W. Lewis, after whom the 'Lewis Transition Model' is named, some 100 million people migrated across international borders during a period of a hundred years spanning the eighteenth and nineteenth centuries, about a million people per year. These migrants were divided into two main groups: Europeans who moved to other places ruled by Europeans and non-Europeans who largely migrated to the colonies (Mintz 1996). The international movement of Europeans was a migration roughly in today's sense of the word, with the United States, Canada, Australia, New Zealand, Argentina, Uruguay, Chile, and South Africa being the main destinations. Many of these white immigrants settled in the politically democratic societies of North and South America. They successfully managed to pass on their family names, histories and identities from one generation to the next and often created schooling systems that transmitted their languages, histories and cultures.

The other group, non-European migrants, did not fare so well. They were from politically failed states or regions under colonial tutelage. They were brought from the African continent, China and India to the Caribbean, the Americas and Southeast Asian colonies (including present-day Malaysia, Indonesia and Singapore) to render their labour for commodity production. Unlike the European immigrants, many did not make their mark in the history of international political economy. Despite this 'invisibility', their labour was essential for transplanting and cultivating new plantation crops.

Tropical linkages

The Columbian Exchange diffused crops, seeds and plants between the western and eastern hemispheres. In the history of humankind, for instance, the movement of horses, cattle and smallpox from the Old World to the New World, and the movement of corn, potatoes and syphilis in the other direction, effectively began in 1492 and accelerated thereafter. Without this global interchange, Italian food today would be devoid of tomatoes, and the Native American Sioux would not have been riding horses (Mintz 1996).

The discovery of a new living space stands for the discovery of a frontier space for commodity production. It is a striking fact that ten years after Columbus's voyage to the Americas, Europeans had already begun to operate plantations in the New World (Mintz 1996). Whereas the Columbian Exchange is generally understood as the transfer between the New World and the Old World, there emerged another spatial linkage along the equatorial zone, where plants-cum-commodities from what is now termed the 'Global South' have been transplanted and harvested by the people from that part of the world. These 'tropical linkages' have been established by white colonizers and have largely been maintained in the hands of multinational corporations in the postcolonial era.

The global reconfiguration of flora has distinctive characteristics. The movements of plantation crops have often taken place horizontally along the equator. The lands of origin and the transplantation sites are located in an equatorial zone, notably classified by climatologist, geographer, meteorologist and botanist Wladimir Köppen (1884) as possessing a 'tropical rainforest climate'. An equatorial zone possesses the most concentrated biome on the surface of the Earth due to a combination of abundant solar energy and high precipitation. Active hydrothermal circulation makes tropical regions fertile ground for the regeneration of biome. In other words, the equatorial zone, a homeland as well as a new cultivation site, is the space where plants grow best and most abundantly. Regions with high levels of biodiversity then became plantation frontiers. In the process, new social relations were institutionalized as a profitable system in which people from the 'Global South' were mobilized, and their labour was expended to transform nature to suit human purposes. The labour circuit of enslaved people and indentured workers thus overlapped with plant trajectories, both connecting regions within the tropics.

In addition to the formation of the tropical labour-plant circuit, patterns of regional specialization emerged. With the advent of new crops and their production systems, a new relationship between regions thereby developed. Massive forestlands were converted to monocultural plantations in some locations. Other areas suitable for grains, such as rice, were exclusively devoted to producing food for people working in plantations. Humans and non-humans were thus mobilized to produce cash crops in tropical plantations, while recalibrated regional configurations emerged.

First came rubber

Plants constitute one of the largest elements of biomass on Earth, some reaching as high as 100 meters and as heavy as 100 tons. They are sedentary by nature and able to sustain their lives through photosynthesis if soil, water and sunshine are available. In the post-Columbian era, however, the movement of people stimulated the transnational migration of plants, changing their fate and relations to local communities and ecologies.

The Pará rubber tree (*Hevea brasiliensis*) is a good example. It was one of the very first global cash crops that altered the political economy of the tropics. The following account briefly reviews its migratory history in order to understand the genesis of the plant-labour circuit in Southeast Asia. Rubber originated in Brazil and was locally collected and traded by people in the Amazon River basin. Its existence was known in Europe and the United States, but it did not become an important cash crop until 1839, when a vulcanization technique was discovered to reduce the softening of the sap or latex and keep it viscous enough to be transported. Initially used as a raw material for raincoats, shoes, bicycle tyres, condoms and other household goods, latex was later in demand for the railway and electrical industries. The development of the automobile industry at the end of the nineteenth century was a major driving force for rubber cultivation (Rawlins 1969, 219).

The origins of rubber in Southeast Asia date back to 1876 when seeds were smuggled from Brazil to Kew Gardens in London, from where about 2,000 seedlings were sent to Ceylon and India and then to Singapore. It is said that most of the rubber planted in the Malay Peninsula, which later became the world's largest producer, originated from these seedlings via Singapore (1969, 219). In response to the increasing demand for resin for vehicle tyres, both large-scale rubber plantations developed with foreign capital and small-scale farms owned by local people emerged in British Malaya, the Dutch East Indies, Ceylon, Burma, India and Indochina in the early part of the twentieth century.

New cash crops penetrated large swathes of rural areas in a very short period of time. During the last quarter of the nineteenth century, by way of illustration, the total cultivated area of the major rubber-producing areas in Southeast Asia expanded some 16,000-fold. After 1900, rubber production further expanded in the region, most notably in Malaya. The total area of Malayan rubber plantations grew from around 2,000 hectares in 1900 to over 500,000 hectares in 1913 (Jackson 1968). Labourers were mostly brought in from southern India. They were mainly Tamils, who were hired in Indian villages and then brought to work in rubber plantations under the terms of indentured labour contracts, supervised by gangs on site (Amrith 2015). As large plantations flourished, smallholder households also grew. Before long, smallholders upscaled their production capacity to collectively match the large-scale plantations in the interwar period (Drabble 1973, 219).

In the economic history of Southeast Asia, the most important industrial commodity after rubber is oil palm. As we will see in the discussion below, this African crop, like rubber from Brazil, spread rapidly across Southeast Asia through both the plantation system and smallholdings. The crop has a unique transfer history and is distinctive in terms of the sheer scale of cultivation and its multifaceted impacts. Oil palm has changed the lives of nomadic peoples in jungles, swidden cultivators in uplands, peasants in peatlands and foreign indentured labourers imported to the region. The following section offers a glimpse of the plant trajectories from West Africa to Southeast Asia.

Oil palm in motion: From African groves to Asian plantations

Although the historical record on the oil palm is 'meagre', there is very strong physical and linguistic evidence for its West African origins (Corley and Tinker 2016, 1). For example, pollen analysis suggests that a close relationship between people and oil palm exists that may date back to 3,000–4,000 years ago in the region (Yamakoshi 2021, 131–3). The geographical distribution of the oil palm is found along the West African coast, concentrated in the highlands of Guinea and from there the palm belt runs southeastwards through Sierra Leone, Liberia, Côte d'Ivoire, Ghana, Togo, Benin and Nigeria, and then to the Central African countries of the Democratic Republic of Congo and Angola.

Oil palm thrives with people in West Africa. Palm groves are densest where the human population is largest: 'It flourishes when humans start to feel the forest, settle there and use the palm and possibly enrich the soil' (Corley and Tinker 2016, 2). Even a cursory journey in the Guinean countryside today offers abundant evidence that oil palm is an indispensable part of the communal natural landscape. Trees stretch as far as the eye can see, from the plains to the tops of the ridges. For the swidden cultivation of cassava, rice and peanuts, local farmers leave the oil palms uncut, and since they are fire-resistant, they survive when fields are burned. Some local oil palm groves have the appearance of plantations.

Farmers in West Africa say that the oil palm is a 'gift from God'. During the swidden farming cycle, oil palms require little labour or active management, and selective breeding is not practised by farmers. The rural landscape maintained through slash-and-burn agriculture seems to provide an ideal environment for semi-cultivated oil palms, where less fire-resistant competing species are regularly eliminated by human hands. Oil palm cultivation is thus relatively unencumbered and useful insofar as the palms can grow in the swidden on their own without incurring any costs to farmers. People and oil palms thus coexist, bringing considerable benefits to each other.

For most of history, oil palm remained domesticated and localized in West Africa. There was virtually no knowledge of it, or of its use elsewhere, or even an accepted name for it in English until 1804. Restrictions on trade, lack of access to the interior for the European traders and the continuing illegal but profitable slave trade to South America and the Caribbean prevented the development of an oil palm

Figure 3.1 West African oil palms, 2022. Courtesy of Noburo Ishikawa.

industry on any significant scale (Corley and Tinker 2016, 4). With the incremental ending of the Atlantic slave trade and then of the institution of slavery itself during the course of the nineteenth century, the export of palm oil initially paralleled that of enslaved people and then became the top export item of the West African forest belt (Wolf 1982, 330). While West Africa exported a mere 130 tons of palm oil to Britain in 1790, exports took off in the 1850s – driven by the great demand for oils in industrializing Europe – and reached about 30,000 tons a year in the 1860s. Palm oil was initially used for soap and subsequently for candles, margarine and lubricants for machinery, with new uses being invented regularly (Metzler 2014, 337–8; Corley and Tinker 2016, 4).

It is at least arguable that the rapid emergence of the oil palm trade – a profitable and thriving alternative commodity – contributed to the final demise of the slave trade. There were other significant political and social consequences for West African societies. The gradual incorporation of oil palm into colonial commodity channels, for example, created what anthropologist Eric Wolf (1982, 330) calls a 'crisis of the aristocracy' as African 'warrior elites and state organizations that had grown powerful and wealthy through the pursuit of slaving' had difficulty in switching over to this new commodity (1982, 330–1). Unlike the slave trade, for which African middlemen had brought enslaved people to the coast for transhipment, European wholesalers established direct contact with local oil palm producers or with their representatives. Consequently, a new African commercial elite, many of whom were ex-slaves educated in European missionary schools, took over the export trade previously handled by the slave traders. The result was a 'market-driven export boom [that] unfolded across coastal West Africa' (Metzler 2014, 336).

Despite the spectacular export boom of the palm oil trade, it was equally susceptible to turbulence in the international political economy. Perhaps the most serious such conjuncture was the financial crisis that began in 1873 – a consequence of speculative investment, rampant inflation and war in Europe – that had far-reaching consequences for the political economy of West Africa, as part of an international 'Great Depression'. During this slump, there was a significant decline in the price of exports with a squeeze on the rate of profits as real wages increased in Europe and the costs of raw materials went up in other parts of the world. In the conditions of such a generalized crisis, there was intensified economic competition and several European states started a concerted search for new investment options and markets. The Great Depression thus propelled European expansionism. In this context, Southeast Asia was one of the new commodity frontiers in the tropics.

Four African seedlings and their descendants

Anthropologist Ann Laura Stoler (1995, 2–3) has identified a 'plantation belt' (*cultuurgebied* in Dutch) that emerged on Sumatra's east coast in the Netherlands East Indies, the area which is also known as Deli (though this name only really referred to one small district). After the Dutch colonial government passed the Agrarian Land Law in 1870 that allowed private foreign investments in their territory – effectively an 'open door policy' – British, North American and Franco-Belgian planters and investors flocked to the area, planting tea, tobacco, rubber, sisal, coconut and oil palm (1995, 14–15). The endeavour generated huge profits for the planters; in fact, these plantation operations were among the most lucrative of all the Western colonial enterprises, earning them the title, the 'Dollar Land of Deli' (1995, 18).

While, as we have seen, West African oil palm producers and traders experienced mixed results of early boom and subsequent decline, Southeast Asian oil palm industries continued to develop very rapidly in the late nineteenth and early twentieth centuries. As one measure of this growth, as early as 1932, oil palms planted in Selangor in Malaya and Sumatra produced more oil than all African counterparts combined (Corley and Tinker 2016).

The earliest record of oil palms being introduced to Southeast Asia was of four seedlings from two different sources planted in Buitenzorg, Java, in 1848. The Botanic Garden at Buitenzorg, created in 1817, played a crucial role in shaping the practice of colonial agriculture in the Netherlands East Indies. Two of the seedlings were from the Amsterdam Botanic Garden, and the other two were from the Botanic Garden at Bourbon on the island of Mauritius in the Indian Ocean (Adam 2020, 10). The palms that sprang from these four seedlings were all quite similar, as they were believed to have all originally been produced in Amsterdam from seeds brought from Africa, while the uniformity of the progeny suggests that all four seedlings originated from a single-parent palm (Corley and Tinker 2016, 6). Some five years later, in 1853, the trees bore fruit. Thereafter, the gardeners at Buitenzorg planted the oil palm seeds widely, usually as decorative plants on streets. More seriously, in-house botanists and chemists began experimenting with the extraction of oils from the fruits. Shortly after, the growing demand in the European market for oil-derived products provided the incentive for experimental stations for palm oil to be set up, including in Palembang, South Sumatra, using progenies of the four original seedlings. They would become, in time, the foundation stock for the Southeast Asian oil palm industry. By the 1870s, oil palm trees had been widely distributed, though economically viable returns were initially modest, not least because colonial government efforts remained focused on expanding and improving the yield of crops such as coffee, sugar cane and indigo (Corley and Tinker 2016, 6; Adam 2020, 10–12). The turning point came in the 1910s, when plantations of oil palm appeared on a large scale, such that by the end of the First World War, there were nineteen plantations scattered along the east coast of Sumatra (Adam 2020, 12). In a parallel history, the oil palm had also arrived in Malaya via several different routes in the 1870s, and the first commercial plantation was established in Selangor in 1917.

While the nascent oil palm industry was consolidated in the interwar years, after the Second World War, Southeast Asian plantation industries had to make a fresh start in new geopolitical and socioeconomic conditions. In newly independent Malaysia, the plantation sector – both in long-established rubber and rapidly expanding oil palm – soon became a major driving force to propel economic development. Ownership of plantations, which had previously been in the hands of foreign companies, shifted significantly to local ownership. A similar development took place in independent Indonesia. However, the most significant post-war change was the shift of plant stock from Deli *dura* palms to *tenera* palms. *Tenera* is a cross-breed between *dura* (thick-shelled) and *pisifera* (shell-less), has a thin shell and produces up to 30 per cent more oil content than its parent varieties (Corley and Tinker 2016, 7). Despite this significant change in the planted stock, the generic basis of the industrial oil palm remained rather narrow, and the unwavering importance of Deli *dura* for the whole industry continued for quite some time.

The production of palm oil has steadily increased over the past fifty years. From just 2 million tons in 1970, global production increased 35-fold to 79 million tons in 2022. Over two-thirds of this is used in foods such as margarine, chocolate, bread and cooking oil; 27 per cent is used in industrial applications and consumer products such as soap, detergent, cosmetics and cleaning agents; the remaining 5 per cent is used as biofuel for transport, electricity or heat. Currently, plantations host improved varieties of oil palm, some of which are hybrids with the American oil palm (*Elaeis oleifera*). Although small amounts of palm oil are produced in many countries, the global market is dominated by only two: Indonesia produces 46.5 million tons and Malaysia 19.8 million tons, accounting for 84 per cent of global production (World Agricultural Production 2022).

Mega-plantations in Malaysia and Indonesia

The massive expansion of oil palm in Indonesia and Malaysia has largely been driven by the agro-industrial mega-plantations that have emerged across the Southeast Asian region, 'plantation development that rapidly and radically transforms landscapes in ways that displace and replace pre-existing human and non-human communities' (Kenny-Lazar and Ishikawa 2019). In Malaysia, the amount of land given over to oil palm has more than quadrupled in the last four decades, and today 5.7 million hectares of land have been converted to plantations. Indonesia has experienced a similar exponential growth; oil palm accounted for only 100,000 hectares in 1970 while in 2021 the figure was a staggering 16.4 million hectares, more than 40 per cent of the country's area of arable land (Jong 2022; Hawkins et al. 2016).

The mode of plantation production in Southeast Asia has some common characteristics. First, it is a monoculture, a form of agriculture in which the land is cultivated with only one crop type. Second, the production model seeks economies of scale. This refers to the nature of plantation production, in which the larger production scale ensures the highest profit margin. As the production volume increases, the proportionate costs of raw materials and labour decrease, and the rates of return are amplified. Economies of scale are thus the rationale for plantations to be large. To materialize this form of economic enterprise, plantation industries also require a large-scale mobilization of labour. Plantations can potentially be developed by a wide range of production arrangement systems, including estates established by government land concessions or outright land purchases, nucleus estates and smallholder arrangements, land-based contract farming, product-based contract farming, managed smallholders and independent smallholders. In the case of Malaysia, the mobilization of cheaper Indonesian workers has been key to the success of plantation operations.

In addition, the plantation industry has primarily derived from converting the ecological environment into a production space through large-scale land grabbing. Historically, this 'accumulation by dispossession' was first pursued under colonial regimes (Harvey 2004). Colonial governments throughout Southeast Asia defined the living space of the local people as *terra nullius* – nobody's land – that could be redistributed at their discretion (Ishikawa 2010). The practice of dispossession has not slackened in the postcolonial period, with native customary lands particularly susceptible to rampant appropriation by palm oil conglomerates, often in collusion with the state. As local societies in the tropics use the land for slash-and-burn rice cultivation based on usufruct management, inhabitants could not prove individual ownership against seizing their traditional land. The result was the expropriation and alienation of land on a massive scale.

The plantation, both as a social complex and an infrastructural form, has also brought about profound transformations to local communities. Oil palm fruits need to be processed within twenty-four hours of harvest to avoid oxidation and to produce a high-quality product in the form of palm oil. It is, therefore, essential that fresh oil palm fruits be treated immediately after harvest to inactivate the lipase, an enzyme originally contained in the seeds, before the oil is extracted. Roads are thus constructed to quickly transport fresh fruit bunches to processing mills, impacting local communities, inadvertently or otherwise, in emerging transportation networks. As a result, the advent of large-scale oil palm plantations not only introduces a new mode of corporate agricultural production but also establishes spatial linkages between upriver cultivation sites and downriver production sites. The road networks and the extension of the supply chain to frontier regions have, in turn, accelerated urban migration from rural areas, leading to rapid depopulation.

Figure 3.2 Clearcut forests and oil palms, 2022. Courtesy of Noburo Ishikawa.

Symbiosis and contestation

While African oil palms remain largely local and vernacular, their Southeast Asian descendants have become part of the global supply chain. African palms in communal groves have maintained symbiotic relations with local communities and the environment, still considered a 'gift from God' shared by local people. In contrast, Southeast Asian palms are a pre-eminent industrial commodity, often antagonistic to local ecologies as well as the social systems local communities have reproduced and maintained for generations.

Such contrasts are readily observable in fieldwork sites. The oil palm groves in Guinea that I first visited in 2011 had no ownership. 'Tu peux le prendre, si tu peux' (You can take it, if you can) is the basic attitude of local people. Climbing the tall trunks of oil palm trees with special tools and harvesting fruits with a machete is quite laborious and dangerous work; ants and snakes are a nuisance too. Here, the 'if you can' attitude is the key to understanding the absence of ownership. After the harvest, fruits must be boiled in water for a long time to extract oil. The task is, therefore, usually communal by which individuals and households work collectively. There is also a gender division of roles in the production process. In other words, harvesting and the production of palm oil in Guinea (and by extension, other sites in West Africa) have been embedded in a web of primordial, communal social relations.

By contrast, Southeast Asian oil palms have been a major driving force for socioeconomic and environmental change. As we have seen, oil palm cultivation and processing require the development of a large-scale infrastructural complex, into which local inhabitants are inevitably incorporated. During the past three decades of my anthropological fieldwork in Sarawak, Malaysian Borneo, I have witnessed the transformation of local communities located in a commodity frontier from the initial moment of clear-cutting to the emergence of oil palm smallholders. When roads were constructed, many residents moved to the roadside, at some distance from their longhouse communities traditionally built along rivers. Then a long stretch of temporary huts was built by local people working to clear the jungle and plant oil palms in order to claim landownership (Ishikawa 2019; Ishikawa and Soda 2019).

The plantation is a social complex that brings local communities into profound contestation. When the plantation system is introduced to a local community, the object of appropriation shifts from the extraction of biomass on land to land itself, and the soil becomes a crucial device for commodity production. This new mode of biomass generation, both in plantations and smallholdings, requires labour mobilization, capital investment and land as a commodity as essential elements for continued operation. The Indigenous logic of swidden agriculture based on non-territorial, usufruct operation has been replaced by the organizational principles of private property and territoriality, with the nation-state as a guardian of this spatial encroachment.

The new mode of oil palm production is also antagonistic to local ecologies. As the plantation operation is based on the clear-cutting of forests and their conversion to monoculture cultivation, multispecies of flora and fauna and the remaining refugia are wiped out. The dispossession of natural resources as well as land from rural communities, especially those of Indigenous peoples, has been one of the most consistent criticisms raised against plantation expansion in the Southeast Asian region (Kenny-Lazar and Ishikawa 2019).

Chimpanzees and orangutans

I had an opportunity to visit the Bossou forests in Guinea, where the Primate Research Institute of Kyoto University has maintained a field station since the mid-1980s. I was most intrigued by the symbiotic relations observable among local people, chimpanzees and oil palms. Oil palm trees, when concentrated in one area, look like a jungle. The oil palms have, for generations, sprouted and multiplied after the fruits were eaten by chimpanzees and spread through their faeces. In Bossou, oil palm is deeply embedded in rural landscapes and local life; as such, it remains useful for both people and wildlife. The forests surrounding villages are inhabited by chimpanzees, revered by villagers as a manifestation of their ancestors. The chimpanzees' habitat is a complex mosaic of sacred forests, burned fallow forests and cultivated lands of cassava, rice, coffee and peanuts. Chimpanzees live side by side with people in these forests, subsisting on the abundant oil palm pulp, endosperm rich in kernel oil, the base of young leaf petioles and tree sap (Yamakoshi 2011).

In fact, the oil palm is a key element in the tripartite coexistence among chimpanzees, oil palms and villagers. There are a large number of oil palm trees around the village that are neither owned nor privately managed. Chimpanzees are, therefore, left to eat oil palms as they never create any serious problems for local agriculture. In the agroecosystem of Bossou, oil palm occupies an important position; it supports and sustains neighbouring communities, both human and non-human.

Once again, in stark contrast, in the tropical forests of Southeast Asia, Bornean orangutans (*Pongo pygmaeus*) are losing habitat and are in critical danger of extinction. Orangutans have been included in the *International Union for Conservation of Nature's Red List of Threatened Species* since 2016 (IUCN

2016). A study conducted in eastern Sabah, Malaysian Borneo, suggests that land conversion to oil palm has left a mosaic landscape of plantations interspersed with fragmented patches of natural forests where orangutans have to survive (Ancrenaz et al. 2014). Although orangutans have adapted to the human-transformed landscapes better than anticipated, the study concludes that oil palm plantations are unable to sustain orangutan populations in the long term. The researchers observe evidence of starvation among orangutans that inhabit small forest patches scattered among vast oil palm estates and their increased conflicts with humans.

Back to West Africa

Today, multinational producers of palm oil from Southeast Asia aim to enter the African market in search of land for cultivation. According to reports from local and international non-governmental organizations that support affected communities, however, palm oil's 'homecoming' has not been as successful as its architects hoped. After years of fierce resistance from communities located inside areas demarcated for oil palm plantation development, at least twenty-seven new plantation projects have either failed or been abandoned. Less than 20 per cent of the 2.74 million hectares of land allocated to the remaining forty-nine have been developed (Mukpo 2019). In 2019, Sime Darby, Malaysia's leading palm oil producer, finally announced its intention to withdraw from Liberia after years of conflict with communities and environmental groups (Chow 2019).

African oil palm has maintained a symbiotic relationship with local communities for more than 4,000 years. The local wisdom of making the seeds accessible to anyone as well as the practice of producing oil through reciprocal labour exchange have prevented land fragmentation and ownership competition within the community. In contrast, when plantations are newly developed on the edge of older settlements, as seen in the Southeast Asian frontier, they constitute an expanding outpost of a new industrial mode of production in the midst of older, conventional modes. The plantation mode of production is based on large-scale land acquisition, implementation of infrastructure, land-use change and labour mobilization, which are all quite antithetical to local modes of subsistence such as swidden cultivation and foraging.

Conclusion

By looking into the trajectories of oil palm from West Africa to Southeast Asia, we witness the entanglements of politico-economic forces, the agency of local people and their communities and a series of historical contingencies that have taken place since the Columbian Exchange. Ironically, Southeast Asian oil palm producers in search of further agricultural frontiers beyond their own oil palm-saturated region now face resistance from African societies as well as critical assessments from civil society and non-governmental groups and appear to be struggling to advance this new expansionary stage.

The comparison of oil palm in its original habitat and new destinations demonstrates vividly the sustained and altered human-nature relationships and their impacts on peoples and communities. Global oil palm trajectories thus enable us to better comprehend such relational changes in world history from the onset of the Columbian Exchange and colonial rule to the contemporary plantocracy. Oil palm has remained an important commodity for people on the tropical frontier albeit in quite distinct

Figure 3.3 An oil palm plantation in Peru, 2022. Courtesy of Noburo Ishikawa.

cross-continental settings and geographies. The plant in and of itself has never changed human-nature relationships, but humans and their capitalist interventions in and appropriation of nature have.

Today oil palms are planted and grown in many countries outside Southeast Asia, including Nigeria, Benin, Cameroon, Ghana, Colombia, Peru, Guatemala and Ecuador, though on a much smaller scale than the palm oil giants, Indonesia and Malaysia. With the formation and intensification of new labour-plant circuits in the zones of optimal conditions suitable for oil palm cultivation, the symbiotic relations between historically established ecology and people will be reorganized, if not vanish completely. Whether the layers of the pollen of oil palms preserved in agricultural frontiers outside Southeast Asia would mark another distinctive geological stratum in human history is for future generations to determine.

References

Adam, Luthfi. 'Cultivating Power: Buitenzorg Botanic Garden and Empire-Building in the Netherlands East Indies, 1745–1917'. PhD diss. Northwestern University, 2020.

Amrith, Sunil. *Crossing the Bay of Bengal: The Furies of Nature and the Fortunes of Migrants*. Cambridge, MA: Harvard University Press, 2015.

Ancrenaz, Marc, et al. 'Of *Pongo*, Palms and Perceptions: A Multidisciplinary Assessment of Bornean Orangutans *Pongo Pygmaeus* in an Oil Palm Context'. *Oryx* 49, no. 3 (2014): 465–72.

Bauer, Andrew M. and Mona Bhan. *Climate Without Nature: A Critical Anthropology of the Anthropocene*. Cambridge: Cambridge University Press, 2018.

Chow, Emily. 'Sime Darby Plantation Considers Exiting West Africa Palm Oil Operations – Sources'. *Reuters*, 22 February 2019. Accessed 29 October 2022. https://www.reuters.com/article/ozatp-us-sime-darby-plant-africa-idAFKCN1QB0UM-OZATP

Corley, R. H. V. and P. B. Tinker. *The Oil Palm*, 5th edn. Chichester: Wiley-Blackwell, 2016.

Drabble, John H. Rubber in Malaya, 1876–1922: The Genesis of the Industry. Kuala Lumpur: Oxford University Press, 1973.

Ellis, Erle C. *Anthropocene: A Very Short Introduction*. Oxford: Oxford University Press, 2018.

Haraway, Donna. 'Anthropocene, Capitalocene, Plantationocene, Chthulucene: Making Kin'. *Environmental Humanities* 6, no. 1 (2015): 159–65.

Haraway, Donna, et al. 'Anthropologists Are Talking – About the Anthropocene'. *Ethnos* 81, no. 3 (2016): 535–64.

Harvey, David. 'The "New" Imperialism: Accumulation by Dispossession'. In *The New Imperial Challenge*, edited by Leo Panitch and Colin Leys. London: Merlin Press, 2004, 63–87.

Hawkins, Doug, Chen, Yingheng and Thomas Wigglesworth. *Indonesian Palm Oil Production Sector: A Wave of Consolidation to Come*. London: Hardman Agribusiness, 2016.

International Union for Conservation of Nature [IUCN]. The Bornean Orangutan (*Pongo pygmaeus*), 2016. Accessed 29 October 2022. https://www.iucnredlist.org/species/17975/123809220#assessment-information

Ishikawa, Noboru. *Between Frontiers: Nation and Identity in a Southeast Asian Borderland*, Singapore: NUS Press, 2010.

Ishikawa, Noboru. 'Into a New Epoch: Capitalist Nature in the Plantationocene.' In *Anthropogenic Tropical Forests: Human-Nature Interfaces on the Plantation Frontier*, edited by Noboru Ishikawa and Ryoji Soda. Singapore: Springer Nature, 2019, 543–62.

Ishikawa, Noboru and Ryoji Soda. *Anthropogenic Tropical Forests: Human-Nature Interfaces on the Plantation Frontier*. Singapore: Springer Nature, 2019.

Jackson, James C. *Planters and Speculators: Chinese and European Agricultural Enterprise in Malaya, 1786–1921*. Kuala Lumpur: University of Malaya Press, 1968.

Jong, Hans Nicholas. 'Proposal Could Redefine Palm Oil-driven Deforestation as Reforestation in Indonesia'.' *Mongabay*, 7 January 2022. Accessed 29 October 2022. https://news.mongabay.com/2022/01/indonesian-proposal-could-redefine-palm-oil-driven-deforestation-as-reforestation/

Kenney-Lazar, Miles and Noboru Ishikawa. 'Mega-plantations in Southeast Asia: Landscapes of Displacement'. *Environment and Society: Advances in Research* 10, no. 1 (2019): 63–82.

Köppen, W. 'The Thermal Zones of the Earth according to the Duration of Hot, Moderate and Cold Periods and of the Impact of Heat on the Organic World'. *Meteorologische Zeitschrift* 1 (1884): 351–60.

Metzler, Mark. 'Revisiting the General Crisis of the Late Nineteenth Century: West Africa and the World Depression'. In *Africa, Empire, and Globalisation: Essays in Honor of A.G. Hopkins*, edited by Toyin Falola and Emily Brownell. Durham, NC: Carolina Academic Press, 2014, 333–55.

Mintz, Sidney. 'The Plantation as a Socio-cultural Type'. In *Plantation Systems of the New World*, edited by Research Institute for the Study of Man and Pan American Union. Washington: Pan American Union, 1959, 42–50.

Mintz, Sidney. *Sweetness and Power: The Place of Sugar in Modern History*. New York: Penguin, 1985.

Mintz, Sidney. *Tasting Food, Tasting Freedom: Excursions into Eating, Culture, and the Past*. Boston: Beacon Press, 1996.

Mukpo, Ashoka. 'Industrial Palm Oil Investors Struggle to Gain Foothold in Africa'. *Mongabay*, 20 September 2019. Accessed 29 October 2022. https://news.mongabay.com/2019/09/industrial-palm-oil-investors-struggle-to-gain-foothold-in-africa/

Rawlins, Joan. *Sarawak, 1839 to 1968*. London: Macmillan, 1969.

Stoler, Ann Laura. *Capitalism and Confrontation in Sumatra's Plantation Belt, 1870–1979*. Ann Arbor: University of Michigan Press, 1995.

Yamakoshi, Gen. 'Jyuuminniyoru Aburayashi Riyou No Genfuukei: Nishiafurika, Ginia No Fiirudokara – [The Original Landscape of Oil Palm Used by Local Residents: From the Field in Guinea, West Africa]'. In *Aburayashi Nouen Mondai No Kenkyu*, Vol. 2: *Nouenkaihatsu To Chiikishakai No Kouzouhenka Wo Ou* [Research on Oil Palm Plantation Issues: Understanding Plantation Development and Changes to Local Society Structure], edited by Hideki Hayashida. Kyoto: Koyoshobo, 2021, 131–3.

Yamakoshi, Gen. 'Pestle-pounding Behavior: The Key to the Coexistence of Humans and Chimpanzees'. In *The Chimpanzees of Bossou and Nimba*, edited by Tetsuro Matsuzawa, Tatyana Humle and Yukimaru Sugiyama. Tokyo: Springer, 2011, 107–15.

Wolf, Eric R. *Europe and the People without History*. Berkeley: University of California Press, 1982.

World Agricultural Production. 'World Palm Oil Production 2022/2023'. September 2022. Accessed 29 October 2022. http://www.worldagriculturalproduction.com/crops/palmoil.aspx

4
THE CALL OF THE CRICKET

Helen Hollyman and James Skeet

Time is a circle. It is orbiting us into the second rotation of the Gilded Age to see if we will transform what is being forced in our hearts this time around differently. In the late 1800s, during the Industrial Revolution, a Western settler in the colonized 'United States' wanted to show a Native Chief the 'great' things – power and technology – and that Westerners were building American cities, so he took him to New York City. As they walked over a bridge, the Chief stopped the settler and asked, 'Wait. Do you hear that?' The settler said, 'What? All I hear is traffic, people talking, and hustling and bustling.' The Chief looked at him and said, 'Listen. Do you hear the crickets?' (Native American Elder Wisdom, Author Unknown). The Indigenous perspective of the world around us always listens to nature's systems and looks for the natural seasons present everywhere, even in cities, because nature is in charge.

We live in a time of imbalance between the yin and yang, the male and female, the prophets and the healers. It is a time that is calling us to return to nature if we listen hard enough. In the past decades, the global agricultural model has accelerated climate emissions, accounting for 72 per cent of all surface and groundwater withdrawals and 23 per cent of global greenhouse gas emissions (FAO 2023). Excessive fertilizer use, overgrazing and intensive animal farming have contributed to soil erosion, compaction and deforestation. It is a painful reality left on our hands when we consider that the health of 13 per cent of global soil has been degraded, including 34 per cent of agricultural land. While regenerative farming practices originally championed by Indigenous communities thousands of years ago are becoming more prevalent from North America to China, they employ no-till, biodiversity and crop rotation, leaving Indigenous expertise and leaders absent from the conversation on climate change and land stewardship.

In industrialized nations, we live in an attention economy, surrendering our agency to technology and leaving us with a false notion of self-sufficiency. This mirage is most evident in cities, where global conglomerates proudly base themselves. Large cities are the most vulnerable places because of their inability to feed themselves, relying on rural farming communities to provide for essential human needs. The circle of time is not linear – right now, a small group of billionaires, including Bernard Arnault, Bill Gates, Jeff Bezos and Elon Musk, own the lion's share of wealth, power and land access that controls the decisions that impact the global community (Inequality Org. 2023). These tech billionaires are perennially rooted in an extractive mindset that drastically changed the world during the Industrial Revolution, marking the most significant period of economic growth, agricultural and technological advancements and population expansion in human history. In the first Gilded Age, J. P. Morgan, Cornelius Vanderbilt,

John D. Rockefeller and Andrew Carnegie gained vast wealth by monopolizing banking, railroad development, steel and oil production. Andrew Carnegie is still considered the wealthiest man in history, with an estimated $310 billion.

The Industrial Revolution was built on an extractive linear model of 'take, make, waste' production that transformed our global economies from small-scale agriculture and handicrafts into economies structured on large-scale industry, mechanized manufacturing and systems focused on efficiency. Our world is currently home to 2,755 billionaires compared to the nearly 8 billion people living on Earth (Peerson-Withorn 2023). According to the World Bank, as of 2021, the world's ten wealthiest billionaires own an astonishing $1.448 trillion combined wealth, a sum greater than the services and goods most nations produce annually. As of 2023, Elon Musk is the second wealthiest person in the world at an estimated $196.5 billion, making headlines in 2022 when he spent $44 billion to buy social media company Twitter. According to the United Nations' World Food Program, a mere 2 per cent of his wealth – $6 billion – could solve world hunger and feed 42 million people dying of starvation. Similarly, Microsoft co-founder Bill Gates is the second largest landowner in the United States, owning a staggering 242,000 acres of farmland (Land Income 2023). By contrast, there are over two million individual farms in America, each with an average farm of 444 acres. A family-owned farm makes roughly $69,000 in profits annually, and since 2021, over 39 per cent of the income generated by farmers comes from tens of billions in government subsidies.

Trying to tune in and hear the cricket under the bridge is a pivotal moment in the current climate crisis that requires us to shift our lenses from a colonized, extractive perspective to one directly connected with nature. In finding solutions to feeding the world through regenerative farming, instead of relying on the latest scientific and technological advances, we must integrate Indigenous perspectives, technologies and wisdom that have existed for thousands of years into systems thinking for climate optimism.

Our current linear economic model is unsustainable; it undermines biodiversity and relies on cheap materials, energy and credit. Alternative economic models such as Cradle-to-Cradle or Circular Economy are inspired by natural systems, aiming to build resilience through biodiversity, renewable energy and systems thinking to create nurturing economies with positive environmental outcomes, shifting away from the extractive mindset. However, these alternative economic models often still reflect industrial frameworks, so we need a more profound examination within ourselves to entirely shift the extractive mindset dominant in the 'Global North'. We must be able to feed our communities through kinship, which can happen through Indigenous practices such as regenerative farming, placing importance on biodiversity and community care. We must place Indigenous voices at the forefront of climate solutions in order to have a deeper engagement with life.

Regenerative farming is not a term for Indigenous people but a sacred worldview. Embracing a regenerative mindset requires non-Indigenous people to understand that the land owns us rather than us owning it. When we die, we will return to it, regenerating over and over again. Indigenous people use the land as a 'commons', carrying the ethics and covenants of the land with them so that they do not destroy it. They coexist with nature by entering a sacred space with great mystery, communicating through meditation and ceremonies. This path represents a journey that takes us into a peaceful state with nature shared among Indigenous people worldwide. Entering this space is what is missing in the conversation of regeneration.

James and Joyce Skeet founded Spirit Farm in 2014, an Indigenous-led regenerative teaching farm, to reclaim Indigenous spiritual and farming practices while incorporating modern techniques to create adaptability, food sovereignty and resilience despite the harsh growing conditions. Located in

Vanderwagen, New Mexico, the farm sits at a towering elevation of 7,149 feet above sea level, an area known for brittle desert conditions that make farming seem impossible. The path to reconnecting with nature's systems has been a challenging road. The soil had 'bad' bacteria when James and Joyce returned to this land. Their predecessors deeply ploughed from one acre to the next for many years until they exhausted the soil, which became evident once they ventured into soil science. Combining soil and Indigenous science is crucial because images and storytelling can merge with research and data. Reaching into the soil with your hands at Spirit Farm feels like running through 'chocolate cake'. The rich dark matter has been remediated through various methods, including nutrient-dense compost and patience.

Spirit Farm is about healing the soil as well as employing ancient ancestral technologies, such as water harvesting, which allow for the redirection and productive use of rainfall. The people working at the farm use agroforestry, the deliberate planting and maintenance of trees, to develop a microclimate that protects crops against extreme conditions. Furthermore, the farm uses intercropping and crop rotation to preserve the soil's productive capacity, minimize pests and diseases, reduce chemical use and manage nutrient density for maximum yield. Intercropping creates biodiversity, attracting beneficial and predatory insects to minimize pests, increase soil organic matter, suppress weed growth and purify soil health. These ancient technologies represent innovation at their best. For example, the Incan Moray or *Muray* in the Quechua language was a terrace system that included different kinds of soil across the Incan Empire. The terracing was so complex that there was a 59°F temperature difference between the central depression and the highest terraces at the edges, allowing for precise climate conditions and rich soil ecology. Archaeologists believe that this way of working the land served as an agricultural testing station so that Indigenous agronomists could experiment with various crops to ensure their community received a balanced diet throughout the winter or during periods of scarcity.

So, how do we re-engage with these ancient technologies in our modern world? Healing the land requires patience and a mindset shift using the heart instead of the head. For example, James and Joyce noticed the dominant presence of invasive weeds such as Russian thistle and bullhead, so they asked themselves, 'How do we approach living in a sacred manner? Do we go in and kill the weeds or ask them why are you here?' As they began asking those questions, they found exciting answers. The succession plants, or so-called 'weeds', had higher nutrient levels than the annual crops they were growing at the time. Their people, the *Diné*, knew and understood the value of wild plants from being trans-nomadic people. Many medicine men and women understood the critical relationship of reciprocity between the land and the plants and what they could do with them. They knew that in order to amend things, they needed to work towards a higher level of biodiversity to create a heat sink to lower scorching temperatures. The microbes create the medicine, help the soil heal and break down organic matter. They started communicating with the soil and understanding the language of the plants. Through this understanding, they realized how detrimental human impact can be. The soil started to live again, producing and providing excellent nutrient levels in the food produced. The microbial sponge on the farm's land creates mini-cycles that capture water torrents, maintaining soil health. A microsponge in the soil creates a hydrome that allows water systems to come in torrents. This approach can be easily applied to a much larger and broader scale, but unfortunately, capitalism favours carbon credits, monocropping and the commodification of foods.

When we understand that the land owns us, we can create kinship. Acknowledging that human beings are not more important than other life forms creates interconnectedness and respect. 'Regeneration' in North America operates on a surface level, and microbes are not honoured. Honour dies when interest

Figure 4.1 Spirit Farm garden, 2023. Courtesy of Spirit Farm. Photo by Mae Salago-King.

is involved, which is a deep conversation among Indigenous people. Worldwide colonization has broken reciprocity and eroded kinship. Indigenous people understand that regeneration has always been a part of nature, which eventually regenerates itself if humans remove themselves from it. Nature will eventually win out if we approach farming from an exploitative or extractive approach. It is sovereign in what it does and where it goes. However, we have tried to dominate it instead of being grateful, ethically sound and understanding fundamental things, such as seasonal and cyclical perspectives. Our understanding should focus on how the land owns us instead of us owning it.

We are part of an ingenious mystery that has vibrated from the beginning of time, connecting Indigenous cyclical worldviews, guiding us away from self-destruction and helping us negotiate pathways so that our journey on Earth is of interconnectedness and beauty. The Diné/Navajo People call it *Hózhó* – a dimension of being grateful, balanced and removed from over-extraction. It begins with the microbes and bacteria in the soil, which have taken centuries to develop into different, complex layers to create an ingenious microbial sponge that produces mini-cycles for the soil to capture water torrents that maintain soil health. The microbial ability to generate a microsponge creates a hydrome that invites water systems to appear in torrents, which are vital for restoring desertified lands and creating heat sinks to lower scorching temperatures. The microbes create the medicine, help the soil heal and break down organic matter. From there, the soil can live, producing and providing vibrant nutrient levels in our food. In honouring the soil, the soil is healing us. Unsurprisingly, recent studies published in the *Microorganisms Journal* have shown a direct connection between soil health and human gut health, containing approximately the same number of active microorganisms. However, the human gut microbiome diversity is only 10 per cent of that of soil biodiversity and has decreased dramatically with modern lifestyles (Blum et al. 2019).

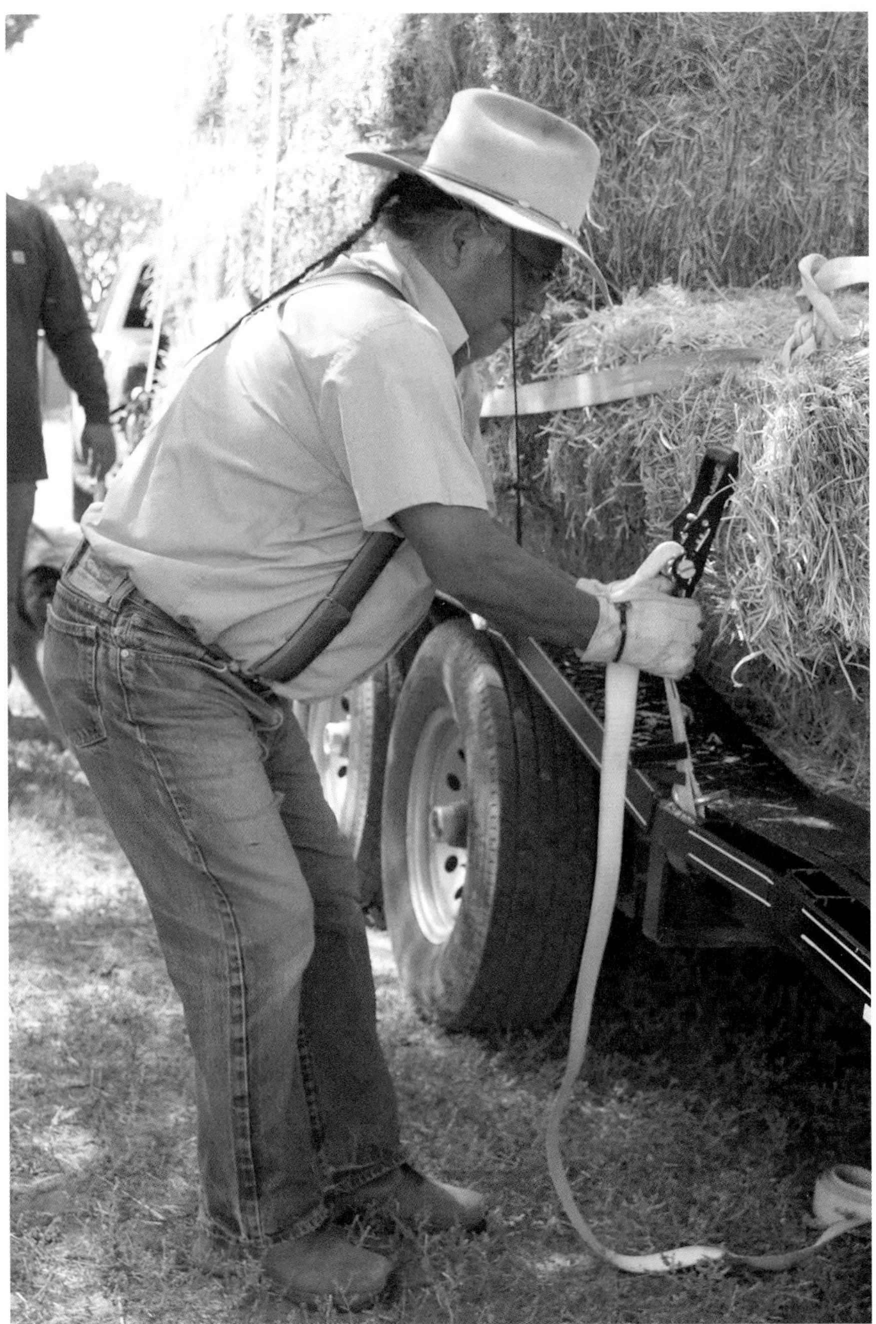

Figure 4.2 James Skeet, 2023. Courtesy of Spirit Farm. Photo by Mae Salago-King.

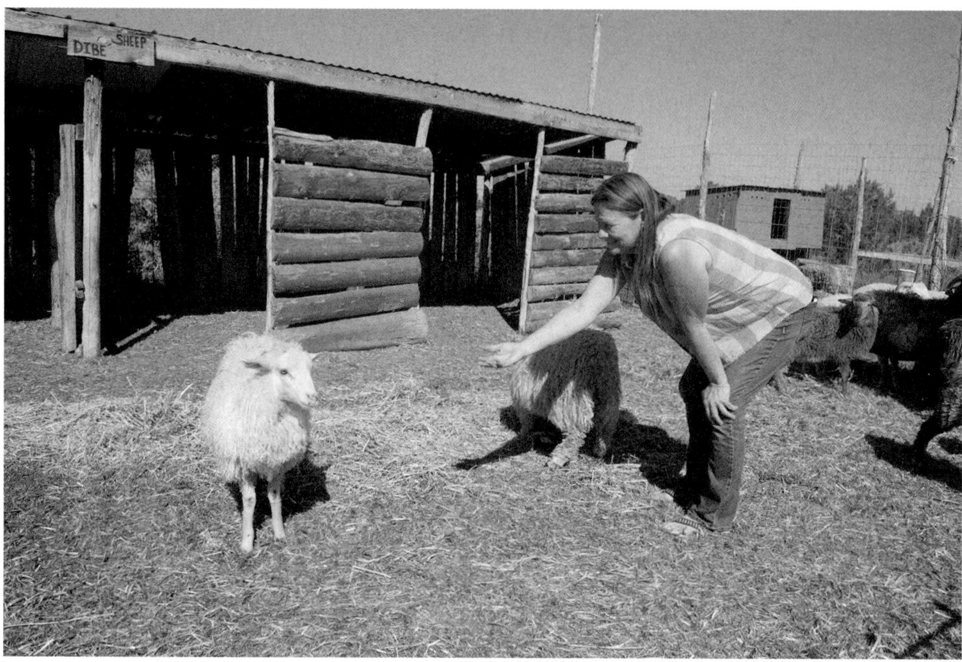

Figure 4.3 Joyce Skeet and sheep, 2023. Courtesy of Spirit Farm. Photo by Mae Salago-King.

Employing ancient ancestral Indigenous technologies creates a limitless loop of nurturing cycles that allow humans to work in harmony with nature and its instinctive rhythm, such as water harvesting through swales and berms, which allows for the redirection and productive use of rainfall. For example, the Agroforestry approach aimed at the planting and maintenance of trees, facilitating a microclimate that protects crops against extreme weather or intercropping and crop rotation (unlike the Big Agriculture approach to monocropping) designed to preserve the soil's productive capacity, minimize pests and diseases, reduce chemical use and manage nutrient density for maximum yield. This approach to biodiversity attracts a variety of insects and animals, which help to minimize pests and increase soil organic matter, suppress weed growth and maintain soil health, contributing to the effort towards land stewardship and maintaining a sense of balance between the ground and its surroundings. These ancestral techniques have been passed down from generation to generation, sharing a thriving reciprocity exchange with nature by looking after microorganisms, pollinators, plants and animals.

Regenerative agriculture increases organic matter, texture, fertility and water retention and supports microorganisms, which protect the roots and plants. Conventional agriculture, on the other hand, is the child of an extractive mindset, which treats the soil as a medium that is forced into sickness by being treated with fertilizers and chemicals in order to increase and optimize productivity. The soil is ploughed, tilled or disked multiple times a year, destroying millennia of intelligence found in microorganisms. Herbicides kill and clear out the threat of weeds, insects (often pollinators) are destroyed with pesticides and rust or blight is sprayed with fungicides. There is also the challenge of drought, which is compensated with intensive irrigation, causing soil salinization and tilling, which contribute to releasing the carbon that plants have captured.

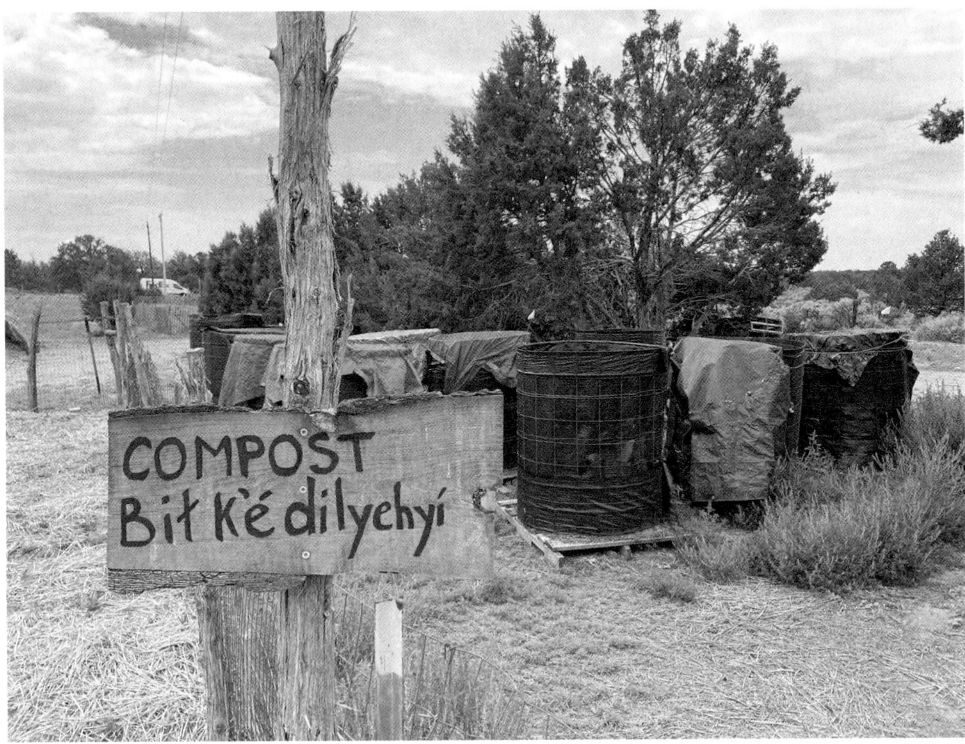

Figure 4.4 Spirit Farm compost, 2023. Courtesy of Spirit Farm. Photo by Mae Salago-King.

We are all paying a devastating price to feed the world right now. When a farmer ignores caring for the soil health, the land becomes infertile, diseased and dead. Consuming the plants and animals produced from this model makes us ill. According to the non-profit organization Project Drawdown, the world's leading resource for climate solutions, from an estimated 108 million acres of current adoption, regenerative agriculture could increase to a total of 1 billion acres by 2050 (Project Drawdown 2022). The rapid adoption estimation is based on the historical rate of organic agriculture and the projected conversion of regenerative agriculture over time. The impact of radically shifting the model to one of regenerative practices could result in a total reduction of 23.2 gigatons of carbon dioxide from sequestration and reduced emissions. Regenerative agriculture could provide a $1.9 trillion financial return by 2050 on an investment of $57 billion. Replacing the conventional agricultural model with regenerative techniques could address all issues associated with pests, drought, fertility, weeds and crop production to feed the world. However, today's farming movement is still deeply entangled in the industrial, commodity-based economy that requires large-scale intensive production, ignoring nature's repair ability. Farming for Indigenous people is about sharing, not production. We can apply thousands of years of Indigenous intelligence to industrial farming, but 150 years of conventional and extractive European-based farming systems will still dominate unless Indigenous worldviews are considered – it is time to honour them!

Capitalism favours monetary and technological solutions aimed at controlling and mastering nature. Take, for example, carbon credits aimed at fixing what we have broken in the first place. In contrast, restoring land has always worked for Indigenous communities. There is a real opportunity for contemporary science and Indigenous knowledge to work together. Climate scientists should learn from Indigenous

Figure 4.5 Spirit Farm hoop house, 2023. Courtesy of Spirit Farm. Photo by Mae Salago-King.

Figure 4.6 Spirit Farm sheep, 2023. Courtesy of Spirit Farm. Photo by Mae Salago-King.

Figure 4.7 Spirit Farm tomatoes, 2023. Courtesy of Spirit Farm. Photo by Mae Salago-King

communities and their 40,000 years of history instead of searching for the latest technological solutions. Integrating Indigenous wisdom into systems thinking requires centring Indigenous voices at the forefront of climate solutions. In order to discuss climate solutions, we need to consider humans' relationship with the natural world rather than an economic system that reduces nature into monetary transactions.

Our planet has been exploited with little consideration for the fungi, bacteria and natural systems that evolved and developed over millennia. It would be wonderful to return to full indigeneity, but sadly, colonization has hampered much of the passing down of generational wisdom in the modern world. When an elder dies, generations of wisdom die. We need to relearn how to coexist with nature and take responsibility for how our food is produced and how it affects the soil. It is vital to carry the wisdom of our ancestors in order to plan for the next generations. Returning to indigeneity is the way forward. Global indigeneity is the ability to return to a sense of balance with nature and understand who we are when we are in nature. Anyone can do this anywhere.

Can you hear the cricket in the city if you stop listening hard enough? Nature will continue to do what it needs to, whether or not we exist, as it will do when we are all long gone. The task at hand is to coexist and become one with nature so that we can regenerate our Earth and live in harmony with it. Indigenous regenerative intelligence is about observing nature and its rhythms. It includes thousands of years of coexistence with plants. We need to rediscover what was possible in order to move forward. Many Indigenous communities have used ceremonies to honour, celebrate and initiate plants and seeds into harvest. Elders of the past knew it was a way to manoeuvre time and space across the land and emulate the seasonal perspective that nature holistically guides. We have yet to honour the land, the microbes in the soil or the water droplets that come from the sky to create new life. Whether you are Indigenous or not, to initiate new ceremonies we must open our hearts to rediscover what we have lost.

References

Blum, Winfried E.H., Sophie Zechmeister-Boltenstern and Katharina M. Keiblinger. 'Does Soil Contribute to the Human Gut Microbiome?' *Microorganisms* 7, no. 9 (2019): 287. https://doi.org/10.3390/microorganisms7090287.

Business, Eoin McSweeney and Adam Pourahmadi. '2% of Elon Musk's Wealth Could Solve World Hunger, Says Director of UN Food Scarcity Organization'. *CNN*, 1 November 2021. https://edition.cnn.com/2021/10/26/economy/musk-world-hunger-wfp-intl/index.html.

FAO. The State of Food and Agriculture 2023: Revealing the True Cost of Food to Transform Agrifood Systems. Rome: FAO, 2023. https://openknowledge.fao.org/items/1516eb79-8b43-400e-b3cb-130fd70853b0

History Extra. 'Who Were the Tycoons of the Gilded Age? Meet the Ruthless "Robber Barons" Who Made Millions'. 30 August 2022. https://www.historyextra.com/period/victorian/rise-of-the-robber-barons/.

Inequality Org. 'Global Inequality'. Accessed 3 February 2023. https://inequality.org/facts/global-inequality/.

Land Income. 'Why Is Bill Gates Buying Farmland? You'll be Surprised'. Accessed 12 March 2023. https://landincome.com/blog/why-bill-gates-is-buying-farmland.

Peterson-Withorn, Chase. 'Forbes' 37th Annual World's Billionaires List: Facts and Figures 2023'. Forbes, 4 April 2023. https://www.forbes.com/sites/chasewithorn/2023/04/04/forbes-37th-annual-worlds-billionaires-list-facts-and-figures-2023/

Project Drawdown. 'Project Drawdown'. Accessed 3 February 2022. https://drawdown.org/.

5

DESIGN, EDUCATION AND THE MOULDING OF ALTERNATIVE FUTURES IN THE ANTHROPOCENE

Peter Sutoris

Education and design are two sides of the same coin – we educate through design and design through education. The two share the same ambition: to mould the world and its future. In my research into education at a time of unprecedented environmental crisis, I have asked what role education has played in bringing the world to the brink of environmental collapse and what role it might play in helping humanity to tackle this unprecedented challenge (Sutoris 2022b; 2021). The same questions can be asked of design: have we designed our way to (self-)destruction, and can we design our way to survival?

In this essay, I explore these questions through the concept of the Anthropocene, the proposed new geological epoch in which human beings are now the dominant force shaping the Earth's very physics and chemistry (Crutzen 2002). In much the same way the impact of an asteroid that caused the extinction of two-thirds of the Earth's plant and animal species led to the beginning of a new epoch 66 million years ago, human activity has made an unmistakable imprint on the Earth's composition. The Anthropocene thesis makes us realize that *we* in effect have become the asteroid.

I next consider the questions of responsibility and complexity that arise from the Anthropocene thesis, which also relate to some critiques and proposed alternative concepts. I argue that, like education, the contribution design makes to environmental decay is a symptom of underlying cultural-political forces, rather than their cause. I make this point even though design and education can (and do) help perpetuate these forces by moulding the future in their image. Drawing from activist perspectives I gained doing field research in India and South Africa, I consider what design might learn from conversations about education in the Anthropocene and what education might in turn learn from design. I conclude by suggesting that it might be possible to give life to democracy through design, but that this will require recognizing a third lesson of the Anthropocene alongside responsibility and complexity: that of humility.

The Anthropocene's implications for design: Responsibility and complexity

Unlike some of the other contributors to this volume, my perspective is deliberately human-centric. The *Anthropos* in Anthropocene refers to humanity, not to the non-human or the more-than-human. But why talk about the Anthropocene in a book that seeks to push the conversation *beyond the human*? One reason is that the concept brings into sharp relief the inextricable link between human beings and the planet they inhabit. The Anthropocene is, after all, a two-way street: just as human beings have indelibly altered the planet's composition, so is the planet's future tied to humanity's ability to survive and thrive. As journalist and author Elizabeth Kolbert so eloquently articulated in *Below a White Sky* (2021), human beings might have become very effective at shaping their environment, but they are, so far, much less effective when it comes to fixing the mess caused by their quest for control over nature. Whether or not we subscribe to the idea that nature is external to humanity – the nature-culture dualism (Haila 2000) – the Anthropocene thesis binds the fate of human beings to nature, thus redefining anthropocentrism. In the Anthropocene, placing humans at the centre means inevitably going beyond the human.

As stated in the introduction to this volume, much has been written about the problems with the Anthropocene thesis. This term implies that all human beings are equally responsible for environmental destruction because they are all members of the human species; it fails to differentiate between those perpetrating violence against the environment (and on fellow human beings) and those on the receiving end of that violence. Professor of Inhuman Geography Kathryn Yusoff has summarized this critique:

> This planetary analytic has failed to do the work to properly identify its own histories of colonial earth-writing, to name the masters of broken earths, and to redress the legacy of racialised subjects that geology leaves in its wake. It has failed to grabble with the inheritance of violent dispossession of indigenous land under the auspices of colonial geo-logics or to address the extractive grammars of geology that labour in the instrumentation and instrumentalisation of dominant colonial narratives and their subjective, often subjugating registers that are an ongoing praxis of displacement. (2018, 2)

These troubling colonial undertones of the word 'Anthropocene' have led to a number of proposed alternatives, many of which seek to highlight the ideologies, cultural logics and groups of people disproportionately responsible for the instrumentalization of nature, extractivism and violence that mark this era. These have included the *Capitalocene* (Moore 2017), which points to the underlying logics of capitalist accumulation; the *Anglocene* (Bonneuil and Fressoz 2017), which recognizes the historically disproportionate contribution of the English-speaking world to climate change; the *Plantationocene*, which recognizes the racialization of the plantation in this historical moment; and the *Chthulucene* (Haraway 2016), which focuses on the interconnectedness of human beings and their surroundings.

These proposed alternatives raise important questions and are helpful in tracing the ideological hubris that has led to the planetary condition of what political scientist Karen Litfin (2016) calls the 'environmental multi-crisis'. While I acknowledge the criticism, I have not adopted any of these alternatives and continue to use Anthropocene in my work. I see this term as deeply relevant to a reevaluation of the role of education at a time of unprecedented environmental decay (Sutoris 2022a), and I believe this relevance extends to the field of design.

While the homogenizing logic of the Anthropocene is misleading when considering who is responsible for environmental destruction, it does help illuminate the universality of the environmental multi-crisis, which affects everyone. However, the impact of this multi-crisis is uneven, which also has much to do with deeply unequal colonial, racialized and extractivist histories, and present circumstances, but we would struggle to find a single human being who is not, knowingly or unknowingly, in some way affected. In other words, the *Anthropos* in Anthropocene refers to the human passengers on 'Spaceship Earth' as it heads into oblivion rather than the humans who caused the problem.

This interpretation is congruent with historian Dipesh Chakrabarty's (2021) call for new universalisms in the face of the Anthropocene. One such universalism is, arguably, the question of historical responsibility (Sutoris 2019; Ricœur 1984). Just as Germans who did not agree with Hitler's genocidal schemes but whose tacit support fuelled the Third Reich were asked, 'Why didn't you do more to stop this?', so are future historians likely to ask what action those alive today took, or failed to take, to help avoid an unprecedented catastrophe. Design – both a lens through which to view the world and a tool in humanity's collective toolkit for (re)shaping the world – has, like education, a crucial role to play, not only in making sense of the current generation's historical responsibility but also in equipping us to take meaningful action.[1]

Apart from recognizing humankind's responsibility for a shared future, the Anthropocene raises important questions about complexity. As historians of science and technology Christophe Bonneuil and Jean-Baptiste Fressoz point out, the Anthropocene 'cancels the peaceful and reassuring project of sustainable development' (2017, 22). This is because the concept forces us to confront the fundamental contradiction between the pursuit of economic sustainability – maintaining, ad infinitum, the current global economic system of endless growth fuelled by extractivism (Hickel 2021) – and environmental sustainability, 'a condition of balance, resilience, and interconnectedness that allows human society to satisfy its needs while neither exceeding the capacity of its supporting ecosystems to continue to regenerate the services necessary to meet those needs nor by our actions diminishing biological diversity' (Morelli 2011, 5).

Much contemporary debate about sustainability does not acknowledge this contradiction, as is reflected in the fundamental premise of the United Nations Sustainable Development Goals – that sustainability consists of three dimensions, economic, social and environmental (Elkington 2000), which are not at odds with each other. The rate of extraction of natural resources continues to accelerate, which – along with its impact on biodiversity, climate, soil erosion, forest cover, phosphate, water cycles and other aspects of the global environmental multi-crisis – shows that ideas like 'green growth', 'green transition' and 'green new deal' are used to justify continued economic growth at the expense of environmental sustainability (Hickel and Kallis 2020). Of what use is decarbonization if it further accelerates the loss of biodiversity and increases the likelihood of ecosystem collapse on a catastrophic scale? The Anthropocene forces us to confront the planet we live on as a complex, interconnected system. This is an intellectual and emotional endeavour that does not lend itself to shortcuts and easy solutions, such as replacing dirty technologies with 'clean' ones. It helps bring about a realization that this is a crisis of politics and culture – of the instrumentalization of nature; of a disconnect between human actions and being able to perceive their long-term consequences; of extractivism and the fiction of infinite growth on a finite planet – rather than merely a crisis of science and technology.

This realization has major implications for thinking about design at this historic juncture. If we accept the idea Elio Caccavale and Gordon Hush put forward in their introduction to this book – that human-centred and user-centred design have contributed to environmental decay on a planetary scale due to their focus on Western ways of life, on consumer behaviours and on catering to the individual rather than the collective – the question then arises of what ought to replace these paradigms.

A tempting idea, which resonates with current political and media discourse, would be 'climate-centred design', an approach that would place the climate crisis, rather than the individual human or user, at its centre. But the Anthropocene teaches us that this would be a mistake, for it would promote yet another particularism, an abstraction of a complex reality into a buzzword. It is important to note that the 'golden spikes' – globally detectable traces of environmental change preserved in the Earth's sediments – that have been identified as the potential beginning points of the Anthropocene are not necessarily linked to the climate crisis (Smith and Zeder 2013); all of them are as much a matter of political and cultural developments as they are a consequence of scientific 'progress'. For example, the detonation of nuclear bombs during the arms race between the United States and the Soviet Union, which spread nuclear isotopes that will be detectable globe-wide for millions of years to come (Smith and Zeder 2013), were a direct consequence of Cold War geopolitics (Barker 2013); therefore, the invention of the nuclear bomb alone would not constitute a golden spike.

The existential threat nuclear weapons have posed to the environment is wholly separate from the issue of carbon emissions and global warming, as are several other environmental crises unfolding in parallel with climate change. The design field's response to the Anthropocene should not be a matter of decentring one thing and centring another; it needs to do away with the very concept of centring.

What can design learn from education?

Design and formal education systems have in common a propensity to spotlight specific ideologies embraced by society's elites, thus it makes sense for designers to consider the arguments being made about this tendency in the field of education. Conversations about the changing social role of education in the Anthropocene show that this 'centring' is not simply a pragmatic device for focusing human effort but a symptom of deeper societal dynamics. Many commentators have pointed to the tendency of environmental and sustainability education to depoliticize the discourse around environmental change, be it from the perspective of transgressive pedagogies (Lotz-Sisitka et al. 2015), Indigenous knowledge (Prakash and Esteva 2008) or educator and philosopher Paulo Freire-inspired eco-pedagogy (Misiaszek 2016). Such depoliticization can take many forms, from avoiding the 'touchy' subjects of environmental justice, consumerism and neoliberal capitalism in the classroom to promoting visions of personal and collective success rooted in wealth accumulation. Another key form is the individualization of responsibility that encourages young people to engage with the environmental multi-crisis only through highly localized micro-behaviours, such as recycling, without a deeper reflection on the need for political action and systemic change (Maniates 2001).

And yet, it would be unfair to see formal education as the main culprit, significant as its influence on society might be, because such depoliticization is a consequence of the underlying cultural-political forces. Most education systems are run by governments that are themselves seen to be failing to adequately address the environmental multi-crisis. This suggests that governments prefer to keep education deep in the depoliticized, individualized waters so as to avoid exposing their own failures. But, the political economy of formal education aside, the currents of depoliticization run deep; as Indian writer Amitav Ghosh notes, 'at exactly the time when it has become clear that global warming is in every sense a collective predicament, humanity finds itself in the thrall of a dominant culture in which the idea of the collective has been exiled from politics, economics and literature alike' (2016, 108). In tracing the origins of this dangerous trend, Ghosh notes:

> The acceleration in carbon emissions and the turn away from the collective are both, in one sense, effects of that aspect of modernity that sees time (in Bruno Latour's words) as 'an irreversible arrow, as capitalisation, as progress'. [. . .] [T]his idea of continuous and irreversible forward movement, led by an avant-garde, has been one of the animating forces of the literary and artistic imagination since the start of the twentieth century. A progression of this sort inevitably creates winners and losers. (106)

Design, too, is subject to these wider cultural trends. Like education, design helps to mould the future and can be instrumental in embedding the ideoscapes (Appadurai 1996) of today in the materiality of tomorrow. The capture of human-centred and user-centred design by the forces of consumerism and the West-centric imaginary of progress and development is, in this sense, analogous to the depoliticization of and individualization of environmental and sustainability education.

It would be tempting to pin the responsibility for these trends on capitalism, as the concept of the Capitalocene (Moore 2017) seeks to do. However, as writer and economist Aseem Shrivastava and environmentalist Ashish Kothari aptly point out, 'Under the competitive conditions of industrial modernity, the race towards a socialist utopia paves the way to ecological dystopia no less than the paradise dreamt up by enthusiastic neo-liberals. The ecological debris left behind by the carcass of Soviet communism after its official end in 1990 stands as a testimony to this' (2012, 243). These observations suggest that it may not be the political ideas themselves that we need to pay attention to as we try to make sense of design in the Anthropocene but the ways in which political ideas interact: human-centred design versus climate-centred design; the anti-democratic system of centring a particular idea while excluding others versus a horizontal playing field on which ideas can interact freely and consensus is built from the bottom rather than imposed from the top.

Through my work in education, I have learned much from environmental activists about facing up to the Anthropocene moment. Some of the perspectives these activists have shared with me are also relevant to the field of design, including the question of who the human in 'human-centred design' is. Consider this idea shared with me by an environmental activist fighting industrial air pollution in South Durban, South Africa, in 2017:

> The catalytic issue here is social action. [. . .] I mean, being a transformative agent is not as some people put it, it's not an act of contemplation. You know, you don't imagine yourself like that, you have to be moved to action. And it is when you act that you have to ask the question, but why am I [active]? And once that kind of process is set in motion, the education's impact is dramatic because suddenly you are open to making sense of the impulses.

This perspective contains two important insights: the importance of emotions when responding to environmental decay and the reordering of the conventionally assumed sequence by which we learn before we act. Both insights are also relevant to design; while much design engages the emotional realm, it rarely harnesses the impulses triggered by experiencing environmental destruction. Moreover, the instrumentalization of much contemporary design means that we tend to think of design as inspiring or enabling action rather than as a means of retrospectively making sense of action. This reordering opens up the possibilities for design to take on radically different roles from its instrumentalized position as a promoter of blueprints made by the few to be implemented by the many.

These different visions for design in the Anthropocene can help the field enable outcomes that are not confined to the boundaries of the current socioeconomic system of infinite growth. Another activist I spoke to in South Africa remarked on the need to shift the global imaginaries of formal education, which favour a narrow instrumentality – something education has in common with design:

> We need an education system that does not punish those who have a commitment to their society and are not necessarily obsessed with self-advancement. [. . .] The question to be asked is whether making someone a decent human being is politicising them – you know, they should actually just be mindful that [they] cohabit the world and I should be mindful of the impact of my actions. I mean, if you take that elementary kind of level, then you will have people that think that it is important to be mindful of our impact on the environment, right? [. . .] The point about it is that education represents the common investment of society's young people. See, it is not an economic investment, it's a moral investment, it's a philosophical investment, it's an investment in the ethos of that society.

Just as much of the world's education policy is framed by the language of human capital and economic expansion, so is design frequently seen as a tool for continued capitalist accumulation rather than a way to bring to life the 'ethos of society' (or to stimulate conversations about what the ethos is or ought to be). This is not to say that the role of design should be to generate propaganda or to communicate value judgements intended for uncritical consumption by users. On the contrary, as an anti-dam activist in Northern India told me in an interview in 2018, the point of a good education – and, I would argue, good design – is to encourage independent thinking:

> In school, I didn't learn any politics, I learned mathematics, literature, physics, chemistry, equations, it was very precise. It wasn't that [. . .] the way you learn doesn't make you think or not think, I think that's the thing I'm pointing towards. [. . .] I don't think school should teach you politics, but school should make you think, and if you think you will see the politics around you – you cannot miss it.

Much of the world around us, particularly those of us living in the urban spaces of (post-)industrial modernity, is made by designers. Arguably, much of this world neither makes us think deeply nor helps us see the politics around us. As Professor of Communication Christo Sims points out, 'Design and technoscience can be a way of doing anti-politics [by translating] political problems and concerns [. . .] into seemingly apolitical technoscientific problems that designers and other experts can manage and solve' (2016, 441). These activist perspectives on education offer cues as to the kind of reorientation needed from design in order to help bring to life the responsibility and complexity inherent in the Anthropocene condition.

What can education learn from design?

I am not saying only that design can learn from education; the opposite is also true. To illustrate how education might learn from design, I will summarize a design process in which I recently took part. When distilling the ideas of activists I spoke with during my research, I was faced with a design problem: how to depict the common threads in these ideas using visual vocabularies that would speak to practitioners. I came up with four verbs – grasp (what is at stake), care (an emotional response to what is at stake), imagine (alternative futures) and communicate (these futures to others) – that represent the human abilities education should be harnessing and strengthening in the Anthropocene. However, while boiling down the idea of 'educating for the Anthropocene' to four verbs was helpful, I needed more to communicate this idea clearly to others. I then had a conversation with a designer, who helped me realize that the approach to education I was calling for was not far off the ancient advice to 'know thyself'. All four verbs refer to aspects of being human that come naturally to us; when a baby is born, it quickly starts to grasp at things in its surrounding world; communication, care and imagination soon follow. The designer suggested further that we link these four ideas to parts of the human body – the hand, the heart, the head, the mouth. This enabled us to create a simple drawing that distils the idea of educating for the Anthropocene while highlighting its embodied nature.

When we shared our drawing with others, further ideas emerged. One observer pointed out that action was missing from the image, which made me recall the ideas of historian and political philosopher Hannah Arendt, who argued that action 'is never possible in isolation; to be isolated is to be deprived of the capacity to act' (1998, 188). Thus, we saw that we needed to add a second human to our figure in order to communicate that plurality is a prerequisite for action. When we shared this new version, one observer noticed that our two human figures were identical. We then realized that, to emphasize that action stems from difference, we needed to differentiate between the two figures. That is how we arrived at the version of the drawing that we include in this essay.

This simple design process highlighted for me that the practices of prototyping, testing, iterating, piloting and scaling offer multiple opportunities along the design journey to bring a more holistic human perspective to the fore, to test our ideas and to involve others in debate about imagined futures. Design, in other words, offers many tools that are uniquely suited to help overcome the elitism and social polarization inherent in the elites-masses dichotomy that lies at the heart of many conventional imaginaries of the future. These tools, mindsets and analytic lenses are what designers can use to intervene in education – and in other human endeavours – in the Anthropocene.

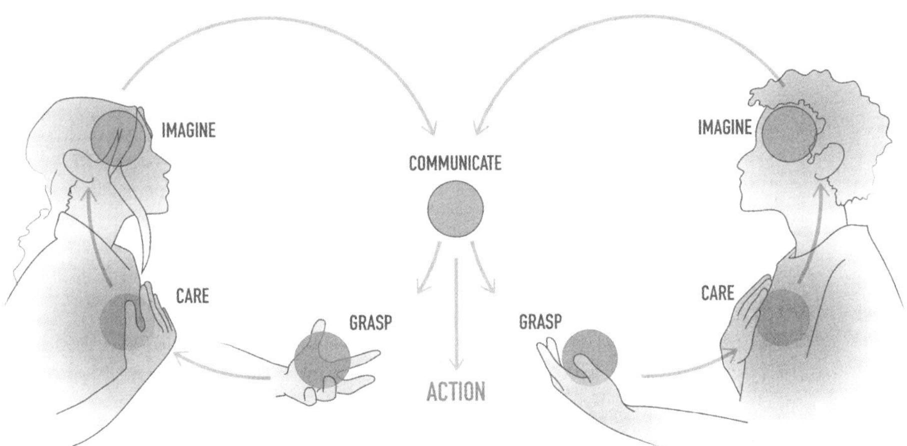

Figure 5.1 Educating for the Anthropocene, 2022. Courtesy of Peter Sutoris. Design by Nuith Morales.

Revisiting the human, (humbly) living democracy through design

Social engineering has come to dominate the worlds of design and education alike, wherein groups of elites (architects, designers, curriculum specialists, policymakers) come up with blueprints for the future that they expect the masses to follow. Such a top-down approach to design is, arguably, somewhat undemocratic, which helps to illustrate the instrumentality with which design is often approached as a means of creating blueprints for the future.

Thus, my fundamental question: Can design help give life to democracy, or are anti-democratic and elitist tendencies an inherent feature of human-centred design? This question might be phrased more helpfully by drawing a parallel with Kathryn Yussof's critique of the discipline of geology that produced the term 'Anthropocene': 'I want to redress how the descriptive qualities of geology's nomenclature produce what Harman calls a "cultivated silence" about the normalcy of those extractive modes as deracialized. To address this silence would be to understand geology as a regime for producing both subjects and material worlds' (2018, 4). So, what does it mean to address the 'cultivated silence' in design?

Aside from responsibility and complexity, the Anthropocene's key lesson for design is humility. The 'cultivated silence' lies in the arrogance – the precursor to elitism and social polarization – of making environmentally harmful products appealing, the arrogance of thinking that the Earth itself can be redesigned, through geoengineering (Vaughan and Lenton 2011), to fulfil the desires of humans. The many contributions design has made to the current environmental multi-crisis, both the willing and the inadvertent ones, are a testament to this arrogance. Human limitations in grasping complexity and forecasting the future are a lesson in humility. If design is to help humanity successfully navigate the unprecedented challenges of an Anthropocene world, it needs to recognize its role as a way of *proposing* rather than *prescribing* solutions (Sims 2016). It also needs to forge alliances with others who might be able to help bring about a different kind of design. In short, it needs to depart from its elitist legacy and embrace humility as its *modus operandi* in the Anthropocene.

Note

1 By 'generation' I mean all those alive in the Anthropocene.

References

Appadurai, Arjun. *Modernity at Large: Cultural Dimensions of Globalisation*. Minneapolis: University of Minnesota Press, 1996.

Arendt, Hannah. *The Human Condition*. Chicago and London: University of Chicago Press, 1998.

Barker, Holly M. *Bravo for the Marshallese: Regaining Control in a Post-Nuclear, Post-Colonial World*. Case Studies on Contemporary Social Issues. Belmont: Wadsworth, 2013.

Bonneuil, Christophe and Jean-Baptiste Fressoz. *The Shock of the Anthropocene*. London: Verso, 2017.

Chakrabarty, Dipesh. *The Climate of History in a Planetary Age*. Chicago: University of Chicago Press, 2021. https://press.uchicago.edu/ucp/books/book/chicago/C/bo8642262.html

Crutzen, Paul J. 'Geology of Mankind'. *Nature* 415 no. 6867 (2002): 23. https://doi.org/10.1038/415023a

Elkington, John. 'Cannibals with Forks: The Triple Bottom Line of 21st Century Business'. *Journal of Business Ethics* 23, no. 2 (2000): 229–31. https://doi.org/10.1023/a:1006129603978

Ghosh, Amitav. *The Great Derangement: Climate Change and the Unthinkable*. New Delhi: Penguin, 2016.

Haila, Yrjö. 'Beyond the Nature-Culture Dualism'. *Biology and Philosophy* 15, no. 2 (2000): 155. https://doi.org/10.1023/A:1006625830102

Haraway, Donna J. *Staying with the Trouble: Making Kin in the Chthulucene*. Experimental Futures. Durham, NC: Duke University Press, 2016.

Hickel, Jason. 'The Anti-Colonial Politics of Degrowth'. *Political Geography* 88 (June 2021): https://doi.org/10.1016/j.polgeo.2021.102404

Hickel, Jason and Giorgos Kallis. 'Is Green Growth Possible?' *New Political Economy* 25, no. 4 (2020): 469–86. https://doi.org/10.1080/13563467.2019.1598964

Kolbert, Elizabeth. *Under a White Sky: The Nature of the Future*. Random House, 2021.

Litfin, Karen. 'Person/Planet Politics: Contemplative Pedagogies for a New Earth'. In *New Earth Politics: Essays from the Anthropocene*, edited by Simon Nicholson and Sikina Jinnah. Cambridge, MA: The MIT Press, 2016, 115–34.

Lotz-Sisitka, Heila, Wals, Arjen EJ, Kronlid, David and Dylan McGarry. 'Transformative, Transgressive Social Learning: Rethinking Higher Education Pedagogy in Times of Systemic Global Dysfunction'. *Current Opinion in Environmental Sustainability*, *Sustainability Science* 16 (2015): 73–80. https://doi.org/10.1016/j.cosust.2015.07.018

Maniates, Michael F. 'Individualisation: Plant a Tree, Buy a Bike, Save the World?' *Global Environmental Politics* 1, no. 3 (2001): 31–52. https://doi.org/10.1162/152638001316881395

Misiaszek, Greg William. 'Ecopedagogy as an Element of Citizenship Education: The Dialectic of Global/Local Spheres of Citizenship and Critical Environmental Pedagogies'. *International Review of Education* 62, no. 5 (2016): 587–607. https://doi.org/10.1007/s11159-016-9587-0

Moore, Jason W. 'The Capitalocene, Part I: On the Nature and Origins of Our Ecological Crisis'. *The Journal of Peasant Studies* 44, no. 3 (2017): 594–630. https://doi.org/10.1080/03066150.2016.1235036

Morelli, John. 'Environmental Sustainability: A Definition for Environmental Professionals'. *Journal of Environmental Sustainability* 1, no. 1 (2011): 2. https://doi.org/10.14448/jes.01.0002

Prakash, Madhu Suri and Gustavo Esteva. *Escaping Education: Living as Learning Within Grassroots Cultures*. New York: Peter Lang, 2008.

Ricœur, Paul. *Time and Narrative*. Chicago: University of Chicago Press, 1984.

Shrivastava, Aseem and Ashish Kothari. *Churning the Earth: The Making of Global India*. New Delhi: Penguin, 2012.

Sims, Christo. 'The Politics of Design, Design as Politics'. In *The Routledge Companion to Digital Ethnography*, edited by Larissa Hjorth, Heather Horst, Anne Galloway, and Genevieve Bell. London: Routledge, 2016, 439–47. https://doi.org/10.4324/9781315673974-58

Smith, Bruce D. and Melinda A. Zeder. 'The Onset of the Anthropocene'. *Anthropocene*, When Humans Dominated the Earth: Archaeological Perspectives on the Anthropocene 4 (December 2013): 8–13. https://doi.org/10.1016/j.ancene.2013.05.001

Sutoris, Peter. *Educating for the Anthropocene: Schooling and Activism in the Face of Slow Violence*. Cambridge: The MIT Press, 2022a.

Sutoris, Peter. 'Environmental Futures through Children's Eyes: Slow Observational Participatory Videomaking and Multi-Sited Ethnography'. *Visual Anthropology Review* 37, no. 2 (2021): 310–32. https://doi.org/10.1111/var.12240

Sutoris, Peter. 'Politicising ESE in Postcolonial Settings: The Power of Historical Responsibility, Action and Ethnography'. *Environmental Education Research* 25, no. 4 (2019): 601–12. https://doi.org/10.1080/13504622.2019.1569204

Sutoris, Peter. 'Slow Violence, Depoliticisation and Hope: Cultural Landscapes of Schooling in Wentworth, South Africa'. *Ethnography*, 2022b. https://doi.org/10.1177/14661381221130278

Vaughan, Naomi E. and Timothy M. Lenton. 'A Review of Climate Geoengineering Proposals'. *Climatic Change* 109, no. 3 (2011): 745–90. https://doi.org/10.1007/s10584-011-0027-7

Yusoff, Kathryn. *A Billion Black Anthropocenes or None*. Minneapolis: University of Minnesota Press, 2018.

PART II

DESIGN BEYOND THE HUMAN

INTRODUCTION: DESIGN BEYOND THE HUMAN

'Design Beyond the Human' provides a theoretical reflection assessing the impact of the anthropocentric conceptualization of design. In transcending the anthropocentrism of the UCD/HCD orthodoxy, design needs to rethink its conceptual framework and must do so as part of a transdisciplinary debate – with philosophy and geology, with ecology, history, and postcolonial critique in order to reimagine what being human *is*. Today, to be human is to understand the ecological system within which you are contained and given life. Where once the Earth was the site of human progress (the actions of conscious design), now we see that the Earth may out-exist humanity, at least in its current civilizational guise, and our future survival may depend upon the transdisciplinary debate that allows us to rethink what it is to be human in the twenty-first century. With this in mind, 'Design Beyond the Human' conceptualizes design through a relational understanding of the world that is rooted in ecological appreciation, rather than economistic ambition, by moving towards a theoretical articulation of design practices that respond more appropriately to planetary (and beyond) conditions and the interrelationships of living beings. This section is characterized by the critical evaluation of the Anglo-European conceptualization of an anthropocentric design, which privileges a selected group of humans, who share and benefit from the same economic and cultural model, while blighting humanity as a whole, along with other species and ecosystems. In bringing new and diverse conversations into a transdisciplinary debate, the historical consequences of our recent past are weighed against the futures of those who have historically been marginalized and without voice.

In 'Design and the Invention of the Modern Human', Professor of Architectural History and Theory Samer Akkach and Visiting Research Fellow in the School of Architecture and the Built Environment at the University of Adelaide John Powell affirm that the human capacity for 'design' is a distinctive means of exercising control and embodying human will and power. They argue that the act of designing is intrinsic to our essence as humans, playing a fundamental role in shaping our 'humanness'. In their contribution, Akkach and Powell offer a historical account detailing significant transformations in the scope and character of human design during the early modern period (sixteenth–nineteenth century). This era witnessed profound shifts marked by the ascent of early modern science and the onset of the European Enlightenment, both of which played pivotal roles in shaping the nature of human design. According to them, these events of global significance took the premodern human on a divergent journey of self-discovery and self-transformation that resulted in the making of the modern human. Akkach and Powell ask readers to consider a fundamental reorientation of human design to change the self-destructive approach modern humans have vigorously pursued over the past 200 years.

In her essay, 'Ecological Design Thinking in the Anthropocene/Ecocene', Senior Lecturer in Design Joanna Boehnert contends that the creation of desirable and achievable futures in the face of climate and ecosystem destabilization requires a profound understanding of ecology and a substantial shift in design priorities. To achieve sustainable design transitions, it is essential to challenge the assumptions and future perspectives inherent in modernity. Ecological literacy extends beyond simple ecological awareness or knowledge – it entails cultivating the skills necessary to actively and effectively promote sustainable change. By utilizing an ecological action framework, ecological design thinking and practices can facilitate adaptation to environmental challenges. Boehnert's chapter introduces concepts at the intersection of ecological literacy and emerging ecological design thinking, with the goal of dismantling the unsustainable logic present in design and beyond.

Design Lecturer at Monash University and Unit Coordinator of the Indigenous Research Methods (Wominjeka Djeembana Lab) Desiree Hernandez Ibinarriaga provides an account of her Mexican Chamula (Mayan), Nahua (Aztec) and Euskaldunak (Basque) heritage and Indigenous relational practice, a new-old approach of design based on relationality between people, Place, and ancestral practices, on Country. Hernandez Ibinarriaga's essay 'Indigenous Design: A Relational Practice between People and Place' unveils her practice through the *Agave* furniture/sculpture, an example of an Indigenous Design project that holds not only materiality and functionality but also cultural significance and ancestral knowledge for the Nahuas and Mayan peoples. Hernandez Ibinarriaga reminds us that Indigenous Design is a creative practice that holds collective knowledge that is relational to Place and its people, encompassing the tangible and intangible, while respecting all living beings on Earth.

In the chapter 'Life-Centred Design: A Sub-Saharan Perspective', design scholar François-Xavier Nzi iyo Nsenga provides an account of the views, practices and aims of design in pre-colonial sub-Saharan Africa, concerning the production and use of artefacts in daily life before globalization. Informed by his personal experience, Nsenga illustrates that prior to Euro-American dominance, design traditions in sub-Saharan Africa approached the relationship between humans and nature with mutual respect and reciprocity among all life forms. This perspective challenges the prevailing 'Global North' techno-scientific tradition, which heavily relies on a dualistic understanding of nature and society. Sub-Saharan African design traditions, in contrast, embody a more interconnected worldview, emphasizing harmony and balance between society and nature.

Curator and Lecturer in Design Criticism and Curatorial Studies at China Central Academy of Fine Arts Naiyi Wang's essay 'Design and Deep Time' examines the complex entanglements of geological time (deep time) and design by drawing on the connection between the materiality of design and the geophysical reality of raw matter-energy. Wang analyses electronic devices by examining their material composition, specifically minerals and their subsequent residues. She traces the life cycle of these devices from the natural minerals, which sediment for millions of years before extraction and processing in the Bayan Obo region of Inner Mongolia. The journey continues through the utilization of these materials and culminates in the deposition of waste in the landfill of Guiyu, China. This exploration provides a comprehensive understanding of electronic devices' temporal and material dimensions and their devastating ecological impact.

In the chapter 'Orbital Debris: Design and Its Extra-Terrestrial Aftermath', Research Professor at the Royal Academy of Art, The Hague, Alice Twemlow considers the phenomenon of space debris. In the text, she uses philosopher Timothy Morton's concept of the 'hyperobject' to explore and comprehend the complex nature of space debris in relation to design. Twemlow critiques the non-sustainable, techno-determinist modes of intervention currently being deployed in the name of remediation and mitigation.

Furthermore, she contemplates the potential contributions of research at the crossroads of art and design practices, history, media archaeology and the environmental humanities by exploring how these interdisciplinary approaches might offer alternative imaginaries to foster a more profound understanding of the issue. This is particularly relevant within the context of the environmental crisis that transcends the confines of Earth, extending into the Earth's orbital commons.

6
DESIGN AND THE INVENTION OF THE MODERN HUMAN

Samer Akkach and John Powell

The great divergence

If we think of the human ability to 'design' – that is, to imagine, create and make tools and objects – as a unique capacity of control, then designing can in many ways be seen as a manifestation of human will and power. And if we think of human will and power as an expression of what makes us human, then our acts of designing are integral to our humanness: what and how we design will always reflect on us and eventually redesign us (Colomina and Wigley 2018). Seen from this standpoint, the scope and nature of human design underwent massive changes during the early modern period (sixteenth–nineteenth centuries) that witnessed the rise of early modern science and the emergence of the European Enlightenment. These events of global significance took the premodern human on a divergent journey of self-discovery and self-transformation that resulted, as this chapter argues, in the making of the modern human (Gaukroger 2006, 2010, 2016).

'Early modernity', as a concept and a historical period, presents a difficult challenge to global and intellectual historians as well as historians of science who are keen on writing history from a non-Eurocentric perspective (Hobson 2006). The challenge lies in such entrenched notions as the 'great divergence', 'European miracle' and 'rise of the West', which refer to profound socioeconomic, intellectual and scientific shifts whereby Europe is shown to have diverged from the premodern path it had shared with other civilizations by inventing a 'modern' approach that eventually led to its emergence as the most powerful, scientifically advanced and wealthy civilization on the planet (Jones 2003; Pomeranz 2000; Gran 2009). The divergence narrative presents the making of the modern world as a European project realized on the foundations of early modern science and the visionary ideals of the European Enlightenment.

Thus understood, 'early modernity' is yet to be integrated into the official historical narratives of non-Western civilizations, especially the Islamic, whose 'early modernity' coincides with a complex intertwining of local dynastic histories. The unity of purpose and global scope of the notion of the 'great divergence' remain absent in non-European historical narratives. As the questions probing the 'great divergence' have focused mainly on the cause and outcome, rather than the problematics of the concept itself, the told historical narratives have been teleologically Eurocentric. Historians have investigated all aspects of the socio-cultural, political, economic and epistemological changes only to explain the reasons behind and consequences of the emergence of Europe as a dominant power on the global stage.

Reflecting on the notion of the great divergence from outside the dominating Western perspective, this chapter focuses on its problematics. It examines how the divergence had led to the invention of the modern human – as a self-centred creature with immense destructive power – thereby taking the debate beyond the conventional rise-and-decline and boom-and-bust polarities. Indirectly, this focus will help us understand why non-Western civilizations had resisted the divergence until it was forced upon them by the divergent Europeans through their imperial projects.

The questions concerning the impact of the great divergence on the human actor that caused the change have remained relatively remote to the debate. Viewed mainly as inventors and agents of change, the humans themselves have remained the same humans. They might have become stronger, wealthier, more civilized and better equipped with advanced scientific tools, but essentially, they themselves have remained unchanged. The act of divergence was seen to be circumstantial. Humans make their own futures, as the official historical narrative goes, all according to their willingness and ability to diverge towards the inevitably liberating and empowering path of modernity. Those who diverged rose, acquired knowledge, power and new fortunes, while those who remained steadfast on the traditional path declined and suffered the consequences of traditional restrictions and cultural inhibitions (Huff 2010).

The invention of the human

In *Are We Human?* (Colomina and Wigley 2018) architectural theorists Beatriz Colomina and Mark Wigley appear to have diverged from the universal narrative of the great divergence by posing a different set of provocative questions. In a series of brief reflections, or 'field notes', they drew attention to the evolving nature of humanity as an inevitable consequence of their inherent design ability and the intimate relationship humans have with their tools. 'If the human is a question mark', they postulated, then 'design is the way that question is engaged'. In Chapter 4, 'The Invention of the Human', they argued that the emergence of the human occurs through the continuous invention of tools, artefacts and technological advancement: 'the human does not simply invent tools. Tools invent the human.'

If we accept the proposition that tools invent the human, then the quantum leap in scientific and technological advancement during the early modern period, which is unprecedented in global history, must have brought about a profound remaking of the human. Consequently, the 'early modern' and 'modern human' must be essentially different from 'premodern human', whose tools and design abilities were remarkably different. In their analysis, Colomina and Wigley have adopted a broad, counter-Darwinian perspective that traces the emergence of the human as a distinctly capable species on planet Earth through the consideration of a long evolutionary timeline (Colomina and Wigley 2018, ch. 3). This wide evolutionary perspective focuses mainly on biological transformations without taking into account the narrower timeline of the recent technological divergence that has shaped the invention of the modern human through specific techno-cultural and epistemological moulds over the past five centuries.

Starting with Colomina and Wigley's proposition that 'the human becomes human in seeing itself in the things it makes, or seeing its possibility in those things', this chapter examines the emergence of early modern science in Europe as a context for the invention of the modern human. The emergence of early modern science has been associated with the invention of the idea of 'European exceptionalism', which has recently resurfaced within a new discourse based on what has been termed 'neo-Eurocentrism' (Hobson 2006; Akkach 2021). Viewing the emergence of early modern science as essentially an invention of the modern human introduces a new understanding of this transformative event that helps us transcend the conventional narrative of the great divergence currently dominating the fields of global, intellectual and economic history as well as the history of science. Such understanding offers a new theoretical framework to consider, for example, why the Islamic civilization, which was the most advanced at the time, resisted following the early modern European adventures for nearly 300 years.

At the core of the invention of the modern human, this study argues, lies profound changes to the ways in which humans saw the nature of their will and power, the human anchors of design. The modern human confronted divinity unprecedentedly to remove contingencies beyond their understanding, declare their unrestricted free will and assert their dominant control over nature. As intellectual historian Margaret J. Osler has argued, rethinking the nature of contingency and necessity was central to this confrontation (Osler 1994). The core questions were: 'Is the world contingent on forces beyond the possibility of human understanding and control? Or does the world necessarily conform to rationally intelligible principles?' (Osler 1994, 1–2). The new answers to these questions not only destroyed the traditional understanding of the nature of causality, providing a new scope for natural philosophy (i.e., science), but, as a consequence, also changed humans who have since continued to claim for themselves a widening scope of will and power, that had long been considered divine prerogatives.

Rethinking the human in a mechanical universe

Throughout history, scholars from various disciplines endeavoured to read the mind of God. They were keen to understand the universe's order, unravel the purpose of existence and foresee humanity's fate. The mode and extent of God's activities in the universe emerged as an area of dispute and contention. While seeking uniformity, consistency and predictability in the workings of nature, theologians and mystics, for example, were keener than philosophers on keeping a space for the miraculous, the free exercise of divine power and the unpredictability of divine providence. Sharing Aristotle's philosophy and physics and Ptolemy's geography and astronomy, medieval Christian and Muslim worldviews were close in understanding the nature of the divine activities in the universe despite their creedal differences and the diversity of ideas both had espoused.

In the seventeenth and eighteenth centuries, European thinkers broke off on new tangents. As a result, the metaphor of a living organism that formed the basis of understanding the universe's workings for centuries was replaced with the metaphor of the clockwork. The microcosm-macrocosm analogy that was for centuries anchored in viewing the world as a large human, and the human as a small world, was replaced with mechanistic physics that assimilated natural processes to the precision and self-regulating control of machinery. While all animal and natural operations were reduced to their mechanics, only disembodied reason was granted a privileged status (Brooke 1991, ch. 4). The implications of this shift were profound. The notion of 'power' underwent a profound transformation in the mechanical universe. In the Ptolemaic-Aristotelian worldview, the original source of power that made things move, the Immovable Mover, lay beyond the physical world: it was intangible and unmeasurable. In the Galilean-

Newtonian worldview, this power became immanent in the world: it became tangible and measurable and eventually coincided with the forces of nature (Dupré 2004, ch. 2).

The mysterious animating spirit that enlivened the world became visible in the mechanics of the clock. The medieval understanding of God's infinite, unmeasurable and inexplicable power that regulates the world from its largest to its smallest entity began to give way to an understanding of a creator who set all the immutable laws of nature and retired to His transcendental retreat, disinterested in the triviality of daily events. In this new scheme, humans were no longer the original idea in the image of which the universe was fashioned, but the rational master uniquely poised to unravel the mysteries of the universe and *redesign* it according to their vision and needs.

In this context, 'nature' appeared as *the* new focus of *human* enquiry. During the Enlightenment, the conceptualization of 'nature' became a scholarly obsession. Everyone spoke in the name of nature, whether in arts or science, politics or aesthetics, religion or philosophy. Ideas about 'nature' and the 'natural' permeated most discussions (Hayland et al. 2003, ch. 4). The spectrum of definitions encompassed a wide range of meanings that shared the common view of 'nature' as a resourceful storehouse as well as a consistent, self-regulating force of the universe. At the perceptual level, 'a new conception emerged of what was real in the world. Particles of matter in motion-defined the new reality. The world of appearances, of colours, odours, tastes was reduced to secondary status – as merely the effect of the interaction of particles on the human sensory apparatus' (Brooke 1991, 118).

Human nature reconfigured

The great appeal of nature and the natural during the Enlightenment inspired a demand for a science of *human* nature. In *A Treatise of Human Nature*, the Scottish philosopher David Hume (1711–76) stressed 'that all the sciences have a relation, greater or less, to human nature' (Hayland et al. 2003, 3). In contrast to the medieval focus on the universalities of human reality, the Enlightenment thinkers became preoccupied with the particularities of the soul's conduct and the processes of the mind. Passions, feelings and emotions became the object of intense and unprecedented types of study and a new sense of selfhood emerged. 'Despite the persistence and development of rationalist trends, the Enlightenment could more accurately be described as an age of self-consciousness' (Dupré 2004, 53).

Scholars from every discipline of study were engaged in a wholesale rethinking of human nature, exploring new and exciting terrains of social sciences and charting new domains of anthropology, psychology and sociology. This marked a radical shift from the medieval Christian preoccupation with humanity primarily as a privileged species created in the image of divinity and made to dwell at the centre of a purpose-designed universe. The Christian sacred history of creation predicated on the idea of original sin and the biblical story of the fall began to give way to a new secular history of humanity that was self-centred and almost irrelevant to the interests of divinity and its promise of salvation.

In his *Leviathan*, the atheist English thinker Thomas Hobbes (1588–1679), a graduate from Oxford, argued 'that men are naturally and fundamentally self-seeking, individually existing units, who have to learn to co-operate within a society' (Hayland et al. 2003, 4). In his view, social existence is a necessity that protects individuals and supports their selfish interests. Likewise, in *Man a Machine*, the French physician and philosopher Julien Offray La Mattrie (1709–51) dismissed the projective conception of man by preceding philosophers, arguing that the only way to understand human nature was by

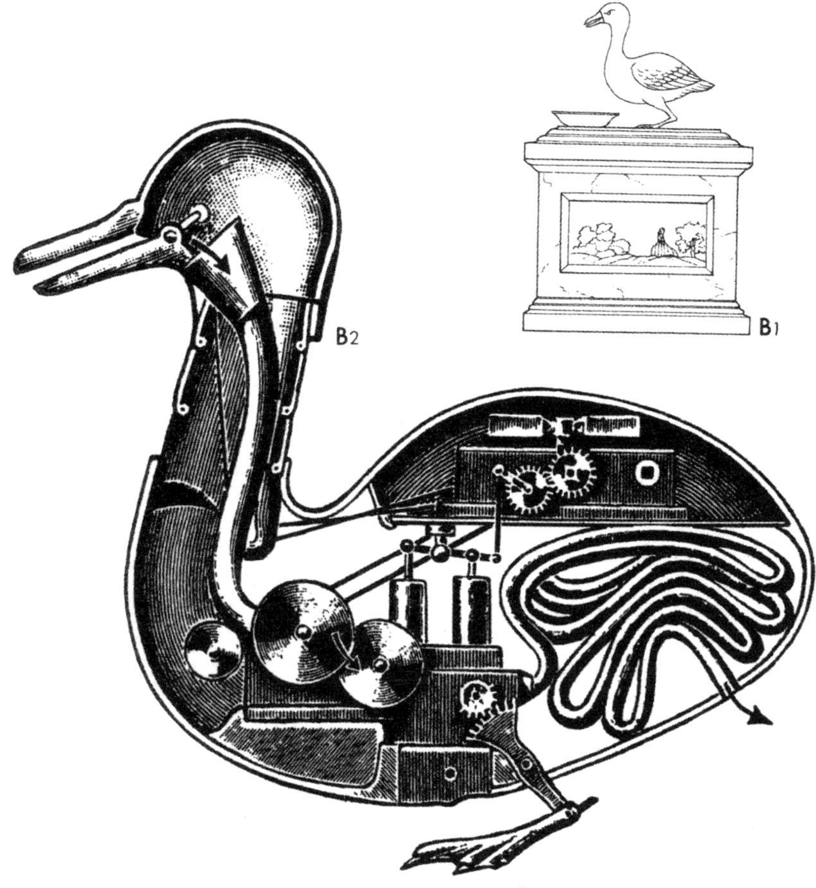

Figure 6.1 *Digesting Duck* by Jacques de Vaucanson, 1739. Internet, public domain.

empirical retrospective analysis based on experience and observation. He concluded that humans, in their individual and social existence, are governed entirely by physical impulses and that their moral values are subjective and arbitrary. In his famous and widely circulated poem titled *An Essay on Man*, Alexander Pope (1688–1744), England's leading poet of the early Enlightenment, summed up eloquently the prevailing sentiment of the age that witnessed the emergence of a keen interest in unveiling the hidden mysteries of this doubtful yet powerful creature and of new approaches to understanding the workings of his both sublime and mundane nature. He wrote:

> Know then thyself, presume not God to scan;
> The proper study of Mankind is Man.
> Plac'd on this isthmus of a middle state,
> A being darkly wise, and rudely great;
> With too much knowledge for the Sceptic side,
> With too much weakness for the Stoic pride,

> He hangs between; in doubt to act, or to rest,
> In doubt to deem himself a God, or Beast;
> In doubt his Mind or Body to prefer,
> Born but to die, and reas'ning but to err;. . .
> Go, wond'rous creature! mount where Science guides,
> Go, measure earth, weigh air, and state the tides,
> Instruct the planets in what orbs to run,
> Correct old Time, and regulate the sun. (Hayland et al. 2003, 12–13)

Cartesian dreams

The most profound change to understanding human nature, and consequently the invention of the modern human, was initiated by the works of the celebrated French philosopher René Descartes, a believer who delighted in mathematics and enjoyed meditating alone in stove-heated rooms. One night at the age of twenty-three, he had three visionary dreams that were said to have inspired him to initiate a decisive rethinking of human nature that radically changed the main orientation of European philosophy. His influential meditations on the nature of the mind, the body and the external world are recognized for providing the philosophical framework for modern scientific methodology, which is anchored in his effective separation of the subjective and objective realms. He defined man as a 'conscious being' and saw human engagement with the world as self-conscious minds (subjects) confronting and coming to terms with autonomous, extended bodies that exist out there (objects) (Anscombe and Geach1970, 2nd and 6th Meditation). In his rethinking of human nature, Descartes began by questioning what he meant when he referred to himself in daily speech as 'I'. He wanted to understand the relationship between his ego, the 'I', and his body. After a series of self-interrogations, he said: 'I can validly infer that my essence consists simply in the fact that I am a conscious being' (Anscombe and Geach 1970, 114). Having equated his ego with his self-conscious mind, he concluded: 'So it is certain that I am really distinct from my body, and could exist without it' (Anscombe 1970, 115). He then went on to explain the basis of his conclusion:

> Body is of its nature always divisible; mind is wholly indivisible. When I consider the mind – that is, myself, in so far as I am merely a conscious being – I can distinguish no part within myself; I understand myself to be a single and complete thing. Although the whole mind seems to be united to the whole body; yet when a foot or an arm or any other part of the body is cut off I am not aware that any subtraction has been made from the mind. Nor can the faculties of will, feeling, understanding and so on be called its parts; for it is one and the same mind that wills, feels, and understands. (Anscombe 1970, 121)

Based on this sharp distinction between the mind and the body, Descartes effectively separated the realm of subjectivity, of inner thoughts, emotions and desires, from the objective reality that embodied autonomous sets of measurable and quantifiable properties. This separation was critical for the development of the scientific methodology that flourished during the Enlightenment and was exemplified in the pioneering work of the great English mathematician and physicist Sir Isaac Newton (1643–1727).

Nature as forces and objects

Nature's workings and manifestations at the physical, social and psychic levels became the main preoccupations of scholars and scientists. With this shift, the world began to gradually lose its mysteries, as the enlightened man set out to conquer nature and dispel all unfounded fears of, and superstitions about her. 'Natural philosophy' – the empirical as well as reflective study of nature – became then roughly equivalent to what we today call 'science'. Newton's famous book on planetary orbits and gravitational theory was titled *Mathematical Principles of Natural Philosophy*, and many writers even regarded travel literature as an important source of knowledge for natural philosophy. Along with natural philosophy, there appeared 'natural theology', which represented the attempts to provide proofs and arguments for the existence of God based on reason and ordinary experience, in contrast to the traditional 'revealed theology' that was anchored in divine revelations, scripture and spiritual experiences. Both natural philosophy and natural theology found support in the 'mechanical philosophy', which was based on the generally agreed view that the universe was entirely made up of small particles that constantly moved and changed direction as they restlessly bumped into each other. The mechanical philosophy dominated most scholarly discussions, presenting a view of the world as a perfectly designed clock which, once set to work, will go on working in a self-regulating, self-sustaining manner. Likewise, the world was made of particles of matter that had been created and set in motion by a God who thereafter made no interventions.

The clock's elaborate mechanics were analogous to nature's intricate laws. The mechanical philosophy excluded the psychic from nature, explained all natural phenomena in terms of matter and motion and regarded material things as inert. It owed much to Descartes' separation of conscious subjects from inert objects and to Newton's discovery of the laws of motion that reinforced its propositions' validity. While forming the intangible core of a universal, self-regulating and self-sustaining system, nature was nonetheless seen as quantifiable and measurable by means of numbers and weights. Observation and experimentation were considered to be the best method to understand its workings. There were many attempts to explain how God operates in a clockwork universe, wherein autonomy of nature and uniformity of causality became the bounds in conformity with which divine activities took place.

The mechanics of causality

In the sixteenth–eighteenth-century Islamic spheres of thought, there was no place for a mechanical universe. The period reveals a wide preoccupation with, and intense debates of, the theology and philosophy of the Unity of Being (Akkach 2010) that offers no possibility for a self-regulating universe independent of God's direct engagement. However, the rationalism that enabled the clockwork metaphor's emergence was not alien to Islamic thought. Early in the second century of Islam (eighth century CE), a group of rationalist scholars concerned with the nature of power at the divine and human levels led one of Islam's most important theological movements. They were known as the *Mu'tazila*, 'those who separate themselves' or 'who stand aside', so named because of the way in which they distanced themselves from conventional theological interpretations. The *Mu'tazila* tried to provide a rational understanding of the ways in which God engages with the world. The nature of causality and human free will were among the core

Figure 6.2 Automaton, 2022. Internet, public domain.

problematic issues they attempted to address. Some of the perennial theological problems they grappled with were: What is God's role in the cause-and-effect relationship? When a cause produces an effect, is it nature or God at work? Similarly, when humans choose or act, who is at work, their free will and own power or those of God? How can the workings of God, man and nature be reconciled and understood?

The implicit questions were: If God is responsible for all events and occurrences in the world, including human actions, then what is the point of punishment and reward? If human choices are already predestined in God's eternal knowledge and their actions subsumed in his infinite power, then what is the nature of divine justice? (Akkach 2007, 82). To address these issues, the *Mu'tazila* attempted, in a manner similar to those of the Enlightenment thinkers, to argue for God's transcendence, the autonomy of the natural world and the individual's free will. Negating the existence of divine attributes as mediators between God and the world was one core principle of their philosophy; the other was the view that all anthropomorphic descriptions of divinity are symbolic and should be interpreted metaphorically. Their main aims were to keep an infinitely good and just God detached and distanced from the corporeal world's vices, injustices and ailments, and to render humans fully responsible and accountable for their choices and actions.

Although the Muslim philosophers' argument against God's knowledge of the changing trivialities of daily events was available to them, the *Mu'tazila* tried to provide rational explanations of how God can at once be distanced yet in control of everything. Their polemics did not convince everyone, and their rationalism eventually gave way to another school of thought, the *Ash'ariyya* (after the founder *Abu al-Hasan al-Ash'ari*, d. 935/6), that has since prevailed throughout the Islamic world.

The *Ash'ariyya* confirmed the existence of divine attributes that keep God connected with the world and introduced polemical twists into the interpretations of the nature of causality that made sense to most Muslims. Their main aim was to keep God actively engaged in world affairs, be they good or bad, but in a way that grants both humans and natural causes relative autonomy in the manner they operate. To achieve that, they argued that God intervenes *at* the cause and not *with* it, meaning that God creates an effect *at* the cause's ability to produce such an effect but not *with* it. When a person stands up, for example, God does not create the act of standing by using the person as a passive instrument, but creates the act of standing by making the person able to stand and providing him with the free will to choose when to do so. Yet, God always remains in action, albeit indirectly. From this perspective, relative autonomy is given to the world and natural phenomena, since God is seen not to dictate directly what happens and when; however, He ultimately remains in control of all the happenings (Akkach 2007, 83).

The *Ash'ariyya* dominated Islamic thought, although the debate over the nature of God's relationships to both human actions and natural causes continued. Within the sphere of the *Ash'ariyya* thought, the Ptolemaic-Aristotelian concept of 'power' did not undergo a profound transformation as it did in Europe. The Immovable Mover remained entrenched in His metaphysical realm, intangible and unmeasurable yet in charge of every tangible and measurable thing. In other words, God remained interested in the trivial events of daily life, and nature never entertained the same sense of autonomy and authority as she did in Europe. This ensured that traditional Islamic cosmology and its structure of the world remained unchallenged until the nineteenth century.

Effects by divine permission

In the seventeenth and eighteenth centuries, the *Ash'ariyya* view on causality was subject to rethinking by some scholars, although much is yet to be uncovered in this area before we can determine how profound and wide this rethinking was. An exchange between two pre-eminent figures of the period, Abd al-Ghani al-Nabulusi (1641–1731) and Ibrahim al-Kurani (1615–1690), points to a wider debate. Al-Kurani, a leading scholar and influential mystic based in Medina, has been identified as a key figure in a wide circle of religious renewal and reform. He wrote two treatises on the nature of voluntary human actions to which al-Nabulusi responded with a lengthy critique (Akkach 2007, 2010). From al-Nabulusi's response, it appears that al-Kurani was somewhat uncomfortable with the relative autonomy the *Ash'ariyya* had ascribed to natural causes, and he wanted to reaffirm God's active role in the phenomenal world.

To do so, al-Kurani introduced the notion of divine 'permission' or 'authorization', arguing that the individual's power and natural causes produce their effects by the mediation of God's permission and not autonomously. In other words, when a person stands up, the person does so not just because of the person's own power and free will but also because of the divine permission that allows the person to stand up. The notion of divine 'permission', though similar to the *Ash'ariyya*'s automatic divine mediation, differs by introducing an unpredictable factor into causality and natural processes that deprive them of the relative autonomy they had entertained under the *Ash'ariyya* theology. Hinging everything on divine permission that is necessarily inexplicable and unpredictable not only increases God's dominance over the natural world but also undermines the autonomy of natural processes and the predictability inherent in the consistency and uniformity of natural laws.

Al-Kurani supported the mystical theology of the 'Unity of Being', which tends to blur the boundary between God's immanence and transcendence. In certain respects, Unity of Being offers neither space for God to retreat to nor a possibility for the world to be autonomous: God and the world are fused together to form an indissoluble whole. This partly explains the intellectual basis of al-Kurani's concept of 'permission' that aims at maintaining God's active engagement with and ultimate control over the world. Yet, al-Kurani's concept of 'permission' introduces new polemical twists into the already complicated view of the world, further limiting the rational space of scientific thinking, in contrast to the increasing scientific rationalism within the sphere of mechanical philosophy in Europe.

The light of Being and the night of becoming

Al-Kurani's rethinking of the *Ash'ariyya*'s theology that enhanced God's involvement in the trivialities of everyday life had a broad appeal among Muslims, despite the criticism it faced from some scholars and mystics. At the age of thirty-eight, al-Nabulusi wrote to the revered *imam*, criticizing his theory and exposing its inconsistency with the sources al-Kurani claimed to have used. Al-Nabulusi's main points of contention were, first, al-Kurani's view that the power of an individual causes an effect with divine permission and not autonomously, and, second, that this view is based on the Quran, the prophetic traditions and the teaching of the *Ash'ariyya*. In his rebuttal, al-Nabulusi appeared concerned that al-Kurani not only misinterpreted his sources but also presented his ideas as being universally shared by Sunni Muslims.

To explain his position, al-Nabulusi presents a Quran-based analogy using the sun and the moon modes of illumination. Just as the moon's light is an effect of the sun's light, he explained, so is human's power in relation to God's. 'If one reflects carefully on this', he wrote, 'one would realise that one's individual power is an effect of his Lord's universal power. One would also realise how actions occur with God's sole power working at one's power, not with it' (Akkach 2010, 73–7).

Viewing humans' power as essentially an effect rather than a cause maintains God as the sole cause of all effects in the world, including one's voluntary actions. An effect can be a cause in itself, producing another effect, such as when the light of the moon dispels the darkness of the night. Yet, the moon's capacity to dispel the darkness is inherently dependent on the sun's power, even though the latter is invisible at night. This is how God's ultimate power is always at work despite being 'veiled by its effect, which is the servant's power' (Akkach 2010, 73–7).

Highlighting the difference between the light of Being and the night of becoming, al-Nabulusi further explains that what appears in the night of becoming is the moon of the servant's power, illuminating with a secondary illumination that conceals the appearance of the illuminating Sun of God's power. So, when one says it is the light of the moon that dispels the darkness of the night, according to what appears to the senses, one, wittingly or unwittingly, means that what dispels the darkness of the night is the light of the sun alone that enables the moon to reflect light, *at* the moon's capacity to shine (not *with* it). The attribution of the dispelling power to the light of the moon is only true insofar as it is being supported by the sun's light, and insofar that the appearance of this dispelling power is *at* that support, not *with* it. And so are the voluntary actions; God creates them *at* the individual power, not *with* it (Akkach 2010, 73–7).

Conclusion

Modern cosmology that prevailed after the critical shifts that took place in the early modern period has not only changed the structure of the universe and our place in it but has also changed human nature along with our fundamental understanding of what it is that makes us human. Using al-Nabulusi's analogy of the light of Being and night of becoming, it can be argued that during this critically transformative period the divergent Europeans sought to live under the moonlight and to prosper in the night of becoming. By contrast, the Muslims were striving to remain under the sunlight of Being. With the prevalence of the European preference, the modern human has emerged as one that prefers to live, think and function in the night of possibilities, wherein only the moonlight of human reason, will and power constantly shines to dispel the darkness of ignorance, incivility and irrationality. In the night of becoming, humans are self-empowered by their own desires to control, possess and consume in order to sustain and perpetuate their dominant existence. In the night of becoming, change and possibilities are boundless, design has no limits and human-constructed morality is non-binding: all possibilities can be explored and exhausted for immediate benefits and with little concern for the universal consequences. Al-Nabulusi advocated for a balance: humans should not surrender their effective agency completely to the divine, nor should they be self-centred and self-empowered. This balance is not about religiosity or maintaining belief in deity, but about acknowledging the presence of the *spirit of the game* (Gadamer 1975; Akkach 2010, 34–42), that state of being transcends human consciousness and worldly conditions. As Gadamer has shown, humans create the spirit of the game but only to become subject to its dynamic control. The spirit of the game directs the consequences of the players' actions independent of their intention and objectives. As the current state of the game indicates, fundamental reorientation is required in order to change the self-destructive style of play modern humans have vigorously pursued over the past 200 years, in the slim hope that a sense of humanity with a viable future can be restored.

References

Akkach, Samer. *Islam and the Enlightenment: ʿAbd al-Ghani al-Nabulusi*. Oxford: Oneworld, 2007.

Akkach, Samer. *Letters of a Sufi Scholar. The Correspondence of ʿAbd al-Ghani al-Nabulusi (1641–173).* Leiden: Brill, 2010.

Akkach, Samer. 'Neo-Eurocentrism and Science: Implications for the Historiography of Islamic Art and Architecture'. *International Journal for Islamic Architecture* 10, no. 1 (2021): 203–15.

Anscombe, Elizabeth and Peter T. Geach. *Descartes: Philosophical Writings*. Middlesex: Thomas Nelson, 1970.

Brooke, John H. *Science and Religion: Some Historical Perspectives*. Cambridge: Cambridge University Press, 1991.

Colomina, Beatriz and Mark Wigley. *Are We Human? Notes on an Archaeology of Design*. Zürich: Lars Müller Publishers, 2018.

Dupré, Louis. *The Enlightenment and the Intellectual Foundations of Modern Culture*. New Haven: Yale University Press, 2004.

Gadamer, Hans-Georg. *Truth and Method*. London: Sheed and Ward, 1975.

Gaukroger, Stephen. *The Collapse of Mechanism and the Rise of Sensibility: Science and the Shaping of Modernity 1680–1760*. Oxford: Oxford University Press, 2010.

Gaukroger, Stephen. *The Emergence of a Scientific Culture: Science and the Shaping of Modernity 1210–1685*. Oxford: Oxford University Press, 2006.

Gaukroger, Stephen. *The Natural and the Human: Science and the Shaping of the Modernity 1739–1841*. Oxford: Oxford University Press, 2016.

Gran, Peter. *The Rise of the Rich: A New View of Modern World History*. Syracuse: Syracuse University Press, 2009.

Hayland, Paul, Olga Gomez, and Francesca Greensides. (eds). *The Enlightenment: A Source Book and Reader*. London: Routledge, 2003.

Hobson, John. 'Global Dialogical History and the Challenge of Neo-Eurocentricity'. In *Asia, Europe, and the Emergence of Modern Science*, edited by Arun Bala. Basingstoke: Palgrave Macmillan, 2006, 13–35.

Huff, Toby E. *The Rise of Early Modern Science: Islam, China, and the West*. Cambridge: Cambridge University Press, 2nd edn. 2010.

Jones, Eric. *The European Miracle: Environments, Economies and Geopolitics in the History of Europe and Asia*. Cambridge: Cambridge University Press, 3rd edn. 2003.

Osler, Margaret J. *Divine Will and the Mechanical Philosophy: Cassendi and Descartes on Contingency and Necessity in the Created World*. Cambridge: Cambridge University Press, 1994.

Pomeranz, Kenneth. *The Great Divergence: China, Europe, and the Making of the Modern World Economy*. Princeton: Princeton University Press, 2000.

7
ECOLOGICAL DESIGN THINKING IN THE ANTHROPOCENE/ECOCENE

Joanna Boehnert

Introduction

The Anthropocene is plural, unpredictable and complex. Humans, more-than-humans, socio-technical systems and environmental ecosystems are entangled in ways that are currently undermining prospects. The faster and more thoroughly we move beyond anthropocentric assumptions of modernity, the more scope we will have in creating desirable and viable futures. Approaching the world as relational and participatory is a foundation for enacting the potential of sustainable, regenerative and responsible design. The concept of ecological literacy was first proposed by Professor of Environmental Studies David Orr (1992, 2002) and scientist and activist Fritjof Capra (1995). It captures the paradigm-breaking challenge ecological thought presents to modernist reason (Plumwood 1993, 2002). Neither environmental awareness nor environmental knowledge, on their own, is ecological literacy. Ecological literacy involves developing capacities to effectively assess and address systemic ecological problems through processes of enacting transitions. The theory is only the starting point. It is one thing to say that humans are ecologically embedded and entangled with each other, within cultures, within technological systems, within socio-political institutions, with other species and within ecosystems at various scales on planet Earth. It is quite another thing to organize our thoughts, and to govern, and to design worlds based on these premises and associated ecological sensibilities. Ecological literacy is the action frame – and the foundation for emergent ecological design thinking in transitions for sustainability.

Ecological literacy is a learning theory that foregrounds ecological knowledge (Orr 1992, 2002; Capra 1995; Sterling 2001, 2003; Boehnert 2013, 2018a) with frames of mind and action that facilitate transition work (Boehnert 2018a, 2024). Ecological theory describes the world as composed of complex systems of different types whose components interact in multiple, often unpredictable ways and follow local rules leading to nonlinearity, randomness, collective dynamics, hierarchy and emergence (Capra and Luisi 2014). Change happens on multiple levels across domains in ways that are not predictable. We are participants in the systems in which we are embedded, so as we change systems, they, in turn, change us.

Transition design theorist Gideon Kossoff describes a process of moving away from reductive perspectives towards engagement with wicked problems to make sense of social and ecological complexity. Wicked problems were first identified as complex systems problems with no straightforward solution (Rittel and Webber 1973). They are interconnected across scale and 'planetary in scope yet manifesting in place and culture-specific ways' (Kossoff 2024, 28). Traditional problem-solving approaches driven by mechanistic logics reliant on 'decontextualised problem frames and linear cause-and-effect processes' (Kossoff 2024, 30) are ill-equipped to respond to current eco-social changes. The complexity of the eco-social problems requires ecological literacy. Wicked problems are a class of problems characterized by systems governed by feedback looks. This complexity can be more effectively addressed with systemic and relational approaches.

Ecological design thinking emerges from ecological literacy with future-oriented and participatory knowledge. Future knowledge systems need to be 'collaborative, open, diverse, egalitarian and able to work with values and systemic issues' as they challenge deeply held assumptions to support the navigation of systemic transformations (Fazey et al, 2020, 5, 11–2). Ecological design knowledge draws on transdisciplinary scholarship on human-nature relationships where the basic framing of relational and ecological transitions has fundamental similarities across fields including philosophy (Plumwood 1993, 2002; Haraway 1988, 2006, 2015), Sociology (Santos 2014, 2018; Bacevic 2021), geography (Sultana 2022; Moore 2015), politics (Bennett 2010; Connolly 2013; Chandler 2018), economics (Daly 91; Jackson 2009; D'Alisa, Demaria and Kallis 2014), psychology and psychoanalysis (Guattari 1989; Sewall 1999; Kahn and Hasbach 2012), anthropology (Bateson 1972; Sullivan 2017), history (Roszak 1992; Moore 2015), education (Orr 1992; Sterling 2001) and the arts and humanities (Latour 2014; Morton 2016; Demos 2017). The ecological-relational turn described by this work creates a basis for adaptive responses to complex eco-social challenges and crises.

In design, scholars have described these relational-ecological changes in theory as ontological shifts (Willis 2006; Fry 2009; Escobar 2018; Tonkinwise 2022). Feminist theorist Karen Barad describes onto-epistemology as a concept that captures the interrelationship between ethics, ontology and epistemology in knowledge production (2007). Ecological and relational onto-epistemologies are transforming knowledge and practice across disciplines as a basis for adaptive responses to complex problems. Design is rising to the challenge by expanding its scope of engagement by revising some of its most outdated assumptions inherited from less ecologically fragile and aware times.

Gregory Bateson's ecologies of mind

Anthropologist and cybernetician Gregory Bateson (1904–80) described the long-standing erasure of the ecological in the Western mindset as a fundamental epistemological error (1972, 493). This error forms 'a systemic false consciousness of our relation to nature' (Goodbun 2011, 42) and distorts understanding across knowledge domains. Bateson proposes attention to relation with the ecological context:

> I suggest that the last 100 years or so have demonstrated empirically that if an organism or aggregate of organisms sets to work with a focus on its own survival and thinks that is the way to select its adaptive moves, its 'progress' ends up with a destroyed environment. If an organism ends up destroying its environment, it has in fact destroyed itself. (1972, 457)

For Bateson, the error of the systemic dismissal of the ecological is compounded by 'erroneous instrumentalising tendencies' (Goodbun 2011, 41) that reduce the vitality of ecological contexts and human relationships. The living world is made up of assemblages of mind: multiple intelligences, constituted relationally as networks of relationships bound by communication (Goodbun 2011, 42; Nachmanovitch 1984, 7). Ecosystems include 'non-human and more-than-human ecological intelligences or eco-mental systems' (Goodbun 2022, 1) entangled with flows of energy, materials and information. This cybernetic vision of human-nature relationships based on complex networks and feedback systems is a basis for systemic design.

Bateson's work describes intelligences and mind as extended beyond the human. Jon Goodbun describes some of the more radical implications of this theory: 'For Bateson, the fact that our minds are ecologically extended allows him to propose a powerful thesis regarding the effects of environmental damage upon the human psyche, and a radical reformulation of environmental damage as a form of mental illness' (2011, 42). Notably, Bateson's most influential work, *Steps to an Ecology of Mind* (1972), includes chapters with theory developed from work in a psychiatric hospital in Palo Alto in California. Bateson used his work with patients suffering mental breakdowns to build a theory of mind describing civilizational problems emerging from epistemological errors. Along with problems generated at a personal level, these errors have far-reaching consequences as economic policies, technologies and design are all based on these foundational assumptions.

One of the enduring values of Bateson's work is its contribution towards action frames for ecological transitions. Human survival depends not only on an evolution in human conceptualization of relationships, ecosystems and ecological order but also on the embodiment and enactment of these premises (Harries-Jones 1995, 8). Bateson used strategies such as dialogue and aesthetics practices to provoke ecological understanding (Harries-Jones 1995, 14). Ecological aesthetics have subsequently been described as a means of opening ecological sensibilities (Harries-Jones 1995; Stern 2018). In experiencing and embodying relational dynamics, ecological subjectivities and sensibilities are emergent. I will describe later towards the end of this essay philosopher Felix Guattari's descriptions of the roles aesthetics and cultural practices play in generating new ecological subjectivities.

Defuturing in ecological design theory

Anthropologist Arturo Escobar describes the environmental crisis as a design crisis (2021, 44). Similarly, design theorist and philosopher Tony Fry describes design defuturing (2009, 2020) as it destroys prospects with its current role in the creation of unsustainable ways of living. Modernity's aspirations to permanence take material form in designed worlds that are breaching planetary boundaries and creating increasingly fragile civilizational conditions. The historic and contemporary context is one where ecological knowledge has been widely ignored in design. With this foundational error, the ecological domain is made available for exploitation. Designers remain unable to create genuine systemic sustainable solutions until able 'to read the forms and map the causal picture of the unsustainable in active relations of the on-going designing of the defutured' (Fry 2020, 239). Designing viable futures depends on coming to terms with errors in current understandings and unlearning defuturing ideas and practices that sustain the unsustainable (Fry 2009; Boehnert and Dewberry 2023). Developing new design priorities and practices relies on recognizing that 'using defuturing to make present that which defutures is the first act of informed futuring' (Fry 2020, 239). The unsustainability of current ways of living requires redesigning design itself – with redirected practice, informed futuring and '"contra-innovation," i.e., innovation to counter innovation that defutures' (Perera and Fry 2022, 1). Since design creates material artefacts, systems and services that determine how we live, and what we design goes on designing (Fry 2022), the work of transforming design from a defuturing practice is an urgent task.

Entanglement within ultra-modernist thought

Unfortunately, even some interpretations of ecological thought can reproduce modernist assumptions. For example, when former director of the MIT Media Lab Joichi Ito claims that 'nature and the artificial are merging' (2016) he describes a position that erases ecological concerns. This conceptualization of entanglement is reinforced by some of the other authors in MIT Press's *Journal of Design and Science* Issue 1 (2016) – computer scientist Danny Hillis's and designer Neri Oxman's papers follow the same logic. Theorizing the entanglement as a coalescence of the natural and the artificial obscures what is at stake. Humans have historically naively assumed we could dump greenhouse gases (GHGs) in the atmosphere, microplastics in the ocean and toxic chemicals in rivers. Incautious conceptualizations of entanglement entrench the historic dismissal of ecological interests enabling continued extractive and exploitative ways of thinking and ways of organizing society. These manifest as modes of organizing and designing ways of living on the planet. The concept of an entanglement of the natural and artificial must not involve a further erasure of nature and the ecological (Boehnert 2018c, 96). Mindful ecological entanglement recognizes the dangers of the virulent modernist assumptions with their polluting and world-destroying entanglements.

While posthumanism comes in a variety of constructions (see Forlano 2017) and most contribute to ecological thought, philosopher Kate Soper warns of obscuring formulations. In resisting binary categories and integrating the human and the non-human, posthumanism considers socio-technical systems as 'both socially constructed and society shaping' (Soper 2020, 20). But in the rush to decentre humans, Soper warns of the merging, blurring and collapse of distinction in some posthumanist thought as it attempts to shed human exceptionalism (2020, 20–3). Human biological systems and the ecosystems we inhabit all have boundaries that must be respected. Planetary thresholds have been breached (Steffen et al. 2018) with disastrous consequences. The technosphere generates pollution and ecosystem destruction that are distinct from the ecological domain with ecosystems that have allowed civilizations to flourish on a biodiverse Earth over time. Posthumanist theory that conceptualizes entanglement as an oversimplistic merging of the ecological and the artificial fails to distinguish healthy and unhealthy consequences of destructive development and technologies – including such harms as disease, death, extinction and ecosystem collapse.

Ecological theorists have described work that fails to challenge the core discontinuities of modernity (in this case naive concepts and entanglements that reproduce exploitative and extractive assumptions), mimics and even amplifies modernist reason and its erasure of the ecological in ways that should be described as 'hyper'-modern or 'ultra'-modern (Griffin 1992; Spretnak 1997, 223; Sterling 2003, 222). While acknowledging the constructed nature of social beliefs, the emphasis on social construction can serve to further marginalize the material and the ecological. Positivist modernity places itself both outside and in control of nature. Ultra-modernism focuses exclusively on the social. Both maintain ecology-denying assumptions (Boehnert 2018a 52, 55–6). Ultra-modernity creates frames that allow the continued dismissal of ecological consequences of technologies and design in ways that have led to even more harmful positions. These errors are evident in the influential techno-utopian ideologies in the

TESCREAL bundle – Transhumanism, Extropianism, Singularitarianism, Cosmism, Rationalism, Effective Altruism and Longtermism (Torres 2023) – which are reliant on dramatic increases in GHG emissions and extraction of natural resources.

Relationality and situated knowledge for just transitions

Relationality has become a key concept across disciplines as it has become evident that 'life is not lived under the conditions of separation' but of 'radical independence of everything that exists, or relationality' (Escobar 2021, 26). In design, Tony Fry advises designers to step back, noting what we are learning and doing (in error) by learning to see things in time and space, relationally (2020, 2022). Relationality-oriented work focuses on repair, healing, caring (Escobar 2021, 26) while supporting struggles of autonomy against the 'pervasive unsustainability and defuturing effected by modern globalised words and their deleterious, albeit deeply naturalised, modes of making and existing' (Escobar 2021, 39). Relational practice reveals interdependencies and dynamics (Nielsen and Bjerck 2022, 1061) supporting situated and participatory design.

The foregrounding of situated perspectives has evolved from the need for more socially inclusive types of design knowledge – but it also applies to ecological concerns. Feminist standpoint theory describes knowledge as socially situated – emphasizing the location, position and site of rational knowledge claims (Haraway 1988; Harding 1991). Social knowledge can be best understood as a view generated in a particular situation (rather than a claim to universal truth) as it allows for different perspectives to be considered. This approach reveals emotive and other contextual factors along with inequities and unjust norms. While the opinions, experiences, knowledge, interests and histories of marginalized individuals or groups have often been historically erased or excluded from knowledge systems, situated approaches focus on individual narratives to draw out these perspectives and reveal (supposedly) 'unintended consequences' of unexamined norms. Design educator Lesley-Ann Noel encourages designers to declare positionality and uses a 'positionality wheel' as a tool to prompt reflection and better understand power, agency and relationality (2022b). 'Sited, situated and situating' research is foundation for inclusive social innovation (Kaszynska, Kimbell and Bailey 2022, 27) as a basis for multilevel process and novel solutions (van Wijk et al. 2018, 3). The emphasis on the experience of a subject in a particular situation places value on knowledge embedded in customs, practices, languages and cultures.

Meanwhile, situated approaches can also address unintended, or unexplored, ecological consequences of design practice. These have also been historically erased and excluded from decision-making through a failure to take ecological concerns into account. Environmental ecosystems cannot advocate for themselves. Addressing their interests requires asking questions and devoting time to research anticipated and potential consequences of design and development. Asking situated questions about the materials, energy use, pollution and any other associated ecological impact can be done with exercises and tools such as the Design Ecologies Exercise and the Innovation Landscape Matrix (Dewberry, Boehnert, Sinclair 2024). Another example of the value of situated approaches in advancing sustainability is the identification of sustainability delay (Boehnert and Dewberry 2023) in a design education for sustainability context and climate delay (Lamb et al. 2020) in climate communication. These delays in sustainable transitions are evidence that deconstructing power hierarchies reproduce unsustainable norms. In both social and ecological contexts, situated approaches support inclusive and justice-oriented transition work. An emphasis on situated knowledge also encourages participatory approaches within knowledge generation and design processes. Participatory methods create richer and more complete understandings of design problems, including the needs of users and unintended consequences for humans, more-than-humans and the environmental ecological context.

Participation and democratization in eco-social design

All too often so-called 'unintended consequences' are unexplored consequences or even known consequences that are dismissed as unimportant in the rush to serve the interests of affluent constituencies. Participation and democratization can help address this problem. Participatory design, collaborative design and co-creation respond to both the need for inclusive forms of research and design and an understanding of reality as a participative where designers are part of the world that we want to influence. Decentring the user and 'designing for a participatory ecological worldview requires design thinking that transcends a mechanistic, interventionist and control outlook to one that reflects the values of ecological systems, emergence, complexity and uncertainty' (Dewberry 2011, 8). With this approach agencies are expanded from: 'customer, consumer, user, participant, adapter, maker to co-creator' (Sanders 2006). Participatory design brings publics together to co-create new systems and services. Enabling wider participation, participatory processes better respond to the issues of power, representation and politics (Ceschin and Gaziulusoy 2019, 109). Movements such as Peer to Peer, crowdsourced design, commoning, open design, Open-Source Ecology, co-realization and so on enable participation. Participants can 'not only purchase and use products and services, but creatively appropriate, hack, redesign and even innovate in them' (Kohtala, Hyysalo and Whalen 2020, 27–8). Designers and other participants 'collaborate to achieve common ends, or to co-produce shared value' (Balamir 2021, 77). This collaborative focus builds capacities to address complex sustainability challenges that depend on change across a variety of scales and domains. By 'rediscovering design as a generalisable human attribute' designers can build collaborative agencies to potentially co-design and build 'survivable post-carbon economies' (White 2021, 200). Participation democratizes design as it enables wider sets of interests to be served (such that justice-oriented approaches can be developed) and facilitates processes that require collective action, such as reducing GHG emissions.

Anthropocene ontopolitics and design

The conceit of human exceptionalism is being challenged across disciplines. Political theorist David Chandler describes 'the human subject as relationally embedded or entangled rather than as an autonomous rational subject distinct from the world' (2018, 23). Chandler's theory of Anthropocene ontopolitics starts 'from an empirical reality of the world as it appears rather than from assumptions of modernist progress, universal knowledge or linear causality' (2018, 4). With the claim that traditional science 'based on stability, laws and regularities, can no longer negotiate the problem' (2018, 10), Chandler proposes practices of mapping, sensing and hacking as modes of governance made necessary by Anthropocene ontopolitics. Mapping, sensing and hacking are equally relevant as responsive strategies for design (Boehnert 2022, 2024; Reason 2023).

> Mapping reveals multi-dimensional contextual information in complex systems facilitating navigation and planning in complex systems. . . . Sensing monitors variables to catch emergent phenomena – creating greater capacities to adapt and respond to uncertainty. Finally, within systems that have not been designed to operate in the context of decarbonisation, hacking can increase agency, participation, and disrupt the strategic goals of larger systems. (Boehnert 2024, 9)

Knowledge and practices across fields are in flux as the complexity of the polycrisis (Tooze 2022) demands not only new ways of knowing but also new practices to adapt to complexity. Critical strategies of Anthropocene ontopolitics navigate tensions in ecological transitions.

The slow violence of political economies of design and sustainability delay

Designers face wide-ranging obstacles in enacting ecological transitions. Waste and pollution are structural in design industries oriented towards consumption – often conspicuous consumption with planned obsolescence. While there are impressive attempts at circularity and sustainability in small pockets, designed worlds are more wasteful now than ever (Stastica 2024). This waste is a result of design economies that systemically prioritize profit at the expense of other values. Political economies determine what is designed in the first place, that is, whose interests are attended to and whose interests are ignored; and which ecosystems are saved, and which can be sacrificed. Designers are institutionally and politically entangled with market relations in ways that limit agency of design practice (White 2021,199). Changing direction on a scale that will make a difference for climate change and other ecological crises involves changes in the governance and the political economies of design, that is, the economic factors that determine the values and priorities in the design industry (Boehnert 2014, 2018a, 2018b, 2023; Orr 2018; White 2015; Nardi 2019; Balamir 2021). While new ecologically literate ways of knowing are emergent and these create new capacities for transformative design practice, this work remains a profound socio-political challenge. Resistance to politicized design manifests as a reactionary rejection of all serious attempts to address social and economic inequities and injustices and an embrace of facile, uncritical approaches to sustainability-associated greenwash and other strategies of climate and sustainability delay.

Design institutions often present economic concerns as imperatives far more important than social or ecological concerns. This hierarchy of priorities seems impenetrable until eco-social conditions become full-on crises that disrupt or collapse economies at various scales. Meanwhile economic issues are increasingly complex, and social conditions are characterized by fragility. Historically oppressed groups are most vulnerable to accelerating social problems and the slow violence of the Anthropocene, that is, 'the gradual, "invisible" destruction of the planet and its marginal peoples' (Sutoris 2022, 8, on Nixon 2011). Slow violence is manufactured not just by corporations and self-serving politicians but by perfectly well-meaning people through processes of bureaucratization and depoliticization (Sutoris 2022, 14, 22). Depoliticized design is a site of slow violence as it reproduces modernist assumptions, outdated ideas and facilitates continued defuturing design practice with its increasingly severe eco-social and political consequences. Design education is at the crux of this dynamic (Boehnert and Dewberry 2023). Since those who currently benefit from the traditional social order have a vested interest in denying the severity of the current situation (in the short term at least), strategies of climate and sustainability delay (Lamb et al. 2020; Boehnert and Dewberry 2023) are part of the challenge of building ecological literacy to enable ecological design thinking.

The polycrisis and the rise of the far right

Design's concentration on the human with low or no regard for the environmental implications of this narrow focus of attention should be understood as an aspect of imperial modes of living (Brand and Wissen 2021) at the expense of contemporary and future victims of climate change and ecological disasters. The design outcomes are necessarily cloaked with greenwash. Greenwash is produced by designers to avoid drawing attention to ecological harms to designed products and services. Ecological problems are also social problems, generating social tensions. Ever more authoritarian responses to social tensions create calamitous feedback loops. As social conditions deteriorate with not only ecological crises but also an accelerated polarization of wealth (Credit Suisse 2024), the far right is rising globally (ISD 2024).

Design can help address these trends with liberatory approaches. The source of polycrisis is ecological, social and political and not, as described by the many political commentators, the fault of migrants, who are increasingly the victims of climate change. Climate change and other ecological problems will intensify and make widespread ecological learning necessary not only for effective strategic work for sustainable transitions but also to help global populations understand the origins of social problems when governments and social institutions fail to enable equitable and just transitions. Reliable ecological and justice-oriented interpretations of eco-social events need to be available to explain eco-social problems and possible solutions. These ideas are not as widely available as they need to be. Political theorists on the right and the left both emphasize the importance of access to appropriate ideas in moments of crises and transition (Friedman 1982, ix; Klein 2014). Design has a critical role to play in the coming decades as it can support ecological learning and ecological transitions. Since design is also involved with creating and camouflaging slow violence, there is no guarantee that ecological design thinking will prevail.

Ecological design thinking in the cultural war

Ecological design thinking must be defended. The politics of design is under transformation as feminist, pluriversal, decolonial and ecological-oriented designers and scholars attend to wider sets of interests. This work challenges traditional power hierarchies. It is not always welcome by those currently in positions of power and those who identify with roles that reproduce exploitative and extractive defuturing design. Transitions can provoke reactionary attacks against both ideas and individuals highlighting problems and suggesting alternatives. The communicative forms of design are situated at the crux of this struggle – typically inextricably involved with representing capitalism as green and benevolent. Despite the growing awareness, resistance to change is often fierce at a variety of scales – personal, institutional, cultural, national and so on. Some design institutions attempt to avoid politicized design by retreating into more technocratic and less contextual and critically engaged forms of design practice and design education (Boehnert, Sinclair and Dewberry 2022). These places entrench old ideas, polluting practices- and obscure irresponsible practice with white- or greenwash. In this context, only part of the process of creating more sustainable future societies is creating types of knowledge and practices that would allow designers to end our complicity with the re-production of unsustainable ways of living. The other part of the process is negotiating institutional deadlock and surviving attacks by bureaucratic and reactionary forces who will not like any of this to be said, written or acted upon.

Many cenes in the ecological pluriverse

The pluriverse is a means of envisioning and designing worlds differently based on liberatory ideals, opposing domination and starting with a lens of marginalized and oppressed groups (Noel 2022b). Addressing the historic erasure of the Southern knowledge traditions, the pluriverse foregrounds resistance to cultural homogenization of colonialism (Leitão 2023, 17) and critically evaluates the ways in which design theory has excluded groups (Noel 2022a, 208) and the majority world. Design researcher Renata M. Leitão describes the pluriverse framework as a recognition that colonialism, imperialism and capitalist modernity have brought immense suffering to numerous societies. Pluriversality can be a creative pathway to change in which new alternative realities can be imagined and acted upon, particularly by the subaltern groups who defend other models of living (2023, 23).

Alternative pluriversal worlds emerge from 'learning that the South exists . . . outside of the episteme of modernity', making these worlds visible, and learning to understand and 'take action from the South and with the South'. Leitão here uses the South as metaphor for privilege, not a geographic concept (2023, 33). The pluriverse and decolonizing movements prioritize harmonious relationships with nature of traditional ecological knowledge and Indigenous cultures (Watson 2019; Kimmerer 2013; Liboiron 2021). Over the past decade, the pluriverse and decolonizing design movements have brought radically new ideas into design and constructed models for inclusive and regenerative practices. Hybrid knowledges offered by pluriverse perspectives are gateways for ecological learning that have developed within diverse Indigenous knowledge systems.

Pluriversal perspectives understand that 'Anthropos', that is, humans, as a generalized category, are not responsible for the intersecting polycrises of the Anthropocene. Some human societies have developed sustainable or even regenerative ways of living over long periods of time. The Anthropocene concept is 'troubling unspecific: the term says nothing about the vastly different ecological footprint of different nations, classes and individuals' and naturalizes capitalist priorities that present the 'ecological catastrophe now facing the planet as an almost inevitable by-product of human economic activity, ignoring the specific influence of a particular mode of production' (Soper 2020, 15). For these reasons, the concept limits the scope of transformative change. Environmental historian Jason Moore's Capitalocene describes contemporary crises emerging from specific ways of organizing human activities. Modes of governance generate types of social relations that drive extractive and exploitative economic processes. Constructing these modes of governance is a political process. They can also be reconstructed.

The recognition that the framing of the new epoch influences responsive actions has resulted in numerous alternative proposals. Anthropologist Franciszek Chwałczyk has documented ninety-two various alternative 'cenes' as 'constructive and creative' critiques of the Anthropocene concept (2020, 2). The Capitalocene concept (Moore 2015) is one of numerous proposals including Donna Haraway's

Chthulucene (2015), Alf Hornborg's Technocene (2015), Richard Norgaard's Econocene (2015), Kate Raworth's Manthropocene (2014), Katerina Chertkovskaya and Alexander Paulsson's Growthocene (2016), Christophe Bonneuil and Jean-Baptiste Fressoz's Anglocene (2016), Glen Albrecht's Symbiocene (2016), Alexandra Pirici and Raluca Voinea's (2015) Gynecene and suchlike (Chwałczyk 2020, 23–9). The diversity of interpretations is testament to a wide range of creative and critical responses to generate alternative framings and transitions pathways. Chwałczyk suggests that diverse approaches are necessary because none of these propositions alone sufficiently 'explain the Anthropocene-phenomenon' (2020, 23). This plurality can be seen as an example of the pluraliverse, that is, plural ways of understanding and re-making the world (Escobar 2021, 7). These proposals reflect diverse, but compatible, future imaginaries addressing diverse aspects of the contemporary polycrisis.

Adaptive, imaginative, responsive and responsible design approaches are emergent. New transformative design strategies include redirected (Fry 2009), regenerative (Wahl 2016), decolonized (Tunstall 2019; Ansari 2021), pluriversal (Escobar 2018; Noel 2022b; Leitão 2023), systemic (Sevaldson and Jones 2019), transition-oriented (Irwin, Tonkinwise and Kossoff 2013) and justice-oriented (Costanza-Chock 2020) design. Design for Sustainability works on various scales from products, services and systems, communities to social-technical systems (Ceschin and Gaziulusoy 2019). New approaches include green design and product ecodesign; emotionally durable design; design for sustainable behaviour; cradle-to-cradle design; biomimicry design; product–service system design for sustainability; design for the base of the pyramid; design for social innovation; systemic design; and design for sustainability (Ceschin and Gaziulusoy 2020, vi–vii). These expansive design methods respond to different aspects of the polycrisis and the urgent need for just transitions. They can all be complementary.

Ecological design thinking in the Ecocene

Ecological design thinking must replace the default dismissal of the ecological in design. The Ecocene concept refers to the ecological turn in both design (Armstrong 2015, 2017; Boehnert 2018a, 2023) and in politics (Tănăsescu 2022). Emphasizing the importance of ecological knowledge in design, the concept was first described by design theorist Rachel Armstrong:

> The side effects of industrialization, with its relentless consumption of natural resources and fouling of our environments, set up feedback loops that destabilize the very systems that sustain us, the hyper complexity, and nonlinear character of the biosphere evades our ambitions to bring these runaway consequences back under our control through the tools of modern synthesis. . . . Yet, the harder we try to 'solve' the unfolding ecological catastrophe, the more it evades our attempts at resolution. Currently, we are reaching the limits of modern technology to address the challenges of 'wayward' nature and are faced with the daunting prospect of reimagining our position within the world and the way we construct the idea of value in the Ecocene. (2017, 188)

Design depends on explicit engagement with ecological knowledge for the development of mutualist, regenerative, responsible design principles. The Ecocene concept draws on ecological and social-feminist ideas and ways of conceptualizing knowledge as relational, situated and participatory. An expansive, politicized Ecocene design practice can be built on the following premises:

1. Transdisciplinary and systemic design
2. Critical ecological design thinking
3. Intersectional feminist: linking the 'isms'
4. Redirected political economies of design
5. Expanded, regenerative, and pluriversal design

(Boehnert 2023, 79)

Design movements embody these premises that are growing. The Ecocene vision commits to collaborative, ecological, intersectional feminist and anti-racist practice with a redirection of incentives towards human and planetary health and wellbeing. This expansive orientation to design includes social and political transitions. Allies and social movements help make these alternatives possible. Design activism is meaningful when these principles are engaged and designers are working in solidarity with social movements and/or institutions.

Reinventing the motors of subjectivity

Building on Gregory Bateson's ecological theory, in *The Three Ecologies* (1989) Felix Guattari describes the role of an 'ethico-political articulation' or 'ecosophy – between the three ecological registers (the environment, social relations and human subjectivity' (Guattari 2000/1989, 28) in responding to ecological crises. Guattari calls on all cultural practices 'in a position to intervene in individual and collective psychical proceedings' (Guattari 1989/2000, 39) to participate in this aesthetic project to nurture a new subjectivity. Guattari evokes an 'ethico-aesthethic' (Guattari 1989/2000, 41) ecological revolution that uses 'domains of sensibility, intelligence, and desire' (1989/2000, 28):

> Literally reconstructing the modalities of 'group-being' . . . not only through 'communicational' interventions but through existential mutations driven by the motor of subjectivity. Instead of clinging to general recommendations we would be implementing effective practices of experimentation, as much on a microsocial level as on a larger institutional scale. (Guattari 2000, 34–35)

Design is well placed to respond to Guattari's call to action. As a practice involved with the creation of seductive images, artefacts and experiences, design is already involved with nurturing cultural ideas and new sensibilities. Designers can nurture ecological sensibilities by making ecological relationships visible, tangible and part of everyday life. As a domain involved in the generation of new material circumstances, often through visualization practices and the creation of new physical experiences, design routinely encourages particular types of ideas, sensibilities and behaviours. New perceptual habits are routinely learned. The perceptual habit of noticing and learning to see relationships is a basis for ecological perception (Sewall 1999; Boehnert 2018a, 113–31). Visual languages and other design strategies can be a means of provoking new ordering sensibilities and understandings. Designers can help audiences and users perceive and experience themselves in relationship and embedded within ecological contexts. Design is a field with capacities to navigate desire, subjectivity, aesthetic sensibilities and perception for transformative cultural, social and political change.

Conclusion

Emergent ecological design thinking can be a basis for viable futures. But ecological thinking and theories do not do transition work on their own. Victor Papanek wrote *Design for the Real World* over fifty years ago describing how design must respond to ecological imperatives. While the necessity for ecological transition is now widely accepted in theory, it is much less likely to be evident in practice. Today, design remains complicit in reproducing unsustainable ways of living with practices such as planned obsolescence, encouraging excessive consumption, the creation of excessive waste and GHG emissions and so on. Despite accumulative social and technological innovation, extractive and polluting design remains the norm.

Ecological literacy can make the difference between reproducing ecological harms and changes in trajectory towards responsible design. Desirable and viable futures depend on a redesign of ways of living on planet Earth. Ecological literacy includes an ability to identify causes of ecological harms and enact transitions alternatives with practices. The current trajectory can be redirected with ecological design thinking supported by strong commitments in design education, institutions and industry. Ecological learning will become increasingly urgent. Responsible and regenerative practices can emerge where institutions are somehow compelled to value the environmental context. The longer the delay, the more dangerous reactionary forces emerge as eco-social crises proliferate. Addressing environmental and social problems at scale demands disruptive ideas and practices in both design and the socio-political contexts that determine how design economies function.

References

Albrecht, Gleen and Gavin Van Horn. 'Exiting the Anthropocene and Entering the Symbiocene'. *Minding Nature* 2, no . 9 (2016): 12–5.

Armstrong, Rachel. 'From Hell to Babel: Creating Value in the Ecocene'. *Journal of Biourbanism* 1, no. 2 (2017): 187–99.

Armstrong, Rachel. 'Urban Ecologies.' Ontario College of Art and Design Symposium, Toronto, Canada, 18 June 2015.

Ansari, Ahmed. 'Design's Missing Others and Their Incommensurate Worlds'. In *Design in Crisis New Worlds, Philosophies and Practices,* edited by Tony Fry and Adam Nocek. New York: Routledge, 2021.

Bacevi, Jana Bacevic. 'Unthinking Knowledge Production: From Post-Covid to Post-Carbon Futures.' *Globalisations* 18, no. 7 (2021): 1206–18. https://doi.org/10.1080/14747731.2020.1807855

Balamir, Selçuk. 'Unsustaining the Commodity-Machine: Commonin Practices in Postcapitalist Design'. PhD diss. Amsterdam School for Cultural Analysis, 2021.

Barad, Karen. *Meeting the Universe Halfway: Quantum Physics and the Entanglement of Matter and Meaning*. London: Duke University Press, 2007.

Bateson, Gregory. *A Sacred Unity: Further Steps to An Ecology of Mind*. Edited by. Rodney E. Donaldson. New York: Harper Collins, 1991.

Bateson, Gregory. *Steps to An Ecology of Mind*. Chicago: University of Chicago Press, 1972.

Bennett, Jane. *Vibrant Matter: A Political Ecology of Things*. Durham: Duke University Press, 2010.

Boehnert, Joanna. 'Anthropocene Economics and Design: Heterodox Economics for Design Transitions'. *She Ji: The Journal of Design, Economics, and Innovation* 4, no. 4 (2018b): 355–74.

Boehnert, Joanna. 'Beyond the Anthropocene: Design Politics in the Ecocene'. *In Future Ecologies Series, Material Trajectories*, edited by Claudia Mareis, Petra Löffler and Florian Sprenger. Berlin: Meson Press, 2023.

Boehnert, Joanna. *Design, Ecology, Politics: Towards the Ecocene*. London: Bloomsbury Academic, 2018a.

Boehnert, Joanna. 'Design for the Design Industry'. *Design Philosophy Papers*, 12, no . 2 (2014): 119–36.

Boehnert, Joanna. *Ecological Literacy in Design Education: A Foundation for Sustainable Design*. In *DRS // Cumulus: Design Learning for Tomorrow*, edited by J. B. Reitan, P. Lloyd, E. Bohemia, L. M. Nielsen, I. Digranes, and E. Lutnæs, 14–17 May 2013, Oslo, Norway. Oslo: Design Research Society, 2013. https://doi .org/10.21606/learnxdesign.2013.014.

Boehnert, Joanna. 'Ecological Theory in Design: Participant Designers in An Age of Entanglement'. In *Routledge Handbook of Sustainable Design*, edited by Rachel Beth Egenhoefer. London: Routledge, 2018c, 86–98.

Boehnert, Joanna. 'Transition Templates: Pathways to Net Zero+'. Rivers of Conversations. Relating Systems Thinking and Design. October 2024.

Boehnert, Joanna and Emma Dewberry. 'Design Politics in the Anthropocene'. In *Future Ecologies Series, Material Trajectories*, edited by Claudia Mareis, Petra Löffler and Florian Sprenger. Berlin: Meson Press, 2023.

Boehnert, Joanna and Emma Dewberry. *Unlearning Unsustainability in Design Education*, edited by Derek Jones, Naz Borekci, Violeta Clemente, James Corazzo, Nicole Lotz, Liv Merete Nielsen, Lesley-Ann Noel. The 7th International Conference for Design Education Researchers, 29 November – 1 December 2023, London, 2023.

Boehnert, Joanna, Alistair Alexander and Matt Sinclair. 'Against Dystopias with Ecological Literacy'. *Notebooks of the Center for Design and Communication Studies*, 222. https://doi.org/ 10.18682/cdc.vi222.11202

Boehnert, Joanna, Matt Sinclair and Emma Dewberry. 'Sustainable and Responsible Design Education: Tensions in Transitions'. *Sustainability*, 14, no. 11 (2022): 6397.

Bonneuil, Christophe and Jean-Baptiste Fressoz. *The Shock of the Anthropocene: The Earth. History and Us*. London: Verso, 2016.

Brand, Ulrich and Wissen, Markus. *The Imperial Mode of Living: Everyday Life and the Ecological Crisis of Capitalism*. London: Verso, 2021.

Capra, Fritjof. *The Web of Life*. London: HarperCollins, 1995.

Capra, Fritjof and Pier Luigi Luisi. *The Systems View of Life: A Unifying Vision*. Cambridge University Press, 2014.

Ceschin, Fabrizio and Idil Gaziulusoy. *Design for Sustainability: A Multilevel Framework from Products to Socio-Technical Systems*. London: Routledge, 2019.

Chandler, David. *Ontopolitics in the Anthropocene: An Introduction to Mapping, Sensing and Hacking*. London: Routledge, 2018.

Chertkovskaya, Akaterina and Alexander Paulsson. 'The Growthocene: Thinking Through What Degrowth is Criticising'. *European Network of Political Ecology (ENTITLE)*, 2016.

Chwałczyk, Franciszek. 'Around the Anthropocene in Eighty Names – Considering the Urbanocene Proposition'. *Sustainability* 12, no. 11 (2020): 4458. https://doi.org/10.3390/su12114458

Connolly, William. *The Fragility of Things*. London: Duke University Press, 2013.

Costanza-Chock, Sasha. *Design Justice: Community-Led Practices to Build the Worlds We Need*. Cambridge, MA: MIT Press, 2020.

Credit Suisse. 'Global Wealth Report 2024', edited by Enrico Börger, 2024. UBS. https://www.credit-suisse.com/about-us/en/reports-research/global-wealth-report.html

D'Alisa, Giacomo, Demaria, Federico and Giorgos Kallis. *Degrowth: A Vocabulary for a New Era Abingdon*. London: Routledge, 2014.

Daly, Herman. *Steady-State Economics,* 2nd edn. Washington: Island Press, 1991.

Demos, T. J. *Against the Anthropocene*. London: Sternberg Press, 2017.

Dewberry, Emma Louise. 'Developing an Ecology of Mind in Design'. The 18th International Conference in Engineering Design, Copenhagen, Denmark, 15–8 August, 2011.

Dewberry, Emma, Joanna Boehnert and Matt Sinclair. 'Design Ecologies Exercise: The Innovation Landscape Matrix'. *Routledge Handbook of Sustainable Design*, 2nd edn. London: Routlege, 2024, 86–98.

Fry, Tony. 'Defuturing: A New Design Philosophy'. In *Defuturing: A New Design Philosophy*. London: Bloomsbury, 2020.

Escobar, Arturo. *Design for the Pluriverse*. London: Duke University Press, 2018.

Escobar, Arturo. 'Designing a Futural Praxis for the Healing of the Web of Life'. In *Design in Crisis New Worlds, Philosophies and Practices*, edited by Tony Fry and Adam Nocek. New York: Routledge, 2021.

Fazey, Loan, et al. 'Transforming Knowledge Systems for Life on Earth: Visions of Future Systems and How to Get There'. *Energy Research & Social Science*, 70 (2020): 101724.

Forlano, L. 'Posthumanism and Design'. *She Ji: The Journal of Design, Economics, and Innovation* 3, no. 1 (2017): 16–29.

Friedman, Milton. *Capitalism and Freedom*. Chicago: University of Chicago Press, 1982.

Fry, Tony. *Defuturing: A New Design Philosophy*. London: Bloomsbury, 2020.

Fry, Tony. *Design Futuring*. Oxford: Berg, 2009.

Fry, Tony. 'Seeing RSD11's Seven Foci Relationally'. *Relating Systems Thinking and Design (RSDX*11), Brighton, UK, 13–16 October 2022. https://rsdsymposium.org/seeing-rsd11s-seven-foci-relationally/

Fry, Tony and Adam Nocek. *Design in Crisis New Worlds, Philosophies and Practices*. New York: Routledge, 2021.

Guattari, Felix. *The Three Ecologies*. Translated by Ian Pindar & Paul Simon. London: Continuum, 1989/2000.

Goodbun, Jon. 'Gregory Bateson's Ecological Aesthetics – An Addendum to Urban Political Ecology'. Field: A Free Journal for Architecture 4, no. 1 (2011): 35–48.

Goodbun, Jon. 'How Many Ecologies? From Bateson to Guattari and Back Again'. *Relating Systems Thinking and Design (RSDX*11), Brighton, UK, 13–16 October 2022.

Griffin, David Ray. 'Introduction to Suny Series in Construction Postmodern Thought'. In *Ecological Literacy*, edited by David W. Orr. Albany: Suny Press, 1992, xi–xvi .

Guattari, Felix. *The Three Ecologies*. Translated by Ian Pindar and Paul Simon. London: Continuum, 1989/2000.

Haraway, Donna. 'Anthropocene, Capitalocene, Plantationocene, Chthulucene: Making Kin'. *Environmental Humanities* 6, no. 1 (2015): 159–65.

Haraway, Donna. 'A Cyborg Manifesto: Science, Technology, and Socialist-Feminism in the Late 20th Century'. In *The International Handbook of Virtual Learning Environments*, edited by Joel Weiss, Ben Schneidermann , L. P. J. L. Peter and S. H. M. Peter . New York: Springer, 2006.

Haraway, Donna. *Simians, Cyborgs, and Women: The Reinvention of Nature.* London: Routledge, 1991.

Haraway, Donna. 'Situated Knowledge: The Science Question in Feminism and the Privilege of Partial Perspective'. *Feminist Studies* 14, no.3 (1998): 575–99.

Harding, Sandra. *Whose Science? Whose Knowledge? Thinking from Women's Lives*. Ithaca, NY: Cornell University Press, 1991.

Harries-Jones, Peter. *A Recursive Vision: Ecological Understanding and Gregory Bateson*. Toronto: University of Toronto Press, 1995. https://doi.org/10.3138/9781442670440.

Hornborg, Alf. 'The Political Ecology of the Technocene: Uncovering Ecologically Unequal Exchange in the World-System'. In *The Anthropocene and the Global Environmental Crisis: Rethinking Modernity in a New Epoch*, edited by Clive Hamilton, Francois Gemenne and Christophe Bonneuil. London: Earthscan/Routledge, 2015, 57–69.

Irwin, Terry, Cameron Tonkinwise and Gideon Kossoff. 'Transition Design: Re-conceptualising Whole Lifestyles. Head, Heart, Hand'. AIGA Design Conference, Minneapolis, USA, 12 October 2013. Accessed 12 December 2021. http://www.aiga.org/video-HHH-2013-irwin-kossoff-tonkinwise

ISD – Institute for Strategic Dialogue. Far-Right Extremism. 2024. https://www.isdglobal.org/extremism/far-right/

Ito, Joichi. 'Design and Science. Can Design Advance Science, and Can Science Advance Design? The End of the Artificial'. *MIT Press Journal of Design and Science*, 2016. Accessed 28 October 2022. https://jods.mitpress.mit.edu/pub/designandscience/release/2

Jackson, Tim. *Chasing Progress – beyond Measuring Economic Growth*. London: New Economics Foundation, 2004.

Jackson, Tim. *Prosperity Without Growth: Economics for a Finite Planet*. New York: Earthscan, 2009.

Kahn, Peter H. Jr. and Patricia H. Hasbach. *Ecopsychology: Science, Totems and the Technological Species*. London: MIT Press, 2012.

Kaszynska, Patrycja, Lucy Kimbell and Jocelyn Bailey. 'Practice Research in Design: Towards a Novel Definition'. *Social Design Institute Working Paper*. London: University of the Arts London, 2022.

Klein, Naomi. *This Changes Everything.* Toronto: Simon and Schuster, 2014.

Kimmerer, Robin Wall. *Braiding Sweetgrass: Indigenous Wisdom, Scientific Knowledge and the Teachings of Plants*. Minneapolis: Milkweed Editions, 2013.

Kohtala, Cindy, Sampsa Hyysalo and Jack Whalen. 'A Taxonomy of Users' Active Design Engagement in the 21st Century'. *Design Studies* 67 (2020): 27–54.

Kossoff, Gideon. 'Embracing an Ecological Worldview and Cosmopolitan Localism for Sustainable Transitions toward More Equitable Futures'. *Cuaderno* 222 (2024): 27–37.

Kossoff, Gideon and Irwin, Terry. 'Transition Design as a Strategy for Addressing Urban Wicked Problems'. In *Cities After Capitalism*. Abingdon: Routledge, 2022, 90–102.

Lamb, William F., Giulio Mattioli, Sebastian Levi, J. Timmons Roberts, Stuart Capstick, Felix Creutzig, Jan C. Minx, Finn Müller-Hansen, Trevor Culhane and Julia K. Steinberger. 'Discourses of Climate Delay'. *Global Sustainability*, 3 (2020): e17. https://doi.org/10.1017/sus.2020.13.

Latour, Bruno. 'Anthropology at the Time of the Anthropocene: A Personal View of What Is to be Studied'. 113th AAA meeting, Washington, USA, 2014. 5 November 2014. http://www.bruno-latour.fr/sites/default/files/139-AAA-Washington.pdf

Latour, Bruno. 'Anthropology at the Time of the Anthropocene: A Personal View of What is to Be Studied'. In *The Anthropology of Sustainability: Beyond Development and Progress*, edited by March Brightman and Jerome Lewis. New York: Palgrave Macmillan, 2017, 35–49.

Leitão, Renata M.'Pluriversal Worlding'. *AM Journal*, 30 (2023): 17–35.

Liboiron, Max. *Pollution Is Colonialism*. Durham: Duke University Press, 2021.

Moore, Jason W. *Capitalism and the Web of Life*. London: Verso, 2015.

Morton, Timothy. *Dark Ecology: For a Logic of Future Coexistence.* New York: Columbia University Press, 2016.

Nachmanovitch, Stephen. 'Gregory Bateson: Old Men Ought to be Explorers'. *Leonardo*, 17, no. 2 (1984): 113–8.

Nardi, Bonnie. 'Design in the Age of Climate Change'. *She Ji: The Journal of Design, Economics, and Innovation*, 5, no. 1 (2019): 6–7, 14.

Nielsen, Britta Fladvad and Mari Bjerck. *Relational Design*. Proceedings of the Design Society Volume 2: Design 2022. https://doi.org/10.1017/pds.2022.108

Nixon, Rob. *Slow Violence and the Environmentalism of the Poor*. Cambridge, MA: Harvard University Press, 2011.

Noel, Lesley-Ann. Critical and Pluriversal Design for a World in Crisis. RSD11 Keynote *Proceedings of Relating Systems Thinking and Design (RSDX*11), 2022b. Brighton, UK, October 2022. Accessed 28 October 2022. https://rsdsymposium.org/lesley-ann-noel-topic-to-be-announced/

Noel, Lesley-Ann. 'Designing New Futures for Design Education'. *Design and Culture* 14, no. 3 (2022a): 277–91. https://doi.org/10.1080/17547075.2022.2105524

Norgaard, Richard. 'The Church of Economism and Its Discontents'. *Great Transition Initiative*, 2015. Accessed 28 October 28 2022.

Orr, David. *Ecological Literacy*. Albany: State of New York Press, 1992.

Orr, David. *The Nature of Design*. Oxford: Oxford University Press, 2002.

Orr, David. 'The Political Economy of Design in a Hotter Time'. In *Routledge Handbook of Sustainable Design*, edited by Rachel Berth Egenhoefer. Abingdon: Routledge, 2018, 4, 7–8.

Papanek, Victor. *Design for the Real World: Human Ecology and Social Change*. Chicago: Academy Chicago Publishers, 1985.

Perera, Dulmini and Tony Fry. 'Ontra-Innovation: Expanding the Innovation Imperative in the Context of Futuring, Defuturing and Fictioning'. *Contexts – The Systemic Design Journal*, 1 (2022): 1–17.

Pirici, Alexandra and Raluca Voinea. Manifesto for the Gynecene – Sketch of a New Geological Era'. *LevArt*, 2015. Accessed 10 April 2020. http://ro.tranzit.org/file/MANIFESTO-for-the-Gynecene.pdf

Plumwood, Val. *Environmental Culture: The Ecological Crisis of Reason*. Oxon: Routledge, 2002.

Plumwood, Val. *Feminism and the Mastery of Nature*. London: Taylor & Francis, 1993.

Raworth, Kate. *Doughnut Economics: Seven Ways to Think Like a 21st-Century Economist*. London: Random House, 2017.

Raworth, Kate. Must the Anthropocene be a Manthropocene?' *The Guardian*, 24 October 2014. Accessed 28 October 2022. https://www.theguardian.com/commentisfree/2014/oct/20/anthropoceneworking-group-science-gender-bias

Reason, Ben. *Design in The Anthropecene*. European Conference on Information Architecture and User Experience Design. Amsterdam, 22 September 2023.
Rittel, Horst W. J. and Melvin M. Webber. 'Dilemmas in a General Theory of Planning'. *Policy Sciences* 4, no. 2 (1973): 155–69.
Roszak, Theodore. *The Voice of the Earth.* London: Bantam Books, 1992.
Sanders, Elizabeth B.-N. 'Scaffolds for Building Everyday Creativity'. In *Design for Effective Communications: Creating Contexts for Clarity and Meaning*, edited by Jorge Frascara. New York: Allworth Press, 2006.
Santos, Boaventura. *The End of the Cognitive Empire: The Coming of Age of Epistemologies of the South*. Durham: Duke University Press, 2018.
Santos, Boaventura. *Epistemologies of the South: Justice Against Epistemicide*. New York: Routledge, 2014.
Sevaldson, Birger and Peter H. Jones. 'An Interdiscipline Emerges: Pathways to Systemic Design'. *She Jī: The Journal of Design, Economy, and Innovation* 5 (2019): 75–84.
Sewall, Laura. *Sight and Sensibility: The Ecopsychology of Perception*. New York: Putnam, 1999.
Soper, Kate. *Post-Growth Living: For an Alternative Hedonism.* London: Verso, 2020.
Spretnak, Charlene. *The Resurgence of the Real*. New York: Addison-Wesley, 1997.
Stahel, Walter R. 'The Product Life Factor'. In *An Inquiry into the Nature of Sustainable Societies: The Role of the Private Sector*, edited by Susan Grinton Orr. Houston: Houston Research Center, 1982.
Stastica. 'Global Waste Generation – Statistics and Facts', 2024. https://www.statista.com/topics/4983/waste-generation-worldwide/
Steffen, Will, et al. 'Trajectories of the Earth System in the Anthropocene'. *Proceedings of the National Academy of Sciences*, 115, no. 33 (2018): 8252–9. https://doi.org/10.1073/pnas.1810141115
Sterling, Stephen. *Sustainable Education – Re-Visioning Learning and Change. Schumacher Briefing No. 6*. Dartington: Schumacher Society/Green Books, 2001.
Sterling, Stephen. 'Whole Systems Thinking as a Basis for Paradigm Change in Education'. PhD diss. University of Bath, 2003.
Stern, Nathaniel. *Ecological Aesthetics: Artful Tactics for Humans, Nature, and Politics*. Hanover, NH: Dartmouth College Press, 2018.
Sullivan, Sian. 'What's Ontology Got to Do with It? On Nature and Knowledge in a Political Ecology of the Green Economy'. Edited by Connor Cavanagh and Tor Benjaminsen. Political Ecologies of the Green Economy Special Issue, *Political Ecology* 24 (2017): 200–341.
Sultana, Farhana. "Critical Climate Justice." *The Geographical Journal* 188, no. 1 (2022): 118–24. https://doi.org/10.1111/geoj.12417.
Sutoris, Peter. *Educating for the Anthropocene: Schooling and Activism in the Face of Slow Violence*. Cambridge, MA: The MIT Press, 2022.
Tănăsescu, Mihnea. *Ecocene Politics*. Open Book Publishers, 2022. https://www.openbookpublishers.com/books/10.11647/obp.0274
Tonkinwise, Cameron. 'Before Design, More-than-Design: Elucidating Ontological Design'. *Design and Culture* 14, no. 3 (2022): 341–59.
Tooze, Adam. 'Welcome to the World of the Polycrisis'. *Financial Times*, 28 October 2022.
Torres, Émile P.'Why Effective Altruism and 'Longtermism' Are Toxic Ideologies'. *Current Affairs*, 7 May 2023. https://www.currentaffairs.org/news/2023/05/why-effective-altruism-and-longtermism-are-toxic-ideologies.
Tunstall, Elizabeth. 'Decolonizing Design Innovation: Design Anthropology, Critical Anthropology, and Indigenous Knowledge'. In *The Social Design Reader*, edited by Elizabeth Resnick. London: Bloomsbury, 2019.
van Wijk, Jakomijn, et al. 'Social Innovation: Integrating Micro, Meso, and Macro Level Insights from Institutional Theory'. *Business & Society* 58, no. 5 (2019): 887–918.
Wahl, Daniel Christian. *Designing Regenerative Culture*. Axminster: Triarchy Press, 2016.
Watson, Julia. *Lo-TEK: Design by Radical Indigenism*. London: Thames & Hudson, 2019
White, Damian. 'The Institutional Gap in Critical Design Studies'. In *Design in Crisis New Worlds, Philosophies and Practices*, edited by Tony Fry and Adam Nocek. New York: Routledge, 2021.
White, Damian, Alan Rudy and Brian Gareau. *Environments, Natures, and Social Theory: Towards a Critical Hybridity*. London: Palgrave, 2015.
Willis, Anne-Marie. 'Ontological Designing'. *Design Philosophy Papers*, 4 (2006): 69–92.

8
INDIGENOUS DESIGN
A RELATIONAL PRACTICE BETWEEN PEOPLE AND PLACE

Desiree Hernandez Ibinarriaga

Indigenous knowledge and ways of knowing and doing can give new design perspectives towards more sustainable and respectful futures and practices for Mother Earth. Indigenous design introduces a new-old approach based on relationality between people, Place, the material and immaterial, and the ancestral knowledge and practices that exist towards designing *for* and *on* Country. It views design far from an Anthropocentric and Eurocentric perspective and more as a practice that nourishes Mother Earth, or what I call *Tonantsintlalli* in Nahuatl language from the Aztecs/Mexicas or *Madrecita Tierra* in Spanish. Indigenous design is a relational practice grounded in Country to privilege Indigenous knowledge systems and Place. Place refers to physicality, time and space, including the metaphysical (Graham 2006). Indigenous design is not only a theory, a concept or a philosophy but also an embodied experience about doing, practising and making alongside the transformative knowledge values attached to the process. Information becomes knowledge and wisdom once practised with respect and values.

This chapter introduces the foundation of Indigenous design through my cultural identity and positionality of my design practice and research. Furthermore, it reveals and unveils diverse Indigenous methodologies and ways of doing and illustrates a tangible example of Indigenous design, *The Agave* furniture/sculpture that holds aesthetics and functionality and cultural significance in the Nahua and Maya cultures while embracing the revival and conservation of Indigenous knowledge.

Positionality

I want to acknowledge Country and the traditional custodians of the lands, waters and sky where I was born, The Great Tenochtitlan, Nahua Country, and its peoples (today Mexico City), and where I work and live, the BoonWurrung Country and its peoples in the Kullin Nations (Melbourne, Australia). I thank my ancestors for all the strength they hold and the ancestral knowledge they pass on to us to be resilient. I am also thankful for all the knowledge and wisdom I hold in my body and my strong connection to the lands, waters, air, fire, sky, non-human and the immaterial; my spirit and body are built throughout these relationships.

'Positioning is vital in Indigenist research' (Martin 2017, 7) and for Indigenous design and partnerships. It postulates the relationship between reality, practice and philosophy, as opposed to the imaginary relationship to existence proposed by Western philosophical discourses. Positionality is essential to Indigenous design as Country, cultural identity, lived experience and knowledge. It shapes your own way of being, reality, values and creative practice. I position myself as an Indigenous Mexican mestiza woman with Chamula (Mayan), Nahua (Aztec/Mexica), Euskaldunak (Basque) and Spanish heritage. Mestiza refers to the result of biological or cultural mixtures described as empirical and 'conceptual hybridity' (de la Cadena 2005, 259), which reveals alternatives for mestizo positionality, including forms of Indigeneity.

My cultural identity, upbringing, values and lived experience have shaped my design practice, research and purpose. My beliefs and purpose come from my onto-epistemology, way of being, knowing and doing. These beliefs include how I view reality (ontology), how I know reality (epistemology), how I form values and morals (axiology) and how I gain more knowledge and experience about reality (methodology) while positioning myself (Wilson 2008) towards creating new sustainable and relational futures. My home-based education is grounded in giving and receiving respect, relational accountability, love, a healthy lifestyle, learning to respect myself and others, being resilient and constantly unlearning and relearning. Through all the new knowledge I have experienced, through learning and sharing different cultures, languages and worldviews, I managed to keep unlearning and find plenitude, abundance and happiness while continuously working towards defining my life's purpose.

When my personal life meets my professional life, I am a creative practitioner, collaborative and social designer, maker and thinker. I am a Lecturer at Monash Art Design and Architecture (MADA) and Coordinator of the Indigenous Higher Degrees by Research at the Wominjeka Djeembana Indigenous Research Lab, where I practise Indigenous design, research and creative practices merging Art, Design and Architecture. Throughout my career, I have worked in furniture and interior design, social design, design for sustainability, decolonizing design and most recently, Indigenous design and research. My current practice focuses on building capacity for Indigenous peoples and creating meaningful ways to collaborate and communicate between them and non-Indigenous people through design. My responsibility lies in acknowledging, recognizing and practising relationality between people and Place, the material and immaterial, while privileging Indigenous knowledge. Furthermore, it aims to enhance biocultural diversity conservation and regeneration towards collaborative resilience, cultural identity and sustainability through academia, education and research.

Throughout my work at the Wominjeka Djeembana Indigenous Research Lab at MADA, an Indigenous space where deep listening, sharing and learning with obligation, respect and responsibility to Place and community are practised, I have come to realize the importance and essence of my responsibility towards ways of being, knowing and doing of Indigenous communities. I have learned that by loving Mother Earth, we can recover, preserve and regenerate biocultural diversity and Indigenous knowledge and empower Indigenous peoples and ways of knowing and doing.

Indigenous design

To understand Indigenous design and decolonial design, we need to go back in time and understand coloniality, what the colonial system and people have done to our People and the difference between decolonial design and Indigenous design. Indigenous design started prior to colonization but has recently been recognized in academia. 'Indigenous design refers to design led by Indigenous designers and peoples, which is based on Indigenous knowledge, methodologies and methods' (Munroe and Hernandez Ibinarriaga 2022, 2). Indigenous design is grounded on Country (Holmes and Jampijinpa 2013; Uncle Charles Moran, Uncle Greg Harrington, and Sheehan 2018), Place (Graham 2009) and relationality (Martin and Mirraboopa 2003) between the human and non-human, the material and immaterial (Hernandez Ibinarriaga 2022). Indigenous design is embodied and practised on Country with values and respect through deep listening, observing and making. Its purpose is to enhance the relationships between people and Place and to understand that knowledge lives and is embedded on Country; therefore, Country and knowledge have agency.

> Relationality, practice, and design have agency.
>
> (Hernandez Ibinarriaga and Martin 2021, 273)

Each Country or Indigenous community is different; has different knowledge, language, energy, humans, culture, practices, nature, Earth, air and waters; and receives the sun and fire differently. This can be called biocultural diversity, and we need this diversity to survive. The colonial project has tried to erase this diversity (we, Indigenous peoples included) through the Eurocentric and globalized way of living, doing and thinking. Indigenous peoples have been affected physically, emotionally, linguistically and culturally (Chilisa 2011; Tuhiwai Smith 2012) because of genocide, racism, globalization and capitalism. The colonization process is still ongoing with the modern economy, power relationships and the societal changes of separation and individuality imposed by colonial design; this has damaged and is still damaging our culture, customs and biocultural diversity to the point that many of these cultures, knowledge and languages have disappeared. 'Colonisation is a "denaturing project" that can be recognised by its pattern of disregard and self-regard' (Hernandez Ibinarriaga and Martin 2021, 257).

Imposition and power relations of colonizers must change to overcome the long-term effects and problems of colonization, such as racism, inequality, discrimination, sexual abuse, health issues, access to healthcare, poverty, dispossession of lands and resources, lack of information, education deficiency, malnutrition, environmental problems, lack of access to safe water and integration into dominant cultures (United Nations 2009; Carpenter 2014). The many problems that colonization brings create a loss of language, detachment to land/Country, cultural annihilation and disruption of the relationality between people and Place.

The decolonial design project is social; it proposes new ways of thinking and values different from the Eurocentric mindset to coexist in Place. Sometimes, it can be seen as progress towards acknowledging, recognizing, and applying knowledge and values from Indigenous cultures. However, it can also be seen as a shallow understanding of Indigenous design as only a few people deeply understand the connection to Country and land as a way of being, seeing reality and as an embodied experience. 'Decolonisation means changing structures as much as building new structures as a way of becoming in the current society' (Munroe and Hernandez Ibinarriaga 2022, 19). Decolonial designers can adapt certain methodologies and methods from decolonial or Indigenous methodologies through critical and reflective thinking. However, the challenge to the change is the deeper understanding and embodied experience of relationality on Country.

> If design starts operating with decolonial theory, will this become another label to attract attention, build a career or establish a brand? We live in the proximity of many designed concepts and products that reform, reorientate, and resituate, so do we need another (decolonised) tag?
>
> (Uncle Charles Moran, Uncle Greg Harrington and Sheehan 2018, 72)

Colonial design embraces a settler way of being based on power relations, separation and individuality, globalization, consumerism, depletion of resources, appropriation and capitalism; it focuses on humans to create and solve problems, and endless consumption. Decolonial design focuses on society and societal change. Decolonial design embraces the adoption of decolonial and Indigenous methodologies through consultation with Indigenous people but often fails to acknowledge intellectual property rights, copyright law and collective knowledge fairness and difference (Janke 2005). Also, using Indigenous peoples as participants in design research with allegedly written consent raises the issue of Indigenous communication, which is not written down but maintained verbally and through traditional cultural practices.

Indigenous design embraces relationality on Country. It favours partnerships and collaborations, ancestral knowledge, the material and immaterial while enhancing Mother Earth with its relationships; the purpose of Indigenous Design is Country and its relationships. Uncle Charles Moran, Uncle Greg Harrington and Sheehan (2018, 76) call it *Respectful Design*, which celebrates the value of respect; 'Respectful Design is founded on the understanding that design is ancestral and alive in Country.' Indigenous Design is an embodied experience in relationality with Country and acknowledges and considers the sacred structures within ancestral knowledge. Furthermore, it provides an understanding of different worldviews and ways of thinking immersed in relational and respectful design. For this, designers need to learn how to unlearn Eurocentric paradigms and experience the embodiment of different 'ways of being, knowing and doing' (Martin and Mirraboopa 2003). Indigenous design embraces the conservation and regeneration of biocultural diversity and ways of being, knowing and doing, which are against globalization and the colonial system.

Relationality

Relationality is an essential element in Indigenous design; relationality is the connection between the material and immaterial through the agency and interconnectedness of all things, together and/or separate; this is illustrated through the *Agave* Indigenous design project described in this chapter. All entities are interconnected through a system of relationality (Martin and Mirraboopa 2003), with the immaterial underpinning the material, such as energy, spirituality, totems, dreams and law, which are fundamental to the immaterial and the human and non-human. This relationality can be understood thoroughly through deeply embodied practices and lived experiences between body, Place and practices on Country.

The 'way of being, knowing and doing' (Martin and Mirraboopa 2003) in Indigenous design is based on the relationships that exist on Country, the knowledge and agency the land holds, the respectful practices and ceremonies that are performed within certain Place and the understanding and reflection of the methods and process to learn, unlearn and relearn. For instance, in Nahua culture, we are in relationships and dynamics with the non-human; the rocks are our grandmothers; they guide us in the ceremony and teach us during the ancestral shamanic ritual *Temazcal* (sweat lodge). We ask them questions, and they answer and heal us through energy, natural elements, fire, steam and water interacting with the body and soul through non-verbal communication; they purify our bodies, mind and soul. They connect us to other dimensions. This happens through the practice of connection between body, Place and the immaterial.

> Indigenous people are not in relationships; they are relationships.
>
> Shawn Wilson (Coates et al. 2013)

In this sense, we can understand relationality as not linear but cyclical and iterative, not through separation but we as one. We understand Country as one, be in oneness with Mother Earth.

> *I am relationality, relationality is me.*

Values attached to design practice

In order to perform ethical decolonial and Indigenous design practices, values must be present in the design process. Indigenous communities have laws and values attached to cultural practices that are significant to creating balance and harmony on Country and Mother Earth. These values include trust, respect, equity, empowerment, collaboration, balanced agency, power relationships between the material and immaterial, integrity, mutual benefits, mutual learning and building of deep relationships.

Two examples of decolonial and Indigenous design methodologies that involve values attached to the core of the methodology and methods are *The Seven Grandfathers' Teachings* (Munroe and Hernandez Ibinarriaga 2022) and *Critical Co-Design* (Hernandez Ibinarriaga and Martin 2021; Hernandez Ibinarriaga 2022). Munroe and Hernandez Ibinarriaga (2022) propose *The Seven Grandfathers' Teachings* as an Indigenous design methodology based on North American Indigenous knowledge related to an Indigenous value system. This methodology facilitates future responsible design opportunities integrating Indigenous knowledge, ancestral knowledge history and embodied experiences for a more sustainable and biocultural diverse world. The values guiding the iterative process of *The Seven Grandfathers' Teachings* as a design methodology (attached to animals while understanding their purpose in life) are: design with wisdom (Otter), research and analyse with respect (Buffalo), ideate with courage (Bear), select with honesty (Raven), implement with love (Eagle), evaluate with humility (Wolf), repeat for truth (Turtle).

Critical Co-Design (CCoD) is a decolonial methodology based on relationality, interaction and collaboration, which respects diverse ways of communication. CCoD acts as a way for non-Indigenous peoples to enter a relational positioning with Indigenous peoples. Furthermore, it favours relational collaboration while privileging ancestral knowledge, values and Indigenous people's capacity-building. In order to guide respectful collaboration between non-Indigenous people and Indigenous peoples, fourteen principles and values have been developed to ensure ethical interactions, mutual benefits and a mutual learning experience over the process (Hernandez Ibinarriaga and Martin 2021; Hernandez Ibinarriaga 2022). To develop a new way of

Indigenous design thinking and a more ethical way of doing and thinking, it is essential to incorporate values into the design process and relationships. This relatedness, interaction and collaboration should be based on respect (Martin 2017), humility, reciprocity, responsibility, safety, love/care, empathy and compassion for each other's generosity, empathy and nurturing (Hernandez Ibinarriaga 2022).

An example of Indigenous relational design – The Agave (*Metl*)

The Agave o Maguey (*Metl* in Nahuatl language) is an ancestral and traditional plant in the Nahua and Maya culture. This ancestral healing plant is used in Mexico to heal the spirit and connect with other dimensions, the land and the immaterial world. For us, it means long life and health and represents dancing and fertility. Significantly, we use the Agave to make rituals, ceremonies, *Mezcal*, pulque, tequila, food, *aguamiel* ('honey water'), ropes, shoes, textiles and tools, to name a few. There are more than 300 species, and each one of them is used for different practices.

Agave,
the butterfly freedoms her wings,
fly around spreading the pollen,
our waters come from the sky,
the goddess Mayahuel is born,
Agave.

Agave, connected to the ground with strength,
stand still,
resistant and hard on the outside,
resilient and soft in the inside.

Spiritually connected to our brown land,
subtle connected to the soft wind,
strongly connected to the sun and sky,
artistically connected to my eyes,

Watery and juicy body,
I want to feel her,
soft green/blue velvet skin connected to my body,
warrior spines if you challenge and disrespect her.

Mayahuel gives her life for us to connect to other dimensions,
to connect with our ancestors,

Her roots are strong,
they survive in harsh and dry soil, as we people survive to colonisation.

The body and the skin hold water to survive in the desert and arid places,
such as us in the colonial system.

She gives her main organ for us to heal our bodies with its nutrient and healing sweet water, the
Agave gives her heart when is mature and ripe,
we warm and cook her heart while taking care of her,
she holds wisdom and ancestral knowledge.

I honour Mayahuel, I feel her in my body and soul,
I drink her juice and connect to my ancestors and land through her,
Mayahuel, the Agave, Metl.

The *Agave* furniture/sculpture – An embodied relational practice

The *Agave* was designed for an exhibition titled *Tonantsintlalli, Our Multidimensional Mother Earth* held at Blak Dot Gallery in 2022 in Melbourne, Australia. The *Agave* furniture/sculpture project exemplifies Indigenous design, embodying relationality between people and Place. Furthermore, it represents ancestral knowledge, holding cultural significance functionally and visually, and facilitates space for Indigenous practices and ceremonies. The *Agave* embodies material and immaterial elements and cultural significance through its tangible manifestation.

The *Agave* is also an example of design practice and methodology which embodies the narrative of *The Seven Grandfathers' Teachings* (Munroe and Hernandez Ibinarriaga 2022) – it holds design with wisdom while respectfully reviving and conserving biocultural diversity and ancestral knowledge from the Nahua culture and disseminating and sharing a different worldview. The project was developed to acknowledge the connection to the land, waters, sky, ancestral knowledge and our *Abuelitos* (Elders). The furniture/sculpture *Agave* was intended to challenge Western beliefs and embrace my cultural identity to allow people to work, practise ceremonies, play and relax. It was designed with honesty, respecting the cyclical and relational *Seven Grandfathers' Teachings* as a methodology. I implemented the materiality with all my love and shared it with the co-creators/co-makers; through this process, we built respect, collaboration and commitment. We evaluated and reflected collectively and individually about the challenges, possibilities, processes, abilities and limitations. We co-created, listened, observed, made and balanced each other. We iterated through experimentation and trusted each other. We designed using a relational approach. The *Agave* is an Indigenous design, a relational embodied experience and knowledge connecting people and Place.

The *Agave* was co-created/co-made with Dan Tanner (Monash MADA), Dan Truscott (Monash MADA) and Carlo Gigliotti (Upholster). We used bent plywood for the leaves, stainless steel for the structure and upholstered fabric for the cushions. Materiality is about the design process, the co-making, the communication and experimentation in creating the prototype using the most appropriate materials for the design, aesthetic and functionality (see Figure 8.1).

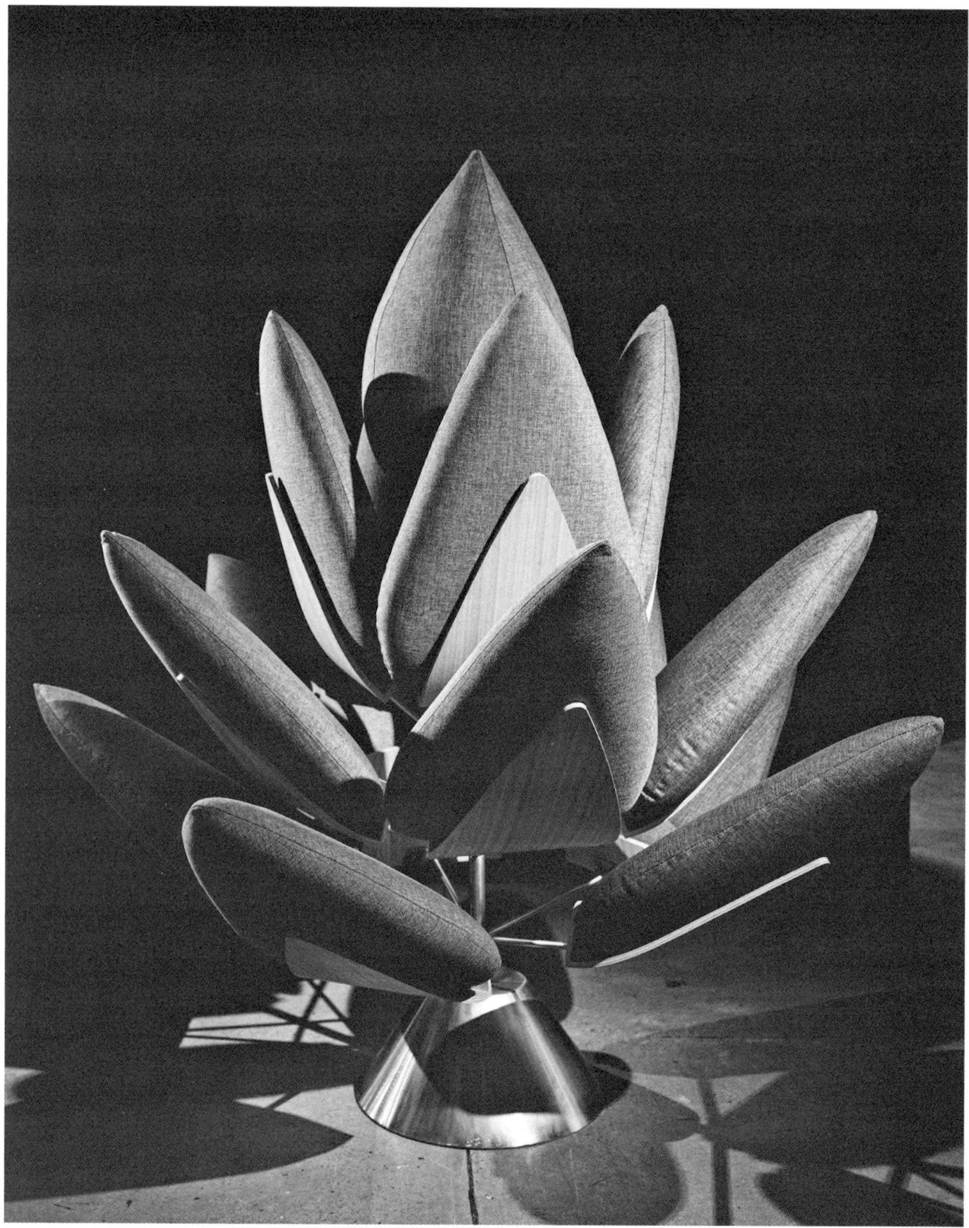

Figure 8.1 *Agave* (*Metl*) – furniture/sculpture, 2022. Courtesy of Desiree Hernandez Ibinarriaga. Photo by Wani.

Figure 8.2 Working in angles for the metal structure, 2021. Photo by Desiree Hernandez Ibinarriaga.

Agave – A culturally significant furniture/sculpture from Nahua and Maya cultures

Legend of *Metl* (Agave/Maguey)

Agave o Maguey comes from *Mayáhuel*, the goddess of the maguey, the fertility and inebriation for the Mexicas (Nahuas). Ancestral knowledge is passed on through many ways of knowing and forms of communication, such as storytelling, yarning, dancing, singing, ceremonies, ancestral practices, planting, making food and so on. On this occasion, I want to use storytelling to share the *Metl* (Agave/Maguey) legend from the Nahua cosmology and culture.

A long time ago on Earth, there was much sadness, and the humans seemed to have no life, so the sacred energies told themselves that they would send the *Metl* woman to give them medicine. One day as planned, *Metl* came and enjoyed being with Mother Earth. However, she saw much sadness in humanity; she spoke to a man passing by and told him to follow her guidance. She transformed into a beautiful Maguey/Agave plant with a marvellous green skirt; she told the man to gently scrape her leaves and carve a hole. The following day, the man returned, so *Metl* told him to drink the juice from the hole. After a while, the man started feeling great happiness in his heart, so he danced. *Metl* told him to share the juice with other people as it would make them happy too. This man did so; he shared the juice

Figure 8.3 Agave and creative practitioner Desiree Ibinarriaga, 2022. Photo by Desiree Hernandez Ibinarriaga.

that *Metl* had given him, so humanity regained happiness, and everyone lived happily ever after. This medicine today is called Mezcal and comes from the Agave.

Language is embedded on Country. It is constructed through deep observation, listening, living things, ancestral practices and understanding the Place, so it is important that I share my culture and tell the story in Nahuatl, one of my ancestor's languages (try to say it out loud and feel the vibrations in your body).

Kipia miak tonalli nikan pan tlaltepaktli onkayaya miak tekipacholli uan maseualmej nesiyaya ken miktoyan, uajka moiljuikej tlen teoajakamej kititlanisej ichpokatsin Metl uan ya kinmas tlen ipajui. Uan se tonalli ijkinon elki Metl ualajki uan nejnelia kipakti itstok nikan kampa tonantsintlalli, kitak nejnelia maseualmej kipiyayaj miak tekipacholli; uajka kinojnotski se tlakatl tlen panoyaya nopika uan kiljui ma kichiua tlen ya kiljuis. Uajka Metl mokuapki se yeyejktsin tlaixxualli ka iyoyon nochipa xoxuik uan killi ni tlakatl ma kichiua kampika uan ma kiixkopeua uan ma kitsintlalanana uan tlen ia kipia itsintla makiji uan ma kinmaka seyokej inniuanpoyaouaj. Ni tlakatl ijkinon kichijki uan nelia keman kijik iatsin Metl tlachixki ka miak tlatepak uan nochipa yolpajki uan mijtotiti. Sempa ni tlakatl kinmajmato nochipa maseualmej ni pajtli tlen iaxka Metl kimatoya uan ijkinon kikaxanillijekj inninkuesolli, tekitij san sejko uan ka miak pakillis itstoyaj san sentik.

The *Agave* – Cultural significance

The *Agave* furniture/sculpture's Indigenous design is material and immaterial. It brings together cosmovision, stories, ancestral knowledge, plywood, metal, fabric and functionality to allow fourteen people to sit together, but it also creates knowledge while using it for events, such as ceremonies, yarning circles, discussions and readings, among others. The *Agave* deeply connects with Country and all the elements – Earth, water, wind and fire. It grows on the soil, and its roots are embedded in the Earth; it is nurtured by water by holding it in its flesh and body; it breathes air while standing still and growing slowly; it has a relationship with the sun, which makes it grow faster; it is connected to fire when a drink is created containing all the elements. As you know by now, Agave is not just about its materiality. It is about the cultural significance and the energy that it holds. *Agave* creates and tells stories about our people, allowing us to connect with our ancestors to preserve knowledge and share our experiences with others.

> The Agave belongs to Country
> The Agave is Country,
> The Agave is energy and ancestral knowledge,
> I am the Agave,
> The Agave is me.

This is an example of a 'way of co-becoming' (Country et al. 2016) and cultural significance in Indigenous relational design where Country, knowledge and people are inextricable and deeply interconnected for the same purpose, Country and its people.

Conclusion

This chapter is about relationality with Country and its people. Furthermore, it is an opportunity to understand Indigenous design and its difference from decolonial design. A co-reflection is needed by understanding and acknowledging new ways of being and cosmologies. Learning to unlearn and relearn is essential. Decolonial design is about collaboration, not consultation. It is about deep learning ancestral knowledge and building new futures, not appropriation. Indigenous and decolonial methodologies are about respectful and ethical design practices supporting biocultural diversity, conservation and regeneration.

Indigenous design way of being is relational, grounded on Country, embodied through lived experience and connects to the human with non-human and 'the immaterial that underpins the material' (Hernandez Ibinarriaga and Martin 2021, 270). Indigenous design is tangible and intangible, creating projects of cultural significance beyond the human. Indigenous design is performed or guided by Indigenous peoples and incorporates values and Indigenous knowledge through its process. Indigenous design aims to enhance Mother Earth and its relationships; it gives new perspectives and diversity in the design process towards more sustainable and respectful futures, privileging Indigenous knowledge and peoples. Indigenous design is an embodied experience connected to the land, waters, skies and fire with all its relationships. It creates a relational and embodied design practice connecting the body and Place with multicultural and pluriverse futures, privileging diverse Indigenous knowledge as a way of becoming.

Positionality is essential to decolonial and Indigenous design to understand our heritage, where we were born (which is different), our way of being, knowing and doing and our purpose in the Country. The *Agave* furniture/sculpture exemplifies my cultural identity, my body on Country and my practice connected to my way of being, knowing and doing within the material and immaterial worlds in the Nahua and Mayan cosmology. I am an Indigenous designer, thinker and maker, a proud Mayan, Nahua, Basque, Spanish woman born in The Great Tenochtitlan.

Figure 8.4 Yarning circle in the exhibition *Tonantsintlalli*, 2022. Courtesy of Desiree Hernandez Ibinarriaga. Photo by Wani.

References

Carpenter, David O. 'Environmental Exposure in Indigenous Communities: An International Perspective'. *Reviews On Environmental Health* 29, no. 1–2 (2014): 3–4. http://www.degruyter.com/view/j/reveh.2014.29.issue-1-2/reveh-2014-0004/reveh-2014-0004.xml

Chilisa, Bagele. *Indigenous Research Methodologies*. Thousand Oaks: Sage Publications, 2011.

Coates, John, Mel Gray and Michael Yellow Bird. *Decolonizing Social Work*. Burlington: Ashgate Publishing Company, 2013.

Country, Bawaka, et al. 'Co-Becoming Bawaka: Towards a Relational Understanding of Place/Space'. *Progress in Human Geography* 40, no. 4 (2016): 455–75.

De la Cadena, Marisol. 'Are Mestizos Hybrids? The Conceptual Politics of Andean Identities'. *Journal of Latin American Studies*, 37, no. 2 (2005): 259–84.

Graham, Mary. *Introduction to Kummara Conceptual Framework on Place: A Discourse On A Proposed Aboriginal Research Methodology*. Brisbane: Kummara Association, 2006.

Graham, Mary. 'Understanding Human Agency in Terms of Place: A Proposed Aboriginal Research Methodology'. *PAN: Philosophy Activism Nature*, 6 (2009): 71–8.

Hernandez Ibinarriaga, Desiree. 'Critical Co-Design Methodology: Privileging Indigenous Knowledge and Biocultural Diversity (Australia/Mexico)'. PhD diss. Deakin University, 2022.

Hernandez Ibinarriaga, Desiree and Martin Brian. 'Critical Co-Design and Agency of the Real'. *Design and Culture* 13, no. 3 (2021): 253–76. https://doi.org/10.1080/17547075.2021.1966731

Holmes, Miles C. C. and Wanta (Stephen Patrick) Jampijinpa. 'Law for Country: The Structure of Warlpiri Ecological Knowledge and Its Application to Natural Resource Management and Ecosystem Stewardship'. *Ecology & Society* 18, no. 3 (2013): 19.

Janke, Terri. 'Managing Indigenous Knowledge and Indigenous Cultural and Intellectual Property'. *Australian Academic and Research Libraries* 36, no. 2 (2005): 95–107.

Martin, Brian. 'Methodology is Content: Indigenous Approaches to Research and Knowledge'. *Educational Philosophy and Theory* 49, no. 15 (2017): 1–9. https://doi.org/10.1080/00131857.2017.1298034

Martin, Karen and Booran Mirraboopa. 'Ways of Knowing, Being and Doing: A Theoretical Framework and Methods for Indigenous and Indigenist Research'. *Journal of Australian Studies*, 27, no. 76 (2003): 203. http://ezproxy.deakin.edu.au/login?url=http://search.ebscohost.com/login.aspx?direct=true&db=edb&AN=75544051&site=eds-live&scope=site

Moran, Uncle Charles, Harrington, Uncle Greg and Norm Sheehan. 'On Country Learning'. *Design and Culture* 10, no. 1 (2018): 71–9. https://doi.org/10.1080/17547075.2018.1430996

Munroe, Howard and Desiree Hernandez Ibinarriaga. 'Indigenising Design: The Seven Grandfathers' Teachings as a Design Methodology'. *The Design Journal* 25, no. 3 (2022): 1–22. https://doi.org/10.1080/14606925.2022.2058680

Tuhiwai Smith, Linda. *Decolonizing Methodologies: Research and Indigenous Peoples*. London: Zed Books, 2012.

United Nations. *State of the World's Indigenous Peoples*. United Nations Publications, 2009. https://www.un.org/development/desa/indigenouspeoples/publications/state-of-the-worlds-indigenous-peoples.html

Wilson, Shawn. *Research is Ceremony: Indigenous Research Methods*. Black Point: Fernwood Publishing, 2008.

9
LIFE-CENTRED DESIGN
A SUB-SAHARAN PERSPECTIVE

François-Xavier Nzi iyo Nsenga

This chapter is a follow-up from and elaboration upon a short essay titled 'Beyond McWorld Design', which I wrote for the journal *Design Philosophy Papers* (2003). The essay was a response to design historian Anne-Marie Willis's editorial question, 'How can the other (non-Euro-American) design and designing be made visible and engaged without being measured against Eurocentric norms?' (2003, 299). In returning to this theme, some twenty years later, I wish to highlight certain thoughts, reflections and ideas in relation to the time that has passed and ideas which have emerged subsequent to the original publication. Consequently, the chapter is divided into four sections, as I revisit my thoughts in light of contemporary events and debates. The first provides an overview of the origin and the implementation of 'Eurocentric norms' expressed through designed artefacts and the education of those who design these. The second describes how some individuals and institutions, including those within the design community in Europe and America, have started questioning those supposedly 'universal' norms and begun developing very different pedagogical curricula, arguing for a 'pluriversal' (Escobar 2018) conceptualization of design and its practice. Section 3 discusses traditional sub-Saharan Africa's design and an ethos which I associate with it, as an example of non-Euro-American approaches. The final section argues for a 'life-centred' approach and ethos as a means to challenge the capitalist and market-driven 'McWorld Design', which too often prioritizes consumer needs, excluding the natural world. By 'life centred', I mean thoughtfully applied, seeking to fulfil core human needs and acknowledge the consequences of our mode of production.

Section 1

Western European historians tell us that until the eleventh century, society was organized into peasantry, aristocracy and clergy, with merchants, tradesmen and artisans progressively forming a fourth class, the *bourgeoisie*. Over the centuries, this new social class gradually developed, across Europe, into the dominant global class we see today, running the planet's socioeconomic and political affairs and centred upon the capitalist market as its organizing principle. Today, most of our existence is shaped by the Euro-American 'inventions' of consumer capitalism that promise an easy, free and happy life. In this context, the ultimate goal is to 'freely' make money in the shortest possible time, maximizing monetary returns on invested capital and its returns, whether it has been gained through work, inheritance or savings.

We are persuaded and trained to become efficient and obedient consumers, following 'orders' to buy goods and services sold in the marketplace and reminding us that through uncontested consumption we will enjoy a 'good life' until death. We are made to believe that a 'good life' equals working hard and earning money, so that we can consume uncontestably and buy more and more products and services offered by the marketplace. The origins of this modern European conceptualization of *human* existence, with the individual as a political entity, can be seen in celebrated thinkers, such as John Locke (1632–1704) who argued that all individuals possess the inalienable rights to 'life, liberty and estate (property)' (Laslett 1963, 289).

The concept of 'free' possession, production and consumption is fundamental to the capitalist market and its relations of exchange and also to the Euro-American *way of life*, which is also expressed through the concept of 'democracy'. This Euro-American ideal has become seemingly 'universal', promoting the freedom to produce, own and 'consume' without limitation. However, many would question these 'positive values' of the West, drawing attention to the negative legacy upon which it was founded and evolved: slavery as opposed to equality; mass killings as opposed to the value of the individual; individualism, along with egotism and greed, as opposed to justice; totalitarianism and tyranny as vitiating practices to universality.

The marketplace has inspired 'ideal' equality for all, in everything and everywhere, gradually implemented throughout civil society, not least by the higher education institutions in Europe and America, which are responsible for shaping younger generations and their political imaginations. The 'offsprings' of artisans, traders and workers have now been allowed into those institutions of higher learning, which were initially created to train the children of the bourgeois elite, exclusively. Among those newcomers to the academies of learning are today's designers, who originally were concerned with artisanal crafts but are now admitted into those traditionally exclusive institutions to learn how to methodically design material artefacts for the marketplace. However, over the last two decades, many design education institutions have started to explore an intellectual and research dimension beyond 'materiality' to align design disciplines more closely to the Social Sciences and Humanities.

Both in Europe and the United States, a network of newly trained design thinkers has been reflecting on the notion and nature of so-called 'wicked problems' (Rittel and Webber, 1973). This represents an attempt to move away from the obsolete and reductive approach of 'tamed' problems and their seeming solutions, which too often celebrate a narrow 'quick fix', most of the time materialized with 'dubious' products and services. Such 'wicked' or complex social and environmental problems, or challenges, directly and indirectly caused by mass production and consumption have become a concern for some designers of this academic group. However, given the inherent complexity of 'wicked problems' and the almost impossible task of addressing them, assessing their success with the task at hand is difficult. These complex problems cannot be attributed to one specific issue (and so lend themselves to easy remedy), even if they may originate at an individual scale, and so they quickly metastasize, affecting humanity and the natural world.

Among the many people who are trying to address these issues are design researcher and author Don Norman, anthropologist Arturo Escobar and IBM Global Vice President and Industry Professor at

McMaster University, and former President of the World Design Organization, Karel Vredenburg, who have embarked upon an educational project entitled *The Future of Design Education Initiative* to explore a 'pluriversal' *perspective* for which designers ought to be designing. Their initiative has gained momentum across the globe, with many designers and academics joining in and aiding in their ambition, which according to the project's website, aims 'to provide an in-depth, evidence-driven academic foundation for design decisions, helping designers to become advocates for social and environmental responsibility' (collected and published as Davis, 2023). The project consists of eleven online workgroups, including one addressing 'Disparate Cultures and World Viewpoints', which has informed the development of a set of principles, among them:

- Every community practices the design of itself, independent of expert knowledge. People in these communities are practitioners of their own knowledge.
- Design WITH and BY, not FOR people.
- Strategies for the future should preserve and/or advance the existing culture, intrinsic to its ways of being, rather than impose a design monoculture that reflects one idea of progress.
- People act in response to the specific, concrete circumstances of the culture. Direct observation of this culturally situated improvisation should precede design theories and plans.
- Designing for resilience means guiding a process of adaptation or transformation, sometimes in response to disruption, while also retaining the essence of what people value in where and how they live.
- Resilience is not sustainable if design ignores the ecosystem in which the community resides and the possible trajectories of external forces.
- The development of local design industries should consider place-based incentives and consequences in the utilization and distribution of resources. It should reflect the value assigned to goods, how the community benefits from production and exchange, and how people best cooperate with one another in achieving negotiated goals. (futureofdesigneducation.org)

The outcome of Don Norman and his colleagues' initiative is eagerly awaited (Future of Design Education 2024).

Simultaneously, in Europe and the United States, other design scholars are also experimenting with historically and academically new curricula, exploring how to address complex 'wicked problems'. One of these initiatives is taking place with the Transition Design course at the School of Design, Carnegie Mellon University, who seek to start a 'new area of design research, practice and study that proposes design-led societal transition toward more sustainable futures' (Irwin 2015, 229). Another notable example is at Delft University of Technology (TU Delft) with the Faculty of Industrial Design Engineering, who are focusing 'on human flourishing and human well-being'. Here, students are trained to:

> Consciously and deliberately use their design skills to contribute to the happiness of individuals and communities. Rather than being a fortuitous by-product of design, well-being is firmly anchored in the heart of these students' design intentions . . .
>
> Some designers focus on individuals, others on groups. Some help us to rediscover our talents, some support us in forming meaningful relationships, and others enable us to invest in our happiness and the people we care about. (Desmet 2018, 5)

According to Professor of Design for Experience Pieter Desmet, who has contributed to a series of publications titled *Positive Design*, Delft students design for our wellbeing, learning to enhance the advantages and diminish the adverse effects of goods and services. An example of this approach is the student project titled *Me & My Smartphone: A Study into the Well-being Paradox of Phones* (2019) developed by Matthijs de Koning. The project was inspired by his personal experience with his smartphone, revealing the 'paradox' of using a product that is experienced as 'both liberating and addictive'. His project addresses the hidden risks and consequences of two often unnoticed and un-addressed contemporary phenomena: *neomania*, the addiction to receiving new stimuli at least every five minutes, and *nomophobia*, the excessive fear of not being reachable by mobile phone all the time. As part of this project, de Koning developed a series of artefacts that incite users to 'think, stimulate debate, and trigger reactions', aiming to hopefully balance the ills against the obvious advantages in using smartphones. The goal of his project is to help people to face a planetary predicament which, according to British philosopher Alain de Botton, highlights the fact that many of us today are more interested in smartphones than in each other, directly.

Such exploratory curricula provide opportunities for graduates to create and propose positive change in the world, through the practice of design, unveiling both the advantages and unintended consequences of design artefacts. Institutions such as TU Delft and Carnegie Mellon are creating new opportunities for designers to break away from the vicious circle of production and consumption and to develop new initiatives towards more beneficial products and services no longer distracted by the pervasive concept of 'passive consumption'.

Section 2

Each one of us, human or non-human, is naturally endowed with the capacity to create, to design and make tools. Every living entity, such as birds or other animals, designs their own habitat, which is an innate imperative for survival. However, the relative value assigned to different forms of making and creating – in particular, the complexity or simplicity, material or conceptual refinement, and the systems, machines, tools or implements utilized – are ranked intellectually, professionally and economically. However, since the rise and influence of the European bourgeois ethos and its market orientation, humans have lost the ostensibly natural capacity to design 'tools', especially among city dwellers where market institutions and associated activities occur. Instead, professional designers are trained and made available for hire, paid to design products, services, processes, experiences and environments, essentially to be sold and bought via the marketplace, as they freely trade their labour and talents for monetary recompense. This 'mode' and way of life have created a generalized way of living, supposedly creating comfort and wellness. Designers are, therefore, trained in higher education academies to design for 'consumers', responding to 'imaginary' needs and desires to maximize profits for the corporations who own the rights to the patents, design or intellectual property of the artefacts manufactured. Subsequently, mass production and mass consumption occur globally without many of those involved considering how the mode of economic production might affect humans and other living entities.

We live with those consequences and with the exponential consumption of goods and services offered by the globalized marketplace, which promotes limitless economic growth, short-term monetary gains and large returns on capital investment. However, at times, concerns have been raised during the late nineteenth century and the early twentieth century, notably by designer William Morris and his followers, criticizing the frenzy of mass production and mass consumption spurred by the bourgeoisie (1896). These concerns have also been captured by political activist, author and father of the consumer movement Robert Mayer in his book *Consumer Movement: Guardians of the Marketplace* (1989).

Despite these growing concerns, through various consumer movements in Europe and North America during the twentieth and twenty-first centuries, Euro-American bourgeois corporations and the economic model they represent have become generally accepted as indispensable by providing jobs and contributing to the global economy. This Euro-American bourgeois ideology is now widespread all over the planet under the banner of progress, modernity and development. Even when it has been proven that many 'purely imagined' products and services are harmful, multinational corporations are allowed, encouraged and supported to continue their operations under false and hypocritical claims of the bourgeois motto, laissez faire. The major argument is that they are contributing to humanity's life improvement, through the provision of material goods, technology and services. However, with a notoriously short-sighted view focusing on quick monetary profit, the proponents of this view fail to consider the true and full meaning of 'planetary well-being'.

During the late 1960s and early 1970s, this myopic worldview raised concerns among Euro-American intellectuals, countercultural groups and some avant-garde professional designers, such as Victor Papanek, who castigated designers for being among the most harmful of all occupations.

> There are professions more harmful than industrial design, but only a very few of them. And possibly only one profession is phonier. Advertising design, in persuading people to buy things they don't need, with money they don't have, in order to impress others who don't care, is probably the phoniest field in existence today. (1972, 14)

The effects of mass production and consumption at a planetary level were voiced by members of organizations such as the Club of Rome, with their awakening publication, *The Limits to Growth* (1972). Also, statistician, economist and founder of the Appropriate Technology Movement Ernst Friedrich Schumacher argued against the limitless growth in his book *Small Is Beautiful: A Study of Economics as If People Mattered* (2010). Many designer scholars and practitioners have joined this debate, distancing themselves from the pervasive, unethical mass-production and mass-consumption corporate ethos, discourse and attitude. This debate is still in its infancy, but many members of the global design community are building solid intellectual networks to oppose the bourgeois ethos and its continuing impact upon both people and planet. For instance, design historian John Heskett closes an article titled 'Creating Economic Value by Design' by calling upon design researchers 'to elaborate – new – concepts of economics through the prism of design theory and practice' (2008, 83). However, this call is not yet widely or uniformly spread and heard. In our present transitional period, it is understandable that some design practitioners, for diverse personal reasons, cling to their corporate positions and assignments, to what they were taught and trained in. They were educated to deal with 'tame' problems created by their employers and to devise fast and simple solutions which are functional, appealing and ideally highly profitable. Again, it does not matter what social, health and environmental adverse effects might emerge before, during and after production or through consumption. Quoting political scientist Herbert Simon, John Heskett reminds us:

> The centre of interest in traditional economics . . . is markets and not individuals. . . . A serious problem is thereby raised at the outset: two important considerations relating to design – how goods

> and services are developed for the marketplace and how they are used – receive scant attention. (2008, 71)

From the early 1950s, design considerations of how goods and services are developed for the marketplace were looked at through scientific research under the emergent discipline of Ergonomics and Human Factors. These disciplines were founded in the United Kingdom and the United States almost solely to reduce human error, increase productivity and enhance workers' safety, system availability and comfort in factories and offices or other specific places such as aeroplane cockpits. According to the International Ergonomics Association in the United States, Human Factors:

> Uses a holistic systems approach to apply theory, principles, and data from many relevant disciplines to the design and evaluation of tasks, jobs, products, environments, and systems. HFE – Human Factors/Ergonomics – takes into account physical, cognitive, sociotechnical, organisational, environmental and other relevant factors. (Wikipedia 2022)

It can be argued that Human Factors and Ergonomics are mainly concerned with industrial and bureaucratic processes, controlled production environments, but what about individuals at home, in the street, in school and everyday life environments beyond work? Also, how buyers purchase goods and services is the domain of another discipline, which has been gradually developing since the proliferation of mass communication media in the early twentieth century. The Marketing discipline became institutionalized in academia during the 1940s and 1950s, but Victor Papanek and a few others accused the marketing act of deliberately inciting people to buy and own goods that are not 'good' for them or other living entities, of promoting 'evil'. Papanek voiced what many people thought and are still thinking today, that the formalization of the 'bourgeois ethos' and its market-based capitalism in the curricula of the educational academies of the Western and the 'Global North' was focused upon profitability at the expense of planetary wellbeing.

Section 3

While it is important that new curricula are emerging in the 'Global North', as I have already discussed in Section 1, designers also need to learn about the traditional and Indigenous cultures of the 'Global South'. However, one might argue that not much is left after six centuries of colonization, stifling and plundering. In traditional, pre-colonial sub-Saharan Africa, for example, any kind of artefact was first and foremost conceived to facilitate social interactions by directly exchanging goods or services for other goods or services without using a medium of exchange, such as money – this way of life is known as the barter system. Artefacts were never for sale, a stark contrast with the current monetized conception of the 'modern' world espoused by inhabitants of the market-based global economy. Besides, in all these traditional cultures, artefacts were exchanged as *gifts* (as examined and defined by many anthropologists) and used to nurture life-enhancing and convivial relationships among all living entities – as well as to respond to physical, social and societal needs or ambitions.

Why should Western and Westernized designers be interested in those foreign and 'archaic', 'backward', 'quality-wanting' and 'outmoded' artefacts, when the overall world trend is towards a limitless forward 'progress' and 'growth' – promised and abundantly delivered through the neat rationality of Western production? Life has changed, the past is gone and it is no longer of use, in present times, even less for the future! Contemporary designers have much to learn from Africa and other non-Euro-American 'ways of knowing' to challenge the 'capitalist ethos' and its seeming universality. Just like anthropologists, designers, too, have the potential to learn from traditional and Indigenous cultures, to create wisdom and build caring communities beyond the 'modern' mode of existence and its reliance upon commodities sourced from a global supply chain. In this sense, 'design wisdom' is not used to increase monetary profits, but instead, it is thoughtfully and methodically deployed to develop tangible and intangible artefacts, safeguarding life in all its evolving manifestations. Furthermore, designers and the products of their labour can contribute to enhancing the human condition by creating new modes of existence, 'colliding in mutual love'.

Philosopher and design theorist Jamie Brassett argues that without anticipation, there is no life; this is why designers have the opportunity to develop a 'sympathetic process anticipating a better future for the planet' (Brassett 2021, 5) and move away from a way of designing which has been proven not to be 'good' for human wellbeing. Consequently, these 'designs', long despised and denigrated, consigned to history and apparently archaic cultures, urgently need to be salvaged, revitalized and reinstated on a worldwide scale, side by side with the dominant design mode.

Conclusion

In the context of the current hegemony of Western (Euro-American) thought, economic artefacts, modes of production and use (along with their associated norms and worldviews), is there any room left for other ways of *making* based on different worldviews, cultural traditions and norms? On what grounds would these 'other ways' deserve a certain interest and call for engagement? A new type of design and designer practice is urgently needed to challenge the Euro-American pervasive design's conceptualization and communication via the curriculum – I am optimistic that we are on the right track.

Instead of treating people as consumers, we should start to design by considering what it means to be living on a planet where every single surviving life form appears, in some fundamental way, to be related to every other life form. While a 'life-centred' design perspective is still in the making, we need to start building alliances with different ways of learning, understanding and knowing, and we must foster dialogue across knowledge areas and lived experiences. As design commentator and writer John Thackara puts it, we need 'to describe where we want to be – and work backwards from there. Where we want to be is in *a new kind of economy* that is not just centered on what humans need, but is centered on all forms of life, and the conditions that support life' (2010, emphasis added). Design should be a 'thinking and merging' discipline just like philosophy, combining 'modern' Euro-American knowledge with thousands of years of non-Euro-American traditions – provided that these traditions are respected, safeguarded and rehabilitated, following six centuries of disparagement and plunder. This *new designing* should be neither 'Euro-Centred' nor particular to any world culture. Rather, it should be a hybrid of both.

As I have previously discussed in my essay 'Beyond McWorld Design', cultures are no longer relatively hermetically closed, as they had been for centuries, prior to European colonialism and mass industrialization (Nzi iyo Nsenga 2003). Many individuals now move out to explore, physically and mentally (some more easily than others), other lands and different cultures around the planet. Consequently, non-Western cultures and traditional circles in the West as well are now equally under pressure: from those *inside,* from individuals 'suffocating', longing to break away from Western tradition and embrace indiscriminately whatever arrives from beyond their social and cultural experience. Such Indigenous cultures are also threatened from the outside, by inoculated aliens carrying infection, claiming equal recognition and privileges, including that of spreading their own modes of life within local host cultures. Traditional cultures are thus being opened to individuals from all corners of the planet; they all are becoming 'universalized' to some degree, provided that they are not simply reappropriated and 're-colonized' as merely 'fashionable' knowledge and experience commodities as tourism.

It is time for design to engage with 'cosmopolitan localism' thinking and 'a lifestyle that is place-based and regional, yet global in its awareness and exchange of information and technology' (Irwin 2015, 229). We are bound to find ways to refer to both modes of designing and, hopefully, come up with a new way, the most appropriate, re-imagining education, creating new curricula and ways of learning, and designing life-centred and life-facilitating approaches to design appropriate to all the inhabitants of the planet, for the twenty-first century and beyond.

References

Brassett, Jamie. 'Anticipating the Work to be Done'. *Futures* 134 (2021): 5.

Consumer Movement, United States. Wikipedia. Accessed 12 April 2022.

Davis, Maredith. 'The Future of Design Education: Rethinking Design Education for the 21st Century'. *She Ji: The Journal of Design, Economics and Innovation* 9, no. 2 (2023): 91–308.

de Koning, Matthijs. *Me & My Smartphone: A Study into the Well-being Paradox of Phones*. Faculty of Industrial Design Engineering Delft University of Technology The Netherlands, 2019.

Desmet, Pieter. *Positive Design: Delft Students Design for Our Well-Being*. Delft University of Technology, April 2018.

Escobar, Arturo. *Designs for the Pluriverse: Radical Interdependence, Autonomy, and the Making of Worlds*. Durham, NC: Duke University Press, 2018.

Future of Design Education Initiative. 'Why Design Education Needs to Change'. https://www.futureofdesigneducation.org

Heskett, John. 'Creating Economic Value by Design'. *International Journal of Design* 3, no. 1 (2008): 71–84.

Irwin, Terry. 'Transition Design: A Proposal for a New Area of Design Practice, Study, and Research'. *Design and Culture* 7 (2015): 229-46.

Irwin, Terry. 'Wicked Problems and the Relationship Triad'. In *Grow Small, Think Beautiful: Ideas for a Sustainable World from Schumacher College*, edited by Stephen Harding. Edinburgh: Floris Books, 2012, 232–259.

Laslett, Peter. *Locke's Two Treaties of Government: A Critical Edition with Introduction and Notes*. Cambridge, MA: Cambridge University Press, 1963.

Latour, Bruno. *An Inquiry into Modes of Existence. An Anthropology of the Moderns*, translated by Catherine Porter. Cambridge, MA: Harvard University, 2018.

Marenko, Betti and Brassett, Jamie. *Deleuze and Design*. Edinburgh University Press, 2015.

Mathee, Thinus. Presentation at the 12th National Design Education Forum Conference Proceedings, 4-5 November 2009, Graaff Reinet, South Africa'. *The Design Education Forum of Southern Africa*, 2009.

Mayer, Robert N. *The Consumer Movement: Guardians of the Marketplace*. Boston: Twayne, 1989, 13.

Meadows, Dennis H., et al. *The Limits to Growth: A Report for the Club of Rome's Project on the Predicament of Mankind*. New York: Macmillan, 1979.

Moore, Jason W. *Anthropocene or Capitalocene? Nature, History, and the Crisis of Capitalism*. Oakland: PM Press, 2016.

Morris, William. *How I Became a Socialist*. London: Twentieth Century Press, 1896.

Nzi iyo Nsenga, François-Xavier. 'Beyond McWorld Design'. *Design Philosophy Papers* 1, no. 6 (2003): 327–35.
Papanek, Victor. *Design for the Real World: Human Ecology and Social Change*. New York: Pantheon, 1972.
Rittel, Horst W. and Melvin W. Webber. 'Dilemmas in a General Theory of Planning'. *Policy Sciences* 4 (1973): 155–69.
Schumacher, E. F. *Small is Beautiful: Economics as if People Mattered*. London: Harper Perennial, 2010.
Simon, Herbert A. *The Sciences of the Artificial*, 1969 and Richard Buckminster Fuller *Synergetics*, 1975.
Thackara, John. *Design for a Restorative Economy* in *Design Harvests. An Acupuncture Design Research Approach Towards Sustainability*, ed. Valsecchi, Francesca, Lou, Yongqi and Diaz, Clarisa Gothenburg: Mistra Urban Futures, 2013. Cumulus Conference, Tongji University, 6–10 September 2010.
Willis, Anne-Marie. 'Design's Other'. *Design Philosophy Papers* 1, no. 6 (2003): 299–303.

10
DESIGN AND DEEP TIME

Naiyi Wang

In a satellite image of the Ulanqab Prairie of Inner Mongolia, the crown jewel of the Chilechuan Prairie located at the northern foot of the Yin Mountains, the pasture appears mostly like a green carpet. However, in the northwest of the prairie, where endless undulating hills used to awe the herdsmen with their vastness, two conspicuous concave 'fingerprints' have been stamped with discernible 'friction ridges', not unlike those on a human finger. In fact, these 'fingerprints' are two gigantic mines in the Bayan Obo Mining District. Originally described in Mongolian as 'a rich sacred mountain', Bayan Obo boasts the largest deposits of rare earth elements (REEs) yet found worldwide. Since its earliest excavation in 1957, a hill in Bayan Obo, with an elevation of 1,783, metres was artificially excavated, gradually forming the main mine with a length of 1,500 metres, a width of 1,100 metres and a depth of more than 200 metres. Another smaller yet deeper mine is located right next to the main mine with a depth of nearly 300 metres.

REE is the general term for seventeen metallic elements consisting of lanthanides, scandium and yttrium. As non-renewable, scarce and strategic resources, REEs are also referred to as 'industrial vitamins'. Because of their physical and chemical properties, rare earths are widely used in fields like new energy, new materials, environmentally friendly energy conservation, aerospace and electronic information. Their applications range from smartphones to electronic vehicles, missiles, radars, submarines and more – REEs are everywhere. REEs are widely distributed across the Earth's crust, but in very uneven deposits. China is relatively rich in these resources, accounting for about 23 per cent of the world's total REE reserves. Among them, the Bayan Obo Mining District ranks first in the world for the largest deposits of rare earth resources and is the only mining district in the world that contains seventeen REEs.

After seven decades of excavation and accumulation, the mines and tailings of Bayan Obo have profoundly reshaped the texture of the city's suburban landscape, which has become a quasi-wilderness mingling ancient geological time with modern industrial time. Meanwhile, the mines have also generated a series of geopolitical disputes and are harshly criticized for natural resource exploitation. One cannot discuss the ecological vicissitudes of Bayan Obo without delving into the myriad of times and spaces created by deep geological time, the historical mutations of the twentieth century and people's individual perceptions and imaginations of the future. Looking down from the edge of such man-made spectacles, one could perceive the Earth's history evolving through deep time. On a broader scale, the strata themselves have become massive databases recording the evolution and mutation of the Earth through hundreds of millions of years.

As 'vessels of time', the ores are not only a technological medium but also a medium of imagination connecting the past with the future. As new media theorist Jussi Parikka noted, the deep time resources of the Earth are the basis for all technological development, every element of which has undergone hundreds of millions of years of evolution (2015). From the perspective of deep time, what we are doing now is nothing short of depleting the entire reservoir of the Earth's historical sediment to facilitate a series of transitory technological developments and mass-produce electronic devices with very short life cycles. Minerals and materials take a significantly prolonged ecological process to form, which are then excavated, refined, processed and consumed in a matter of years or even months. The current state of digitalization has incurred a severe ecological crisis alongside generating countless amounts of electronic waste, which will become 'future fossils', a sort of planetary memory that is part of the stratigraphical features of the Anthropocene.

The Anthropocene is a new geological epoch in which humans have been considered as the dominant force impacting the Earth's geology (Steffen, Crutzen and McNeill 2007, 614–21). For the past decade, the Humanities have been faced with challenges posed by the notion of the Anthropocene. Historians encounter in their practice the same theoretical and methodological challenges; the first attempt to deeply reflect on the Anthropocene's challenges, historian Dipesh Chakrabarty's 'The Climate of History: Four Theses', was published in *Critical Inquiry* in 2009. In it, Chakrabarty has pointed out that consideration of humanity as a geological force troubles the distinction between natural and human history, forcing us into a new kind of historicity (2009, 201). This proposition interrogates the traditional perception that humans are history's sole agents. The realization that 'humans are both biological and geological agents' rules out that cherished anthropocentric illusion, as well as calls for a post-anthropocentric turn in history. In this context, humans are actors but not always at the centre; on the contrary, various different elements come together to form a 'hybrid' (206–7). To incorporate this interrelated web of relationships between humans and non-human entities such as plants, animals and larger forces, 'we will need to develop multiple-track narratives', as Chakrabarty again reminds us, so that 'the story of the ontologically-endowed, justice-driven human can be told alongside the other agency that we also are – a species that has now acquired the potency of a geophysical force, and thus is blind, at this level, to its own perennial concerns with justice that otherwise forms the staple of humanist narratives' (2010, 3).

The notion of the Anthropocene creates 'an entry point of deep time' (McKay 2008)[1] and opens up a new space for a radical critique of inherited dualisms such as human and non-human, nature and culture, subjectivity and objectivity, the animate and the inanimate. From the perspective of this geological era, design cannot simply be considered as a passive object made by or for humans, but referred to as an active agent in the ontological and epistemological sense. As environmentalist Melinda H. Benson has argued, 'the Anthropocene is not simply a new geological epoch but an opportunity to embrace a new ontology' (2019, 252). It is within this context that I argue the notion of the Anthropocene presents new understandings of time, matter and agency for design as a geological actor capable of geomorphic and stratigraphic acts. From the perspective of the negative consequences of design, the impact it has produced is profound (Fry, Dilnot and Stewart 2015, 8–9). As design theorist Ben Highmore has observed, 'it is hard not to see global warming and climate change as a consequence of a variety of design processes, design values and design products' (2009, 1).

If, as some claim, the Anthropocene obliterates the distinction between geological time (deep time) and historical time, what does the geological discourse of the Anthropocene mean for design and its histories? The historical timelines situate us in a continuum that focuses exclusively on designs (electronics) made by or for humans whereas the materials (deep time resources) used to make them are millions of years old, such as rare earth minerals. The profound depletion of non-renewable resources used in the production and circulation of design, the energy required in the extraction as well as the emissions produced, all contain different entities and involve completely different temporalities than the human-scale ones. Even if they are thrown away, the toxic materiality they retain surpasses the usual timescales design historians are used to working with. As ecological theorist Timothy Morton points out, there is really no 'away' (2013). To better understand this 'hybridity' (Latour 1993)[2] is to accept the fact that all entities are ontologically equal and involved in multi-scaled periodizations of their own. What methodologies should design historians use to address these multiscalar temporalities in which different entities are inextricably embroiled? Realizing these temporal entanglements and design's impact on a geological scale requires us to consider an expanded notion of timescale in relation to design.

At a distance of 2,500 kilometres from Bayan Obo Mining District, an entire street along the river in Guiyu, Guangdong, is piled with bags of circuit boards and rows of furnaces. Since the late 1980s, 70 per cent of the world's electronic waste has been sold across oceans to this town on the coast of Guangdong, China.[3] In the Guiyu Cycle Economic Industrial Park, the clangorous cacophony of metal rings in the air, as sacks of these scrap materials are thrown from containers and scattered across the area. To process electronic waste and extract rare metals, locals go through rudimentary and crude rounds of disassembly, heat plates, acid washing, incineration and landfill disposal. Guiyu is entangled in a weird temporality, as these methods come from the craftsmanship of nineteenth-century alchemists, yet are being employed to deal with the overflows of the twenty-first century. Furthermore, toxic chemicals and waste fluids brought about by the disposal of electronic waste seep into the ground, directly polluting and eroding local soil and water sources. The geography of Guiyu adds difficulty to the situation, as the uneven, hilly terrain makes it hard for harmful gases and particulate matter to disperse from the area naturally. All of these constituent factors loom over Guiyu year-round, where people are victim to every layer of the hostile environment, from the underground to the atmosphere. In social scientist Jennifer Gabrys's words, 'electronics are not only matter, unfolding through minerals, chemicals, bodies, soil, water, environments, and temporalities. They also provide traces of the economic, cultural, and political contexts in which they circulate' (2011, 7).

These minerals, initially matter that has come into existence through ages of geological evolution, assume transient lives as parts of electronic devices before ending up at Guiyu, the largest e-waste dumping site on Earth. After going through the 'urban mining' process, where only a few rare metals are extracted and collected, tons of e-waste are buried in bulk beneath the earth, mingling and sedimenting with each other in various strata, waiting for future archaeologists and geologists to excavate. From the rare earth mines of Bayan Obo of Inner Mongolia to the e-waste dumping site at Guiyu in Guangdong, such a leap in time and space involves a complex cycle of human intervention, including mining, refining, processing and dumping, which constantly repeats itself. Meanwhile, the timescale of human perception moves alongside planetary geological time, which goes back aeons and tends to escape people's attention. Therefore, whatever takes place in our time and space could be interpreted as either a development or a regression. Moreover, such timescales unrolling in different dimensions could help us to weave the times of geological formation together with historical narratives, thereby creating cracks in between where one can re-assess and re-negotiate long-established paradigms, premises, theories and methodologies of history. It also establishes a critical threshold, compelling us to interrogate scales of time and space to rethink design and its histories.

In order to address the tension between geological (deep) time – both the time before minerals are excavated, refined or processed and the time it takes for the dumped waste to become future fossils – and historical time, it is crucial to examine the complex materiality of electronics. Focusing on minerals excavated from beneath the earth and future fossils that have returned to the earth, this chapter considers substances and residues as a useful basis for discussing the mineral ontology of contemporary design and conceptualizing the relationship between design and deep time. By proposing a 'new material' (Coole and Frost 2010) understanding to the relationship between geophysical realities and design beyond anthropocentrism, it also explores whether such interdisciplinary perspectives can provide an appropriate theoretical framework and methodological concept for exploring the complex materiality and temporality of electronics and new ways for navigating the interconnected trajectories of deep time, design and its histories.

Sony Walkman

What drives this enquiry is a close examination of the Sony Walkman, the first portable music device released in 1979. With this unit, music was able to accompany a person anywhere they went. Gone were the restrictions of a stationary player. Sony can shrink the form of the device due to ever smaller, stronger magnets, specifically those made from the rare earth element samarium. Deep time resources of the Earth enabled the Walkman to be born, and after a short use-period, obsolete devices become part of the materiality of electronic waste, which requires geological time spans to decompose. The life cycle of the Walkman – from birth in a geological process, through life as a consumer product and ultimately to death in a landfill – indicates complex materialities and temporalities. How would its history look if we approached it not through the end-products made for human use, but through its substances and residues which are concretely geological? What methodologies should design historians use to unfold these deep layers for analytical purposes? Although significant research on the Sony Walkman has been carried out within broader cultural, social and economic contexts, it has not acknowledged itself as part of the Earth's geology. What role design and its histories play in geological time, and how to explore their relationship are still contested topics in need of elaboration.

These questions lead me to track the importance of rare earth minerals as a geo-entity in constructing electronics: the literal deep times and deep places of electronic devices in mines and landfills. The geological materials (rare earth minerals) are mined from their strata and assembled in electronics, while the subsequent residues feed back to earth as 'fossils of the future'. Thinking about geological, extractive, deposition and sedimentation processes requires considering alternative temporalities in which design and its histories are involved. Hence, this chapter argues that different temporalities – the long-term durations of geological formations, mineralization, as well as the millions of years of decomposition and sedimentation – must be considered alongside a history of design. Given these interdependencies, design and its histories can no longer be embedded in the frame of human time but accept the existence of multiple timescales. From this perspective, new methodologies have to take into account alternative temporalities, other times than that of humans – from thousands to hundreds of thousands of years.

To interrogate these deep layers, the concept of 'deep time' (Hutton 1959, 200),[4] or geological time, coined by geologist James Hutton in the eighteenth century, serves as a useful base for thinking about design for more-than-human temporalities. Besides a geological concept, it has been adopted in media archaeology by German media theorist Siegfried Zielinski (2006). Zielinski's deep time is a methodology

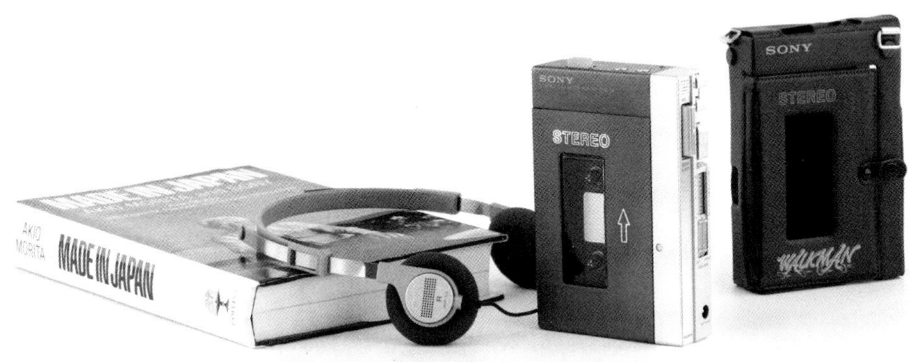

Figure 10.1 Sony Walkman, portable cassette player (model TPS-L2), 1979. Courtesy of Naiyi Wang.

that bypasses the 'canonised' narratives of media history and is interested in 'digging out secret paths in history' (Huhtamo and Parikka 2011, 10).[5] With the ongoing discussion of the Anthropocene and the 'materiality turn' in media studies, much research focuses on exploring the relationship between geological materiality and media devices. Design historians may find that media archaeology can provide an appropriate methodological concept for studying electronics. According to Parikka's assertion, 'media history is millions, even billions, of years old' (2015, 35). He takes the notion of 'deep time' as a way to explore the earthly components that precede media themselves. Another way to approach this depth is Jennifer Gabrys's *A Natural History of Electronics*, which explores the materiality of electronics through the multiple forms of waste. The notion of 'deep time' is commonly adopted within critical discourse around e-waste matter. In recent years, there seems to be an increasing interest within design practices to address the problematics of e-waste – with emerging projects such as design duo Formafantasma's *Ore Streams* (2017–2019) and artists/designers Revital Cohen and Tuur Van Balen's *H / AlCuTaAu* (2014), to name just a few.

How to 'excavate' (Huhtamo and Parikka 2011, 3) both literally and metaphorically into this depth and interrogate these temporal entanglements? By looking in particular at materials of REEs which are essential for electronics, this analysis traces its life as what philosopher Jane Bennett calls vital material, from natural minerals that are sedimented for millions of years before being mined and processed to the deposition of material in the landfill. By drawing inspiration from Parikka's work on the geology of media, this chapter argues that it is the earth (minerals and materials) that provides for electronics and enables them; moreover, their afterlife should also take into account this aspect of the earth, becoming a sedimented layer of fossils left for future archaeologists to excavate. In the words of political theorist Jane Bennett, 'materiality continues its activities even as a discarded or unwanted commodity' (Bennet 2010, 6). By drawing on the connection between the materiality of electronics and the geophysical realities, it seeks to excavate the deep layer of design, not only through geological materiality but temporality.

While a range of scholars have begun to redraw the materiality of electronics, less attention has been paid to this geophysical reality raw matter-energy.[6] Furthermore, design historians have yet to show much concern for multiscalar temporalities embedded in design and its histories as mentioned earlier. Most studies are restricted to conventional ideas about electronics as devices whose meanings are inscribed by their social, cultural and economic contexts, apparently lacking in material substance. The relentless focus on the end-product blinds them to the fact that the materiality of design 'creates its own times and spaces which do not necessarily coincide with those of predetermined contexts and relations' (de Almeida Meroz 2017).[7] For instance, Sony Walkman can be a case of this problematic.

Much research into the Sony Walkman has been carried out within the 'wider context', of which arguably the most famous is *Doing Cultural Studies: The Story of the Sony Walkman*, which was first published in 1997. In this book, cultural theorists have historically examined the Walkman through a theoretical model of 'cultural circuit': representation, identity, production, consumption and regulation, identifying how cultural forms and social relations shaped the meaning of the Walkman. Although this study has been criticized for its relational model which limits the analysis to certain predetermining frameworks, it has provided a useful analytical perspective for design historians, who have been searching for a contextual understanding of design to rule out the 'art historical template' and the 'heroic approach' since the 1970s (Fallan 2010, 4–11). In terms of a culture studies approach to design history, Paul du Gay and colleagues' contribution to design history is indisputable; such an approach has provided access to understanding 'design as a cultural phenomenon', as Kjetil Fallan has asserted that 'design history can be approached as cultural history' (2010, 33). In fact, this proposition can be traced back to Penny Sparke's study *An Introduction to Design and Culture: 1900 to the Present*, published in 1986. Sparke replaced 'history' with 'culture' as the context of narrating design. She emphasized that 'as a cultural concept, design is determined by the outside forces that have shaped it and by the contexts within which it has manifested itself' (2013, xii). Furthermore, Guy Julier's advocacy of design culture can be seen as a continuation of this proposition (2008).

The trend towards a broader analytic context of design has certainly provided fertile ground for developing new design histories while serving as a catalyst for interdisciplinary approaches to design history. However, it has also covertly introduced a potential 'contextual determinism' approach (Heskett 1980, 7–9), which is overly concerned with the influence of cultural forms and social relations upon design, implying a view of design as a passive vessel whose meanings are inscribed by its contexts, where their physical materiality is disregarded or greatly underestimated. As an essential feature of the Walkman, the pursuit of eminently portable became the dominant factor in its development, and such portability can be seen as the reason why the Walkman was considered as a representative of the central discourse of 'autonomy and mobility' in the 1980s (Hosokawa 1984, 165–80; Chamber 1990, 1–4; du Gay et al. 1997; Bull 2001, 179–97). Design researcher, theorist and historian Juliette Kristensen, together with scholars Santiago Acosta Maya, Susan Sanderson and Mustafa Uzumeri, have emphasized that technological evolution was important for the Walkman development in their studies, indicating that Sony's pursuit of technological miniaturization is based on existing technology: the development of transistors (1950s) and the microchip (1980s) have made the Walkman possible and underlay the development of its capabilities (Sanderson and Uzumeri 1995, 761–82; Maya 2000, 20; Kristensen 2014, 226–9).[8] However, such innovation of lighter, smaller and higher fidelity apparatus is inseparable from the application of key materials, which unfortunately has not been mentioned in the existing studies of the Walkman.[9]

Materials such as germanium, silicon and REEs were central to the emergence of such technologies and the development of electronic devices. Nevertheless, scholars have yet to emphasize this aspect as an analytical category in their accounts of technological developments, and therefore the various circumstances of their agency have been greatly underestimated. They give little attention to how 'raw materials' are integrated into production systems and thus ignore the processes of mining, processing and standardizing minerals before they are assembled into finished mass-consumer devices. In fact, these processes also deserve to be recognized as designs that are vital for a historical understanding of the Walkman. This is not to advocate for a material determinism but embodies important questions about the relationship between design and the materials and material capabilities that shape it and exposes the neglect of the design's materiality in these existing studies of the Walkman. It also questions whether (material) culture studies approach is an appropriate framework to satisfactorily address the materiality of design. In the enriched second edition of *Doing Cultural Studies: The Story of the Sony Walkman*, which was published in 2013, the authors focused on the 'material turn' approach and particularly introduced philosopher, anthropologist and sociologist Bruno Latour's Actor-Network Theory (ANT) in the session labelled as 'Back to the Future', which can be seen as a response to the inattention to materiality of the Walkman in cultural discourses, as well as a testament to 'Latour's focus on materiality [which] has been seen as a challenge to the cultural turn' (du Gay et al. 2013, xviii). Their reflection also echoes a more systematic exploration of the 'material turn' or the 'materiality turn' begun in the field of social and cultural studies since 2010.

A 'new materialist' perspective

Working from the case study of Sony Walkman, this chapter aims to propose a 'new materialist' framework which seeks to extend the material notions of electronics thoroughly towards deeper materialities and temporalities. As a critical engagement with this 'linguistic' or 'culturalist' approach to materiality, theories marked as 'new materialism' work against the notion of considering matter as inert, while embracing the vitality of matter. As philosopher Karen Barad once pointed out, 'Matter itself is not a substrate or a medium for the flow of desire. Materiality itself is always already a desiring dynamism, a reiterative reconfiguring, energised and energising, enlivened and enlivening' (2012, 59). This chapter draws from key concepts and debates to interrogate the notion of material agency as well as to rethink entrenched dichotomies between human and non-human, nature and culture, subject and object, the animate and the inanimate within discourses of the Anthropocene.

Since the late 1990s, theorists from heterogeneous backgrounds such as Manuel DeLanda, Barad and Rosi Braidotti have been involved in a theoretical turn with 'matter' as the central claim. Their theories are catalogued under the umbrella term 'new materialism' which is by no means a consistent genealogy but an emerging field with various propositions and assumptions which continue to proliferate. Intersecting with theories such as posthumanism, object-oriented ontology and its umbrella philosophy, speculative realism,[10] what all have in common is their rejection of anthropocentrism and examination of material agency.[11,12] Collectively, this vital field seeks a monist perspective, although there is a philosophical divergence between each theory. Within this context, I explore a key concept from the interdisciplinary field of new materialism to present as a theoretical framework through which we can think about the complex materialities and temporalities of design in the geological epoch of the Anthropocene. By drawing in particular on the notion of 'arche-fossil', which is a term coined by philosopher Quentin Meillassoux in *After Finitude (*2010), I argue that such an approach can contribute not only to understanding the excavations of materiality of electronics from the earth, but it also lends support to discussions of electronics as future fossils in the geologic strata of the Anthropocene.

In the opening chapter of *After Finitude*, Meillassoux used a famous thought experiment based on cosmological/archaeological evidence ('arche-fossil') and 'ancienneté' to surpass the philosophical framework of correlationism and to imagine an objective, real-world anterior to the emergence of human life or every recognized form of life. In fact, 'arche-fossil' does not simply refer to fossils that have come before in time. Because no matter how radical one defines this 'beforeness' of arche-fossil in time (i.e., before humans, before life, before matter or even before the existence of the universe), it still will not be able to surpass correlationism if the pre-human 'beforeness' still bears any relation (causational, evolutional or any other relations) to the 'here and now' of the human world. Therefore, it was in this sense that Meillassoux rejected realism, which, in all its forms, always assumes an adequation between the human and the world. On the other hand, materialism pushes the discussion in a much more radical direction, proposing that matter exists not only anterior to and independent of humans but as something categorically different from humans (as complete, absolute alterity). That is the reason why Meillassoux added the qualificative 'arche-' before 'fossil' to indicate that it is not a fossil in the human sense; nor does it record any human 'traces' or 'origins' that can be retraced by any contemporary artificial perceptive and technological devices. For Meillasoux, this notion serves as a rejection of 'correlationism' attitude in post-Kantian philosophy, which advocates humans cannot exist without the world nor the world without humans (2010, 13–4). An 'arche-fossil', in his words, 'is not just materials indicating the traces of past life, according to the familiar sense of the term fossil, but materials indicating the existence of an ancestral reality or event; one that is anterior to terrestrial life' (2010, 22).[13] It is an absolute, which 'presents itself to us as non-relative to us, and hence as capable of existing whether we exist or not' (2010, 49).

The notion of 'arche-fossil' serves as a theoretical lens in approaching further hidden depths of materiality of electronics and offers a fresh perspective to speculate on the 'fossils of the future' mentioned above. It exists beyond human perception, measurement or even contemplation, independent of any human scales of time (whether it is physical time, psychological time or pure internal time in the phenomenological sense). As Meillassoux points out, 'the arche-fossil enjoins us . . . to get out of ourselves, to grasp the in-itself, to know whether we are or not' (2010, 27). As 'fossil', it testifies to its own existence; as 'memory', it proves the persistence of the universe. As such, it refers to deep time 'as a past that has never been present . . . this wordless prehistorical time, independent of any subject, is precisely the time of the elements, of ashes and dust' (Toadvine 2014, 266). In this chapter, 'ore' refers to ultimate 'anteriority' and 'beforeness', while 'future fossil' involves imaginations of the apocalypse. These embedded implications echo Meillassoux's speculative materialism, which underscores the persistence and alterity of matter.

To summarize, by taking the work of Quentin Meillassoux as exemplary, my effort is to construct a theoretical framework which offers fresh perspectives that can contribute to extending the material notions of electronics thoroughly towards deeper materialities and temporalities. The notion of 'arche-fossil' supports the argument concerning deep time and design, which also opens a new horizon for a design materialist analysis and speculates about the multiplicity of temporalities that constitute a set of very important questions regarding ores and fossils. Insights from new materialist scholarship are diverse, yet their implications for design and its history have, to date, been relatively unexamined. Furthermore, this chapter seeks to illustrate the potential of a 'new materialist' perspective to design and its histories, especially when it echoes the urgent challenges that the Anthropocene poses to it.

Notes

1 Canadian poet Don McKay mentioned during his lecture in 2008 that his poetry focuses on fossils, rocks and narratives about deep time. For further information, see McKay (2012).

2 For Bruno Latour, its 'polytemporal' properties are more important than the morphological properties of 'hybridity'. In his words, 'every cohort of elements may bring together elements from all times'. See Latour (1993), 75.

3 Guiyu is a small town located in Guangdong Province, China. It was once the largest e-waste site on Earth. Since the late 1980s, 70 per cent of the world's e-waste has been dumped to this town. E-waste mainly came from the United States, Japan, and other Western countries. This phenomenon continued until 2017, when China started completely banning foreign e-waste imports.

4 In the book *Theory of the Earth*, Hutton described the temporality of the Earth's metamorphosis as one in which 'we find no vestige of a beginning, – no prospect of an end'. See Hutton (1959), 200.

5 Huhtamo and Parikka, for example, claim that 'Media archaeology should not be confused with archaeology as a discipline. When media archaeologists claim that they are excavating media-cultural phenomena, the word should be understood in a specific way.' See Huhtamo and Parikka (2011), 3.

6 For Manuel DeLanda, Deleuze and Guattari's philosophy of immanence suggests a 'neo-materialism in which raw matter-energy, through a variety of self-organising processes and an intense, immanent power of morphogenesis, generates all the structures that surround us'. See DeLanda (1997).

7 de Almeida Meroz (2017). This argument has its implicit resonances with the way in which Graham Harman has pointed out 'objects' essentially 'escape' from all relationships. In his words, 'if there are objects, then they must exist in some sort of vacuum-like state, since no relation fully deploys them'.

8 See Kristensen (2014), 226–9; Acosta Maya (2000), 20; Sanderson, Susan and Uzumeri (1995), 761–82.

9 See Hosokawa (1984), 165–80; Chambers (1990), 1–4; du Gay et al. (1997); Bull (2001), 179–97.

10 The term 'Speculative Realism' derives from a conference held at Goldsmiths College, University of London, in April 2007. The conference featured presentations by Ray Brassier, Iain Hamilton, Graham Harman and Quentin Meillassoux, who have a shared resistance to what Meillassoux terms 'correlationism'. See Harman (2013, 2018); Bryant, Srnicek and Harman (2011).

11 Object-Oriented Ontology (OOO) is generally regarded as a philosophical school founded by Graham Harman. In addition to Harman, OOO is represented by theorists such as Levi Bryant, Timothy Morton and Ian Bogost. See Harman (2011, 2018); Bryant (2011); Morton (2013); Bogost (2012).

12 The notion of 'humans are not the sole agency' has been elaborated in many theories, including 'non-human/actants' (Latour), 'human-non-human assemblage' (Bennett), 'animism' (Harvey), 'object-oriented ontology' (Harman), 'new materialism' (Coole and Frost) and so on. Collectively, they contest a human-centred concept of agency and aim to break the old subject/object dualism. See Latour (1996), 369–81; Bennett (2010); Harvey (2005); Harman (2018); Coole and Frost (2010).

13 In Meillasoux's words, the term 'ancestral' refers to 'any reality anterior to the emergence of the human species – or even anterior to every recognised form of life on earth'. See Meillasoux (2010), 22.

References

Barad, Karen. 'Interview with Karen Barad'. In *New Materialism: Interviews & Cartographies*, edited by Rick Dolphijn and Iris van der Tuin. London: Open Humanities Press, 2012, 48–70.

Bennett, Jane. *Vibrant Matter: A Political Ecology of Things*. Durham: Duke University Press, 2010, 6.

Bennett, Tony and Patrick Joyce. *Material Powers: Cultural Studies, History and the Material Turn*. London: Routledge, 2010.
Benson, Melinda H. 'New Materialism: An Ontology for the Anthropocene'. *Natural Resources Journal* 59 (2019): 251–80.
Bogost, Ian. *Alien Phenomenology, or What It's Like to Be a Thing*. Minneapolis: The University of Minnesota Press, 2012.
Bolt, Barbara and Barrett, Estelle. *Carnal Knowledge: Towards a 'New Materialism' Through the Arts*. London: I.B. Tauris, 2013.
Bryant, Levi R. *The Democracy of Objects*. London: Open Humanities Press, 2011.
Bryant, Levi, Nick Srnicek and Graham Harman. *The Speculative Turn: Continental Materialism and Realism*. Melbourne: re.press, 2011.
Bull, Michael. 'The World According to Sound: Investigating the World of Walkman Users'. *New Media & Society* 3 (2001): 179–97.
Chakrabarty, Dipesh. 'Brute Force'. *Eurozine* 7 (2010): 1–3.
Chakrabarty, Dipesh. 'The Climate of History: Four Theses'. *Critical Inquiry* 35 (2009): 197–222.
Chambers, Iain. 'A Miniature History of the Walkman'. *New Formations: A Journal of Culture/Theory/Politics* 11 (1990): 1–4.
Coole, Diana and Samantha Frost. *New Materialisms: Ontology, Agency, and Politics*. Durham: Duke University Press, 2010.
DeLanda, Manuel. 'Immanence and Transcendence in the Genesis of Form'. *South Atlantic Quarterly* 96 (1997): 499–514.
Dolphijn, Rick and Iris van der Tuin. *New Materialism: Interviews & Cartographies*. London: Open Humanities Press, 2012.
du Gay, et al. *Doing Cultural Studies: The Story of the Sony Walkman*, 1st edn. London: Sage Publications, 1997.
du Gay, et al. *Doing Cultural Studies: The Story of the Sony Walkman*, 2nd edn. Los Angeles: Sage Publications, 2013, xviii.
Fallan, Kjetil. *Design History: Theory and Method*. Oxford: Berg Publishers, 2010, 4–11, 33.
Fry, Tony, Clive Dilnot and Susan Stewart. *Design and the Question of History*. London: Bloomsbury, 2015, 8–9.
Gabrys, Jennifer. *Digital Rubbish: A Natural History of Electronics*. Ann Arbor: University of Michigan Press, 2011, 7.
Harman, Graham. *Bells and Whistles: More Speculative Realism*. Alresford: Zero Books, 2013.
Harman, Graham. *Guerrilla Metaphysics: Phenomenology and the Carpentry of Things*. Chicago: Open Court, 2005.
Harman, Graham. *Object-Oriented Ontology: A New Theory of Everything*. London: Pelican, 2018.
Harman, Graham. *Speculative Realism: An Introduction*. Cambridge: Polity Press, 2018.
Harman, Graham. *The Quadruple Object*. Alresford: Zero Books, 2011.
Harvey, Graham. *Animism: Respecting the Living World*. New York: Columbia University Press, 2005.
Heskett, John. *Industrial Design*. London: Thames and Hudson, 1980, 7–9.
Highmore, Ben. 'A Sideboard Manifesto: Design Culture in an Artificial World'. In *The Design Culture Reader*, edited by Ben Highmore. London: Routledge, 2009, 1–11.
Hosokawa, Shuhei. 'The Walkman Effect'. *Popular Music*, 4 (1984): 165–80.
Huhtamo, Erkki and Jussi Parikka. *Media Archaeology: Approaches, Applications, and Implications*. Berkeley: University of California Press, 2011, 10.
Hutton, James. *Theory of The Earth*. Codicote: Wheldon and Wesley, 1959.
Julier, Guy. *The Culture of Design*. Los Angeles: SAGE Publications, 2008.
Kristensen, Juliette. 'Sony Walkman, Japan (Nobutoshi Kihara, 1978)'. In *Iconic Designs: 50 Stories About 50 Things*, edited by Grace Lees-Maffei. London: Bloomsbury Visual Arts, 2014, 226–9.
Latour, Bruno. 'On Actor-network Theory: A Few Clarifications'. *Soziale Welt*, 47 (1996): 369–81.
Latour, Bruno. *We Have Never Been Modern*. Cambridge, MA: Harvard University Press, 1993.
Maya, Santiago Acosta. 'The Sony Walkman'. *Revista Universidad EAFIT* 36, no. 117 (2000): 19–27.
McKay, Don. 'Ediacaran and Anthropocene: Poetry as a Reader of Deep Time'. In *Making the Geologic Now*, edited by Elizabeth Ellsworth and Jamie Kruse. New York: Punctum, 2012, 46–55.

Meillasoux, Quentin. *After Finitude: An Essay on the Necessity of Contingency*. London: Continuum, 2010, 27, 49.

Meroz, J. Ozorio de Almeida. 'The Environment as "Context" in Design Historiography'. In Proceedings / Book of Abstracts of the Design History Society, 2017. https://www.academia.edu/34551907/The_Environment_as_Context_in_Design_Historiography.

Morton, Timothy. *Hyperobjects: Philosophy and Ecology After the End of the World*. Minneapolis: University of Minnesota Press, 2013.

Parikka, Jussi. *A Geology of Media*. Minneapolis: University of Minnesota Press, 2015, 35.

Revital Cohen and Tuur Van Balen, *H / AlCuTaAu*, 2014. Accessed 19 March 2021.

Sanderson, Susan and Mustafa Uzumeri. 'Managing Product Families: The Case of the Sony Walkman'. *Research Policy* 24 (1995): 761–82.

Sparke, Penny. *An Introduction to Design and Culture: 1900 to the Present*. London: Routledge, 2013, xii.

Steffen, Will, Paul J. Crutzen and McNeill, John R. 'The Anthropocene: Are Humans Now Overwhelming the Great Forces of Nature?' *AMBIO: A Journal of the Human Environment* 36 (2007): 614–21.

Studio Formafantasma, *Ore Streams, 2017–2019*. Accessed 19 March 2021.http://www.orestreams.com

Toadvine, Ted. 'The Elemental Past'. *Research in Phenomenology* 44 (2014): 262–79.

Zielinski, Siegfried. *Deep Time of the Media: Toward an Archaeology of Hearing and Seeing by Technical Means*. Cambridge, MA: The MIT Press, 2006.

11 ORBITAL DEBRIS

DESIGN AND ITS EXTRA-TERRESTRIAL AFTERMATH

Alice Twemlow

When the sociologist Roland Barthes encountered the new Citroën D.S. at the 1955 Paris Auto Show, he considered it obvious that this 'superlative object' had 'fallen from the sky' (Barthes 1991, 88). The achievements and accoutrements of space travel fuelled the post-war auto industry and the Western imagination of modernity. Whether in Poissy or Detroit, designers channelled Space Age aesthetics for their cars that the artist Richard Hamilton described as being 'fabulously wrought like rocket[s] and space probe[s]' (Hamilton 1963, 53).

Outer space, whether seen as a conceptual *tabula rasa* from which cosmological forms were summoned for application to earthly functions or as a mysterious metaphoric 'world above that of nature' from which vehicles fell, fully manufactured, into cultural discourse, has long provided design with its ultimate reference point and horizon for cognitive as well as actual colonization.

In the sixty years since the publishing of Barthes' now-famous essay, however, space, as a context for design, has been transformed. What was once an infinite expanse of pre-design possibilities is now an increasingly finite dumping zone for pieces of post-design waste. Trillions of pieces, in fact.

From the perspective of French sociologists, science fiction production designers and televised launch viewers, rockets may seem to be made of 'unbroken metal' just as cars were considered to be 'juxtaposed and [held] together by sole virtue of their wondrous shape' (Barthes 1991, 88). But, up close, and after decades in orbit, their surfaces are less like 'cake icing' and more like steampunk artichokes – with dandruff.

In the sixty years since the successful launch of the first artificial satellite, Sputnik 1, almost 15,000 objects (satellites, probes, landers, crewed spacecrafts and space station flight elements) have been propelled into space. About 9,000 of those, in various states of repair, are still operational and orbiting Earth. The rest have been abraded into what was recently estimated to be 100 trillion pieces of space debris whirling around in the Low Earth Orbit (LEO) region (the area of space below an altitude of 2,000 kilometres) (Sample 2023). There are some stray nuts and bolts – errant spatulas, even – but most, like Mylar chips and plastic flakes, are small in size individually. The fact that they circle the planet at 17,500 miles an hour and their population is increasing so rapidly, however, means they frequently collide with one another and create yet more fragments. This phenomenon of 'ablation cascade' was predicted in 1978 by National Aeronautics and Space Administration (NASA) scientist Donald Kessler (Stewart 2016, 108). Kessler, who later became chair of the Orbital Debris Program Office, has observed that 'any attempt to achieve a growth-free small debris environment by eliminating sources of past debris will likely fail because fragments from future collisions will be generated faster than atmospheric drag will remove them' (2019).

Attempting to dodge the proliferation of 'space junk', as it has become known, is expensive and dangerous. The pieces of debris larger than 1 centimetre can cause spacecraft to completely break up and, with each collision, create hundreds to thousands of new debris objects. Even the very small fragments of less than 1 centimetre can render spacecraft inoperable or destroy sensitive components, causing damage to navigation, communication and weather forecasting systems. NASA's chief scientist for orbital debris Nicholas Johnson believes that the most significant risk to space missions is the smallest and least trackable bits of debris, due largely to the uncertainty of when and from where they may strike. Apart from the inconvenience caused to the communications, defence and other emergent space industries that comprise what NASA calls the LEO Economy, the potential for significant scientific study is also being hampered. For example, the International Space Station (ISS) is

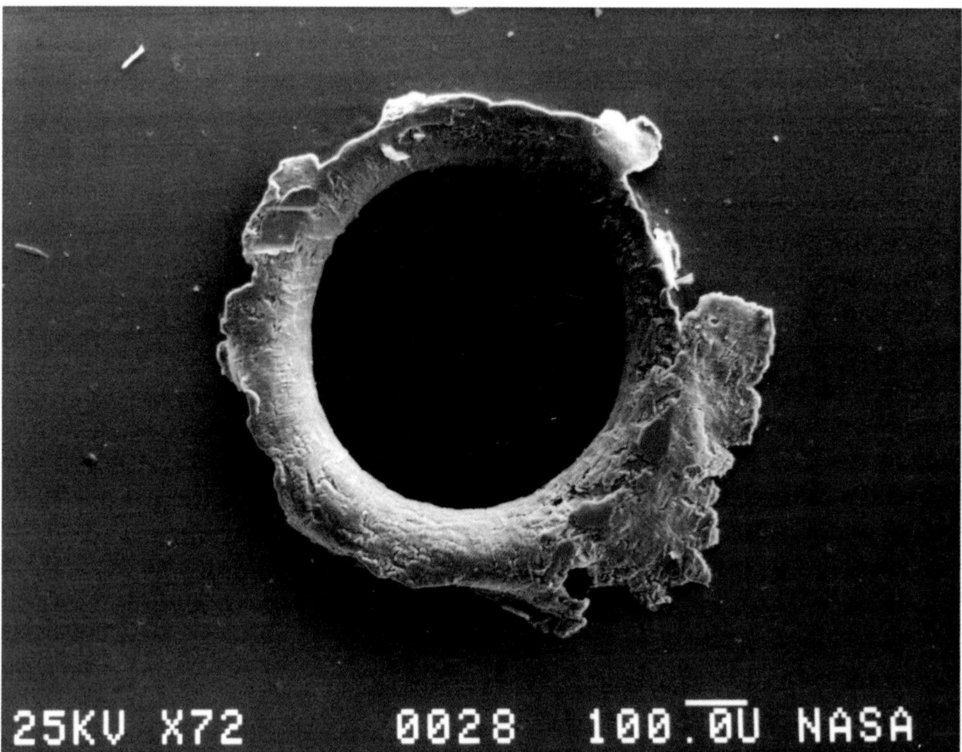

Figure 11.1 Orbital debris hole made in the panel of the Solar Max satellite, 2006. Courtesy of NASA.

vulnerable to damage and on three occasions in 2022 alone, it had to engage in what are termed Debris Avoidance Manoeuvres. October 2014 saw one of the closest shaves at ISS, when six astronauts only just survived a junk collision by sacrificing an automated transfer vehicle to take the impact (Boucher 2014).

Meanwhile, the trend towards mega-constellations of small satellites continues without being checked. The broadband satellite internet services company OneWeb has a constellation of 648, and Elon Musk's spacecraft manufacturer, launcher and satellite communications company SpaceX has launched more than 3,000 Starlink satellites and is planning to launch a further 9,000 by 2026. The latest report from the Inter-Agency Space Debris Coordination Committee posits that the amount of space junk in orbit will double within twenty-five years and, because of the exponentially increasing collisions, could increase a further fifty times by 2100.

* * *

The fallout of capitalist industrial processes, behaviours and ideals has wreaked irreparable damage on our planet's life forms and habitats. In order to practice, teach, learn and research the skills and capacities needed to repair our connection with other beings and entities – let alone to shape liveable futures – we need to attend to alternative understandings of time beyond the Capitalocenic, linear, progressive and globally synchronized, and towards the cyclical, plural and cosmological.

Relevant in this respect is the geological concept of *deep time*, first described by the eighteenth-century Scottish geologist James Hutton, who saw that the cycles of sedimentation and erosion, which had given the planet its stratified topography, must have required a timescale that not only exploded the Biblical creation narrative but also was of a magnitude so vast that in it, 'we find no vestige of a beginning, no prospect of an end' (1788, 223). The Royal Academy of Art Deep Futures Research Group (KABK) (2017–) is based on the premise that this immensity of timescale can be a departure point exploring the ways in which art and design research might contribute to a more nuanced understanding of climate catastrophe, planetary degradation and the loss of biodiversity. The group's collectively generated research is shared via publications, exhibitions and an annual conference (Fault Lines) and includes glossaries of key terms, open-source repositories of references, recipes, resources and essay-making (text, audio, visual and video). Above all, it seeks to develop and experiment with new methods for practice-based research and for embedding it in art and design education – for compositing climate justice imaginaries needed to navigate our post-Capitalocenic, posthuman futures. Just as there is a temporal continuum between the deep time of our planet's geological past and the deep future of the consequences of our design products, processes and values, we also need to conceive spatially of how, and how far, those consequences extend. As a reviewer of *Dr Space Junk Vs The Universe: Archaeology and the Future* notes, 'an entanglement of pastness and futurity is intrinsic to outer space for while the night sky presents us visually with intermingling pasts, the idea of preservation entails a future into which these pasts are cast' (Gorman 2022, 422).

* * *

In 1948 English astronomer Fred Hoyle speculated that 'once a photograph of the Earth, taken from the outside, is available, a new idea as powerful as any in history will be let loose' (Yoder 2022). And, indeed, when the *Earthrise* image taken from the spacecraft Apollo 8 was published in 1969, its power as an idea and icon was co-opted both by an emergent environmental movement and by corporate interests. Its ability to instantly convey the integrated beauty of the planet's natural ecosystem and its fragility helped galvanize a demand for pro-environmental legislation and the inception of the first Earth Day in 1970. It also led to new conceptions of planetary management and imperial control and has become increasingly reinscribed as what Neil Turnbull has referred to as 'a representation of global corporate prowess' (2006, 133).

The 'overview effect', as space philosopher Frank White dubbed it, was the cognitive shift brought about by perceiving Earth from space in which it was possible to have an intense emotional reaction and an increased sense of connection to other people and the Earth as a whole. Even though only a handful of humans experienced this effect directly, the 'stream of transmitted pictures' of Earth and the proliferation of new terminology to convey the sense of being *global* in the 1970s meant that a simulation of this total overview of the planet took shape in the public imaginary. And even as this image of wholeness, integration and relationality was forming, the magnitude of its distribution meant that it was simultaneously shattering, as philosopher Susan Buck-Morss has described, into signals of a new, fragmented global era where exploded structures of history are 'scattering fragments of the past forward into unanticipated locations', creating combinations and juxtapositions that offer 'new readings of the past as a way of charting a different future' (2015).

We cannot photograph the space junk phenomenon in its entirety, but because around 40,000 pieces of debris are catalogued and tracked by the US Space Surveillance Network and maintained in their catalogue, there are plenty of real-time interactive maps through which orbits of particular pieces can be tracked and renderings through which their distribution is plotted. Some of the illustrations in circulation are quite old (one of the most frequently used dates from 2005) and exhibit various peculiarities of representation. The images based on NASA data, for example, are generated from what the image captions describe as 'a distant oblique vantage point' and, in order to optimize their visibility, the plotted dots are scaled not according to the size of the Earth but rather to the image dimensions.

What the various renderings have in common is their depiction of a planet doubly imprisoned by its own trash – 'scattered fragments of its past' – first by a densely packed low-orbit perimeter cloud which in turn is encircled by a looser ring of the higher-orbit pieces. This variant of post-photographic digital self-portrait – albeit more of an avatar or a selfie with all the filters – is enabled by the very orbiting imaging devices that, as they deteriorate, will become part of the captured image itself. It is 'operational' in the sense of filmmaker Harun Farocki's definition – an image that can track, navigate, activate, oversee, control, visualize, detect and identify (Hoel 2018, 12). There is something rather depressing about how easily it has usurped the place of those instantly-visually-graspable-and-ye t-resonant-and-profound analogue images taken by the Apollo 8 and Apollo 17 crews, respectively.

But could it also be that this new species of constantly updating, networked, publicly available, plotting-as-imaging is just as powerful, in its way, and 'operational' not just in the technological sense of the term but also in the way it can 'activate' emotional response in humans? Space archaeologist Alice Gorman has observed during an online article for *Scientific American* that space junk, far from being useless, as the label implies, has an important social function where its 'value comes from shaping people's ideas of what space is and how they are connected to it' (Billings 2019).

The novelist Amitav Ghosh has convincingly argued that our era's 'failure in the face of climate emergency' is a 'failure of the imagination' (2016, 9). Ghosh examines our inability – at the level of history, politics and literature – to comprehend climate events' extreme scale and violence. The pollution of space, while imperceptible to the human eye, is extremely legible and even spectacular to the human imagination. Might the vivid composite of renderings and impressions of our planet, with its ultimate escape route being closed off by a dense cloud of colliding, exploding and self-replicating debris, provide us with the impetus we seem to need to attend to the other invisible and insidious stranglehold on our atmosphere – that of carbon-dioxide?

This chapter explores some of the approaches to the mitigation of space junk. It considers how research at the intersection of art and design practices, history, media archaeology, speculative fiction and the environmental humanities might contribute a needed critique of the non-sustainable, techno-determinist modes of intervention currently being deployed, bring about deeper understanding and offer alternative imaginaries of the extra-terrestrial aftermath of design, in the context of the earth-orbital environmental crises.

* * *

Inquiring minds at dozens of academic research institutes worldwide have been ignited by the challenge of space debris and supported in their endeavours by private venture capital that perceives a viable business opportunity in the SpaceTech niche, as well as by government and regional funding bodies.

Figure 11.2 'Energy flash' produced in a simulation of a piece of orbital debris colliding with a spacecraft in orbit at a speed of up to 17,000 miles an hour. Tested at the Hypervelocity Ballistic Range at NASA's Ames Research Center, 2017. Courtesy of NASA.

Some run simulation experiments to calculate the impact of debris on spacecraft materials and components, while others measure the density of pieces of debris in low earth orbit, so that the extent of damage of impending collisions can be accurately predicted. Elsewhere, the emphasis is on education and public awareness.

Remediation through removal, however, gets the most attention. Among the thousands of patents that have been filed since the early 1990s which purport to solve the problem of space debris removal, recurring tropes emerge: snagging nets and tentacles; shooting lasers and harpoons; sweeping robots; and dragging tethers, parachutes or solar sails. Most of the innovation uses space's natural incinerating zone; the gadgets are meant to nudge, tow, sling-shot or otherwise propel the waste towards Earth's lowest orbit where it will burn up on re-entry. A piece of junk dragged below an altitude of about 500 kilometres will burn up within twenty-five years; if left above that, it would take centuries. However, these figures will have to be adjusted as we continue to emit too much carbon dioxide and the temperature of the Earth's troposphere decreases, making it less dense, which hinders the debris from falling to the threshold of Earth's atmosphere.

Among the technologies being tested during increasing numbers of missions dedicated to this purpose are the European Space Agency Space Debris Office's e.DeOrbit mission to retrieve the derelict satellite Envisat with a double whammy of nets and tentacle-like cables. The mission was taken over by Switzerland's ClearSpace-1 programme, which wanted to demonstrate its Active Debris Removal technology, which its CEO characterized as a 'tow truck' (Piguet 2019). In 2022 the Japanese company Astroscale tested its End-of-Life Services and successfully demonstrated 'tracking of an object from a great distance and rendezvous with an uncontrolled object' as part of its ELSA-d mission (Astroscale 2023). A tiny three-unit CubeSat called OSCaR (Obsolete Spacecraft Capture and Removal), designed to clean up debris with its onboard nets and tethers, and developed at Rensselaer Polytechnic Institute in New York, is scheduled for a five-year mission, after which it is programmed to self-destroy along with the junk it captured. The research team says they 'envision a day where we could send up an entire flock, or squadron, of OSCaRs to work jointly going after large collections of debris' (Anderson 2019).

As these proposed technological solutions proliferate, there is an emerging danger that these autonomous gadgets, if not regulated, will themselves become part of the problem they are trying to solve.

Another type of approach focuses less on removing individual pieces of debris and more on tracking, surveillance and measuring to safeguard operational crafts. The NASA Orbital Debris Program Office, in cooperation with the US Space Force, uses a network of ground-based radar systems to track and catalogue space debris in real-time, creating what they refer to as a 'space fence'. In military aviation, to 'fence in' means you are ready for battle and are entering enemy air space; your weapons are armed, and avionics are in combat mode. This kind of linguistic slippage is typical of the ongoing normalization in political and popular discourse of the enclosure and militarization of orbital and outer space.

* * *

Space debris constitutes a 'hyperobject', in the sense that philosopher and ecological theorist Timothy Morton uses the term as a phenomenon (such as global warming or poverty or plastic waste) so confused and massively distributed in time and space as to transcend spatiotemporal specificity. Hyperobjects, according to Morton are: 'viscous' in that they stick to the things to which they relate; not easy to define and tend to flood discourses; generally, not visible (even if we see something, it is only a part of the hyperobject); and their temporalities exceed the human sense of time (2013, 27–37).

Space debris is also a species of 'super wicked problem'. It is characterized by 'incomplete, contradictory, and changing requirements that are often difficult to recognise' (which renders it 'wicked') and it is additionally burdened by the four criteria of 'super'-resistant problems: the fact there is a time deadline on finding the solution; no central authority is dedicated to finding a solution; those seeking to solve the problem are also causing it; and certain policies irrationally impede future progress (Levin et al. 2012, 123–52).

Whether conceived through the lens of Object-Oriented Ontology or political science, the more-than-global scale of the issue creates the need for international cooperation and international legal regulation. As the race to the moon was gathering momentum in the late 1960s, the United Nations (UN) established a Committee on the Peaceful Uses of Outer Space (UNCOPUOS) to review, among other things, legal problems arising from space-related conduct. It went on to develop five international treaties and five sets of principles governing outer space. Of these, the 1967 Outer Space Treaty (OST) is still relevant today and considered by space lawyers as akin to a constitution. Article IX in the OST requires states to conduct their outer space activities 'with due regard to the corresponding interests of all other States Parties'. But space debris is not explicitly mentioned in any space law treaty.

In 2002 the Inter-Agency Space Debris Coordination Committee (IADC) was founded to address this omission. The Committee organizes conferences and issues documents such as its *Space Debris Mitigation Guidelines*, which were updated in 2021. While its recommendations for mitigation measures have found broad consensus, and thirteen national agencies are members, there is no mechanism to enforce compliance. The Committee still considers there is much to be done to raise awareness of space farers, decision takers and the interested public and develop a common understanding and route towards a sustainable space environment.

It is hard to imagine a binding space debris treaty being agreed upon in today's political climate since, as Christopher Newman, a Professor of Space Law and Policy at Northumbria University, observes, 'the very nations who need to compromise are geopolitical adversaries' (The Guardian 2023). For example, on 15 November 2021, while on Earth Russia was engaged in a full-scale invasion of Ukraine, it launched a direct-ascent anti-satellite test to destroy one of its own defunct satellites. The explosion created a huge amount of new space debris and drew condemnation from the international community, underlining how closely linked are the environmental geopolitics of Earth and outer space (Amos 2021).

One of the most 'super-wicked' and 'hyper' aspects of the challenge of regulating international agreement is that all of our space agencies are inextricably tied to national governments and militaries. As the Future Today Institute chief executive has noted, enforcing space debris prevention guidelines would involve each country divulging exactly what it was launching and when, and this scenario remains 'unlikely' (Webb 2018). The private sector is potentially in a better position to collaborate to build grand-scale orbital cleaning mechanisms, but immediate launches drive their commercial interests, which are often entangled with national governments.

But it seems the real impediment may be less about diplomacy and more about epistemology. In a 2016 interview, former NASA scientist Kessler explained that one of the main impediments to achieving meaningful solutions is located in the lack of a legal, internationally agreed definition of space debris

(Stewart 2016, 103). NASA describes it as 'all man-made objects in orbit about the Earth which no longer serve a useful purpose'. The European Space Agency's definition sounds similar but differs on points of detail: 'all non-functional, artificial objects, including fragments and elements thereof, in Earth orbit or re-entering into Earth's atmosphere'. While individual governments, agencies and corporations are doing the defining, those seeking justification for their non-compliance with the guidelines will always find a loophole or an interpretation to work with. As space becomes increasingly valuable as a resource-commodity-territory-lab, it will raise more complex philosophical and ethical questions about the nature of ownership, nation statehood, governance and the relationship between human beings and the natural environment.

* * *

In all our utopian and dystopian imaginaries, waste is a factor, sometimes conspicuous by its sterile absence but usually by its excessive presence. English Professor Brian Thill notes how waste, trash, the dirty and unclean assert themselves in science fiction as 'signs of the stubborn resistance to total order that advanced societies are supposed to be shepherding us toward' (2015, 48). Space debris, in particular, plays a vital role in both the world-building and world-undoing of science fiction plotting. In many instances, such as the 1970s TV sitcom *Quark*, 1990s hard sci-fi anime *Planetes* and the 2021 Korean movie *Space Sweepers*, the action revolves around multispecies gangs collecting garbage in deep space. Others, such as the 1950s pulp novel *Deadly Litter*, or episode eight of the first season of *Futurama*, depict the 'Armageddon' moment when Earth is threatened by an approaching giant ball of garbage of its own making. The 2013 movie *Gravity* focuses on the threat to individual humans in space who are separated from their craft by a massive cloud of debris. Even documentaries such as *Collision Point: The Race to Clean Up Space* and *Space Junk 3D* lean on science fiction tropes to activate the viewers' imaginative engagement with the topic.

An early instance of a literary imaginary that bridges the earth-orbit divide is the menacing and entropic agency of 'kipple' in the Philip K. Dick novel *Do Androids Dream of Electric Sheep*, published in 1968, and the 1982 *Bladerunner* movie it inspired. Kipple in Dick's post-apocalyptic dystopia is 'useless objects, like junk mail or match folders after you use the last match or gum wrappers or yesterday's homeopape' (1968, 30). At night and when you leave your home, the kipple reproduces itself. JR explains to Pris, whose own home has been overrun, how 'the First Law of Kipple' is that it drives out nonkipple. 'We can roll the kipple-factor back', he says, but ultimately:

> No one can win against kipple [. . .] except temporarily and maybe in one spot, like in my apartment I've sort of created a stasis between the pressure of kipple and nonkipple, for the time being. But eventually I'll die or go away, and then the kipple will again take over. It's a universal principle operating throughout the universe; the entire universe is moving toward a final state of total, absolute kippleization. (1968, 30–1)

An example of the kind of contribution that can be made by visual arts research is *Project Adrift*, a series of films and installations by artists Cath Le Couteur and Nick Ryan. Practice-based research inquiries in art and design have the potential to introduce nuance to the dominant geopolitical narrative, to counter the techno-solutionist approach with critical ambivalence and to contribute an alternative and more-than-visual means of engagement with the space debris hyperobject.

Figure 11.3 *Debris-o-Gram* (live holographic projection of the Earth with each dot in the visualization representing one of 52,829 pieces of catalogued space junk, with its position calculated in real-time), 2017. Courtesy of Nick Ryan and Cath Le Couteur.

Motivated by the enigmatic qualities of orbital debris and the emotions it can evoke, such as awe, fear, loneliness and even love, their work takes account of the senses in seeking to render space junk 'personal, visible, audible'. Five of the artworks from the project were assembled for the exhibition *Cosmos Archaeology – Explorations in Time and Space*, held in late 2022 in the EPFL Pavilions in Lausanne. Among them was *Debris-o-Gram*, where the positions of 52,829 pieces of debris were visualized as part of a live holographic projection of Earth. There is something disturbing and moving about the scale of this installation. Positioned on a plinth at eye level, and as small as a tennis ball, this little Earth is the same size as the *Earthrise* and *Blue Marble* images, and even as its holographic dimensionality invites our caress it denies it.

The best-known part of the project is *Adrift*, a film that combines footage from space missions, interviews with astronomers and the astronaut and meteorologist Piers Sellers (the one who during the 2006 Mission STS-121 says, 'Guys . . . I gotta tell you . . . I think my spatula's escaped') and is narrated from the perspective of Vanguard, the oldest piece of space junk being tracked in orbit. In the most participatory aspect of the project, individual pieces of debris can be 'adopted' via Twitter (@VanguardAdrift, @FengyunAdrift and @SuitSatAdrift tweet status reports and can respond to your questions).

There are seventeen pieces of trash displayed reverently in a velvet-lined vitrine (representatives of a larger collection of 250, each selected by participants for how it symbolized space debris). These bits of tin foil, bicycle wheels and squashed ping pong balls were recorded in action to create a library of sonic signatures.

Based on the activation of open databases that track the movements of orbital debris (such as celestrak.com and celestrak.com/satcat), Machine 9 responds to pieces of tracked debris as they pass over where the machine is located. Using the size of each piece as a guide to pitch, Machine 9 selects a sound from a library of 1,000 foley audio recordings derived from the pieces of 'Earthly Debris' and plays it across a surround sound system of eight speakers. The moment that an object disappears over the detectable horizon, it falls silent.

Visualizations of orbital debris released by the space agencies are becoming ever more accurate and sophisticated. They are compelling, but what is more likely to create the kind of cognitive shift or overview effect needed to incite collective action around climate justice all across the earth-orbit environment continuum is the kind of multidimensional activation of all our senses and the experiential immersion in data that Le Couteur and Ryan are attempting to achieve.

* * *

In 2019 the entrepreneur Elon Musk strapped his $100,000 cherry-red convertible Tesla Roadster to the SpaceX Falcon Heavy (the most powerful operational rocket at that time) and, with the top down and a mannequin at the wheel listening to David Bowie, sent it far into outer space. Its heliocentric progress that crosses the orbit of Mars can be tracked at whereisroadster.com.

Philosopher Roland Barthes was knocked down and fatally injured by a laundry van in 1980. He would probably be intrigued by the fact that in less than the average human lifetime, we have gone from it seeming 'obvious' that a fossil-fuel-run Citroën would fall from space to Earth, to making it possible for a multi-billionaire to muster five million pounds of rocket thrust to send his electrically powered car from Earth 400 million kilometres into space, where it is predicted to orbit for hundreds of millions or even billions of years. Unless, of course, it collides with a piece of space junk.

In 1584, the cosmological theorist Giordano Bruno wrote three *Cosmological Dialogues*, including *Of the Infinite Universe and Worlds*, in which he laid out his thinking about the limited nature of the human perspective:

> The ancient observed, and we also observe, that sometimes things fall to Earth, or some things leave the Earth, or whatever parts we may be near [. . .] something passing from us to the moon would look the opposite to those across from us on the moon; where we would say, something has ascended, those moon people, our anticephali, would say that something has descended. (2014, 260)

In 1600 Bruno was burned to death, deemed a heretic for daring to propose an alternative cosmological perspective beyond the prevailing one of his era. He probably would have been grateful to learn that in 1961 a 22-kilometre-wide impact crater on the moon, with an ejecta radius of up to 150 kilometres, was named in his honour. But he would also be frustrated with how long it has taken us to catch up to his ability to conceive of cosmological pluralism. And, as he pointed out in his careful source citation of 'the ancient', catching up is not necessarily about linear time progression; it might require a circular return.

'If we have learned anything from the exploration of space', wrote historian and political philosopher Hannah Arendt in 1963, 'it is that man is an inhabitant of a small planet, a tiny part of a universe far too vast to be measured or imagined, and that his existence depends upon an understanding of and willingness to adapt to the rest of the universe, which lies beyond his grasp as a sensing organism' (2007, 43–55). She argued that human senses are limited in their ability to grasp the vastness of space, which presents a challenge to human achievement. She details how science leads us to distrust our senses and replaces a 'common sense' objective worldview with a subjective worldview where we treat objects as things that are disposable and changeable by man, and the world as man-made. Her question, 'Has man's conquest of space increased or diminished his stature?' still hangs in the balance. While an anthropocentric worldview might temporarily or illusorily create the impression of an increased stature for man, it also diminishes it, as in the process, humans become objects among many, just as liable as a plastic spatula to disintegrate into flecks of space junk.

Thus far, a conception of design history, which came of age in Britain in the 1970s, has concentrated its efforts on examining design within the frameworks of production, consumption and, more recently, mediation. What happens to design after its period of usefulness is over, however, is studied much less. By expanding the paradigm of design history to incorporate a fourth area of concern, *disposal* (even if that means we need to extend an account of aftermath to billions of years), we can achieve a fuller understanding of material culture's impact on the environment, including the far-reaching, long-lasting consequences of one of the most fascinating, humbling and disturbing of anthropogenic hyperobjects – the accumulation of space junk. As Morton frames it, hyperobjects constitute co-collections, assemblages, metaphors or narratives of other objects or semi-objects. Hyperobjects are also strategies to attempt an understanding of, as Giordano Bruno put it in 1591, 'innumerable things, vastness and the unrepresentable.'

To avoid being consumed by the hyperobjects of our era, design and the research-based, theoretical and historical practices that gather around it will need a more-than-human conception of time and a more-than-geo-centric notion of space. It will also need to interface with more disciplines, such as environmental humanities, media archaeology and artistic research, in order to generate the kinds of imaginative yet rigorous research that addresses the urgent challenges facing the planet and the preservation of that most precious of the planet's commons – its orbital environment.

References

Amos, Jonathan. 'Russian Anti-Satellite Missile Test Draws Condemnation'. *BBC News*, 16 November 2021. Accessed 3 April 2023. https://www.bbc.com/news/science-environment-59299101

Anderson, Kurt. 'Rensselaer Team Developing Tool to Battle Space Debris'. *Rensselaer Polytechnic Institute*, 23 April 2019. Accessed 5 March 2022. https://news.rpi.edu/content/2019/04/23/rensselaer-team-developing-tool-battle-space-debris

Arendt, Hannah. 'The Conquest of Space and the Stature of Man'. *The New Atlantis*, 18 (2007): 43–55.

Astroscale 'Astroscale's ELSA-d Mission Successfully Completes Complex Rendezvous Operation', Accessed 29 March 2023. https://astroscale.com/astroscales-elsa-d-mission-successfully-completes-complex-rendezvous-operation/

Barthes, Roland. *Mythologies*. New York: Noonday Press, 1991, 88.

Boucher, Mark. 'NASA ISS Orbit Status. Space Ref'. *Space Ref*, 24 July 2014. Accessed 30 March 2023. https://spaceref.com/space-stations/nasa-iss-on-orbit-status-23-july-2014/

Buck-Morss, Susan. 'Seeing Global'. 17 October 2015. Accessed 30 March 2023. https://www.susanbuckmorss.info/text/seeing-global/

Dick, Philip K. *Do Androids Dream of Electric Sheep?* New York: Doubleday, 1968, 30.

European Space Agency. 'European Space Agency Space Environment Report 2022'. Accessed 30 March 2023. https://www.esa.int/Space_Safety/Space_Debris/ESA_s_Space_Environment_Report_2022

European Space Agency. 2021. 'Frequently Asked Questions on Space Debris Answered by the Team at ESA's Space Debris Office'. Accessed 4 April 2023. https://www.esa.int/Space_Safety/Space_Debris/FAQ_Frequently_asked_questions

Ghosh, Amitav. *The Great Derangement: Climate Change and the Unthinkable*. Chicago: Chicago University Press, 2016, 9.

Giordano, Bruno. *On the Infinite, the Universe and the Worlds: Five Cosmological Dialogues*, trans. Scott Gosnell. CreateSpace Independent Publishing Platform, 2014, 260.

Gorman, Alice. Quoted in Lee Billings, 'Space Archaeologist Probes History in Orbit'. 25 September 2019. Accessed 30 March 2023. https://www.scientificamerican.com/article/space-archaeologist-probes-history-in-orbit/

Gorman, Alice. 'Review. *Dr Space Junk Vs the Universe: Archaeology and the Future*'. *Journal of Visual Culture* 19, no. 3 (2022): 422.

Hamilton, Richard. 'The Institute of Contemporary Arts'. *Living Arts* 2 (1963): 53.

Hoel, Aud Sissel. 'Operative Images: Inroads to a New Paradigm of Media Theory'. In *Image – Action – Space: Situating the Screen in Visual Practice*, edited by Luisa Feiersinger, Kathrin Friedrich and Moritz Queisner. Berlin: De Gruyter, 2018, 12.

Hutton, James. 'Theory of the Earth; or An Investigation of the Laws Observable in the Composition, Dissolution, and Restoration of Land upon the Globe'. *Transactions of the Royal Society of Edinburgh* 1, no. 2 (1788): 223.

Kessler, Donald. 'The Kessler Syndrome'. *Web Archive*, 8 March 2019. Accessed 30 March 2023. https://web.archive.org/web/20100527195029/http:/webpages.charter.net/dkessler/files/KesSym.html

Levin, Kelly, Cashore, Benjamin, Bernstein, Stevenand, and Graeme Auld. 'Overcoming the Tragedy of Super Wicked Problems: Constraining our Future Selves to Ameliorate Global Climate Change'. *Policy Sci* 45 (2012): 123–52.

Morton, Timothy. *Hyperobjects: Philosophy and Ecology after the End of the World*. Minneapolis: University of Minnesota Press, 2013, 27–37.

NASA. 'Space Debris and Human Spacecraft'. Accessed 4 April 2023. https://www.nasa.gov/mission_pages/station/news/orbital_debris.html

Newman, Christopher. Quoted in Ian Sample, 'Legally Binding Global Treaty Needed to Tackle Space Debris, Say Experts'. *The Guardian*, 9 March 2023. Accessed 30 March 2023. https://www.theguardian.com/science/2023/mar/09/global-treaty-space-debris-earth-orbit-junk

Orbital Debris. 'IADC Space Debris Mitigation Guidelines', IADC-02-01 Rev. 3 June 2021. Accessed 14 March 2023. https://orbitaldebris.jsc.nasa.gov/library/iadc-space-debris-guidelines-revision-2.pdf

Our World in Data. 'Cumulative Number of Objects Launched into Space'. Accessed 30 March 2023. https://ourworldindata.org/grapher/cumulative-number-of-objects-launched-into-outer-space?country=OWID_WRL~USA~RUS~CHN~GBR~JPN~FRA~IND~DEU~European+Space+Agency

Piguet, Luc. 'Esa Commissions World's First Space Debris Removal'. *European Space Agency*, 9 December 2019. Accessed 29 March 2023. https://www.esa.int/Space_Safety/Clean_Space/ESA_commissions_world_s_first_space_debris_removal

'Resolution Adopted by the General Assembly, 2222 (XXI), Treaty on Principles Governing the Activities of States in the Exploration and Use of Outer Space, including the Moon and Other Celestial Bodies'. United Nations Office for Outer Space Affairs. Accessed 14 March 2023. https://www.unoosa.org/oosa/en/ourwork/spacelaw/treaties/outerspacetreaty.html

Sample, Ian. 'Legally Binding Global Treaty Needed to Tackle Space Debris, Say Experts'. *The Guardian*, 9 March 2023. Accessed 30 March 2023. https://www.theguardian.com/science/2023/mar/09/global-treaty-space-debris-earth-orbit-junk

Stewart, Alison. *Junk: Digging Through America's Love Affair with Stuff*. Chicago: Chicago Review Press, 2016, 108.

Thill, Brian. *Waste*. New York: Bloomsbury Academic, 2015, 48.

Turnbull, Neil. 'The Ontological Consequences of Copernicus: Global Being in the Planetary World'. *Theory, Culture & Society* 23, no. 1 (2006): 133.

University of Southampton Space Environment Research Centre (SERC); The Japan Aerospace Exploration Agency (JAXA) Space Debris Office; respectively. https://patents.google.com/?q=(space+debris)&oq=space+debrisGoogle Patents

Webb, Amy. 'Space Oddities: We Need a Plan to Stop Polluting Space Before It's Too Late'. *Wired*, 12 April 2018. Accessed 15 March 2023. https://www.wired.com/story/we-need-a-plan-to-stop-polluting-space-before-its-too-late/

Yoder, Kate. 'The Overview Effect / How the View from Space Might Be Key to Saving the Planet'. *Grist*, 9 February 2022. Accessed 30 March 2023. https://grist.org/climate/overview-effect-view-of-earth-from-space-astronauts-climate-change/

PART III

MEDIATING HUMAN-NON-HUMAN RELATIONS THROUGH DESIGN

INTRODUCTION: MEDIATING HUMAN-NON-HUMAN RELATIONS THROUGH DESIGN

At the heart of *Design Beyond the Human* is a critique of anthropocentrism and economic self-advantage. It also identifies the need for a multidisciplinary and transdisciplinary debate capable of generating a new conceptual platform for design, rooted in relational and ecological understanding. 'Mediating Human-Non-Human Relations through Design' investigates how we translate the theoretical into the experiential, the fact/actuality of 'not being alone' – as a set of interactions and engagements with each other, our ecological neighbours and the planet (as an actant/citizen) whose voice(s)/presence(s) must be acknowledged, incorporated and ensured. This section presents contemporary design practices and projects, which inform modes of enquiry that open up ways of thinking about interdependencies between humans, as well as between humans and non-humans, and challenges conventional notions of what being a designer might mean in the twenty-first century. Contributions cover subjects such as artificial intelligence, biodiversity, biomimicry, biotechnology, cellular agriculture, chemistry, climate change, computing, conservation, creative writing, degrowth, Discursive Design, eco-tourism, ecology, Ethics, Geo Design, human-animal relations, Indigenous design, Indigenous knowledge, lab-grown meat, living architecture, multispecies justice, mythology, physics, poetry, Relational Design, technology and Transition Design. The examples offered transcend existing disciplinary expectations and inform emergent modes of enquiry, which are capable of thinking about how the human and non-human branch out, entangle and crisscross.

Designer J. Paul Neeley's contribution 'Consider Everything: A New Kind of Design for a Computationally Irreducible World' reminds us that most design practices operate within narrow domain spaces and focus predominantly on problems and solution optimizations within the capitalist system, contributing to catastrophic outcomes. Evident challenges, such as climate change, the obesity epidemic and global financial instability, represent the result of this mindset. Neeley advocates for a radical shift in design practice, addressing our complex reality appropriately. He provides an account of his design approach New Kind of Design (NKD) Principles and Practices (e.g. Consider Everything, Universal Responsibility and Grand Priorities), offering new opportunities for designers to rethink how design engages with complexity. This approach is exemplified through a case study from Neeley's design research practice, which uses emerging NKD design principles and practices as ethical constraints. *Night Night Everyone* is a simple line of open-source code that can be used to turn off any website at a specific time each night, prompting users to go to sleep rather than spend time online during bedtime hours. This *modus operandi* allows the website's owner to adopt a 'Universal Responsibility' by acknowledging that web technology can negatively impact public health (e.g. sleep deprivation) and the environment with its large digital carbon footprint.

In their conversational text 'Planetarity: Designing for Coexistence', neuroscientist and Professor of Immersive Media Erinma Ochu and designer Caroline Ward assert that embracing planetarity, or 'thinking with the planet', can encourage us to contemplate the idea that all life forms are interconnected, responsive and susceptible to change. Planetarity, for them, represents an epistemological endeavour aimed at breaking free from the deadlock of a globalized Earth, influenced by nation-state geopolitics and human activities that exceed the limits of Earth's ecosystems. Moreover, planetarity embodies an affirmative ethic that acknowledges more-than-human subjectivity in connection with the planet. This perspective involves actively sustaining life, embracing coexistence with non-human life forms and reflecting a holistic approach that considers the wellbeing of the entire ecosystem, recognizing the interdependence of all living entities. In their exchange, Ochu and Ward discuss the potential of infrastructures that can be built or already exist to support more-than-human life. Their conversation investigates relationality across time and space within design practice and how it can foster a generative dialogue. Indeed, the dialogue between Ochu and Ward endeavours to nurture design approaches that prioritize a deep yearning for a holistic understanding of what it entails to think, feel and act in harmony with and for the planet. Their exploration provides a perspective that transcends anthropocentrism, fostering a more inclusive and interconnected approach to design that considers the wellbeing of the entire planetary ecosystem.

British-Chilean writer, artist, activist and Visiting Lecturer at Schumacher College Felipe Viveros's chapter 'Indigenous Futures: Epistemologies of Care for a World in Crisis' foregrounds the human capacity for cooperation, empathy, solidarity, trans-rationality and right action. Viveros discusses Indigenous epistemologies that emphasize care as a response to the challenges facing our world in crisis. For him, Indigenous communities not only exemplify the possibility of alternative worlds, but they also serve as stewards for 80 per cent of the world's remaining biodiversity, playing a crucial role in preserving and nurturing the planet's ecological diversity. Viveros examines the practical applications of various ways of knowing and being within Indigenous epistemologies to offer valuable guidance for individuals seeking to navigate and embrace the inevitable transition towards a post-capitalist world. He suggests that incorporating these perspectives can contribute to a more sustainable and harmonious relationship with the natural world and each other. His essay is an inquiry into emerging global phenomena such as Indigenous Futures, Traditional Ecological Knowledge, Transition Design, Artificial Intelligence and post-growth alternatives. By exploring these diverse perspectives, he contributes to a broader understanding of the evolving landscape and potential pathways towards a more sustainable and equitable future.

Nepali-Canadian multispecies designer, educator and scholar Priyanka Bista's essay 'A Bottom-up Approach to Conservation: The Vertical University, Nepal' provides a response to biodiversity loss in Nepal through the Vertical University (VU) project. This initiative aims to support Indigenous communities residing in the 8,000-metre vertical gradient of Eastern Nepal, seeking to safeguard the biodiversity integral to their habitat. Across this vertical belt, the VU project is creating spaces to facilitate empathic understanding between human and non-human inhabitants and to encourage a deeper awareness, comprehension and reciprocal stewardship of the environment. Simultaneously, the project strives to promote ecologically sensitive livelihoods for rural farmers, fostering a harmonious coexistence between communities and their natural surroundings.

Educator, writer and Programme Director at the Yunhe Centre Xinlin Song, inspired by philosopher, environmentalist and conservationist Aldo Leopold's essay 'Thinking Like a Mountain', reminds us that throughout human history, mountains participated in the formation of the planet and our human story through interweaving biology and mythology. Following this reflection, her chapter 'Design That Thinks Like a Mountain' tells the story of changing viewpoints, discussing the historical account of the human-nature relationship and the ongoing regional regeneration work in progress in Danba County, which sits within Sichuan's Garze Tibetan Autonomous Region in China. Song's contribution reveals how design and education assist this process by developing a relationship with the Indigenous communities whose livelihood and cultural identity are deeply intertwined with nature.

In examining a practice inspired by philosopher Val Plumwood that challenges human-centred perspectives, Professor of Sustainability, Design and Fashion Systems, Manchester School of Art & Design, Manchester Metropolitan University, Kate Fletcher describes the journey of creating five short texts written from the viewpoint of Earth beings. In the essay 'A Larger, Less Humanised Design Community', the author shares and reflects on her writing process, exploring how adopting the perspective of non-human entities contributes to a broader understanding of the interconnectedness and interdependence of all life forms. Fletcher's 'life writing' practice encourages a shift from human-centric perspectives, fostering a more inclusive and holistic worldview vocabulary for design.

Design editor, curator and Lecturer in the History of Design Domitilla Dardi's text 'Talking Materials – A Discursive Design Practice for a Design Beyond the Human' asks us to consider the following question, 'What if materials could talk back to us and reveal information and data on their use and provenance to inform environmentally aware sustainable design practices?' Her contribution provides an account of Formafantasma's Design Studio, which in recent years has given 'voice' to materials to enhance our understanding of design's impact on nature. The research projects developed by Andrea Trimarchi and Simone Farresin explore materials such as wood and wool, reflecting on their use in industrial and craft production chains. Their approach reveals fundamental issues that should be examined when considering natural and artificial materials or sustainable and unsustainable production. Furthermore, it underlines a critical and timely characteristic: the evolution of a design practice into a design research agency interested in a 'discursive' materials investigation, which combines environmentally aware theoretical research, educational practices and consultancy.

Professor of Experimental Architecture Rachel Armstrong's chapter 'Towards a Culture of Life: A New Synthesis for the Living World' discusses human exceptionalism and its role in the Anthropocene and the detrimental impacts of the climate emergency. The notion of human exceptionalism, which places humans at a superior and separate position from the natural world, has hindered our ability to adequately recognize and appreciate the essential contributions made by more-than-human entities to the vibrancy of the world. The failure to acknowledge the interconnectedness and interdependence of all living entities has contributed to the environmental crises and challenges we face today. Armstrong draws on implicit concepts found in metaphysical perspectives such as new materialism and posthumanism, incorporating the more-than-human realm into their value system. Combined with insights from advanced (bio) technology and the versatile characteristics of microbes, Armstrong introduces a variety of experimental 'living' architecture projects to pave the way for the establishment of cities built on a culture of life, where the principles of sustainable coexistence with the environment are deeply ingrained in the design and functionality of urban spaces.

Last but not least, Cellular Agriculture Society's founder Kris Spiros's essay 'Designing the Future of Agriculture' offers a compelling argument for a transformative shift in intensive animal farming. He advocates for replacing traditional factory farming methods with Cellular Agriculture (CellAg), a practice that involves growing cells outside of living animals, eliminating the necessity of raising and exploiting animals for human consumption. Spiros argues that CellAg holds the potential to tackle significant issues in public health, environmental sustainability and human/animal rights on a remarkable and essential scale. His perspective positions CellAg as a transformative solution with far-reaching implications for various interconnected challenges in the realm of animal farming and food production. Spiros investigates the concept of CellAg from both an introductory perspective (What, Why, How), and also the manner by which CellAg's positioning, as it relates to design and the creative sphere overall, could impact education, the understanding of food and its production and the eventual possible consumer acceptance and behavioural change. Moreover, Spiros explores tangible experiences within the realm of CellAg and examines how they can contribute to the success of CellAg, particularly in addressing the technological, cultural and social challenges. This perspective highlights the importance of translating the concept of CellAg into tangible and accessible experiences that can resonate with citizens and consumers on various levels.

12 CONSIDER EVERYTHING

A NEW KIND OF DESIGN FOR A COMPUTATIONALLY IRREDUCIBLE WORLD

J. Paul Neeley

The problem

In 2007, I worked as a Service Designer and Researcher at the Mayo Clinic in the United States. The Mayo Clinic is a large not-for-profit academic medical centre and is considered by many to be the best hospital in the world (Cooper 2022). The Department of Medicine at the Clinic had put together a small team of designers and researchers, initially called the SPARC Innovation Program, to explore how design could be used to prototype, improve and enhance the patient experience (Neren 2010). Several years into my design practice, I was thrilled with the opportunities to work with world-class experts in medicine and other fields to address complex and meaningful healthcare problems. The team was excellent, and it was great to work with such dedicated and driven professionals working to enhance the delivery of world-class care. I loved my time at the Mayo Clinic and learned so much about how design can contribute to innovation in these settings. However, there was one thing that I struggled with as a designer during this time. I was constantly frustrated by our colliding into the edges of any project's defined scope or purview.

Imagine you have been invited to improve the experience of someone with a particular condition, say diabetes. Through the research, you soon learn that each medical condition often sits alongside several other medical conditions, so you cannot look at any one medical condition alone in isolation. Next, you find that diabetes' impact was felt far beyond the individual patient's medical terms; it rippled throughout their lives and even on to their family and friends. You next realize the changes in care delivery needed were not only within the department that initiated the project, but several other departments with varied expertise across the clinic would need to be involved, and radical new kinds of coordination would be required. But even then, much of the care that you were looking to provide was being shaped by complex policies that sat far from the patient, inside insurance companies or government agencies and legislations, much of which was focused on broad population metrics for the narrowly defined initial condition and did not fit well with specific individual cases. And finally, you discover that many of the needed lifestyle changes were not really in the individual's control and beyond the clinic's ability to provide care, but required widespread behavioural and market changes within society (Montori 2016). This sort of frustration was frequent, together with the feeling of being overwhelmed by the complexity of each project. But more than that, it was a feeling of helplessness because the most considerate solutions we could see required a broader systemic understanding and intervention which our small design team could not address appropriately.

After my time at the Mayo Clinic, this personal tension and fascination with scope, domains and boundaries continued as I returned to study at the Royal College of Art (RCA) on the MA Design Interactions Course led by designers and scholars Tony Dunne and Fiona Raby, authors of the book *Speculative Everything* (2013). Over the following two years, I worked with Speculative Design approaches, where we would design future products and services to explore the impact of emerging technologies. Again, as at the Mayo Clinic, I continued to find that our design methods failed to engage with the complexity of the issues. In our narrowing of scope, we were ignoring many meaningful connections. During this time, I came across the concept of 'Computational Irreducibility', developed by the mathematician and scientist Stephen Wolfram and described in his book *New Kind of Science* (2002). The idea of Computational Irreducibility is that there are some systems where the entire system is the computation. Any abstraction or simplification of the problem, narrowing of scope and focusing on one particular element means that you are ignoring vital information that would be essential to understand the system. You cannot simplify the computation as the entire system is the computation. When I first came across this concept, it perfectly described the healthcare space I was involved with and the many emerging technology spaces I was exploring with Speculative Design.

Most design methods and approaches are generally based on abstraction and simplification of problems they are trying to address. They start with a definition of scope, usually relatively narrow, fitting within the project's budget or timeframe aligned with the client's or company's objective or the designer's interests, failing to have a real impact because it is something we cannot fully understand or tackle. But as a matter of fact, this narrowing and simplification are antithetical and do not reflect life's complex reality and our infinitely interconnected world. Traditional design approaches fail us as we try to create a meaningful impact. Not only that, but when we fail to understand this complexity, our design interventions often create unintended negative externalities outside the initial project's scope, the cumulative effect of which can be catastrophic for the entire system. Think climate change, global financial instability or the Western obesity epidemic; each is an outcome of the cumulative effects of our modern design and business interventions. Our design and optimization of parts lead to something other than an optimized whole, but rather a devastated one. With this in mind, if we were to engage with our complex reality, I realized we needed a new way of designing that avoided simplification, abstraction and narrowing focus and scope.

New Kind of Design

In order to address this issue, I developed what I call *New Kind of Design* (*NKD*) in a nod to Stephen Wolfram's *New Kind of Science* work. *NKD* is a design approach I have been exploring since 2010 that considers the complexity of the world we exist within and design for. *NKD* is based on the premise that we need new mindsets and methods to avoid abstraction and simplification. It rejects traditional boundaries, allowing us to engage with the complex reality we design within. *NKD* has two main parts, a set of *Principles* and an evolving set of *Practices*. It begins by defining seven principles that articulate a basic understanding needed to engage with our complex reality. The seven principles of *NKD* look at the nature of the world and outline attributes that are critical for us to consider in a design context. They are acknowledgements that must be made before we begin acting in our world. I will share them here and talk about each briefly.

NKD_1 – 'Anytime we consider anything less than everything, we are missing something.'

NKD_1 aims to shift our thinking from what we know about a subject to acknowledging what we do not know. With our narrow view of the world, we are always missing something. Acknowledging what we don't know means approaching every problem and every design with humility. We can only be fully confident about our interventions if we consider 'everything'.

NKD_2 – 'Nothing can ever be isolated from anything because it is always connected to everything.' Whenever we draw a line around something or create some edge or boundary, that line is false. *NKD_2* points out that every time we try to isolate parts, we need to comprehend the interconnections of everything.

NKD_3 – 'Good is good and bad, and bad is bad and good, and often we can't tell the difference.'

NKD_3 – It helps us remember that good and bad are moral judgements that are based on the position and context of the individual making the judgement. What is bad to one person or group is good to another; what is bad today is good tomorrow. We often say that technology is neither good nor evil and is all about how we use it. This thinking is dangerous, and a twist on this concept is more complete. All designs and technology are simultaneously good and bad, with all affordances and possible use brought into the world and all possible moral positions brought into existence upon the technology's creation. This principle suggests that this is true and that most of the time we do not have enough information to fully understand judgements of good and bad, and such assertions cannot be made with great confidence.

NKD_4 – 'Anytime we do something, we do not know exactly what we have done.'

NKD_4 – It points out that when we act in the world, because of our limited information, we cannot ever know all of the impacts of our designs. We can hope for our intended outcomes, but there are many other consequences both seen and unseen, many unintended, that will emerge as well as a result of our intervention in the world. A perfect understanding of the impact of our design is never possible.

NKD_5 – 'We will never know everything, and never even know everything we do not know.' In a sort of known knowns, known unknowns, unknown knowns and unknown unknowns world, we have to acknowledge the limitations of our knowledge. We will always be missing important information. And this applies to all moments of the design process. We can never fully understand the problem space we are working in, the people we are designing for and the systems they are operating within, the social and cultural underpinnings of their worldview. *NKD_5* requires us to approach every learning and design decision with deep humility.

NKD_6 – 'We will never know what will happen tomorrow, until tomorrow.' *NKD_6* speaks to the nature of the limitations of our knowledge over time. Because of our limited information, and the complex and chaotic and adaptive nature of the world, the only way to know exactly what will happen tomorrow is to let the whole system run until tomorrow. We can never perfectly simulate or predict, so our prediction and foresight will always be limited. We need to accept the incompleteness of and inherent uncertainty in the predictions that we make. This is not to say our predictions are not useful, but just to acknowledge their limitations.

NKD_7 – 'A theory of everything, applied to everything, is our only hope of saving everything.' The first six principles speak to the nature of the world as it is and outline acknowledgements that we all must make as we approach each design in this world. The final principle, *NKD_7* lays out a broad hypothesis for a way forward. *NKD_7* suggests that the only way to design within and solve the current state is to never limit your scope, and that design methods for understanding and engaging with 'everything' are needed.

When properly understood, these *NKD* principles can shape new approaches that consider our complex reality more faithfully. I have been experimenting with several new *NKD* practices in my design work over the years, which are constantly evolving as my understanding of the issues outlined in the *NKD Principles* develops through experience. For this chapter, I want to share with the reader three of these emerging practices that have started to impact my design practice profoundly: *Consider Everything* (*NKD_CE*), *Universal Responsibility* (*NKD_UR*), and *Grand Priorities* (*NKD_GP*).

Consider Everything (NKD_CE)

Hypothetically, if you wanted to be a design 'God', creating 'perfect' design outcomes, then you must consider everything that a 'God' would consider in your design. Omniscient and omnipresent, an imaginary being with a perfect understanding of the world would be capable of overcoming all the constraints outlined in the *NKD Principles*. They would be able to know and explore all issues related to the problem, simultaneously, at all scales, while understanding all interconnections and future interactions perfectly. They would consider everything in their design choices. While a fun thought experiment, in practical terms, considering everything would never be possible. On every front, we are radically limited in our ability to fully know and understand the entire context which we are designing within. But what is exciting here is that attempting to consider everything radically transforms our thinking meaningfully.

This attempt means a radical expansion of our consideration sets and purview. It means that because everything is connected to everything else and nothing exists in isolation, we are required to go beyond the edges of scope that feel comfortable. Furthermore, it means that traditional ways of designing in isolation, with a narrow space, and optimized for parts, have never worked. It also means that we invest more time trying to understand the nature of the issues and the context we are dealing with. It means that we are open to throwing out established problem domains and solution disciplines in search of a broader understanding. It means we accept all possible outcomes of our work and consider interactions at all degrees of separation. It means we cannot see any part of our design without seeing everything else.

Try to consider everything and see how it transforms the problems you are working on.

Universal Responsibility (NKD_UR)

Once everything has been considered, the next opportunity is to take universal responsibility for the impact of our actions in this total system. Universal responsibility is the idea that as designers, businesses and technology creators, we must take responsibility for *all* of the outcomes of our creations, no matter how many degrees of separation exist from our design intervention. Generally, when we operate in the world as designers, we think of things in terms of limited liability. We only take responsibility for the direct impacts of our actions. Take, for example, the fact that alcoholic beverage companies do not take responsibility for consumers beyond the warning 'drink responsibly', and they do not take responsibility for any effect their products have in the world, that is, increased domestic violence, addiction, substance abuse, motor vehicle accidents and so on (Moss 2013). In the UK, the National Health Service hospitals have been overwhelmed by alcohol-related accidents and injuries, costing the health system millions in treatment costs (Boseley 2019). There is an enormous cost to society here, which is afforded and largely ignored by the alcohol industry.

In an *NKD* world where we take *Universal Responsibility*, we identify all of the interconnections and knock-on effects of any particular action, product or service by taking responsibility for the totality of the impacts. In the example above, the alcoholic beverages industry would pay for some portion of the societal health cost from the knock-on effects of their product. We desire to create great product experiences for people, but we also have a universal responsibility to care for their general wellbeing, health and happiness. And we have a universal responsibility to all other systems impacted by our interventions, including non-human species, ecosystems, the environment, the climate, the planet and the future.

Try taking universal responsibility for all of the knock-on effects of your designs and see how this changes your design decisions.

Grand Priorities (NKD_GP)

Once everything has been considered and we take universal responsibility for our design outcomes, our priorities radically shift and change. What was a problem is now seen as a benefit, what was good is now clearly a problem and what was inconsequential is now a critical component of the whole system. We more perfectly consider what was previously ignored as externalities and can better see the relationships between all things. This view lets us explore root causes and helps us better understand the task at hand. With this new view, a list of *Grand Priorities* begins to emerge. A grand priority is the prioritization of something within all other things. Regardless of what we are designing, it will sit against and within the context of all other critical issues required to consider with the entire system. As a set, understanding this single list is important as it reveals an order that must be respected. Some of these lists have begun to emerge, for example, the United Nations' Sustainable Development Goals, Singularity University's Grand Challenges and economist Kate Raworth's Donut Economics, to name a few (United Nations; Nail 2018; Doughnut Economics Action Lab 2022). Another example is psychologist Abraham Maslow's Hierarchy of Needs (2022) which I often use in my design work. While not perfect, these lists and frameworks represent a positive start to understanding the whole we are designing within and the essential issues that should first be addressed for the entire system's health.

The question of *Grand Priorities* falls with why would we work on any given 'X' if any critical 'Y' is not yet solved? Why would we work on satisfying higher-order needs if the fundamentals still need to be satisfied? Why would I help someone with their fashion choices if they do not yet have access to clean drinking water? In this way, we focus on basic evolutionary needs, fundamentals of civil society and sustainable systems before addressing other issues that may arise from a capitalist and profit-driven worldview.

Can we consider the Grand Priorities the planet faces through design?

An *NKD* case study

While the ideas behind *NKD* and *NKD* practices may seem grand, theoretical or abstract, I want to share a case study to illustrate how these design practices can play out practically while addressing an actual design challenge. As part of my research work at the RCA to better understand the idea of computational irreducibility and complex issues, I decided to undertake an experiment by imagining a future where I could consider everything. This technologically enabled future society would be able to accurately measure, map and predict all systems and flows of materials, energy and life. The question then became: What am I optimizing for in this hypothetical world? What is the design intent of everything? Through this exploration, I concluded that happiness was the ultimate design intent and that all of our other design goals, such as faster, better, stronger, more beautiful, easier to use, slower, softer and more sustainable, are only considered because they give us the illusion that achieving them will make us better off or happier. With this in mind, I wondered what our world would look like if I focused on what I saw as the ultimate end goal of happiness instead of focusing on these intermediary goals. What if I designed my entire life, and the world, for happiness (Neeley 2013)?

Over the course of the following year, I started an experiment by trying to redesign every aspect of my life through the lens of optimized happiness, from my breathing to my eating and exercise, my sleep, my material possessions and even my personal and social relationships. I created daily measures for all these factors and made adjustments based on how I felt and how my understanding of any particular factor impacted my happiness. These experiments proved life-changing and completely shifted how I thought about happiness and the purpose of my design intent. It also made me reconsider every design project I was taking on. Why am I worried about this if I can see that work in other spaces will better impact my happiness and others? It changed my design practice for good, and many of the insights and habits I developed over that time on personal happiness have stayed with me until the present day.

When I share the project and my experience with others, people often say to me, 'This is great. I love everything you did, but what is the one thing that I can do that can have the biggest impact on my happiness?' It is an important question but highlights our general bias towards quick, simple, singular fixes. I learned that *everything* I did impacted my happiness in some way. Every system, every interaction, every behaviour, every person I met, everything and everyone had some effect on my happiness. And this points back to our need for *NKD* to better engage with this kind of everything and avoid narrowing and simplification. But when I am pressed on the question of the 'one thing', I look at all of my interventions as if they were a *Grand Priority* list related to personal happiness, and I tell people to start by looking at their sleep. And my explorations in *NKD* and sleep led to the project I want to share with you now.

Sleep debt

Sleep is a critical biological process for survival and dramatically impacts our health, wellbeing and happiness. When we do not get enough sleep at night, it is called sleep debt (Wikipedia 2022). For example, one-third of Americans do not get enough sleep; in some parts of the country, this is as high as 50 per cent (Chew 2016). After just one night of missed sleep, you perform cognitively as if intoxicated (National Institute for Occupational Safety and Health 2020), and the cumulative impact over time is devastating. This lack of sleep is quite often associated with increased stress and depression, hypertension, heart and kidney disease, motor vehicle accidents and suicide (National Institute of Health: National Heart, Lung, and Blood Institute 2022). One of the best things you can do to improve almost every aspect of your life is to improve your sleep. During my happiness experiments, I was able to design my life to support almost perfect sleep hygiene and experience amazing sleep for months. It was a transformative experience, and I realized I had not slept so comfortably since I was in my early teens. I am serious; go to sleep! It is awesome!

There are many reasons why getting enough sleep and good sleep hygiene is difficult; it is a complex issue. Our modern behaviours, beliefs and culture relating to sleep are generally unsupportive. It is considered cool to pull an all-nighter; these are celebrated at many universities and seen as a rite of passage in many design or architecture schools (instead of being seen as a failure of planning and efficiency and a failure to protect the individual from unreasonable workloads). We celebrate Fortune 500 CEOs who wake up at 4.00 pm and operate on just four hours of sleep, viewing them as heroes for their work ethic, drive and dedication (Connley 2018). We look at teenagers that sleep a lot and consider them lazy (despite current research suggesting more sleep during those ages is part of critical cognitive development for adolescents) (Johns Hopkins Medicine 2022). Furthermore, the world we live in is not designed for sleep. Artificial lights, city and home soundscapes, food, modern living schedules, mobile phones and apps, screens, social activities and so on generally fail to support healthy sleep habits. The cumulative effect is devastating for our sleep generally. A significant change is needed in designing all these elements of our lives if we were to create a world supporting sleep. I will share just one curious intervention that highlights *NKD* thinking and one step we could each take to improve the world's sleep radically. I start by asking the question: What if we put the web to sleep at night?

NIGHT NIGHT Everyone

NIGHT NIGHT みんな (*みんな* is Japanese for 'everyone') is a simple piece of software I designed and coded with Norwegian developer Håkon Eide, that allows to put any website to sleep at bedtime, encouraging the website visitors to go to bed, better supporting their health, wellbeing and happiness (Masamichi Souzou 2016).

NIGHT NIGHT allows the website to run normally throughout the day. Then, looking at the time on the website visitor's computer, *NIGHT NIGHT* will 'put the website to sleep' at a selected bedtime (Defaulting to 10.00 pm). A black window then pops up, stating, 'Nothing we can offer you is as important as your sleep. Sleep well, sweet dreams, and we will catch you in the morning.' At 6.00 am, the website wakes up, the black window disappears and visitors can use the website as usual. And because *NIGHT NIGHT* considers the individual's computer time, it will work anywhere in the world and in any time zone. *NIGHT NIGHT* also has an opt-out function that lets users continue using the site if they need to do something that cannot wait until morning. The goal is not to take away people's freedom but prompt visitors to sleep. *NIGHT NIGHT* reminds people of the trade-off between the value of what they are doing online and the value of the sleep they could be having. Website owners can install *NIGHT NIGHT* by placing a single line of code just above the *</body> tag* on any HTML page. Alternatively, if they prefer, website

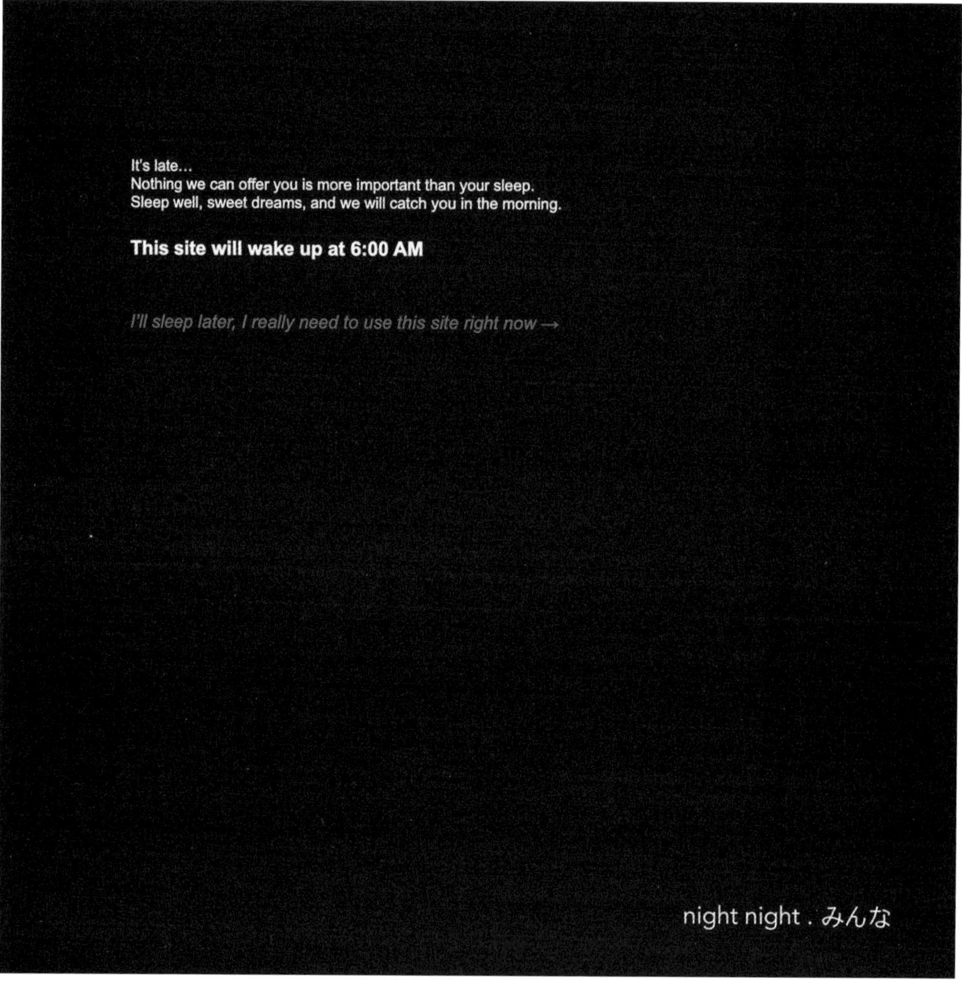

Figure 12.1 *NIGHT NIGHT Everyone* home screen, 2016. Courtesy of J. Paul Neeley.

owners can also self-host the code as *NIGHT NIGHT* is an open-source software distributed under the MIT License.

The crux

NIGHT NIGHT Everyone was created to shift the responsibility for sleep away from the website user and onto the website's designer and owner. If the designer were to consider everything by considering both the needs and goals of the website and all of the needs of the website's visitors, and then take *Universal Responsibility* for the design's impact, then they have an obligation to support all aspects of the website visitors' lives, that is, the visitor's sleep is probably further up the *Grand Priority* list than the particular objective of the website or company.

night night . みんな

```
<script async src="https://code.nightnight.xn--q9jyb4c/js/2200/0600/nightnight.js"></script>
```

```
/** nightnight.みんな v1.0 | MIT License | https://git.io/vwz9N */

window.nightnightHide = function() {
        var banners = document.getElementsByClassName('nightnight');

        for (var i = 0; i < banners.length; i++) {
                banners[i].style.display = 'none';
        }
};

(function(){
        var d = new Date();
        var m = d.getHours() * 60 + d.getMinutes();
        var bh = 22, bm = 0;
        var eh = 6, em = 0;

        var use12HourClock = true;

        var b = bh * 60 + bm;
        var e = eh * 60 + em;

        if (b < e) {
                console.log("WARNING: NightNight: invalid time interval: sleep time is earlier in the day than wakeup time");
                return
        }

        if (m >= b || m <= e) {
                console.log('NightNight activated')

                // Inject CSS
                var css = '.nightnight {background: #000; font-family: Arial, sans-serif; color: #fff; font-size: 12px; padding: 10%; position: fixed; margin: 0; top: 0; left: 0; right: 0; bottom: 0;
z-index: 9999; } .nightnight-skip a {padding: 10px 0; } .nightnight a:link {color: #555; } .nightnight a:visited {color: #555; } .nightnight a:hover {color: #FFF; } .nightnight-timing {font-size:
15px; font-weight: 900; margin-top: 20px; } .nightnight-skip {font-style: italic; font-size: 14px; margin-top: 40px; } .nightnight-credits {position: fixed; bottom: 20px; right: 20px; margin-top:
40px; font-size:9px; }';
                var head = document.head || document.getElementsByTagName('head')[0];
                var style = document.createElement('style');
                style.type = 'text/css';
                if (style.styleSheet){
                        style.styleSheet.cssText = css;
                } else {
                        style.appendChild(document.createTextNode(css));
                }
                head.appendChild(style);

                // Format time
                var time = ''
                if (use12HourClock) {
                        var suffix = eh < 12 ? "AM" : "PM"
                        time = (eh % 13) + ":" + ("0"+em).slice(-2) + " " + suffix;
                } else {
                        time = ("0"+eh).slice(-2) + ":" + ("0"+em).slice(-2)
                }

                // Inject DIV
                var wrapper = document.createElement('div');
                wrapper.innerHTML = '<div class="nightnight"><div>It&rsquo;s late&hellip;</div><div> Nothing we can offer you is more important than your sleep.</div> <div> Sleep
well, sweet dreams, and we will catch you in the morning.</div> <div class="nightnight-timing">This site will wake up at ' +
                        time +
                        '</div> <div class="nightnight-skip"> <a href="javascript:nightnightHide()">I&rsquo;ll sleep later, I really need to use this site right now &rightarrow;</a> </div>
<div class="nightnight-credits"> <a href="https://www.nightnight.xn--q9jyb4c"><img src="https://code.nightnight.xn--q9jyb4c/static/night_night_everyone_white.png" alt="night
night" height="32" width="161"></a></div> </div>';
                document.body.appendChild(wrapper);
        }
})();
```

Figure 12.2 Code to be included by the website owners to enable *NIGHT NIGHT Everyone*, 2016. Courtesy of J. Paul Neeley.

As technology creators, we build tools that delight, engage and create profit. Unfortunately, the 'success' of the experiences we create can also hurt the people that use them, negatively impacting other aspects of their lives, like their focus, finances, relationships, health and sleep. A website optimized for engagement might be brilliant for a company but can be a disaster for the circadian rhythms of the people using it. By putting a website to sleep at bedtime and encouraging users to go to bed, we better support their health, wellbeing and happiness. We are caring about them and putting their needs first. With an intervention like *NIGHT NIGHT Everyone*, we are *Considering Everything*, taking *Universal Responsibility* for the effect of a website on others, and engaging with *Grand Priorities;* we are taking a small but essential step to improve the world we live in.

Reactions

There have been a lot of fascinating reactions to the *NIGHT NIGHT Everyone* project, from public talks where I shared the concept to discussions about the project on Hacker News. The reactions broadly fall into two groups, with one side usually approving of the approach and intent of the project and the other vocally opposing the idea. On the 'I like it' side, we see people who understand the dangers of sleep deprivation. Medical professionals, teachers or individuals who have suffered from sleep deprivation are excited by the intervention's potential to impact public health positively.

There is also some excitement for the idea related to *Universal Responsibility*, that businesses can take responsibility for their actions and the implications of those actions in the world beyond their profit-taking goals. *Universal Responsibility* becomes a way to acknowledge the externalities in the current capitalist system and the exploitation that takes place in many of these exchanges. A responsible business that avoids many of these adverse public outcomes would represent a new kind of caring business that many perhaps hope for but has not been realized in our current capitalist market-driven system as it exists today. Related to this, I had a conversation with a woman who said she began crying when she first came across the *NIGHT NIGHT Everyone* project while visiting the School of Critical Design website. She mentioned that she was overwhelmed by it as she never experienced such a caring and human moment on the web before. On the negative side, there have been critiques highlighting the implications of the *NIGHT NIGHT* intervention for people who work night shifts or have the need to use a website at various hours. Both of these issues are valid and may have been considered by including, for example, an opt-out option on the website. Other types of personalization can be considered as the *NIGHT NIGHT* project evolves. The more considerable negative critique has been from people who are generally angry about the idea as it is seen to take away an individual's freedom by a 'nanny state'. This critique does not consider the severity of the sleep debt epidemic and its impacts on society and perhaps emerges from a failure to consider everything. If people truly understood the severity of the sleep debt issue, they would feel differently about potential interventions.

Implications at scale

What is also exciting about ideas like *NIGHT NIGHT Everyone* is to think of a design intervention at scale. What would happen if *NIGHT NIGHT Everyone* was used universally by website creators? Consider the impact of putting the web to sleep on global sleep debt reduction. From a public health perspective, the

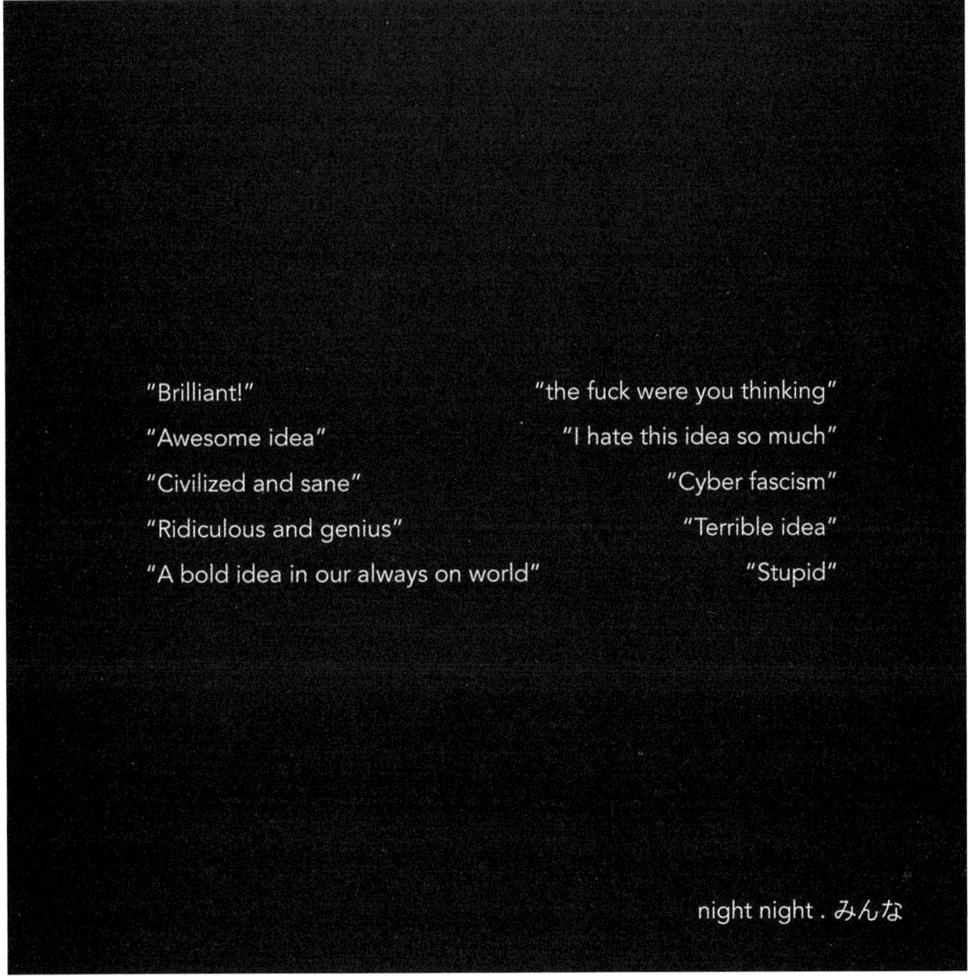

Figure 12.3 Range of reactions to *NIGHT NIGHT Everyone*, 2016. Courtesy of J. Paul Neeley.

upside to improving sleep at a population level is enormous. 'Up to $680 Billion is lost each year across five OECD countries due to insufficient sleep', causing lower workers' productivity or missed days at work (Hafner et al. 2017). And 'Insufficient sleep increases mortality risk by up to 13 per cent' (Hafner et al. 2016, x).

Sleep Debt Reduction looks at the narrow and direct implications of sleep, but as we consider everything, there are other broader implications for the *NIGHT NIGHT Everyone* concept's impact at scale. Take for example, global CO2 emissions, 'The carbon footprint of our gadgets, the internet and the systems supporting them account for about 3.7 per cent of global greenhouse emissions, according to some estimates. It is similar to the amount produced by the airline industry globally. . . . And these emissions are predicted to double by 2025' (Griffiths 2020). And by my rough estimate, approximately 20 per cent of our internet activities take place between 10.00 pm and 6.00 am (Kafka 2011), the default *NIGHT NIGHT Everyone* sleep hours. And if you used *NIGHT NIGHT Everyone* to

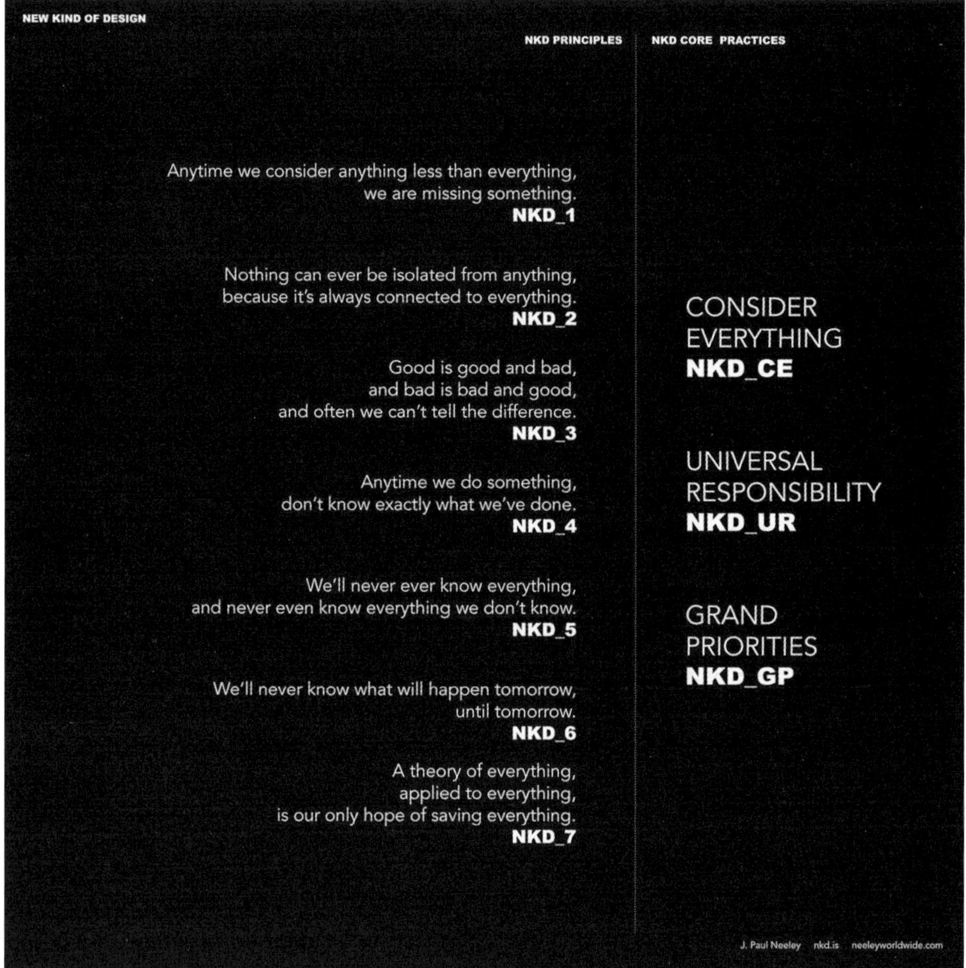

Figure 12.4 *New Kind of Design* – principles and core practices, 2011. Courtesy of J. Paul Neeley.

prompt sleep in the two hours before 10.00 pm, which would fall in line with many sleep experts' suggestions to avoid screen time before bed (Pacheco 2022), you would capture an additional 14 per cent of internet usage. That equates to almost a third of all internet usage during those critical sleep hours.

Could a simple intervention like *NIGHT NIGHT Everyone*, just a few lines of code, at scale, have an almost unimaginable positive global impact? I will not put an exact figure here, but we can comfortably say that the health and environmental impact at scale would be significant. *NIGHT NIGHT Everyone* represents just a small intervention emerging from an *NKD* approach. Now imagine a world where these connections were built into the design approach, a world where we have *Considered Everything*, and decisions around optimization were taken with a *Universal Responsibility* approach and actions prioritized along *Grand Priorities*.

It is important to note that the *NIGHT NIGHT* project was first launched in 2016, and since that time, some progress has been made in supporting consumers' habits, particularly on mobile phones, for example, screen time measurements, lighting changes late at night, sleep modes that silence notifications and sleep tracking (Welch 2018; Gebhart 2020; Mitroff 2022).

The one unique thing here is that generally, they are introduced by a 'middleman', say the phone hardware producer, and not by companies whose apps or business models may be affected by a *NIGHT NIGHT Everyone*-like intervention, which is the whole point. *Universal Responsibility* means we disadvantage ourselves and our own businesses because we are trying to better support 'Everything'.

A *New Kind of Design* world

I have come to believe (and hope that through this chapter, you now feel it too) that the primary design approaches we rely on today, based on simplification and abstraction, generally leave us ill-equipped to deal with the complex nature of our reality, a world where everything is interconnected and nothing exists in isolation.

If we want to tackle today's complex challenges, we need a *New Kind of Design*. In the design of anything, we must consider everything, and in doing so, we must radically rethink goals, frames, methods, purview, scope, interventions and so on. We must take *Universal Responsibility* for our designs and understand and take responsibility for our actions no matter how many degrees of separation from our initial intervention. We must begin to understand our work within a set of *Grand Priorities*, ensuring our design work contributes meaningfully to the whole. I believe that exploring an *NKD* will allow us to realize future dreams for humanity.

References

Boseley, Sarah. 'New Report Reveals Staggering Cost to NHS of Alcohol Abuse'. *The Guardian*, 4 July 2019. Accessed 15 July 2022. https://www.theguardian.com/society/2019/jul/04/staggering-cost-nhs-alcohol-abuse-report

Chew, J. '1 In 3 American Adults Are Not Sleeping Enough'. *Fortune*, 19 February 2016. Accessed 25 July 2022. https://fortune.com/2016/02/19/sleep-americans-study/

Connley, Courtney. 'Tim Cook Wakes Up at 4 am – Here's the Rest of the Morning Routine That Sets Him Up for Success'. *CNBC Make it*, 17 November 2018. Accessed 25 July 2022. https://www.cnbc.com/2018/11/27/tim-cook-reveals-the-morning-routine-that-sets-him-up-for-success.html

Cooper, Nancy. 'The World's Best Hospitals 2022'. *Newsweek*, 2022. Accessed 12 April 2022. https://www.newsweek.com/worlds-best-hospitals-2022

Doughnut Economics Action Lab. 'About Doughnut Economics.'. Accessed 1 October 2022. https://doughnuteconomics.org/about-doughnut-economics

Gebhart, Andrew. 'Apple Wind Down Mode Wants You to Get to Bed on Time'. *CNET*, 22 June 2020. Accessed 23 September 2022. *https://www.cnet.com/tech/mobile/apple-wind-down-mode-wants-you-to-get-to-bed-on-time/

Griffiths, Sarah. 'Why Your Internet Habits Are Not As Clean As You Think'. *BBC*, 6 March 2020. Accessed 23 September 2022. https://www.bbc.com/future/article/20200305-why-your-internet-habits-are-not-as-clean-as-you-think

Hafner, Marco, et al. 'Why Sleep Matters'. *Rand Health Quarterly*, 1 January 2017. Accessed 25 July 2022. https://www.ncbi.nlm.nih.gov/pmc/articles/PMC5627640/

Hafner, Marco, et al. 'Why Sleep Matters: Quantifying the Economic Costs of Insufficient Sleep'. *RAND*, 30 November 2016. Accessed 25 July 2022. https://www.rand.org/randeurope/research/projects/the-value-of-the-sleep-economy.html

'Impairments Due to Sleep Deprivation are Similar to Impairments Due to Alcohol Intoxication!' National Institute for Occupational Safety and Health, last review 31 March 2020. Accessed 25 July 2022. https://www.cdc.gov/niosh/work-hour-training-for-nurses/longhours/mod3/08.html

Kafka, Peter. 'The Night Time Is the Right Time for Watching TV, Surfing the Web, Playing With Apps'. *All Things D*, 29 September 2011. Accessed 23 September 2022. https://allthingsd.com/20110929/the-night-time-is-the-right-time-for-watching-tv-surfing-the-web-playing-with-apps/

'Maslow's Hierarchy of Needs.' *Wikipedia Foundation*, 4 August 2022. Accessed 1 October 2022. https://en.wikipedia.org/wiki/Maslow%27s_hierarchy_of_needs

Mayo Foundation for Medical Education and Research. 'The SPARC Innovation Program at Mayo Clinic, Transforming the Patient Care Experience Through Research and Innovation'. SPARC Innovation Program, 2007. Accessed 5 September 2022. https://vol10.cases.som.yale.edu/sites/default/files/cases/Design%20at%20Mayo/Sparc%20Development%20Brochure.pdf

Mitroff, Sarah. 'Apple Watch OS 9's New Features Include Sleep Tracking, Medication Reminders'. *CNET*, 6 June 2022. Accessed 23 September 2022. https://www.cnet.com/health/medical/apple-watchos-9-offers-new-features-sleep-tracking-medication-reminders-and-more/

Montori, Victor. 'The Proposal for a Patient Revolution'. *TED X ZumbroRiver*, 22 November 2016. Accessed 3 October 2022. https://www.youtube.com/watch?v=kYW6bC3unLM

Moss, Hahard B. 'The Impact of Alcohol on Society: A Brief Overview'. *Social Work in Public Health* 28, no. 3–4 (2013): 175–7. https://doi.org/10.1080/19371918.2013.758987

Nail, Rob. 'Singularity University at Ten Years: The Global Grand Challenges'. *Singularity Group*, 30 September 2018. Accessed 1 October 2022. https://www.su.org/blog/singularity-university-at-ten-years-the-global-grand-challenges

Neeley, J. Paul. 'Can We Put the Web to Sleep?' *Mayo Clinic Transform*, 20 December 2016. Accessed 25 July 2022. https://www.youtube.com/watch?v=MBjbhT37ZoM

Neeley, J. Paul. 'Designing for Happiness in a Complex World'. *Mayo Clinic Transform*, 2013. 13 May 2012. Accessed 15 June 2022. https://www.youtube.com/watch?v=n2rpljWGeUY

Neren, Uri. 'How the Mayo Clinic Invests in its Next Century of Innovation'. *Harvard Business Review*, 27 October 2010. Accessed 5 September 2022. https://hbr.org/2010/10/how-the-mayo-clinic-invests-in

'NIGHT NIGHT Everyone'. *Github*, last updated 3 June 2021. Accessed 25 July 2022. https://github.com/nww/nightnight

'NIGHT NIGHT Everyone'. *Masamichi Souzou*, 2016. Accessed 25 July 2022. https://www.nightnight.みんな/details

'Night Shift (software)'. *Wikipedia Foundation*, last edited 16 December 2021. Accessed 23 September 2022. https://en.wikipedia.org/wiki/Night_Shift_(software)

Pacheco, Danielle. 'How Electronics Affect Sleep'. *The Sleep Foundation*, updated 1 April 2022. Accessed 23 September 2022. https://www.sleepfoundation.org/how-sleep-works/how-electronics-affect-sleep

'Should I Put My Website to Sleep?'. *Hacker News*, 10 May 2021. Accessed 25 July 2022. https://news.ycombinator.com/item?id=27110263

'Sleep Debt'. *Wikipedia Foundation*, last edited 6 June 2022. Accessed 25 July 2022. https://en.wikipedia.org/wiki/Sleep_debt

'Teenagers and Sleep: How Much Sleep Is Enough?' *Johns Hopkins Medicine*, 2022. Accessed 25 July 2022. https://www.hopkinsmedicine.org/health/wellness-and-prevention/teenagers-and-sleep-how-much-sleep-is-enough

'The School of Critical Design'. *Neeley Worldwide Ltd*, 2017. Accessed 2 August 2022. https://www.critical.design/

United Nations. 'The 17 Goals'. Accessed 10 August 2022. https://sdgs.un.org/goals

Welch, Chris 'How to Ese Apple's New Screen Time and App Limits Features in iOS 12'. *The Verge*, 7 September 2018. Accessed 23 September 2022. https://www.theverge.com/2018/9/17/17870126/ios-12-screen-time-app-limits-downtime-features-how-to-use

'What Are Sleep Deprivation and Deficiency?' *National Institute of Health: National Heart, Lung, and Blood Institute*, last updated 24 March 2022. Accessed 25 July 2022. https://www.nhlbi.nih.gov/health/sleep-deprivation

Wolfram, Stephen. *A New Kind of Science*. Champaign: Wolfram Media, 2002. Accessed 18 June 2022. https://www.wolframscience.com/nks/p737--computational-irreducibility/

13
PLANETARITY
DESIGNING FOR COEXISTENCE

Erinma Ochu and Caroline Ward

Erinma: By way of introduction and to give a sense of where we are coming from, let's introduce ourselves and our motivations for having a conversation focused on cultivating design approaches that surface what it means to think, feel and act collectively with care.

Caroline: My practice spans design, research and filmmaking. I am cross-disciplinary in my thinking, and I move across boundaries and borders very quickly and easily.

Erinma: If I might ask then, what value does design bring to being cross-disciplinary?

Caroline: Design is political in that it has contributed to how we have arrived at the current conjecture. On the one hand, it is collaborative in nature with a laser focus on the user who often behaves in a non-linear way, and on the other hand, design has the capacity to bring the lived experience of both human and non-human users into the mix. Design can also weave different disciplines together, often in unusual and generative ways. I am thinking here about a project we did collaborating with community growers, plant scientists, architects, engineers, coffee shops and city residents to imagine the future of food in cities. Design played a crucial transdisciplinary role in bringing biological knowledge from scientists working on climate change into contact with community knowledge of what crops could be grown in existing hotter, wetter climates and then imagining together what could be grown in the event that we have completely exhausted soil and have limited space in cities in which to grow food.

Erinma: On the exhausted soil front, I recall that we co-designed a process with mushroom growers to turn used coffee waste from coffee shops into food by seeding oyster mushroom spawn into coffee waste for people to take home a bag of this 'seeded' waste. The mycelium that grew from the spawn was able to turn the coffee waste into energy in the form of mushrooms which people could eat and cook at home. The whole process took about seven to ten days.

Figure 13.1 Waste coffee grounds, 2016. Courtesy of Squirrel Nation. Photo by Caroline Ward.

Caroline: That regenerative potential of slowly turning waste into energy could become a bigger part of everyday living. Demonstrating that kind of value chain in cities and extending it to where people live, cook and eat food is a way of building a platform or infrastructure from which to collectively imagine the possibilities.

Erinma: It creates a desire and produces those 'new visions and blueprints' (2022) that philosopher Rosi Braidotti is talking about. I really enjoy that speculative, yet within the realms of the possible aspect of our work. I think there are interesting parallels here with the shift away from the universalism of Human-Centred Design, and the problem of Enlightenment.

Caroline: Can you say a bit more about how those parallels manifested for you?

Erinma: My background is as an applied biologist, specializing and practising as a neuroscientist working in a laboratory. But neuroscience, at the time, was not able to satisfy the questions I had about conscious experience and how our sense of reality emerges from the interactions that we have, and how that can wildly differ from one context to another, and how we are positioned. Imperial science often fails to consider positionality or localized contexts, and I often found myself deciding to do science experiments that questioned the rationale of standardized time-based protocols. For some reason, we always had to work with nerve cells that had been growing for fifteen days in cell culture. I would think, let's see what happens when you work with younger or older cells, what happens then? And of course, I would find new subpopulations of cells that did not follow the expected pattern or published norm for these types of cells. These edge populations or subcultures often get erased when you stick to the protocol that has always been used just because it is how things are done and established in the scientific literature.

Caroline: And what about now? Now that you have left science?

Erinma: I still think of myself as a biologist, albeit attempting to work from an anti-colonial standpoint in conversation with the arts, through design practice. This offers another way into considering collective consciousness and how we become immersed within a belief system. I still stay connected to science through ecologists and biologists who see the value of working with local communities that bring stories and place-based knowledge to recontextualize climate and biodiversity modelling. A key vehicle for that transition from science into being in dialogue with the arts, through design, has been via our collaborative practice.

Caroline: Were there other factors?

Erinma: Crucially, my lived experience of racism and sexism from an early age made quite an impression. How was it possible for people to be so entrenched in a particular set of values and beliefs and how had this become so normalized through mainstream culture? I went to university and realized that biology, and the conscious creation of racism, sexism, ableism and speciesism, had a lot to answer for.

Caroline: Was there anything that kind of broke you out of that thinking?

Erinma: Fortunately, there are always alternative ways of schooling and getting educated outside of the mainstream canons. Alongside studying biology at university, black studies found me when I volunteered to teach excluded young people at a West Indian community centre in the north-west of England. The books, poetry and talks that I was exposed to there included revolutionaries like political activist and philosopher Angela Davis and human rights activist Malcolm X, poets and writers like Langston Hughes and James Baldwin, and inventors like Lewis Latimer and Dr Rebecca Crumpler, who respectively broke boundaries within electrical engineering and medicine. My entire canon of knowledge was refreshed by these people by becoming part of this community. This felt incongruent to my training as a scientist and at the same time, it exposed me to how a community can work together to source alternative blueprints to the universalizing forces that impose a standardized way of categorizing humans and non-humans emerging from the relationship between colonialism, imperial science and industrialization.

Caroline: That perhaps leads us into a starting point for this conversation and what has led us to the emerging and intersecting polycrises that we face: where multiple crises – ecological breakdown, climate change, homogenizing technological forces and heightened inequality – become so deeply entangled with one another that they pose a sustained and critical threat to life and livelihoods as we know them – affecting food, water, waste, energy and habitats. And of course, all of this is felt disproportionately in specific geographies, communities and cultures over others.

> In these climates, one always has to internalize a geography because there may be, depending on where one is located, no external marker that says this is a hazardous place for Black people, or this is a 'safer'

zone, it is a completely embodied experience in that sense. So, we move through these atmospheres quite differently depending on how the body is read, depending on what we know. (Sharpe 2016)

Erinma: We might see these polycrises as causing what Professor of English Literature and Black Studies Christina Sharpe refers to as the 'weather' or the 'totality' (2016) of black people's environments. The weather is totalizing in that the effect of climate change, biodiversity loss and ongoing extraction via industrialization and their associated infrastructures is produced on multiple registers all at once, all the time, feeding into and entangling within one another. Taking a stance of refusal of this status quo is a form of what Sharpe describes as 'wake' (2016) work – in the wake of the slave ship, of climate change and imperialism. This work is, or can be alienating, unless we go to those edges to build solidarity, common ground and knowledge with others facing the dehumanizing effects of such oppressive legacies, which suppress self-determination in the face of erasure. In the middle of the Covid-19 pandemic – which is a symptom of everything that we have been describing – it felt particularly totalizing – and yet, we went out to collect acorns in the autumn months and started to grow oak trees. This was a way to hold on to the possibility of life, in the face of heightened hostility.

Caroline: This reminds me of a story of a college building in Oxford, New College, where they also planted oak saplings, which, over hundreds of years, grew into trees. The idea was that planting these trees was a restoration act of longevity over lifetimes, and the trees could not be cut down as they were being planted in anticipation of when, hundreds of years from now, the oak beams in the buildings would

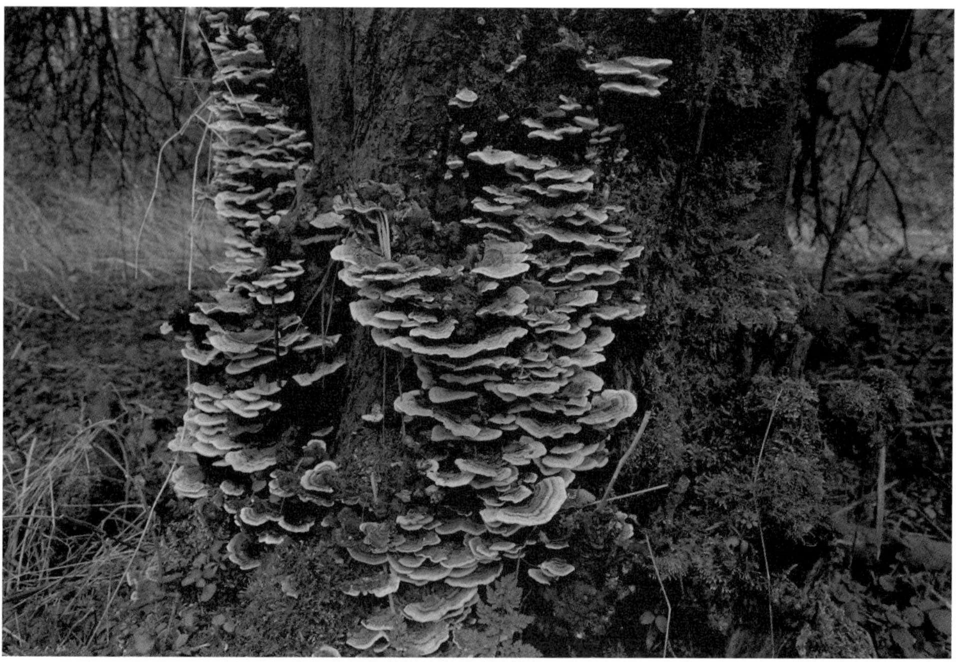

Figure 13.2 Turkey tail mushrooms growing on a tree trunk, 2016. Courtesy of Squirrel Nation. Photo by Caroline Ward.

need to be replaced. It is a way to build that thinking into the design of human and non-human habitats, over the long term.

Erinma: To know that an oak tree can grow and live for 400 to 1,000 years, and that mycelium can turn decaying wood into food, feels like an incredible way to bring into practice the ongoing, dynamic processes of coexistence, which include decay, renewal and regeneration.

Caroline: Of course, the double-edged sword of England's oak trees is that they were also cut down to build ships to go out, conquer and extract resources from overseas. Shipbuilding was a massive source of deforestation in England. At one point around the 1920s, only 5 per cent of our landscapes were covered with forests. Trees can become both a source of life, in creating habitats, as well as a technology of empire, in the form of a slave ship.

Erinma: Perhaps our conversation is looking to surface an epistemological break from design methods centred around human bodies, human perceptions and human desires?

Caroline: And to consider how design practice and the field of design can come to terms with the emergent conditions of the present, which is a kind of agency, that is decentring the human. We can think about how we might collaborate through what Design Researcher Laura Forlano terms 'more-than-human social worlds' (2017) and what that might entail for design. And, what possibilities might such practices present for creating a shared future?

Erinma: And yet I am concerned about what we skip over when we quickly move from human to more-than-human without a consideration of equity and the need for a just transition out of capitalism, and the deep inequities in certain communities and the 'weathering' of certain bodies. How do we do that without considering who or what gets to be considered as human in the first place? How do we address the inherent problem of hierarchy and representation that renders some humans invisible and dispensable? Growing up, I often had playing in my head Billie Holiday's haunting song *Strange Fruit* (1939), and for many years, I had this irrational fear of trees which was connected to lynching practices in America. I am thinking on the one hand about who needs to do what work and the different work that is required to arrive at both a decolonial and an anti-colonial standpoint, to arrive at the common ground of a postcolonial or posthuman position. There is a kind of reorganization and organizing principle or principles that are required.

Caroline: I think we can turn to language and perhaps find some value in considering 'human as a verb' (1984), rather than human as a noun, after novelist and philosopher Sylvia Wynter. This rearrangement brings the possibility of recomposition and a kind of collectivity of life which links quite well with the idea of us 'becoming human' in tandem with 'becoming planet': this is perhaps an ongoing and quite intentional process.

Erinma: I like that as it speaks to the notion that we are part of, not separate from the Earth, and black and disabled and queer perspectives can also be reclaimed as being about embracing life and joy. Here, there can be new forms of solidarity in finding a desire for a different way of living.

Planetarity: Thinking with the planet

Caroline: Planet Earth, as we know, has both a deep history and a future, before and after humanity. In a way we can consider that while we live here, the planet is 'on loan', and we need to reinscribe our relationship outside of globalized capitalism.

Erinma: This includes reinscribing a relationship outside of the imagined globe that is designed on maps or data points on our interconnected computers.

Caroline: To recognize that history as a designer requires a transformational shift beyond the limits of Human-Centred Design and opening up designing, across multiple generations, beyond single human lifespans. To consider this temporal and spatial expansion of the relations and agencies before and after the human, we can turn to a scholar of comparative literature, Gayatri Chakravorty Spivak. Spivak writes about 'planetarity' or 'thinking with the planet' (2005) as both a practice and a relational ethic. It is perhaps a way to imagine multiple futures, moving away from what Professor of English Amy J. Elias and Christian Moraru describe as 'the totalizing paradigm of modern-age globalization' (2015, xi) subject to nation-state geopolitics and human activities that breach the limits of Earth's ecosystems.

Erinma: Lots of people have laid claim to the representation of the planet in various different ways – 'planet as globe', 'planet as object' – but what I find really interesting is this linguistic play of differences between the words 'planetarity' and 'planetary'. I wonder about the linguistic intention of the disruption. Sociologist Jennifer Gabrys picks up on Spivak's intention that 'planetarity' (2005) is a reworking of the term 'planetary' (2018) and its long association with a universalized episteme.

Caroline: Yes, planetarity acknowledges the agential capacity of the planet. And from here we can consider a role for design and for designers to design in relation to the generation of life and Earth's agential capacity. My way into it, initially, is to draw on the philosopher Spinoza's notion of 'what a body can do' (1677) and how we might enhance our capacities to 'affect and be affected' (1677) by relating to and interacting with a variety of different bodies. To go down this road not taken by dominant Western thought has solidarity with Indigenous thought and is counter to species hierarchies and the universal episteme.

Erinma: There is work to be done to come to terms with becoming anti-colonial. We somehow also must get beyond this conversation of the 'Global North' and the 'Global South', in the same way that we attempt to rethink the notion of 'becoming human'. At the same time, and in line with thinking about a just transition away from dependency on fossil fuels, we have to be careful not to skip over the inequities or past harms that clearly still exist in 'weathered' bodies and geographies.

Caroline: Getting beyond the struggle of identity and representation is crucial because, as you say, it opens space for considering the human in a very different way and from there to design from the present in thinking about our collective future and 'becoming planet'. On some level weathering is considered in policy terms, at least, by non-economic loss and damage (NELD).

Erinma: In a way, this allows us to move towards a kind of radical kinship, going beyond the patriarchy of family, or of DNA. This leads us back to what we were considering before – how we can embrace difference and justice at the same time. Planetarity, then, offers a way of relating to and re-inscribing our relationship to the planet, and our human entanglement within it, not as a static object with the Earth 'captured' by humans as an 'image' from outer space, but as lively and dynamic, with many Earths within the Earth, many of which are yet to be imagined.

Caroline: Perhaps a way to build this into design education and practice is to draw inspiration from scholarly perspectives that blur the boundaries and binaries of animal and human, machine and animal. Design can acknowledge philosophers Donna Haraway and Rosi Braidotti and anthropologist Arturo Escobar to offer an emergent design practice, by building relationality and infrastructures beyond human lifespans.

Ruins and the problem of obsolescence

Erinma: We are starting to explore an approach to addressing the problem of obsolescence, but I wonder if you could articulate the pervasiveness of Human-Centred Design and highlight what aspects need to be, or could be, designed differently.

Caroline: Modern landscapes, infrastructures and products like computers and phones, for example, are in effect destructive as soon as they are created. This is in part because they draw from the future as a kind of debt, in the energy and minerals they use to create them and the harm they do when they are discarded and shipped overseas to be 'recycled' into electronic waste. It is a form of speculating into the future for use in the present. Within cities, landscapes might be described as 'ruins' with concealed industrial processes that qualify and quantify which lives matter and which are expendable. Design theorist and philosopher Tony Fry describes this as 'defuturing' (2020), a process by which designed products, services and infrastructures rapidly become obsolete.

Erinma: How do we get to a way of designing that moves away from this offsetting of the future? By way of example, if we acknowledge that all life is interdependent, responsive and subject to change, how does that 'fit' or 'not fit' with Net Zero as a design solution? How do we make space for an alternative vision of what design practice can become, when globalized solutions, like the race to Net Zero, are so entrenched? The electronic devices that we use are all energy intensive, and the data that they draw on makes data centres the equivalent of the modern-day factory, with fossil fuels supplying most of the electricity that powers data centres. Looking things up on the internet, sending text messages and the advent of artificial intelligence within smart devices all have a huge environmental impact in totality.

Caroline: Indeed, the issue with Net Zero is that it upholds the status quo. As a term, 'Net Zero' appears to have been mobilized from environmental science by the World Bank into policy discourse. We cannot rely solely on greenhouse gas offsetting, and Net Zero ignores the fact that it takes time, for example, for a forest to grow, and that we need to cut emissions right now, as well as in the future. And it also ignores the role that local communities might already play through alternative farming practices to maintain or improve biodiversity.

Erinma: Net Zero does not necessarily favour collaborative, place-based approaches that can reconfigure the unequal power relations, of human, animal and machine. Neither does it consider the social differences and landownership and forestation histories. In that way Net Zero is very entrenched in nationalistic thinking and quite forgetful of the imperial histories – deforestation, plantation monoculture and resource extraction – that brought about inequities in the first place.

Caroline: There are similarities here in terms of needing to be more nuanced in for whom and with whom we design. There is an importance of encountering difference, learning from it and having a kind of reciprocity. In terms of interdependence, initially my way into this was through disability and the lived experience that a disabled life requires relationality and reciprocity. Rather than seeing care as a form of dependency and a burden, instead, considering the wider environment and how we are all connected, reliant and entangled. In considering interdependence as a relational ethic, it is not a stretch to expand this notion to care for the Earth, to soil, to minerals and other forms of life.

Designing infrastructures for coexistence

Erinma: There are lots of community-based examples that we visited when we were thinking about our Future of Food (2014) project. For example, East New York Urban Farm in Brooklyn in the United States grows food for the neighbourhood on previously unused space. The farm acts as a kind of community hub where you can develop the skills, use tools and build connections to grow food for the community, which is then sold locally. The farm builds both social infrastructure and local biodiversity, where what previously existed was garbage dumped in empty parking spaces at the back of a community centre.

Caroline: There was a fascinating design approach on East New York Urban Farm, where the drainage infrastructure of the surrounding houses syphoned rainwater into the farm to water the crops. It reminds me of another example in Malmo, Sweden, where design plays a role for enhancing local community participation. The city council was very ambitious about reducing fossil fuel use by creating an effective food waste system that was designed to make it easier for local residents to avoid their food waste going to landfill. Instead, their collective food waste is converted into biogas, which is used to then power local buses and the garbage trucks that collect the food waste.

Erinma: The problem of the race to Net Zero is perhaps illustrated by lithium mining. It is dirty to mine lithium, and there is not enough lithium to resource everyone with electric cars. Rather than this capitalist consumerist model of moving to electric cars as quickly as possible, how do we, as a society, move on a different trajectory towards valuing public transport, moving away from individual ownership and the need to replace cars every few years? Of course, there will always be outliers, and some people will be or feel dependent on using individual cars. These outlying users of course problematize the ethics we are discussing and need to be considered and taken on a journey as well. In that sense, the universal approach just does not work. We need to design for pluriversality.

Erinma: That makes sense, and yet, a key question is what is stopping us? What might incentivize a shift towards a trajectory of collective care, to move us towards planetarity?

Caroline: There is a concept called *Half Earth* (Hiss 2014; Wilson 2015), which is heavily critiqued, but the idea is that half of the Earth's surface is designated free from humans, as a kind of reserve away from humans to preserve biodiversity. It forces us to consider how much land humans should be using for human life and how much we need to allow to regenerate. The previous ideas that we have discussed, which come from the examples in Malmo and in Brooklyn, show that, when we build, we can refit or retrofit while also building in the possibility for coexistence. A simple example might be cohabitation with other species – where swift boxes can easily be built into a building to house birds between their migration periods. These are pockets of practice in the present from which we might collectively imagine the possibilities, as we move into a different climatic state.

Erinma: Are there other larger-scale examples?

Caroline: Another example would be the hydropower dams in Washington in the United States, where salmon need a way to bypass the dam. Designers have built in a 'fish ladder' that hauls the fish upstream or downstream of the dam. Or we might consider wildlife corridors in cities that connect patches of wildlife together and this can allow different species to migrate and flourish in different parts of a city, from one park to another, from one city to another and of course going beyond state borders.

Erinma: An obvious example is fungi, where mycelium create networks with plant roots underground, creating a web structure that brings about decomposition and decay, and ongoing cycles of life. There are analogies there with black, feminist, queer and crip solidarity networks and ways of organizing, taking root 'where the commons give refuge, where refuge gives commons' (2013, 28), as scholars Stefano Harney and Fred Moten assert.

Conclusion

Erinma: We have spoken about planetarity as a *relational design ethic* that considers more-than-human perspectives while at the same time considering justice, which requires equity and transversal solidarity. What kinds of choices do designers need to make such that life is actively sustained and regenerative?

Caroline: As designers, we can choose to design interdependently. We can work with those edge cases. When edge cases become lead users, and we start our design practice from those positions, we can then offer multiple alternative paths to the future.

It is also a question of crossing borders between philosophical genres; epistemological borders, between documentary, scientific, and fictional languages; the borders of gender, the borders between languages and nationalities, those that separate humanity from animality, the living from the dead, the borders between today and history. (Preciado 2019, 41)

Acknowledgements

Caroline Ward and Erinma Ochu (Squirrel Nation) were racial justice AI fellows of the Ada Lovelace Institute and the London School of Economics, funded by UKRI-AHRC. Erinma is supported by a UKRI-NERC grant, Engaging Environments (grant number NE/S017437/1).

References

Blair, James J. A., et al. *Exhausted: How Can We Stop Lithium Mining from Depleting Water Resources, Draining Wetlands and Harming Communities in South America*. New York: NRDC, 2022.
Braidotti, Rosi. *Posthuman Feminism*. Cambridge: Polity Press, 2022.
Büscher, Bram, et al. 'Half-Earth or Whole Earth? Radical Ideas for Conservation, and Their Implications'. *Oryx* 51, no. 3 (2017): 407–10.
Elias, Amy J. and Christian Moraru. *The Planetary Turn: Relationality and Geoaesthetics in the Twenty-First Century*. Evanston: Northwestern University Press, 2015.
Escobar, Arturo. *Design for the Pluriverse: Radical Interdependence, Autonomy, and the Making of Worlds*. Durham: Duke University Press, 2018.
Forlano, Laura. 'Posthumanism and Design'. *She Ji: The Journal of Design, Economics, and Innovation* 3, no. 1 (2017): 16–29. https://doi.org/10.1016/j.sheji.2017.08.001
Fry, Tony. *Defuturing: A New Design Philosophy*. London: Bloomsbury, 2020.
Gabrys, Jennifer. 'Becoming Planetary'. *e-flux Architecture*, 2018.
Gabrys, Jennifer. 'Electronic Environmentalism: Monitoring and Making Ecological Crises'. In *The Routledge Handbook of Ecomedia Studies*, edited by Antoio López, et al. London: Routledge, 2023, 129–36.
Harney, Stefano and Fred Moten. *The Undercommons: Fugitive Planning & Black Study*. London: Minor Compositions, 2013.
Hiss, Tony. 'Can the World Really Set Aside Half of the Planet for Wildlife?' Smithsonian Magazine, September 2014. https://www.smithsonianmag.com/science-nature/can-world-really-set-aside-half-planet-wildlife-180952379/
McKittrick, Katherine. *Dear Science and Other Stories*. Dhuram: Duke University Press, 2021.
paperson, la. *A Third University is Possible*. Minneapolis: University of Minnesota Press, 2017.
Preciado, B. Paul. *An Apartment on Uranus*. London: Firzcarraldo Editions, 2019.
Sharpe, Christina. *In the Wake: On Blackness and Being*. Durham: Duke University Press, 2016.
Spinoza, Baruch. *Ethics*. Translated by Edwin Curley. Princeton, NJ: Princeton University Press, 1994.
Spivak, Gayatri Chakravorty. 'Planetarity'. In *Death of a Discipline*. New York: Columbia Press, 2005, 71–102.
Squirrel Nation. *Everyday Growing Futures*, 2014. https://vimeo.com/71372707
Tooze, Adam. 'Chartbook #130 Defining Polycrisis – From Crisis Pictures to the Crisis Matrix'. 24 June 2024. https://adamtooze.substack.com/p/chartbook-130-defining-polycrisis
Tsing, Anna. *The Mushroom at the End of the World: On the Possibility of Life in Capitalist Ruins*. Princeton: Princeton University Press, 2015.
Wilson, Edward O. Half-Earth: Our Planet's Fight for Life. New York: Liveright Publishing Corporation, 2016.
Wynter, Sylvia. 'The Ceremony Must Be Found: After Humanism'. *Boundary* 2, no. 12/13 (1984): 19–70.
Yusoff, Kathryn. *A Billion Black Anthropocenes or None*. Minneapolis: University of Minnesota Press, 2019.

14
INDIGENOUS FUTURES
EPISTEMOLOGIES OF CARE FOR A WORLD IN CRISIS

Felipe Viveros

One windswept, wintry night in a faded ex-industrial city in the Northern Hemisphere, several hundred lawyers, political activists, artists and technocrats turned their backs on one of the most deeply consequential symposia of our age, where the very future of the world was being fought over. Instead, they sought solace in an alternative form of assembly and an altogether different story of our shared tomorrows within the walls of a nineteenth-century converted church. When the United Nations Conference of Parties 26 (UNCOP 26) began in October 2021 in Glasgow, with the world just shrugging off the shock and quiet of the global pandemic, there seemed to be a collective longing for leaders to fashion a powerful response to the crises that confront us. It was made clear that the survival of our species and countless other life forms were at stake. Scientists had never before so unequivocally made their case: we cannot go on as we have been. Worldwide, young people marched in the streets.

Covid-19 has shown that nation-states could slow down the global economy in the face of a life-threatening emergency. Yet, despite the tireless work of many dedicated people in the negotiating chambers, action fell far short of collective hopes and desperate planetary needs. Why? And how can those of us longing for a different future reckon with that failure? The harsh reality is that in the thirty years since the global community first gathered at the Earth Summit in 1992 in Rio to design a response to globalized, industrial pillage and extraction, there has yet to be an international consensus on how to act. In fact, we have seen the opposite of progress and agreement with worsening emissions, increasing extraction, mass species extinction, growing numbers of climate refugees, the collapse of pollinator species and the continual crossing of more and more planetary boundaries. Vested interests, of course, play no small part. But there is a growing tide of thinkers, designers, artists and writers who suggest a linked but more foundational problem: the very way in which we see and relate to the world.

While UNCOPs generate high political drama, in their current format, they are incapable of generating the deeper reckoning with our past, present and future that is needed to advance change of the necessary magnitude. What is needed is a full redesign of Earth's operating systems: a 'hospicing of modernity' (2021), to borrow Latinx Professor Vanessa Machado de Oliveira's phrasing, and a midwifery of its alternatives. Central to these tasks will be both new and ancient stories, songs, ceremonies and myths about the Earth and our place within it. Within many multinational fora, UNCOPs included, the dominant conception of the Earth is an 'inert repository of resources' (2021), as the writer Amitav Ghosh puts it. This flawed concept allows humanity to perpetuate extraction and pollution on an industrial scale. The key work right now is to dislodge this concept, to forge a genuinely fresh compact with the Earth by embracing ways of feeling and knowing that emphasize how fully alive the Earth is. To paraphrase the Amazonian Indigenous leader Sonia Guajajara, we must reforest our minds and re-indigenize our politics, institutions and operating systems (Guajajara 2022).

Crafting and paying close attention to new stories, myths and practices that might propel us towards a more beautiful future has never been a more urgent task. To do so requires us to see, confront, contest and consciously release ourselves from the dominant, destructive stories, myths and practices that hold us captive. We must focus on the liberation of our cultures, hearts and minds, and bring these revitalized cultures of liberation to our politics, how we come together to organize and how we live our everyday lives. This essay is an attempt to suggest how that might happen, drawing on over twenty years of practice, in ecology, activism and design, showcasing just a few of the ways myself and others are starting to do this, why it is so important and why the time to do it is now.

New mythologies: 'Begin again'

That winter evening at the UNCOP in Glasgow, as shared hopes started to yield to grief, disbelief, anger and resolve, many of us who felt most impatient for concrete political and radical systems change found ourselves forsaking the conference suites to find fellowship and connection in an altogether different modality. We gathered to sing. That we chose to sing at all and the exact song we sang were rejections of the business-as-usual rubric and narrow definitions of spheres of action and agency, belonging and expression that the main UNCOP event modelled. The songs left us spellbound and awake to unseen sentience; we were on the threshold of some new-yet-ancient paradigm that might power meaningful transformation. The group at St Luke's that evening was diverse – we were of all ages, genders, persuasions and creeds. There were organizers, artists, students, policymakers, writers, from every geography. All we had in common was coming together in the midst of the climate crisis, in the midst of our immense grief, disillusionment, fears and hopelessness in fellowship and with a deep sense of openness to the possibility that there might be some value to us being there with our hearts open. Together, we sang a song called *Begin Again*, which includes the following lines:

> There's rain in the river, there's a river running through
> To the sea around these islands crying tears of sorrow and pain
> There's rain in the river, there's a river in my veins . . .
> Living lines of memory drew the markings on my hands
> Ancient lines of living love are waking in this land
> Saying, 'I am in the forest, in the city and the field
> I am in the bounty, come on, know me as I yield

I am in the Falcon, in the Otter and the Stoat
I am in the Turtle Dove with nowhere left to go.'

Begin Again is a song I wrote with my close friend and collaborator, the musician Nick Mulvey, in 2019. We wrote it as an experiment, exploring how we might use music to create ancestral connections and speak about the ecological crisis intuitively and generatively. *Begin Again* is not showy: the musical arrangement consists chiefly of Nick's voice and his guitar. The aim of the song is to open us up to a different sense of selfhood: reminding us that we have an opportunity to reconcile ourselves with our ancestors and the more-than-human world and to remake the world we inhabit. It invites us to imagine a different path.

Every day, we are bombarded by narratives of fear: the spectre of war, climate disaster and economic recession. Many of us feel disempowered and overwhelmed, unsure of what to do. Yet amidst the

Figure 14.1 A machine for plotting ley lines, 2022. Courtesy of Felipe Viveros and Keir Williams.

tragedy are stories of beautiful, alternative tomorrows. Art has the power to present these new stories in a way that can disrupt the status quo, opening the door to new possibilities. Nick and I wrote *Begin Again* with themes of ancestral connection, nature and interbeing to sit between the realms of question and possibility. Humans used to sing songs of reverence for and reciprocity with nature with openness and vigour in public and political fora. Singing together in a church outside Glasgow, we started to ask, how might it reinvigorate global processes if songs such as these were no longer relegated to side events? Of course, it is not only about the songs themselves. Rather, who is singing them, what are they saying, who is listening, how are they received and what weight they hold in the midst of such processes.

Progress-as-arrow versus Indigenous mythology

Three hundred years ago, at the dawn of industrialization, intellectuals of the Enlightenment constructed a mythology of progress-as-arrow, a framing that has underpinned one of the most enduring and pernicious of paradigms – of conquest and exploitative capitalism (and its antecedent: slavery, colonialism, and its spin-off: neoliberalism). Capitalism and the ideology of conquest are founded and rely on several key tenets: the separation of humanity from the natural world, human exceptionalism, white supremacy and patriarchy. Its expression is commodity fetishism, dispossession and perpetual war. The natural world is quantifiable raw material and must be controlled, subjugated, exploited and owned.

Before the arrival of explorer Christopher Columbus in 1492, Indigenous people in North America had identified this ideology as *Wetiko* – a cannibalistic spirit driven by greed (Forbes 2009). And it is Indigenous stories and songs that present us with the clearest articulation of an alternative path to the *Wetiko* ideology. It is a path of remembering. I was born in the Wallmapu, Mapuche Indigenous country, in what is now known as Chile. I am a hybrid, a *mestizo*, a comingling of Indigenous bloodlines and European migrants. It is at this intersection – in the struggle between dominant, traditional and emergent ideas – that I define my practice as an artist, designer, musician, ecologist, writer and organizer. Increasingly, I have been working to embed and transpose Indigenous Knowledge to the industrial lands of my adopted home, the UK; to use the techniques of my ancestors to tackle head-on the insatiable industrial logic that fuels climate disaster.

Reforesting the mind: Reawakening to our earthly entanglements

We need new mythologies to navigate these times. 'Humans', says Swiss psychiatrist Carl Jung, 'have always been mythmakers' (Jung 1964). Myths and ceremonies have allowed humans and the non-human world to communicate with one another for millennia, reinforcing a felt sense of our interdependence down the generations. Also known as the Ethnosphere (Davis 2007), this continuum of songs, rituals, knowledge, myths and stories connects us to the *anima mundi* – Latin for 'the soul of the Earth' (Margulis 2006). As First Nations peoples around the world remind us: we are nature. The web of life is a living dynamic interconnected network, whereby organic and inorganic life forms are constantly interacting, following an infinite pattern of reciprocity. Humans are organic beings, an amalgamation of smaller organisms, deeply enmeshed in an extraordinarily sophisticated living world that abounds with other life forms. We are just one sub-species within the superorganism. We depend on a number of conditions to live, to sustain our bodies and minds: clean air, fresh food, drinkable water, play and leisure. But perhaps most importantly, we rely on a network of mutually supportive relationships – what neuroscientists call 'care and systems of affiliation' (Insel 2001). To put it another way: 'We can be motivated by power and achievement, by consumption and wanting; but we are also motivated just as deeply by care and systems of affiliation' (Singer 2015, 130). Our wellbeing depends on a number of interrelated factors: our capacity to cultivate inner fulfilment, the quality of our social bonds and a healthy environment. We are deeply entangled to each other and to the broader world, within a wider web of nested hierarchies: we *inter-are* (Thich Nhat Hạnh 1998). We echo nature in our bodies. The form of our lungs resembles the shape of trees and river deltas, our very being a fractal of the larger whole.

In the past, our deep-time ancestors understood and spoke the language of nature (de Quincey 2002). Humans thrived in land-based cultures that gradually adapted to their environments, developing complex and sophisticated ecosystem management techniques over time. From this symbiotic relationship with the land 'comes sheer genius' (2019) as the Australian Indigenous academic Tyson Yunkaporta reminds us. A disposition towards awe for the immeasurable entanglements we have been entrusted with is natural for Indigenous and non-Indigenous human beings. According to the American philosopher David Rothenberg, beauty is a key evolutionary principle: 'Life is far more interesting than it needs to be, because the forces that guide it are not merely practical' (Rothenberg 2013).

Tragically, most of us have lost our connection to place and our kinship with the Earth due to modernity. Our memories have been wiped, and our minds, bodies and imaginations have all been steadily and methodically colonized by the dominating Western culture. As novelist Amitav Ghosh explains in an online interview for *Emergence Magazine*: '[In previous ages] in Europe as elsewhere, people had always thought of many other kinds of beings as being capable of making meaning. For many of us, the faculty [to be in communication with non-human beings] has been educated out of us' (2022). Repairing the link with the *anima mundi* is essential. But how do we rekindle and nurture this relationship? *Reforest the mind*, answers Celia Xakriabá, an Indigenous tribal leader with whom I have had the honour of collaborating. Xakriabá writes in an online letter for the Barbican Centre website: 'Reforest the mind is a way of life; it is decolonising our bodies and the land. In our *Xakriabá* language, we say *Smikra Wahira* – the future is ancestral. To save the old is to save the new. You cannot cure an illness with the same disease. . . . We are the cure of the Earth' (2022). Ghosh echoes her analysis: 'European colonisers felt so profoundly threatened by Native American beliefs, most of all by their beliefs in the life of the Earth, or the life of landscapes and the lives of many different kinds of beings. But human beings have had these abilities forever.' He argues that: 'We have to be doubly attentive to those who have not lost that ability. We have to find ways to restore life to the beings of the Earth who have been silenced over the last two hundred years.' He goes on to say that this is 'The biggest artistic and political task of our era' (2022). Reforesting our minds means nothing less than ending our misplaced notions of human superiority, dominance and endless greed. It necessitates our movement towards greater adaptability, resilience and long-term thinking. If we do this with humility, gratitude, sobriety and responsibility, we may yet course-correct.

The Earth, with an incredibly vast and diverse array of living beings, has much to teach us about multiple coexisting perspectives. We can learn, for instance, as the American conservationist Aldo Leopoldo said, to 'think like a mountain' (1949). 'Only if we understand, can we care. Only if we care we will help. Only if we help, we shall be saved' (1999), says the primatologist Jane Goodall. Multispecies perspectives may help us seed post-anthropocentric, decolonial futures and help us rethink what it means to be human within a more-than-human world. The reality is, that whether we realize it or not, our existence is deeply entangled with everything and everyone else. The premise that living organisms significantly affect the climatic system is no longer controversial. Our climate has been relatively stable for the last 9,000 years thanks to the symbiotic and fluid relationship between the living planetary systems and its orchestra of beings. Yet knowledge of these complex and vital processes remains relatively niche outside Indigenous groups and a few scientists. If anything, our changing climate has made the intricate web of relationships between humans and our living world more evident.

Complexity rather than homogeneity is the essence of the living world. This is in exact opposition to the monocultures and standardization of industrialization. Nature is, in the words of the Irish poet Louis MacNeice, 'incorrigibly plural' (2012) – teeming with multitudinous life forms. Or as the Colombian biologist Brigitte Baptistery notes, there is nothing *queerer* than nature. As agriculturalists now know, such multiplicity is the source of resilience. Indigenous peoples have always narrated climate change and their relationships with the natural world through a different lens: through kinship relationships which are based on care, consent and reciprocity (Whyte 2019). These people often have a wider sense of time – enabling a much longer-term sense of responsibility for the future impacts of their actions. 'Every decision that we make [must] relate to the welfare and wellbeing of the seventh generation to come' (1980), as Chief of the Onondaga Nation Oren Lyons advises. How would it change our actions if we were to imagine the impact of human behaviour on our children born 500 years hence? Perhaps the so-called civilized world should become just a little bit more Indigenous, rather than the other way around.

Indigenous technologies: Symbiotic geography and architecture

How can we cultivate awe for the vast entanglements that we have been entrusted with? Where do we look for inspiration to rebuild our innate connection with the more-than-human world? As the philosopher David Abram points out: 'We live immersed in intelligence, enveloped and informed by creativity we cannot fathom' (2010, 129). The challenge, then, is how to unlearn our industrial practices and reawaken to this sense of wonder. A key way in is through our relationship with the land. Indigenous people have maintained a constant wisdom of place and through their *Traditional Ecological Knowledge* (TEK) are living embodiments of how we might avert the climate and ecological crisis. Eighty per cent of the world's remaining biodiversity is safeguarded by Indigenous people globally, despite making up only 5 per cent of the world's population (IUCN 2019). 'It seems like the practices of the Indigenous people enhance biodiversity', as the academics James P. Robson and Fikret Berkes explain. 'Thus, people are factors of landscape regeneration, allowing biological and cultural diversity to flourish' (2010, 844). It is hard to overemphasize what a contrast this makes to the impact of most modern-day humans' interaction with the lands we occupy.

Recent archaeological evidence demonstrates that native peoples in the Americas created sophisticated agroecological systems that allowed them to prosper and maintain a civilization long before the arrival of the Europeans (Heckenberger et al. 2003). Indigenous peoples are not a homogeneous group; their cultural complexity is as diverse as the range of the wildlife in the spaces they inhabit. Take a moment to picture a rainforest overflowing with life, filled with melodic bird songs, wildflowers hanging on the tree canopy enticing a swarm of bees with their fragrance, a crystalline river basin running through. Humans belong to the land and help 'hold the sky in place' (2013), in the words of Yanomami shaman Davi Kopenawa, through offerings, prayers and songs. Yet, these great stewards of nature, at a moment when they offer such powerful hope to humanity, are more under threat than ever before. They are on the frontline of the devastating externalities of capitalism, caught in a seemingly endless cycle of destruction and violence, deforestation, epistemicide (the destruction of knowledge), systematic racism and extermination. Despite all of that, they continue to put their lives on the line, every day and every night, in service to the living world as they have done for hundreds of years, championing a reciprocal and restorative relationship with the Earth that we are all part of.

A flourishing field of academia now works to study, protect and widen appreciation for Indigenous land stewardship through the transdisciplinary codification of TEK. Friket Berkes, an environmental scientist from Canada, defines TEK as 'A cumulative body of knowledge, practice, and belief, evolving by adaptative processes and handed down through generations by cultural transmission, about the relationship of living beings (including humans) with one another and with the environment' (Berkes 1999, 8; Gadgil et al. 1993, 151). TEK sees knowledge as a *process* rather than something static and as a way of life rather than something you do. It has enabled humans to understand and manage ecosystems and adapt to the changing environment using a symbiotic approach to living systems. TEK provides an alternative to the contemporary Western knowledge-practice-belief complex. In the words of the educator and activist Celia Xakriabá:

> Territory is more than just the environment; territory is our whole lives. Our body is the territory and the territory is our body. We should be thinking beyond politics, and think about how we can re-enchant the world again. Awaken our senses. The challenge is to reforest our hearts. (Xakriabá 2020)

There is a continuum between humans and the Earth, where life is interconnected, intertwined with our human bodies, the rainforest, the whisper of the river and our thoughts. This understanding of the continuum between humans and the whole is not exclusive to Indigenous peoples: it can also be found in pre-Christian Europe, in the Sufi mysticism of Islam and Hindu, Buddhist and Taoist traditions (Callicott 1994). Berkes calls the unity between humans and the environment 'Sacred Ecology' (1999). In my practice for accessing the sacred, I have embraced ceremony and ritual as key methods for sensemaking. Ceremony, according to the Potawatomi author and plant scientist Robin Wall Kimmerer, is 'A vehicle for belonging – to a family, to a people and to a land' (2013, 51). Ceremony and ritual have always been part of the sensemaking process, a unique technology that enables us to connect with the more-than-human world, each other and what First Nations call the *great mystery*. Working with the renowned light artist Chris Levine, I have applied some of those learnings in the UK. Chris invited me to explore the hidden energies of the land with him (see Figure 14.2). He was interested in how ancient wisdom and Earth frequencies might help us 'remember' who we truly are and heal disembodied territories and desolate inner landscapes.

Imagine if our design and infrastructure had this continuum as a core design principle. Julia Watson, the Australian architect who coined the term 'Lo-TEK', has done exactly that with her book *Lo-TEK, Design by Radical Indigenism*. In her book, Watson details several case studies covering mountains, forests, deserts and wetlands, of innovative and resilient infrastructures developed by Indigenous people using TEK principles. They offer powerful beacons for what could grow into a flourishing new field of design and architecture that is Earth-entangled, symbiotic and future-proof. In her research, Watson notes that the Apete Forest Islands of the Kayapo people of the Brazilian Amazon appear to have 'No division between the spiritual and daily aspects of life' (2022, 17). The raised platforms of the *Waru Waru*

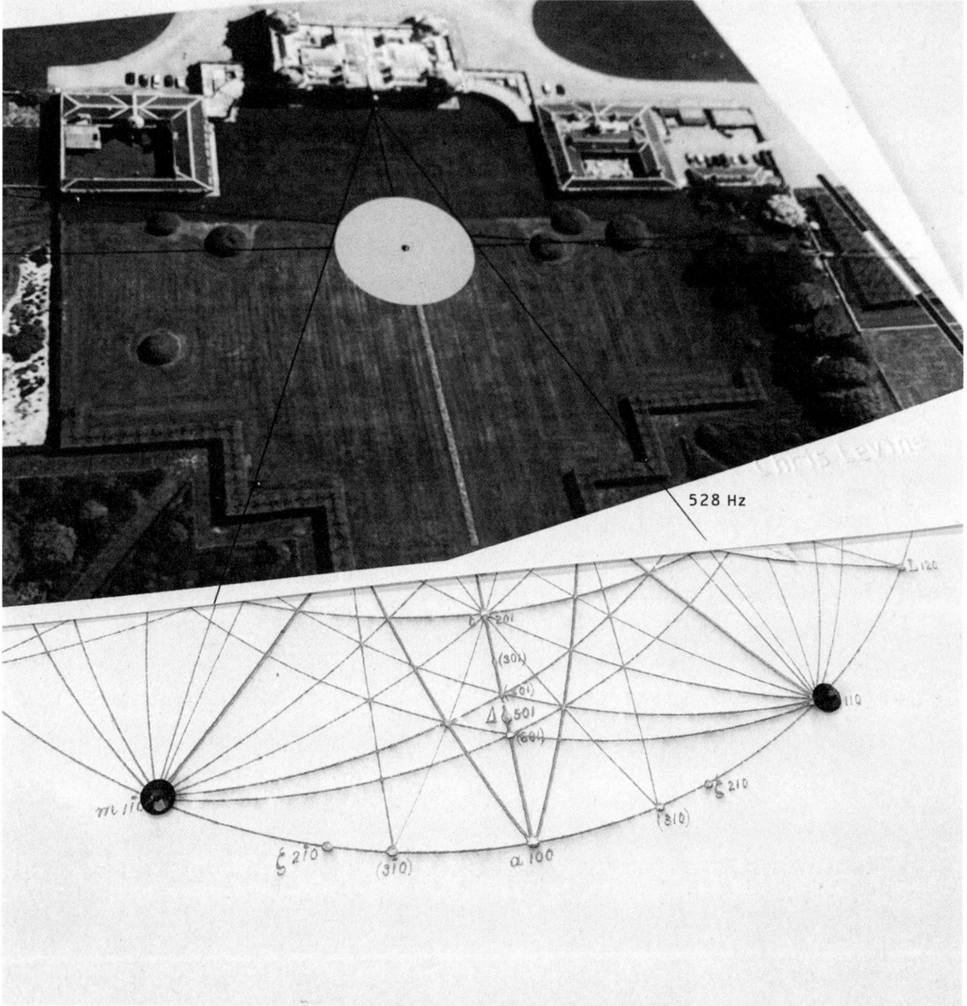

Figure 14.2 *528 Hz Love Frequency*, 2021. Courtesy of Chris Levine.

terraces of the Inca in Peru increase topsoil depth, aeration and drainage. 'This ancient agricultural system has positive localised environmental effects and represents a scalable and sustainable model for modern agriculture' (2022, 18), says Watson. Moreover, at the current pace of environmental degradation, which inevitably triggers unexpected disasters and emergencies that require rapid response, Lo-TEK designs could enable us to be more resilient to future crises.

Whether they like it or not, modern design must consider new weather patterns and planetary dynamics. This presents us with an extraordinary opportunity to redesign our civilization and reckon with the consequences of our energy-intensive way of life. One place already moving towards a more regenerative model of design and community, developed on such Lo-TEK principles, is Tierra Valiente (Brave Earth) in Costa Rica, which describes itself as a centre for applied cultural transition. The land that Brave Earth is built on was purchased and put into a trust, so the community that lives there are stewards rather than private owners. They operate their centre as a not-for-profit cooperative and have co-founded

Figure 14.3 Maloca's skylight, 2022. Courtesy of Tierra Valiente.

a bioregional mutual aid network. With an architectural design primarily informed by biomimicry, and built with natural materials, Tierra Valiente bridges scientific and Indigenous understandings of the world (see Figure 14.3). Many of my emergent findings and most powerful ideas have found inspiration in the jaguar's habitat, the graceful dance of the blue morpho and the fragrance of the wild rainforest orchids. There, humans are the 'rare species' and the subtropical air embraces you.

Tierra Valiente is just one example of many other similar experiments around the world. There is a growing network of alternatives to the current system (see for example: https://ecovillage.org/), gestures, improvisations and purposeful explorations towards the 'beautiful world our heart knows is possible' (Eisenstein 2013).

A new mythology of technology

Notions of reforesting our minds and applying sacred geography may seem fanciful to many twenty-first-century humans, most of whom live urban existences, often in challenging circumstances. A key new frontier, I would argue, is how we incorporate Indigenous perspectives into humanity's newest and most disruptive infrastructure – that of Western-based technology. Unlike the vast systems of agriculture, politics, economics, transport and energy that surround us, which we inherited from earlier ages, this system is still emergent: being invented and refashioned in real time. Wet clay that we might yet still hope to shape.

Technology's design and content currently remain skewed towards rich, Western countries. Most online knowledge is accessible only through colonial languages, predominantly English and Chinese

(Whose Knowledge? 2022). This fundamental imbalance of content and knowledge creation is deeply embedded in the structure of the internet itself. Most importantly, those of us who are the primary consumers of digital content and infrastructure – 75 per cent of the world's online population – come from the 'Global South' and are neither its producers nor the decision-makers when it comes to its content, design and experience. Epistemic colonialism is likely the least well-known type of colonialism and is an invisible but persistent force (Sengupta 2022). What would happen if epistemologies of the geopolitical south including many ways of knowing and being that centre care and reciprocity were embedded in the design process? A working group called *Indigenous AI* is exploring this terrain. 'The artificial intelligence industry-academic complex does not have an ethics problem. It has an epistemology problem' (2021), says the multidisciplinary group's co-founder Professor Jason Edward Lewis in an online article for the publishing platform *Medium*. The group comprises Indigenous experts working in media studies, AI, history, politics, neurobiology and other disciplines interested in questions such as 'How can Indigenous epistemologies and ontologies contribute to the global conversation regarding society and AI?' (Lewis 2020, 26). If groups like this succeed in indigenizing technology, the internet might act as a genuinely transformative infrastructure.

Indigenous futures: Mycelium to fruit the change

In her book *Hope in the Dark* the author Rebecca Solnit talks about the hidden work that leads to dramatic, visible change, arguing that often when nothing seems to be changing, we may be at the cusp of a collective breakthrough. She writes:

> What we call mushrooms, mycologists call the fruiting body of the larger, less visible fungus. Uprisings and revolutions are often considered to be spontaneous, but less visible long-term organising and groundwork – or underground work – often laid the foundation. Changes in ideas and values also result from work done by writers, scholars, public intellectuals, social activists, and participants in social media. It seems insignificant or peripheral until very different outcomes emerge from transformed assumptions about who and what matters, who should be heard and believed, who has rights. (2016, xv–xvi)

Right now, a powerful and vast global interconnected network of underground mycelium is pushing to centre Indigenous principles in an overhaul of operating systems. Our role as artists, academics, activists and simply as citizens of our times is to assist in fruiting Indigenous futures.

The 4.5-billion-year-old superorganism we call Earth is teeming with life. It survived cataclysmic events such as meteorite collisions, five mass extinctions and volcanic eruptions. Our planet remains a resilient whole. To the Earth, the Anthropocene is little more than a glitch, a temporary transitional period. For our species, itself now standing perilously close to the extinction of our own making, our response is of the utmost consequence. We can rewrite our destiny, use this crisis as the impetus for demonstrating humanity's capacity for sensemaking, creativity, solidarity, healing and trans-rationality. The antidote to the Anthropocene lies in embracing other ways of knowing and being outside of the Anglo-European extraction-and-conquest model. As I have set out, we need a new cosmology: changing how we perceive reality and position ourselves in relationship with it. 'What we contemplate here is more than ecological restoration; it is the restoration of the relationship between plants and people. We are dreaming of a time

Figure 14.4 O futuro é indígena, 2022. Courtesy of Alice Aedy.

when the land might give thanks for the people' (2013, 313), says environmental biologist Robin Wall Kimmerer.

We have a duty of care with and for the Earth's community and future generations, an allegiance to Life with a capital L. Expanding our perception and our embodied self is an exciting prospect. After all, the destiny of humanity is to *explore the vastness of ourselves*: symbiosis with the living world is possible if we change our core design principles and practices. We cannot go back in time, but we still have time to create something new, informed by a greater understanding of our role within a living Earth. As I have shown, we can learn from Indigenous peoples and their symbiotic technologies. The current meta-crisis is the perfect rite of passage to demonstrate our capabilities. The only question that matters is: Which future will you help create?

References

Abram, David. Becoming Animal: An Earthly Cosmology. New York: Pantheon Books, 2010.

Baptiste, Brigitte. 'Brigitte Baptiste: It's Time to Reframe Sustainable Work Through a Queer Lens'. *Welcome to the Jungle*, 29 March 2022. https://www.welcometothejungle.com/en/articles/brigitte-baptiste-reframing-work-with-queer-lens

Berkes, Fikret. *Sacred Ecology: Traditional Ecological Knowledge and Resource Management*. London: Taylor & Francis, 1999.

Callicott, J. Baird. *Earth's Insights: A Survey of Ecological Ethics from the Mediterranean Basin to the Australian Outback*. Berkeley: University of California Press, 1994.

Davis, Wade. Light at the Edge of the World: A Journey Through the Realm of Vanishing Cultures. Vancouver: Douglas & McIntyre, 2007.

de Quincey, Christian. *Radical Nature*. Rochester: Park Street Press, 2002.

Eisenstein, Charles. *The More Beautiful World Our Hearts Know Is Possible*. Berkeley: North Atlantic Books, 2013.

Forbes, Jack. *Columbus and Other Cannibals: The Wetiko Disease of Exploitation, Imperialism and Terrorism.* New York: Seven Stories Press, 2009.

Ghosh, Amitav. 'Beings Seen and Unseen'. *Emergence Magazine*, 31 August 2022. https://emergencemagazine.org/interview/beings-seen-and-unseen/

Ghosh, Amitav. The Nutmeg's Curse: Parables for a Planet in Crisis. Chicago: University of Chicago Press, 2021.

Goodall, Jane. *Jane Goodall: 40 years at the Gombe*. New York: Stewart Tabori & Chang Inc, 1999.

Guajajara, Sonia. 'To Indigenize Politics and Reforest Mind'. *Sumauma: Journalism from the Centre of the World*, 27 September 2022. https://sumauma.com/en/aldear-a-politica-e-reflorestar-mentes/

Hanh, Nhất Thich. 'Interrelationship'. *Plum Village*, 7 July 2019. https://plumvillage.org/articles/interrelationship-poem-by-thich-nhat-hanh/

Harding, Stephan. *Animate Earth. Science, Intuition and Gaia*, ed. L. Margulis. Totnes: Green Books, 2006.

Heckenberger, Michael, et al. 'Amazonia 1492: Pristine Forest or Cultural Parkland?' *Science* 301 (2003): 1710–14. https://www.science.org/doi/10.1126/science.1086112

Insel, Thomas R., and Larry J. Young. 'The Neurobiology of Attachment'. Nature Reviews Neuroscience, 2, no. 2 (2001): 129–136.

IUCN. 'IUCN Director General's Statement on International Day of the World's Indigenous Peoples 2019'. August 2019. Iucn.org/news/secretariat/201908/iucn-director-generals-statement-international-day-worlds-indigenous-peoples-2019

Jung, Carl G. Man and His Symbols. New York: Dell, 1964.

Kopenawa, Davi, and Bruce Albert. The Falling Sky: Words of a Yanomami Shaman. Translated by Nicholas Elliott. Cambridge, MA: Harvard University Press, 2013.

Lewis, Jason. 'From Impoverished Intelligence to Abundant Intelligences'. *Medium*, 28 May 2021. https://jasonedwardlewis.medium.com/from-impoverished-intelligence-to-abundant-intelligences-90559f718e7f

Lewis, Jason Edward, ed. Indigenous Protocol and Artificial Intelligence Position Paper. Honolulu: Initiative for Indigenous Futures and Canadian Institute for Advanced Research, 2020.

Lyons, Oren. 'Seven Generation Sustainability'. *Wikipedia*, 1980. https://en.wikipedia.org/wiki/Seven_generation_sustainability#cite_note-2

MacNeice, Louis. *Incorrigibly Plural: Louis MacNeice and his Legacy.* Manchester: Carcanet, 2012.

Robson, James P. and Fikret Berkes. 'Sacred Nature and Community Conserved Areas'. In *Nature and Culture: Rebuilding Lost Connections*, edited by Sarah Pilgrim and Jules Pretty. London: Earthscan, 2010, 197–216.

Rothenberg, David. Survival of the Beautiful: Art, Science, and Evolution. New York: Bloomsbury USA, 2013.

Sengupta, Anasuya. 'Decolonising the World's White Web'. Shuttleworth Foundation, 2022.

Singer, Peter. *The Most Good You Can Do: How Effective Altruism Is Changing Ideas About Living Ethically*. New Haven: Yale University Press, 2015.

Solnit, Rebecca. 'Hope is An Embrace of the Unknown'. *The Guardian*, 16 July 2016. https://www.theguardian.com/books/2016/jul/15/rebecca-solnit-hope-in-the-dark-new-essay-embrace-unknown

Thich Nhat Hanh. The Heart of the Buddha's Teaching: Transforming Suffering into Peace, Joy, and Liberation. New York: Broadway Books, 1998.

Wall Kimmerer, Robin. *Braiding Sweetgrass*. Minneapolis: Milkweed, 2013.

Watson, Julia. *Lo-TEK Design by Radical Indigenism*. London: Taschen, 2022.

Whose Knowledge? Decolonising the Internet's Languages – Summary Report, 2020'. https://whoseknowledge.org/wp-content/uploads/2020/02/DTIL-Report.pdf

Whyte, Kyle. 'Time as Kinship'. In *The Cambridge Companion to Environmental Humanities*, edited by Jeffrey Cohen and Stephanie Foote. Cambridge, MA: Cambridge University Press, 2019, 39–55. https://ssrn.com/abstract=3830025

Xakriabá, Celia. '*Cura da Terra – Celia*'. YouTube. 1 September 2020. https://www.youtube.com/watch?v=lBgYoaiiqac&t=17s

Xakriabá, Celia and Sonia Guajajara. 'We are the Earth. A Letter from Indigenous Leaders'. *Barbican*, 20 April 2022. https://www.barbican.org.uk/read-watch-listen/we-are-the-earth-a-letter-from-indigenous-leaders

Yunkaporta, Tyson. Sand Talk: How Indigenous Thinking Can Save the World. Melbourne: Text Publishing, 2019.

15
A BOTTOM-UP APPROACH TO CONSERVATION

THE VERTICAL UNIVERSITY, NEPAL

Priyanka Bista

Nepal, a landlocked country in South Asia, only 0.09 per cent of the Earth's landmass, encompasses a unique physiography consisting of wide altitudinal variations and diverse climatic conditions ranging from the tropics to the nival regions. As a result, this complex terrain has given birth to an incredible diversity of species, from over 6,000 floral diversities to 891 bird species, over 212 mammal species and 220 fish species. Equally diverse is the human domain, with 125 officially recognized ethnicities speaking 123 languages and 59 Indigenous ethnicities. Today, this mountainous geography is flattening rapidly with road networks and urbanization, leading to the destruction of forests and the simultaneous marginalization of Indigenous communities.

The biodiversity conservation approach adopted by the Government of Nepal follows this devastating trend. In the 1970s, while establishing the national parks, the government imported a Western model of nature's strict protection controlled by the military. The founding of the first national park in Chitwan, as a result, displaced 22,000 local inhabitants. This Eurocentric lens also began viewing the local people who once lived in these landscapes as illegals, extractors, poachers and destroyers. This model discarded the intergenerational links Indigenous communities have fostered with their landscapes. While addressing this issue, the Vertical University (VU) project was born in 2016 as a support mechanism that could enable Indigenous people living within biodiversity-rich landscapes to steward conservation efforts. We have been working with communities living in six nodes across the vertical belt of the Eastern Region of Nepal to spearhead a community-based conservation effort. In the first section of this chapter, I will introduce the community-based pangolin conservation project. In the second section, I will elaborate more on the foundations of the VU project. Finally, in the third section, I will go into more details about the complexities of working in conservation within the new Federal State of Nepal.

Encountering pangolins

Early morning around 6.00 am, Anish Magar, a local youth from Dahar village in Yangshila, came running down the hill knocking on the door of a new office we had just set up, 'They killed a pangolin; they killed a pangolin. Last night, they killed a pangolin in my village. I told them not to kill it, but they only ridiculed me! This has been happening every week.' Unable to reply, his comments left me speechless.

Pangolins are listed as a critically endangered species on the *International Union for Conservation of Nature Red List of Threatened Species* and are also famously known as 'the world's most trafficked mammal' (Aisher 2016). Despite the stringent legal protection pangolins had on paper, in villages like Yangshila, pangolins were being openly and routinely hunted down, killed and sold for their scales, used in traditional medicine, and for their meat, a delicacy among some wealthy individuals. In order to have a better understanding of the problem, we undertook a field survey. It became clear that more than 150–200 pangolins had been poached in just four years. However, based on interviews with local communities, it was also estimated that approximately forty to fifty species might still remain in Yangshila's forests. It was difficult to imagine that this shy, nocturnal, solitary and scaly anteater, a species with an evolutionary history of 56–67 million years (Choo et al. 2016), was in danger of extinction. As ecological engineers, pangolins eat 70 million termites annually, significantly affecting forest termite management (Hua et al. 2015). The Chinese Pangolin (critically endangered (CR)) (*Manis pentadactyla*) and the Indian Pangolin (endangered (EN)) (*Manis crassicaudata*) are also present in Nepal. During the last ten years,

Figure 15.1 Pangolin found in Yangshila, 2022. Courtesy of KTK-BELT.

the Chure Hills of Yangshila and its agricultural fields served as a safe habitat for these species. However, with China as one of the largest pangolin trading hubs, the population has steadily declined (Bashyal et al. 2021). Pangolin trade is common in Nepal, with seizures reported from about one-third of the sixty-one districts where pangolins are found and nearly a quarter of the seventy-seven districts (Bashyal et al. 2021).

Further investigation into the causes of the poaching and the identity of the poachers revealed a far more complex picture. Most poachers came from underprivileged and marginalized backgrounds and used poaching as a means of income. However, young adults or adolescents also engaged in poaching because they had too much free time and not enough work. For these people, poaching was more of a hobby or a way to pass the time rather than a way to make money. Contrary to the prevalent perception of dangerous poachers with extensive underground networks, most of them were just ordinary villagers, many oblivious to the ecological impact they were having by engaging in poaching activities. These people were our primary 'stakeholders' and as such, we could not take legal action, which in our opinion was ineffective. Therefore, in consultation with local elders, we decided to take an educational approach and share our awareness and understanding of this species.

Building a community-based movement

Along with a team of wildlife experts and concerned community members, we started to roam from village to village – bringing awareness about this fascinating creature and its behaviours. We informed villagers about its evolutionary history, role as an 'ecosystem engineer' and curious nocturnal habits and morphology. We forged partnerships with international artists and filmmakers, such as Louise Fletcher and Coral and Oak Studios, to develop creative and imaginative community engagement methods. We started to run playful workshops using painting, drawing, filming and writing and held classes for local students using scientific tools, such as camera traps and Geographic Information Systems (GIS). To coordinate all the workshops and programmes, we recruited and engaged with marginalized and unemployed local youth through the BELT fellows' programme. We trained them in filmmaking, photography, camera trapping, mapping and coordinating and leading community projects. We also held official large-scale gatherings, inviting government officials, policymakers, the army and hundreds of community members, including our poacher 'stakeholders'. In addition, we inaugurated signages and exhibits, distributed thousands of bags with the text 'I am a pangolin protector' printed on them and developed an award system for individuals who were actively involved in protecting our little friends. We did everything possible to make the engagement with pangolins 'the coolest thing in the village'. And it worked!

Now, far from being ridiculed, we were able to talk openly and widely about pangolins and other species facing population decline. Over the next five years, I witnessed poachers turning into conservationists, young men and women turning into pangolin conservation leaders and even children turning into monitors of pangolin habitats. Our indirect, non-confrontational, inclusive and long-term approach was a strategy that had not been adopted before. Thus, I learned through this period that if we provide space, time and open, non-judgemental support structures, we can engage local communities to participate in conservation efforts and environmental stewardship and build a broad base of people who speak for the environment.

Figure 15.2 Pangolin Day with Anish Magar explaining the exhibit, 2022. Courtesy of KTK-BELT.

Indigenous people and biodiversity conservation

What I have described in the first section is a fairly successful process where Indigenous community members who are born, brought up and live in areas of biodiversity-rich regions are provided with a platform to engage in biodiversity conservation. Although it seems like a straightforward process, it is not without ongoing struggles, problems and often even harassment that we have managed to create this atmosphere and space for communities to work in this field. In 1976, environmental journalist Erik Eckholm wrote about Himalayan degradation in the book *Losing Ground: Environmental Stress and World Food Prospects*. He claimed that the introduction of modern medicine in the Terai region of Nepal resulted in unsustainable population growth and 'illegal' migration from India, and deforestation by subsistence farmers, which further resulted in the environmental degradation of not only the Terai region but also the hills and Himalayan landscape. He blamed rural poor people for the total cataclysmic destruction of the Himalayan landscape. Although this idea has been challenged for the lack of empirical evidence, Eckholm's doom and gloom narrative accelerated the response of the Western world and the Nepalese government in developing national parks under strict military protection. This approach was directly imported from the United States with the growing expansion of the American environmental movement (Ghale 2018). Influenced by foreign aid and tourism potential, the government of Nepal accepted this Western model of strict protection of nature controlled by the military, where the local poor people were portrayed as 'illegal' extractors and destroyers of the biodiversity-rich landscape.

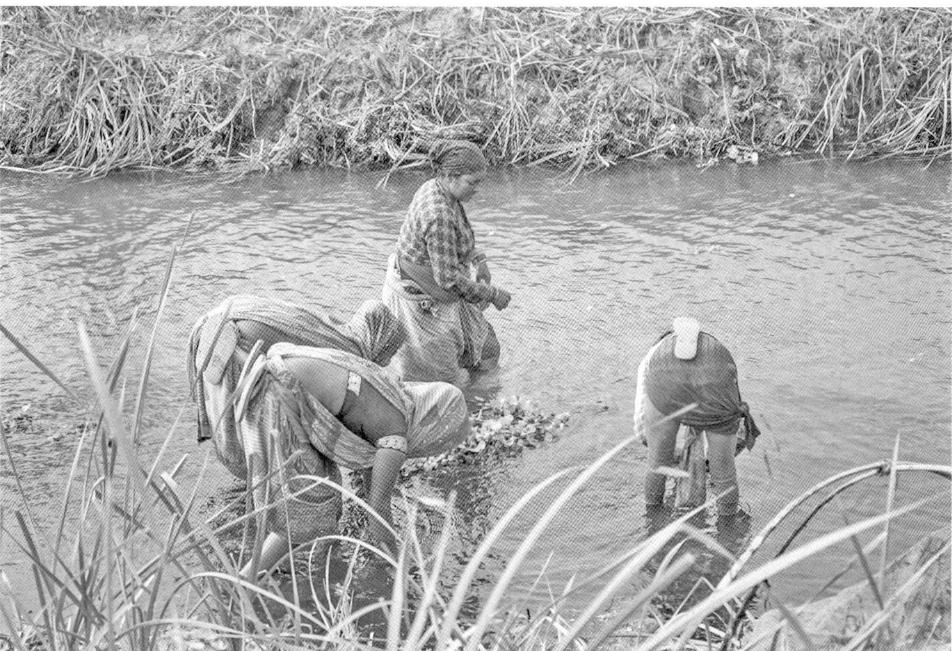

Figure 15.3 Indigenous communities living outside of the Koshi Tappu Wildlife Reserve, 2022. Courtesy of KTK-BELT.

The establishment of the first protected area in Chitwan in 1973 resulted in the removal of 22,000 locals from within the reserve, followed by the creation of the Shuklaphanta Wildlife Reserve, and then Koshi Tappu Wildlife Reserve, which resulted in the dislocation of 12,000 people (Lam 2014). This process created physical and economic displacement by disregarding the Indigenous ways of living with the land. Furthermore, it discarded the intergenerational relationships that the Indigenous communities have established over generations with the landscapes, wildlife and wetlands, creating a breach between Indigenous communities and their biodiversity heritage.

Conceptualizing the Vertical University

The idea for the VU did not start with this macro-level examination of this systemic violence or a desire to challenge Erik Eckolm's theory of Himalayan deterioration (1976). Instead, it began on the ground. It all began with one person, Kumar Bishwakarma. Belonging to the Dalit caste, Kumar Sir was a local leader, a teacher at a village school and a farmer with a deep interest in nature conservation. Before meeting Rajeev Goyal (VU, co-founder) and me, his dream was to take kids into nature and teach them about their natural habitat. When Kumar Sir learned that we were interested in environmental community-based projects, he invited us to visit his village. The initial journey lasted a total of seventeen days. Yangshila is situated in the Chure highlands, with a height range of 180–1,950 metres. As a result, it consists of both subtropical and temperate climatic zones with over 400 unique plant species spanning 96 plant families. The plant diversity reflects how, throughout generations, Indigenous communities have been planting medicinal plants and using these forests as a 'pharmacy'. Historically, the communities in Yangshila have consciously decided to cluster multiple community forests together to create a more extensive presence to safeguard the landscape.

Along with the plants, we met hundreds of farmers who did not have a formal education but had extensive knowledge of medicinal plants and the forest. For them, every tree, every vine and every fern in the forest was medicine, a source of fuel, fodder and building materials. The diversity of their knowledge was deeply tied to the diversity of their landscape. Thus, each forest became a 'classroom' and each farmer a 'professor'. Inspired by the diversity within 14 kilometres of Yangshila, we began to wonder whether it was possible to move beyond these boundaries into the larger north-south corridor of the country, starting from the lowest plains to the highest Himalayas: a gradient consisting of wide altitudinal variations and diverse climatic conditions, with an incredible diversity of species, including over 6,000

Figure 15.4 Map of Yangshila with plant and animal diversity, 2022. Courtesy of KTK-BELT.

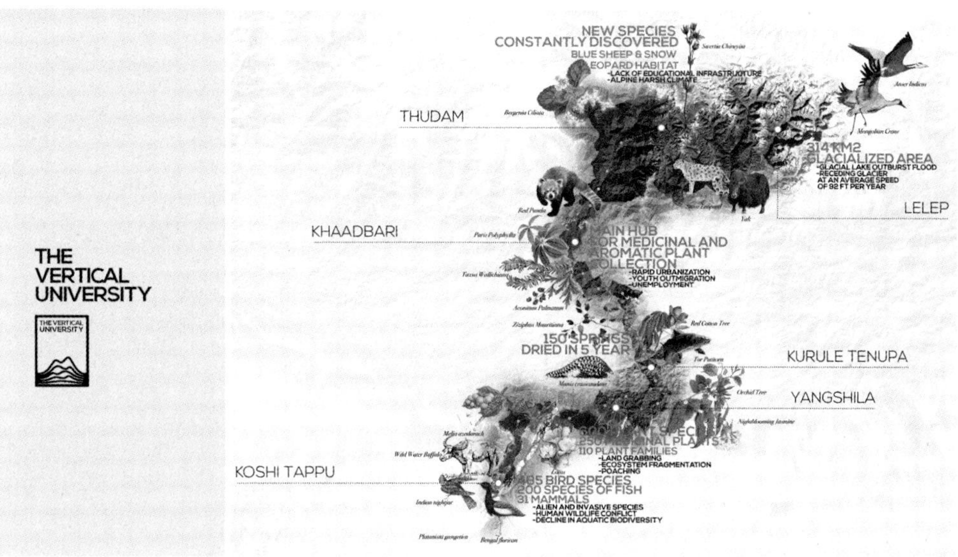

Figure 15.5 Vertical University concept, 2022. Courtesy of KTK-BELT.

floral diversities (Press et al. 2000), 891 bird species (Joshi 2022), over 212 mammal species (Amin et al. 2018) and over 220 fish species (Khatri et al. 2020). Equally diverse was the human population existing in this landscape, with 125 officially recognized ethnicities speaking 123 languages and 59 Indigenous groups (Rajbanshi et al. 2019). By acknowledging this human and non-human diversity, the VU project was conceived. Across this vertical BELT, we anchored ourselves in communities where we met leaders, farmers and teachers like Kumar Sir, who joined us through word of mouth. We collectively started to imagine a larger project.

Building the Vertical University

We had big dreams and envisioned ideas and possibilities with a huge sense of hope. We received a prize for protecting mountains before the event started. We patted ourselves on the back but quickly realized how much work there was to do. So, we moved into a room in Kumar Sir's house and began planning and plotting our project to build the VU – three of us, no money in the bank and no staff. For our first project, we wanted to start recording the knowledge of our 'professors'. And to do the recording, we wanted to start with the local youth – our first students. And so, we launched the VU Youth Fellow Program – and within a week, received three applications – all women. The first two women I interviewed talked about their household chores, goats and babies – and how they did not have time to study. The third applicant, Ganga Limbu, showed up in the office. Initially, I asked her if she had time, and when she said yes, I asked what she wanted to learn – she immediately said, 'AutoCAD'. I asked 'Why?' To my surprise, she said, 'I want to learn everything about technology.'

Ganga was marginalized in every possible way – a daughter of a landless farmer but an ambitious young woman from an Indigenous caste group. We taught her photography, filming and editing. We even trained her in GIS, AutoCAD and SketchUp. Each time testing her interests and abilities, she succeeded in every possible way. Now with one student on board, we returned to our 'professors' and started recording our first Indigenous knowledge video. And then our second, and third and so on. We now have seventy-five videos. We have shown them locally on movie nights. And globally, Ganga has presented the Indigenous Knowledge project to over 300 scientists. And in 2019, she won the Young Naturalist Award, which she dedicated to her late parents and Indigenous 'professors' who taught her how to understand her own landscape. Thus, young men and women of all shapes and sizes, with drive, ambition and tenacity, started to show up from all corners of remote Yangshila – and became builders, accountants, researchers and technicians of the project.

We wanted to broaden this base to an even larger cohort of an even younger generation – local students from government schools born and raised in remote areas. We drafted our first module turning years of place-based research into combining Indigenous and scientific knowledge for grades six first, then seven and then eight. We identified sixty educational opportunities, essentially classrooms, across the topography of Yangshila where kids could learn subjects from astronomy to wetland ecology. We even built our first classroom at the base of this trail and played with many ideas of creating a platform to view the highest and the lowest points of Yangshila.

Building the classroom also functioned as a series of classes for local builders. Lesson 101 was about how to use a measuring tape, draw plans and use case studies. Finally, we even looked at rural toilets in the parks and how the structures framed the landscapes. With hundreds of volunteers from the community – mothers, grandmothers, uncles and aunts – and over thirty local builders and engineers, we completed our first classroom on 15 June 2017. And on 16 June, we opened the classroom and the trail and launched the outdoor education programme. We started the outdoor classes with the basic orientation of the trails and the interpretation points, including lessons about birds, pangolins, ecosystem

Figure 15.6 Ganga Limbu training Amrita Sardar, a youth fellow from Koshi Tappu, 2022. Courtesy of KTK-BELT.

Figure 15.7 Outdoor education with students in Sikti forest, 2022. Courtesy of KTK-BELT.

services and the water cycle. We zoomed in, zoomed out and looked at the same space in multiple ways through multiple lenses. We even brought farmers into the classrooms to teach students about their Indigenous knowledge and trained them to record these events. Our grade six students have graduated to grade eight now. If they engaged with the forest in year one, they would have learned to slow down, document, look, observe, draw and see the intricacies in their landscape.

As the programmes started to take place in communities, within just a few years, we began growing fast – an underground unruly grassroots movement cutting across diverse ecosystems, ethnicities, genders and age groups. We moved out from the one room in Kumar Sir's house and established several offices in Yangshila, Kathmandu, Dharan, Kurule, Khandbari, Taplejung and Koshi Tappu. As we were busy again, congratulating ourselves on witnessing the growth and success of our efforts, the entire political structure of the country changed right before our eyes.

Navigating new complexity

In November 2017, Nepal held its first historic local election after twenty years (Sharma 2017) and, as a result, shifted from a centralized government to a federal state (Bhattarai 2019). During election season, being an apolitical organization, we prided ourselves on being a grassroots and work-oriented organization which focused on building the country instead of rallying with political slogans. However, our naive understanding of the historic change started to impact us almost immediately. For instance, the community members working together up to the announcement of the election's results were suddenly fractured into different political allegiances. Before the election, we had been looking at the map of the country and seeing only the diversity of plants, birds and mammal species, and in the human context – the ethnic minorities and Indigenous communities. However, now we started seeing another layer of Nepal's diversity – the diversity we had deliberately decided to ignore. Nepal now had 116 political parties. Moreover, within the federalist state, our geographically ambitious project now spanned across one province, five districts, nine rural municipalities and over ten wards. Together with the central government, we needed to acknowledge and engage with thirty-nine administrative entities from the central level ministries to the provincial level, district, rural municipalities and the local ward-level administrative bodies.

This new landscape presented new challenges that we had to adapt to. For example, if we had previously spent 80 per cent of our time working in the 'field', we would now have to devote 80 per cent of our time to government relations. Crossing administrative boundaries also meant many more administrative roadblocks than we had previously encountered. Furthermore, managing a project involving eight organizations meant we had an increasing number of lawyers, accountants and administrative staff. So, as incredibly fascinating as it was to be a part of the pangolin project in the early days, over the course of seven years, as we grew, we started to become less organic and more complex with political and bureaucratic ties and donor and government requirements.

Papung

Last but not least, I would like to share the story of Papung – a special project which teaches us to see inspiration from this new (less inspiring) circumstance. In 2017, again through word of mouth, we met Dandu Dhokpya, then Chairman of the Indigenous Federation of Nepal and a community member from Papung. He had heard about our Indigenous Knowledge project and wanted to collaborate with us so that he could document his Indigenous knowledge. Through him, we met parliament members Mingma Dandu Lama and Pasang Sherpa. This area had a strong Indigenous identity and a solid political base at the national level. They declined to join the Kanchenjunga National Park very early on, claiming that they did not need the military or the national government to protect the territory they had been protecting for centuries.

The Dhokpya community is a sub-clan of the Sherpa caste group from Papung. This area also has over 200 high-altitude wetland lakes and an incredible biodiversity of birds, mammals and plants. However, much like the rest of the country, this area is also at threat of encroaching roads, major highways and hydropower projects, and so we started to discuss the possibilities of protecting this landscape. Over the last few years, our team, in collaboration with the Dhokpya community, has been using photographs, videos, stories of their landscapes and even speeches by activist Greta Thunberg to build a momentum encompassing the highest levels of government officials, along with the grassroots community members, youth, yak herders and women. This collective effort has resulted in stopping seventeen new hydropower projects, detouring the route of a highway corridor and making headways to declare Papung as the eleventh and the largest RAMSAR site of Nepal – the Dhokpya RAMSAR Protected Lakes and Wetlands.

Conclusion

The Anthropocene is an era most known for its impact on biodiversity loss. However, as discussed in this essay, it is also negatively impacting Indigenous communities. The disconnect between people

Figure 15.8 High-altitude lakes of Papung, 2022. Courtesy of KTK-BELT.

and nature is further exacerbating the biodiversity crisis inherent in the Anthropocene. The Vertical University project and process have shown us that it is possible to heal the relationship between human and non-human. The project's success and the reason it has continued to survive and expand even after the political restructuring of Nepal are due to the network we helped to build – a network of local people passionate about conservation across this vertical gradient and a network that relies on not just the co-founders but also hundreds of people engaging across the board. Whether it is working on pangolin conservation in Yangshila, birds and wetlands in Koshi Tappu or high-altitude lakes in Papung, we have been able to 'activate' conservation dialogues and policy-level impacts through this network.

Taking an integrated and place-based approach towards conservation was also critical, as the strategies implemented in the upper regions of the project relied more heavily on legislative tools to protect larger landscapes, whereas, in the lower regions, we heavily engaged local communities. Providing both a physical and social space for the community to learn and celebrate local biodiversity or to watch movies has also taken a stronghold. In marginalized rural spaces with limited access to public amenities and facilities, these spaces are providing an alternative space for outdoor, hands-on education, most importantly, spaces that engage local people's curiosities, minds and interests. We did not start with a road map or a blueprint to build the Vertical University – but with each passing year, with each hurdle and challenge, we are learning the ins and outs of working collaboratively with communities, government bodies, youth, students and international partners.

References

Aisher, Alex. 'Scarcity, Alterity and Value: Decline of the Pangolin, the World's Most Trafficked Mammal'. *Conservation and Society* 14, no. 4 (2016): 317–29.

Amin, Rajan, et al. 'The Status of Nepal's Mammals'. *Journal of Threatened Taxa* 10, no. 3 (2018): 11361–78.

Bashyal, Ashish, et al. 'Illegal Trade in Pangolins in Nepal: Extent and Network'. *Global Ecology and Conservation* 32, no. 5 (2021): e01940.

Bhattarai, Prakash. 'The New Federal Structure in Nepal: Challenges and Opportunities for Quality Governance'. *EDP Network*, Centre for Social Change, 2019.

Choo, Siew Woh, et al. 'Pangolin Genomes and the Evolution of Mammalian Scales and Immunity'. *Genome Research* 26, no. 10 (2016): 1312–22.

D'Cruze, Neil, et al. 'A Scio-Economic Survey of Pangolin Hunting in Assam, Northeast India'. *Nature Conservation* 30, no. 3 (2018): 83–105.

Ghale, Shraddha. 'The Pitfalls of Imported Notions'. *The Kathmandu Post*, 15 June 2018. https://kathmandupost.com/opinion/2018/06/05/the-pitfalls-of-imported-notions

Goyal, Rajeev Kumar. *Government Schools as a Land Trust Mechanism to Teach Indigenous Knowledge and Conserve Biodiversity in Eastern Nepal*. Ithaca: Cornell University, 2015.

Hua, Lin, Song Gong, Fang Wang, Wei Li, Yanzhu Ge, Xiaoying Li and Feng Hou. 'Captive Breeding of Pangolins: Current Status, Problems and Future Prospects.' ZooKeys 507 (2015): 99–114.

Joshi, Abhaya Raj. 'Chinese Pond Heron Spotted in Nepal for First Time'. *Monga*, 8 June, 2022. https://news.mongabay.com/2022/06/chinese-pond-heron-spotted-in-nepal-for-first-time/

Khatri, Kumar, et al. 2020. 'Freshwater Fish Diversity and Its Conservation Status in Different Water Bodies of Nepal'. *Nepal Journal of Environmental Science* 8, no. 1 (2022): 39–52.

Lam, Lai Ming and Paul Saumik. 'Disputed Land Rights and Conservation-Led Displacement: A Double Whammy on the Poor'. *Conservation and Society* 12, no. 1 (2014): 65–76.

Pietersen, Darren W., et al. 'Temminck's Pangolin Smutsia Temminckii'. In *Pangolins – Science, Society and Conservation*, edited by Daniel W. S. Challender, Helen C. Nash and Carly Waterman. Cambridge: Academic Press Inc, 2020, 175–93.

Press, John Robert, Krishna Kumar Shrestha and David Andrew Sutton. *Annotated Checklist of the Flowering Plants of Nepal*. London: Natural History Museum Publications, 2000.

Rajbanshi, Neeta and Lal B. Thapa. 'Traditional Knowledge and Practices on Utilizing Medicinal Plants by the Endangered Kisan Ethnic Group of Eastern Nepal'. *Ethnobotany Research and Applications* 18 (2019): 1–9.

Sharma, Gopal. 'Nepal to Hold First Local Elections in 20 Years'. *Reuters*, 20 February 2017. https://www.reuters.com/article/us-nepal-election-idUSKBN15Z1XT

16
DESIGN THAT THINKS LIKE A MOUNTAIN

Xinlin Song

Mountains participated in the formation of the Earth for aeons. As an ecological system, a mountain hosts life, builds vegetation, creates springs, supports lives and provides livelihoods for humankind. It holds the secrets of our planet; it is the backbone of the Earth; it is as alive as you and me. In the essay 'Thinking Like a Mountain' (1974), philosopher, environmentalist and conservationist Aldo Leopold saw the last wolf pack fading in his mountain and experienced the cascade of ecological downfall in the decade following. Without the wolf, deer proliferated and cleaned up the roots of seedlings that stabilized the mountain soil. Without trees and plants, animals disappeared, followed by soil erosion, landslides and dust bowls. Hunters once thought fewer wolves meant more deer, a hunter's paradise. A playground for humans brought temporary excitement, but humans did not realize that removing the wolves from the mountains meant they had to take over their ecological function. The mountain was sad to see the wolves gone and perhaps even sadder to see humans failing to take over their ecological function.

Leopold's essay reminds us to step back, see the bigger picture, ask more profound questions, understand the consequences of our actions and think longer-term – 'Thinking Like a Mountain', as he called us to. How does a mountain think? Ask a twenty-first-century scientist, and he may laugh at you or ask you to read poetry. Today, such a question is essential for us to address, especially for those whose work is to some degree about setting or changing realities: designers, investors, politicians, decision-makers, teachers, mothers, citizens or even consumers. Living in an age of 'environmental red alert', we are called to re-examine our ways of relating to the natural world, each other and, eventually, to ourselves.

This story of my mountain is about changing viewpoints and new ways of relating. As a former researcher of urbanization and human-centred design, I have experienced an ongoing viewpoint shift since 2017, when a series of projects took me away from buildings, malls and highways. I started frequent trips to the Chinese countryside, visiting villages and farms in the nature preservation areas and their bordering communities. Human presence is prolific in an environment with such pristine beauty within one of the most populated countries on the planet.

Human communities are deeply embedded in the natural landscape of China's western mountains. Many of these communities are ethnic groups that are Indigenous to the place with a spiritual worldview and practical knowledge relating to the land. However, such a bond has been challenged in the modern world. Since the 1950s, tensions between man and nature have been building up with nature exploitation, new extractive infrastructures and the ever-growing need for a better quality of life – a too familiar story to all of us. I was drawn to explore topics relating to these regions' economic development and ecological restoration, understanding conflicts and counter-narratives that arise from these local eco-social-techno systems and how a dynamic balance between growth and preservation can be achieved.

Danba County sits within Sichuan's Garze Tibetan Autonomous Region. Facing Mt Mo'erdo and the Dadu River, the county has had a history of mining and lumbering since the 1950s. In 1999, the Mt Mo'erdo Provincial Ecological Preservation area was established in response to the previous year's devastating floods. After over half a century of heavy drilling and chainsaws, the mountain finally returned to peace and started its long-awaited healing. Yunhe Centre was first introduced to this area during this period of recovery and restoration. The centre was founded by Liu Xuan and Rong Yao, a couple specializing in architecture and eco-tourism planning. The intention in establishing the centre was to become a 'community member' and participate in the ongoing ecological and economic transformation, using a sustainable entrepreneurial approach. Since 2015, the centre has initiated a major community-wide transformation, starting with an architectural intervention using green technologies and introducing new skills. An agrotourism cooperative was also established to develop eco-tourism initiatives. The centre also pioneered an 'ecosystem service-based economic model', promoting social entrepreneurship as an engine to stimulate system change.

Figure 16.1 Yunhe Centre in Danba, 2021. Courtesy of Crystal Hao.

In dialogues with the founders, I discussed the connection between Aldo Leopold's 'Thinking Like a Mountain' and Yunhe's work in Danba's mountainous village. Following an initial conversation with Liu Xuan and Rong Yao, I joined the centre as an Educational Programme Developer. Gradually being taken in as a member of this ambitious project, I started to have a slow but steady clear vision of the calls from Leopold about the ecological, spiritual, cultural, social, personal and local implications of 'Thinking Like a Mountain'. This challenge begins by seeing the mountain from different perspectives. In a modernized, globalized, capitalistic world, mountains are resources, capital, property and playgrounds. It is where advantages are waiting to be taken and profits to be made, with disproportionately little payback for nature.

To its Indigenous communities, mountains are homes, temples, food banks, hospitals and schools. The spirit of inter-dependency (instead of independency) prevails, and acts of reciprocity take place. Following this reflection, this chapter tells the story of changing viewpoints, discussing the historical account of the human-nature relationship in Danba and the ongoing regional regeneration work. Furthermore, it describes how design and education assist this process by developing a relationship with the communities whose livelihood and cultural identity are deeply intertwined with nature.

Mica, Cupressus, and watchtowers, Mt Mo'erdo in three stories

Once upon a time, the Mountain God of Himalayas held a contest to decide on the rankings of the mountain gods over the Tibetan plateau. An unexpected winner stood out. Nobody knew who he was or where he had come from. He competed with all other Gods in debating Buddhist scriptures and martial arts, and with his skills, wisdom and bravery he earned the respect of his peers. When he came to receive his reward, he made a deep bow, and everyone was surprised to find out he was the mountain God that once appeared in Buddha's prophecy. In the prophecy, the Buddha once said, 'A mountain God from the eastern Himalayan mountains would rise, which is where the Buddhist teaching would spread.' In Buddha's words, the east land has rich soils and hardworking people, and most distinctively, a realm of golden light radiates above that eastern mountain. That is where the hero would arise. However, how did people find out that he was the winner? When he bowed, he took his hat off, exposing his bald head, which radiated a realm of golden light, just as described in Buddha's prophecy. It was Mt Mo'erdo (Tibetan Folk Legend, Anonymous).

The Indigenous communities which inherited Mt Mo'erdo's stories are the Gyalrong Tibetan tribes. As one of the four major Tibetan branches and Indigenous to the Tibetan Plateau, the Gyalrong differs from other nomadic tribes such as Kangba or Amdo; they live by tending the land and growing buckwheat, beans, potatoes and corn, hunting in the forest and making stone houses with skilful craftsmanship. The origin of the Gyalrong tribes remains a mystery, but one thing is sure, they are mountain people. Gyalrong is a geographical concept, meaning 'people who live in the warm river valleys'. For generations, Gyalrong people lived in the mountains and valleys surrounding Mt Mo'erdo under their mountain God's protection and generous offerings. Many Gyalrong Tibetans dislike the part of the Mt Mo'erdo story where it says their beloved mountain God was bald. Today, however, if you look far towards the top of Mt Mo'erdo or down on the ground, it radiates a shimmering light. Ask any middle-aged local Gyalrong community member, and they will tell you that the shimmer comes from White Mica,[1] an abundant mineral in the

Figure 16.2 A view of Mt Mo'erdo at sunset from the Yunhe Centre, 2021. Courtesy of Yunhe Centre.

geological formation of Mt Mo'erdo. The legend narrative mixed with the geological stratification meet here in Danba, and both are woven into the recent memory of the place.

In 1939, a few large pieces of White Mica from Danba were displayed during the New York World Fair. It was the first time Danba's White Mica made this small town famous to the world, earning the name 'Town of Mica'. In the 1950s, China started establishing Mica mines in the Danba region. The mining industry brought instant prosperity, new communities were built and people moved from all over the country. The state-owned mining facilities also included schools, hospitals and cinemas. Young people were eager to work in the mines for good salaries and a modern lifestyle. Wider social networks, movies and ballroom dance were far more attractive than traditional campfire stories or traditional Guozhuang music and dance.[2] However, this new development, fuelled by economic prosperity, brought mixed feelings in the local communities. On the one hand, mining provided employment and good public services, but on the other hand, according to Tibetan spiritual beliefs, mining sacred mountains was considered disrespectful, resulting in the mountains fighting back. Locals choose the latter between disrespecting God and making a decent living for the family. However, Tibetan miners were still reverent towards Mt Mo'erdo by building stupas and making offerings during their *kora* pilgrimage.

Between the 1950s and 1980s, intensive mining eventually drained one of the Earth's rich and pure White Mica reserves. With the closure of the state-owned Mica mines in the early 1990s, the once flourishing mining town was now a sleepy community. During the golden age of Mica extraction, some people had already noticed that mining activities brought instability to the land, with elders' warnings of potential environmental risks. Still, the warnings did not stop mining. On 12 July 2003, a decade after the mining industry closure, an unusual flood hit the Danba area, causing fifty-one deaths. Since then, each year, a large sum of the local government's financial budget has been allocated to mending the road and reinforcing the mountain bed to prevent landslides. By 2015, according to the Chinese State Council, natural disasters accounted for 20 per cent of the total population's poverty, the second most significant reason for poverty in China.

To date, no scientific studies have been conducted to link Mica mining with environmental disasters. However, we cannot ignore the profound message of Leopold's wolf. If science cannot tell us if there is a correlation between thirty years of mining and continuous mudslides, can the mountain tell us instead? And if so, how do we listen? As an act of reciprocity, the ancestors of Gyalrong passed on a series of spiritual practices. Based on each local and regional mountain story, a particular date is set for a *kora* pilgrimage (circumambulation around a sacred site). *Kora* is traditionally a meditative practice, but in modern times, it has also developed into a community event in a more secular form. Nonetheless, this is still an Indigenous way of knowing and a meaningful way of relating. Each year, on the chosen date, the villagers gather early in the morning to start Mt Mo'erdo's pilgrimage. Once they reach a high-enough peak, the pilgrims stop for a series of ritual ceremonies. They thank the mountain for its generous offering of livelihoods and call for protection for the coming year. As elders chant prayers, smoke offerings are made with freshly collected Cupressus barks and leaves.

Minjiang Cupressus (or *Cupressus Chengiana*) is a tree species unique to the mountain and the Gyalrongs. Indigenous to China's Western Plateau, *Minjiang Cupressus* is an important tree species for water and soil conservation in the upper Yangtze River's arid valley climate. The tree has a widespread root system, holding the soil while preserving rainfall for replenishing the underground aquifer. The Cupressus branches and leaves are also necessary ingredients for the auspicious smoke offering (or the *Sur* offering) as it is considered its primary material. Therefore, planting a Cupressus tree is a good deed to add to 'Merit-making'. In the Tibetan worldview, life is continuous and interchangeable with other forms of beings. 'Making Merit' is a concept linked to the next life and achieving enlightenment. For the mountainous Gyalrong tribes, families used to keep the tradition of tree nursing and planting, a system of forestry stewarding with knowledge passed on over generations through inherited community practices. Danba inherited a vast amount of original forestry from the Hengduan Mountains range, one of the world's thirty-six biodiversity areas, as recognized by the International Union of Conservation of Nature. The lumbering business in the upper Yangtze region had started during the Ming dynasty, but not until the 1950s, with the Great Leap Forward demanding large amounts of firewood, did it cause the forest to be destroyed as never before. In the summer of 1998, an unusually severe flood season occurred in the upstream Yangtze area. According to an online report by the United Nations Office for the Coordination of Humanitarian Affairs:

> The central and southern parts of the country along the banks of the Yangtze River and its tributaries were battered by more than 60 days of heavy flooding . . .
>
> Estimates, 223 million people – one-fifth of China's population were affected, 3,004 people died, and fifteen million were made homeless. Fifteen million farmers lost their crops. The floods caused severe damage to critical facilities such as health clinics, schools, water supply, and other infrastructure such as roads, bridges, irrigation systems, and industrial facilities. At the end of August, direct economic damage was estimated at over US$ 20 billion. (UN 1998)

The Chinese government announced that the damage was partially due to intensive deforestation in the upper Yangtze watershed region, causing severe soil erosion and, in turn, silting. In the same year (1998), the emergency plan National Forest Protection Program (NFPP) policy was put in place in September. Considered one of the world's most significant ecological rehabilitation projects of the early twenty-first century, NFPP focused on stopping lumbering, forest fire prevention and tree plantation, followed by strict legislation and law enforcement. Consistent financial support from the central government was also allocated to local communities annually as eco-compensation. Many former loggers became tree planters and forest rangers through upskilling training programmes. After half a century of devastating mining and lumbering, the mountain has been restored to a long-awaited sanctuary for peaceful regeneration.

When the NFPP policy was launched, the local government was eager to explore new economic possibilities. Starting in the early 1990s, Chinese cultural magazines published images of Danba's Gyalrong Tibetan villages. The images included the distinctive stone watchtowers and traditional Tibetan houses surrounded by terraced fields, the mysterious rite of passage ceremony for girls and the smoke offering, contributing to developing a new tourism industry. Among these images, the stone watchtower was the most distinctive, encouraging many tourists to visit the area. The French explorer Frederique Darragon came across these towers in the late 1990s and started detailed research, archiving and conservation work (Darragon 2005). From the early 2000s, small family hotels started to appear in the region, followed by extensive tourism facilities financed by the government. Expecting this to be the next pillar of the local economy, the government invested heavily in building infrastructures, such as roads and tourist centres. Villages with better views of the stone towers were the first to be developed. Roads were paved and widened for large buses carrying visitors, while water and sewage systems were developed, new public spaces were built and the village's appearance was restored and reinvigorated. However, there was a catch. Following these transformations, a ticketing office was installed at the village entrance, requesting visitors to buy a ticket to visit the village. Initially, this 'amusement park-style' approach brought financial rewards to the local villagers, with many families benefitting from becoming homestay owners. Gradually, the atmosphere changed. Many families moved away, and homestays became boutique hotels owned and managed by people from other places. The remaining community members were very upset about this development, so the tension between business owners and the community was building up.

The local tourism bureau was keen to understand what went wrong with the current model and what could be done to improve it. In 2015, Yunhe was commissioned to evaluate the tourism industry and develop proposals for a more sustainable model and further development. With an interdisciplinary team of eco-tourism experts, community workers, nature educators, architects and planners, the centre spent seven months researching. The research team explored the mountains, traced the watersheds and interviewed local communities, homestay owners, tourism operators and policymakers. During this time, the co-founder of Yunhe Liuxuan explained her findings: 'The tourism industry built on the "ticketing economy" was lacking distribution channels of wealth and resources to its local community.' Furthermore, she also noted that most of the public investments were only used to build tourist infrastructures, such as roads, sewage systems, parking lots and tourism centres, and very little funding was used for community building or upskilling. The ticket office infrastructure model was somewhat linear in its planning and financing. From the entrance to the exit, visiting routes were designed without considering the local Indigenous community, so soon, they started to be alienated by entitled visitors who paid a ticket to visit the village. Most people visited for a few hours to take pictures without staying for the night, and those who stayed would only spend one or two nights. According to Liuxuan, a different view of tourism development was needed. She explained, 'In this tourism model, the stone towers were in the background for pictures rather than a close encounter for appreciation. The local communities can be much more than hotel owners, drivers, or souvenir sellers.'

Mining, lumbering, the evolving mainstream mass tourism and Danba's trajectory in searching for economic pillars over the past fifty years were not unique. It is understandable from an economic perspective, but from a mountain's point of view, it is short-sighted. Reviewing this approach and evaluating the gains and losses over the short, medium and long term were necessary. Success is often described through tangible things that can be measured in numbers. However, something else was missing from the equation. The exploitative nature of this tourist business model harmed local communities and nature. When we exploit the outer world, part of our inner nature is unconsciously harmed. This inner nature, according to Tibetan Meditation Master Chögyam Trungpa, is a basic goodness: 'A great deal of chaos in the world occurs because people do not appreciate themselves. Having never developed empathy or gentleness towards themselves, they cannot experience harmony or peace within themselves, and therefore, what they project to others is also inharmonious and confused' (1984, 35). It is impossible for someone who lived and participated in the businesses of breaking mountains and polluting rivers to experience harmony or true self-appreciation. The exploitation continues until both outer and inner nature approach exhaustion, and the crises become apparent. In short, when we exploit, we take life away from both outer and inner nature. The ongoing crisis, as described in the mainstream news, includes severe biodiversity loss, but what about the crisis of our inner nature's richness and the rapid disappearance of the cultural diversity that nurtures it?

Design for regeneration, from the inner to the outer world

While reading through the recent history of the human-nature relationship in Danba, it was evident that assisting nature's regeneration was much needed. Nevertheless, this regeneration work will only begin if our inner world regenerates. Since Yunhe was invited to assess Danba's tourism industry and create proposals for further development, the team was confident that building an eco-tourism infrastructure, which stimulates local participation, was the way forward. They created reports and proposals and delivered them to the local government responsible for tourism policy, hoping to receive its support. However, after several meetings, the proposal did not gain momentum.

In 2015, China's mass tourism was booming. It was impossible to avoid the lucrative ticketing income, not to mention the public funding available to support its infrastructures. Yunhe's vision was not convincing because it did not align with mainstream approaches. With this in mind, Yunhe Centre's founders Liu Xuan and Rong Yao started a small, self-funded project, addressing three main challenges: (1) to transform the recent history of nature exploitation into a new story that assists the region's ongoing ecological regeneration; (2) to promote a worldview shift that assists an inner restoration for all stakeholders, from employees to community members to visitors; (3) to search for a sustainable pathway for an ecological transition for the local economy and promote social entrepreneurship among the youth community. With a team of designers, educators and community workers, Yunhe rented a traditional Tibetan house at the highest point of the mountainous village of Zhonglu to be the home of the centre. An architectural transformation began to address the built environment transition under the pressure of mass tourism. Yunhe's architects managed to keep the spirit and design of the original Gyalrong Tibetan house while making a spatial transition to its structure and interior only when and where necessary. Various green technologies, such as central water treatment systems, composting toilets and solar heat collection systems, were implemented. These green infrastructures were selected to fit the local conditions and to demonstrate that appropriate technology could play a positive role in ecological restoration. Unlike construction in a city, managing construction in an Indigenous mountainous village was difficult beyond imagination.

The local community relies on a communal labour-sharing tradition; families help each other with agricultural work, construction or even wedding events. As a newly arrived community member, Yunhe's construction work had to wait for its turn, resulting in two and a half years to complete the architectural renovation, with work finishing in 2015. This is relatively slow in relation to China's fast-paced development. However, after seven years, the founders believed that through this long process of working with the local community, a deeper trust and understanding between the centre and local people was formed, which opened up possibilities for further communication. For many villagers who had negative memories from the period when the county was busy with mining and lumbering, it was refreshing to participate in a project sensitive to its surrounding environment and community.

Plans for the centre's future programming emerged through the first years of construction work. Villagers were interested in participating in the eco-tourism vision, not only as homestay operators or drivers but also as storytellers, traditional craft teachers or 'nature facilitators'. 'They are natural teachers, and all they need is merely some assistance in presentation skills', Liu reflected. A training programme was introduced for anyone who wanted to participate in the tourism infrastructures. Experienced educators, naturalists and scientists came to offer workshops, teaching what was needed for the local community. Encouraging respect towards the non-human world and Indigenous knowledge among urban visitors was also important. With this in mind, the learning programme developed at Yunhe Centre included a mountain smoke-offering ceremony led by the local community youth. This activity was adapted from a traditional smoke-offering ritual using a four-dimensional programming development map (spiritual, ecological, cultural and communal). Before the ritual started, stories of the mountains were told by local facilitators, followed by a discussion about the Tibetan worldview of wellbeing and longevity. A *Thangka* painting of *The Six Symbols of Longevity* was used to facilitate discussions and scientific facts were shared about the area, such as biodiversity hotspots, the Earth's water cycle and climate change. As the programme developed, the recent mining and lumbering history was also introduced. Local narratives were shared as references to avoid simplifying conversations dealing with nature's exploitation and economic development. These were aimed at stimulating a constructive mindset for the visitors to consider, 'What can I do to help?' Many of our programmes ended with visitors helping with some community conservation work, such as restoring old watermills and village water channels or planting *Minjiang Cupressus* trees.

As a part of the design exploration, the programming, its local network building and the economic model that values and restores human-non-human relationships were as important as building the house and gardens. This approach provided an opportunity to demonstrate to the local community and the tourism bureau that a new path for economic development was possible and necessary. With the guidance of the Beijing Global Environment Institute, Yunhe Centre became a research-action lab for an 'ecosystem service-based economy' (Sukhdev et al. 2014). Within this model, ecosystem-based products and services were developed, and the income generated from them was used back in the community to support ecosystem infrastructures and train new people. This approach resulted in an economy based on (not separate from) assisting the regeneration of nature and local communities.

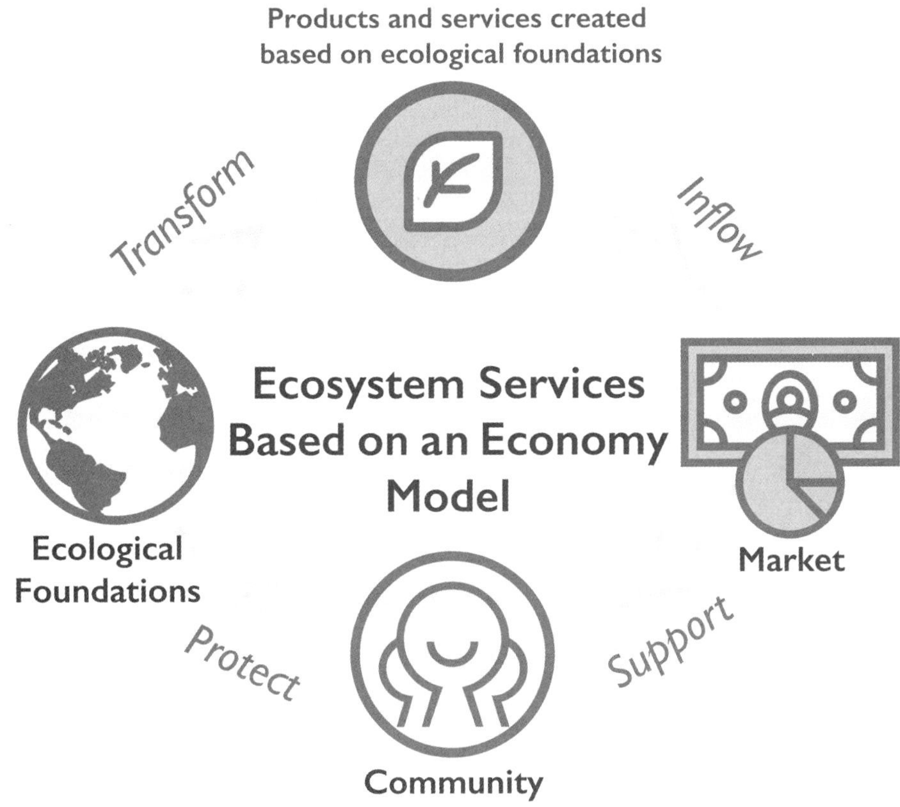

Figure 16.3 Ecosystem services based on an economy model, 2021. Courtesy of Yunhe Centre. Illustration by Shuang Song.

Design that thinks like a mountain

What is the ecological and cultural implication of mountains in our modern society? What wisdom have mountains tried to teach us, but we have failed to listen? Moreover, to receive this teaching, what do we have to leave behind? Are we, as designers, willing to listen to what a mountain has to teach? What is the role of designers in the Earth's regeneration? Mountains and their Indigenous communities may bring us insights into these questions. A designer who thinks like a mountain can learn from human-non-human relationships by respecting the Earth and life in all its diversity, by entering a space for unlearning and relearning. The Yunhe Centre has taught us that Indigenous communities are willing to offer guidance and be co-creators along this process.

Learning to respect life also reminds us that our presence on Earth is not a coincidence but a gift from an ever-evolving process of biology and mythology. Trust ourselves and each other, (so) that we can be a positive presence on Earth. This is different from being confident that we will win the war on climate crises. We may not win a war if there is a war to begin with. We will, however, in this effort, be able to

Figure 16.4 Visitors and students participating in a mountain ceremony led by a village elder, 2021. Courtesy of Yunhe Centre.

re-join the interconnected web of life and find new ways of relating. The story of Yunhe and Mt Mo'erdo are still in the process of 'becoming' – local communities around the world are doing positive work for inner-outer world regeneration. A collective 'becoming' (Bergson, Deleuze) is in process.

Notes

1 White Mica is a type of silicate mineral. It is used widely in the automobile, cosmetic and food industries for its shimmering and elastic properties.

2 Traditional Tibetan dance form.

References

Darragon, Frederique. *Secret Towers of the Himalayas*. Shenzhen Boyejituan Publishing House, 2005.

Flader, Susan. *Thinking Like a Mountain: Aldo Leopold and the Evolution of an Ecological Attitude Toward Deer, Wolves, and Forests*. Columbia: University of Missouri Press, 1974.

Gentiloni, Fabrizio, et al. 'Final Report on 1998 Floods in the People's Republic of China'. United Nations UN Office for the Coordination of Humanitarian Affairs, 29 September 1998. https://reliefweb.int/report/china/final-report-1998-floods-peoples-republic-china

Sukhdev, Pavan, et al. 'The Economics of Ecosystems and Biodiversity (TEEB): Challenges and Responses.' In *Nature in the Balance: The Economics of Biodiversity*, edited by Dieter Helm and Cameron Hepburn. Oxford: Oxford Academic, 2014, 135–152.

Tibetan Folk Legend, Anonymous. http://www.gzz.gov.cn/gzzrmzf/c100008/201204/6116324b4ab443e09a0b462271d9f9f5.shtml

Trungpa, Chögyam. *Shambhala: The Sacred Path of the Warrior*. Boston: Shambhala Publications, 1984.

Wikipedia contributors. 'Thangka.' Wikipedia, The Free Encyclopedia. https://en.wikipedia.org/wiki/Thangka.

Yunhe Centre – https://www.yunhecentre.com

17
A LARGER, LESS HUMANIZED DESIGN COMMUNITY

Kate Fletcher

This chapter is deeply inspired by the work of the ecological and feminist philosopher Val Plumwood, particularly her essay 'Nature in the Active Voice' (2013). In it, she argues for an epistemic shift in how humans see, talk about, think about and treat nature and its resources. In this chapter, I explore this shift for design. Plumwood sets out the imperative of approaching nature as alive, with mindlike qualities, with self-inventiveness and agency and of value beyond its usefulness to humans. She talks in terms of nature being made up of multiple centres of striving, of lives that go on independent of human ideas and ways of valuing. These arguments have been rehearsed many times. At their root lies a critique of human-centredness, a philosophical position that is pervasive and endemic within the Modern West. A position that is also prevalent in the design disciplines, where nature is often approached as background and as a source of inspiration and materials over which the mastery of design has dominion. This approach, based on domination and extraction, is, following Plumwood, at the root of the ecological crisis.

In this chapter, I share five short texts 1 as a response to human-centredness, which I wrote as an exercise within a larger, ongoing practice. For the best part of a decade, I have been writing in first person and from direct experience about fashion and nature, looking to root clothing in place, as part of life and living, and using garments as a 'way in' to growing ecological literacy and awareness of biophysical limits. I see nature writing – or 'life writing', as I usually call it – as a practice of design for sustainability, and specifically as a practice of design and nature. I see it as a way to situate knowledge, presenting 'a view from somewhere' (Haraway 1998) in which what is known is recognized as partial, subjective, culturally bound and equivocal. I also see it as a way to ground design and nature practices in everyday experiences: the challenges of caring for kids, doing the laundry, cultivating friendships, being part of a community and more. These things cannot be separated. Certainly, life writing is not the typical modus *operandi* for sustainability work in design, yet I experience it as a powerful route to a changed relationship between self, society and the natural environment and our experience of connectedness within it. As far as I am aware, it is the only nature writing that uses designed artefacts as its point of departure. The work has been published widely (Fletcher and Mort 2022; Fletcher 2019), and I have also written about life writing as both a research method (Fletcher 2022) and a design practice (Fletcher 2023; St. Pierre and Fletcher 2023). One feature of the work (as well as it being about clothing) is that I am at the centre of it – it involves my life experience, my design sensibility, my technical and ecological understanding, my knowledge about fashion and sustainability – with the upshot that the stories I tell are largely about me. It is not that I think I am interesting (I am not), more that writing in this way gets me closer to the places in which I live and the others who also are there. Further, the stories are often of common experiences and behaviours that people recognize from their own lives, therefore making them about many of us. In this way, they build widely distributed narratives of design and nature that are based on direct experience, not shopping for new pieces. Then came a time when I was sketching and scribbling at the foot of an ancient ash tree that I visit often. It is near where I live in the north of England, land that has been shaped by human habitation for thousands of years. The ash has branches the size of other trees' trunks and a trunk the size of other trees' crowns. I take little gifts when I visit, tokens of my appreciation: sprigs of rosemary, posies of wildflowers, hedgerow wool and apricots, leaving them at the tree's roots, tucked into the folds of her bark. Whenever I visit next, these things have always disappeared. At first, I used to search for them, trying to piece together what might have happened to the items that I, in my mind at least, had gifted to the tree. A crow perhaps? Squirrels? Could it be mice? And then I realized that I was the only one seeing things so narrowly, seeing this me-and-the-tree relationship as exclusive. The receiver of the gifts was never just the tree, it was the whole community, everyone that lived here and around here, transient, stationary and more. In this larger view, I was but a tiny part of the happening. And so, I turned over the page in my notebook, the place where I had been doodling about the funny and the odd experiences I have had while hanging out at the base of Great Grandmother Ash, this ancestor being, and I sought to make myself smaller, to make this less about me. This chapter is the story of this exercise.

Positionality

At the outset, I wish to acknowledge where I am coming from in doing this work. I identify as a White British, able-bodied cis woman who has worked in universities for nearly thirty years, and I recognize my many privileges as a member today of not one but two Western educational institutions, both in extremely wealthy countries. This was not always my reality. I was born and raised in a working-class community in a disadvantaged city in the north of the United Kingdom, an experience that imprinted me with a strong sense of fairness, with practice of graft, struggle and political radicalness, and has meant that I often find myself working in challenging edge zones of the domain. Above all, through my work, I seek to affect systemic change in fashion sustainability and to find the right relationship with the natural world.

Context

As the ecological crisis intensifies, so does the urgency of uncovering new knowledge that enables awareness and action, including for the design disciplines. Latter-day design training rarely includes context-based learning about design in relationship with the living world. Instead, what is more common are educational curricula that perpetuate an approach to design rooted in Euro-American mechanistic and modernist traditions, which favour rationalism, mastery, progress and innovation, including towards natural systems. Here, in a continuation of colonial power dynamics, nature is seen in terms of extraction and conquest, as a source of 'dead' resources, primarily available for use by humans. Design scholar Joanne Boehnert (2018, 57) reminds us that ecological theory finds this reductionist, mechanical paradigm insufficient: 'The case against the dominant Western worldview is that it no longer constitutes an adequate reflection of reality – particularly ecological reality. The map is wrong.' Yet, as design scholar Louise St. Pierre (2019, 94) explains in her essay 'Design and Nature: A History', despite its inadequacy in, or perhaps because of it, much design practice persists in approaching nature superficially or instrumentally or both, seeing nature as inspiration for design, a source of ideas for pattern, colour, construction possibilities, efficient ways of organizing production and so on. Yet, even in these situations – when nature is 'on design's mind' – design's relationship with it is typically approached through the lens of design as master. St. Pierre continues: 'call[s] to design with nature had great resonance for designers, but were diminished by human-centric applications . . . nature remained an "other" for mankind's pleasure or manipulation' (2019, 95).

Leaving behind design processes where nature is both othered and exclusively centred around human interests is an ongoing challenge. The questioning of human-centredness, so essential to action around design and nature, intersects with decolonial (Escobar 2018), feminist (Haraway 2016) and anti-racist (Ahmed 2017) discourses, putting forward ideas and practices of design that respond critically to the logic of domination. Another part of this ongoing challenge is how to seed changed nature relationships within design culture, education and system structures most obviously by diversifying ways of knowing about design. In this way, insight, such as that gleaned from direct experience and sensory engagement with natural systems, forms the basis for how humans and greater-than-humans can flourish in mutually enhancing ways and becomes the starting point for design action.

The *Multi-Centred Worlds* exercise

Following my realization at the roots of Great Grandmother Ash, I started experimenting with giving more voice to the greater-than-human world and, consequently, less to myself. Design actions rely on the gifts of the Earth. These collected gifts have their own ways of being, their own intentions and contributions to the world and their own rights to live, and yet these qualities are often denied to non-humans. Val Plumwood guides us in this matter: 'I am not talking about inventing fairies at the bottom of the garden. It is a matter of being open to experiences of nature as powerful, agentic and creative, making space in our culture for an animating sensibility and vocabulary' (2013, 451).

In the spirit of making space for this animating sensibility, I set about writing short pieces that locate action, awareness and experience in five earth beings. In writing as tree, sheep, stone, nettle and bird, common materials used in design – timber, wool, stone, plant fibre and feathers – can carry forward their gifts, surrounding us with intelligences other than our own. In each of the texts, I looked to describe Earth's intentional and mindlike qualities and its agency through sensory description and without human metaphor. This was a purposeful decision. In portraying the animate lives of other beings without human reference points or related to human priorities, nature is experienced as a means to its own relational ends and not as a resource for the achievements of human reason, culture and design. My concern is with a life-centred view for design in which we humans are invited to act as if we are *just* a part of nature, one of many centres of striving rather than the main one.

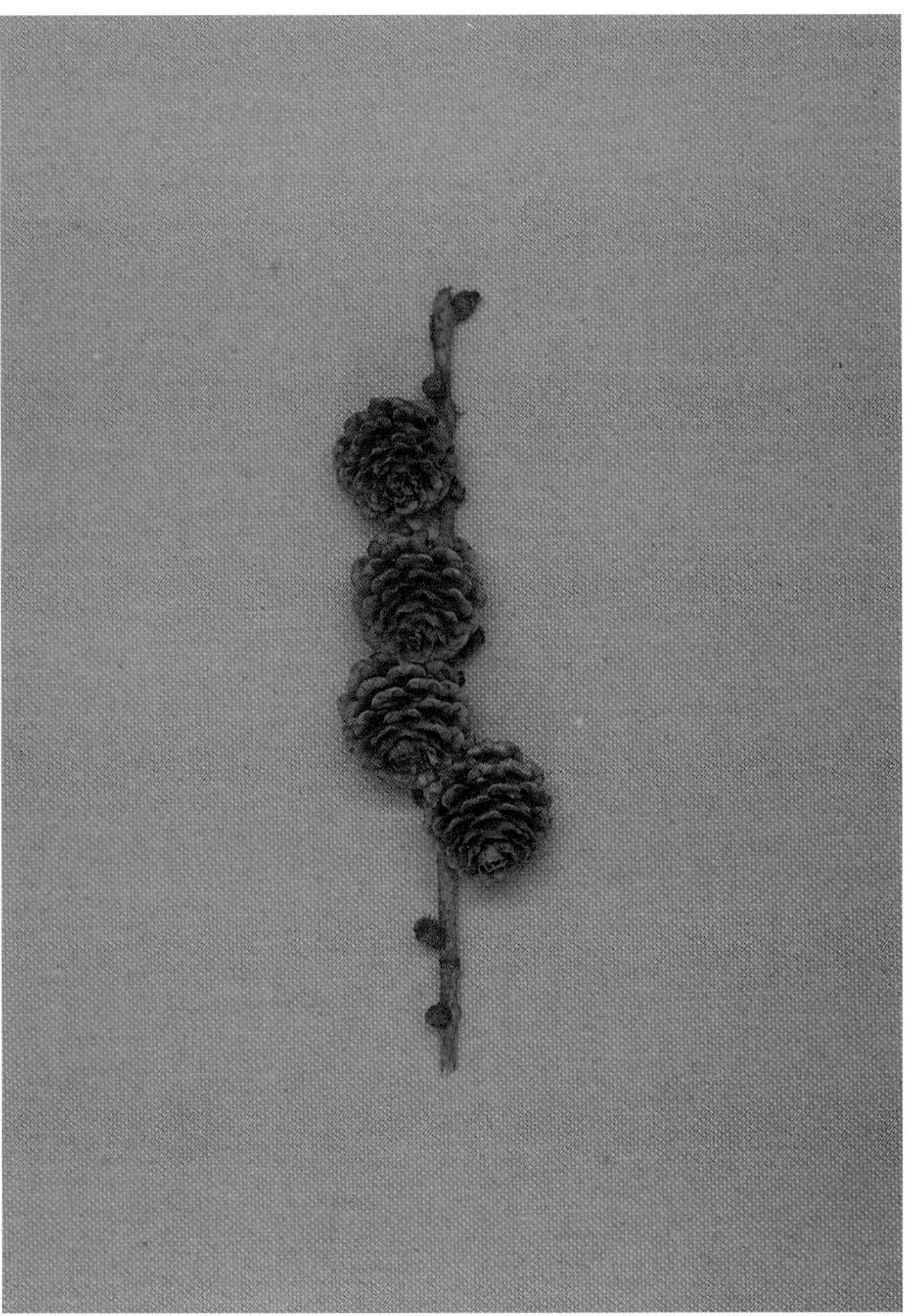

Figure 17.1 *Multi-Centred Worlds*, 2023. Courtesy of Kate Fletcher. Photo by Simone Aslek.

While the five texts were written without reference to humans and human experience, it is not because I am seeking to take humans out of nature or romanticize wilderness untouched by human activity. On the contrary, I see them as an inviolable part of each other, entangled. Yet, in order to get a better deal for non-humans, I sought to engage in an exercise to dislodge the privilege often given to human interests, making more space for other voices and experiences. Writing the pieces taught me differently to the ways in which I have been taught before. The lessons I learned were about respect, closeness, complexity, aliveness and an intentionality that is distributed widely. If a feature of the human-centred worldview is that it 'makes the least of the non-human other' (Plumwood 2013, 447), then this exercise deals in its opposite.

* * *

Tree-centred

This day, like every other day, we live as pure sensation.

We are racing, seeking, sinking. We are small and big movements. We are stillness. Noise. Touch. We live where we stand in a series of slow poses. First this one. Then this. Then this. Time moves in decades. Our trunks swell. Leaves bud and fall.

The quiet depths of shadows press coldly into our bodies. Moisture drops out of cool air, settling itself into gradients along our branches. The vapour has little energy left. It descends into our bark and tissue, cooling us to the same ice crystal temperatures as the night sky. Above, the moon's light is pale, old ivory. It falls across our high branches, lying there, tender.

Heaviness, solidity, rootedness. Reachingness, branchingness, light. Gravity holds us, it guides us down, deeply. The sun, then, by contrast, gives us wings. In between the two, the tearing hands of the air and the wind grab and caress our bodies in movements of many pauses and then, suddenly, of passion. The downing of a limb, the shimmering of an entire forest of aspen leaves, the clacking of branches one against the other; these things ululate through our lands as messages. And then there is the flow of water. It tugs hard on every fibre, every cell. We shape towards it, craning our roots to its rumblings, its vital music.

Bird language bubbles up. It claws through our tops and our middles. The songs cross our bark thresholds as vibration. Felt sound. We feel the feet of birds as pressure. Their nests as heat. When a buzzard lands on a leading shoot, our tops bend. The bird lifts off, our shoots straighten.

Colour passes into our bodies as radiating energy. Arsenic-green lichen is a cool diffuse breath. The mauve of winter leaves, a quiet hum. The blanket grey-white light of winter sun, a day-long exhale.

Sheep world

At night we sleep apart. We tuck ourselves against a wall, lie on a path, in the reeds. The dark sky spins above us, bodies separate but somehow together. Our weight flattens stems. Icy surfaces tear fibres from our coats when we rise. We wake with the light, with a call, a cough, the bark of a pheasant.

Figure 17.2 'Tree-Centred', 2023. Courtesy of Kate Fletcher. Photo by Simone Aslek.

We graze like we sleep, apart. We are near but not close, our flanks not touching. We tear at the grass, rasping it with our hunger. Then an alarm is raised, one of us hears a sound and our separateness dissolves. We start to move, to run, to bunch. As we flee, we are one body, a herd. As we have always been.

Our nerves keep us alive. Panic is what coils the wool on our backs, fries it into springs, makes us jumpy. We stare at the world through pill-shaped pupils, holding our gaze like we hold our vulnerability, tight. We process all against nervy instincts. And then our babies come. The most ancient, primal force arches our backs, turns our eyes upwards and we stop running. We birth where we stand and lick our young into life, butting and nuzzling them to the teat. Protectors now, we stamp a foot, hold some ground. Providers now, we sleep together, bodies spooned, as close on the outside as we were in the womb. As our young grow, so does their fear. But not until the sun is hot and we search out shade and claw the hot fleece off our bodies on hawthorn bushes. In our rest we are still on edge and call for them, our children, when the alarm comes. We call them to our sides as our pulses race and our bodies skit. Then there is a time when they do not come. We call through dark and light. And again, we sleep apart.

Stonelife

Cold

Old

Tough

Proud

Slow

Heat

Sun

Bake

Crack

Cool

Heat

Split

Tear

Fracture

Fissure

Open

Centre

Soft

Dust

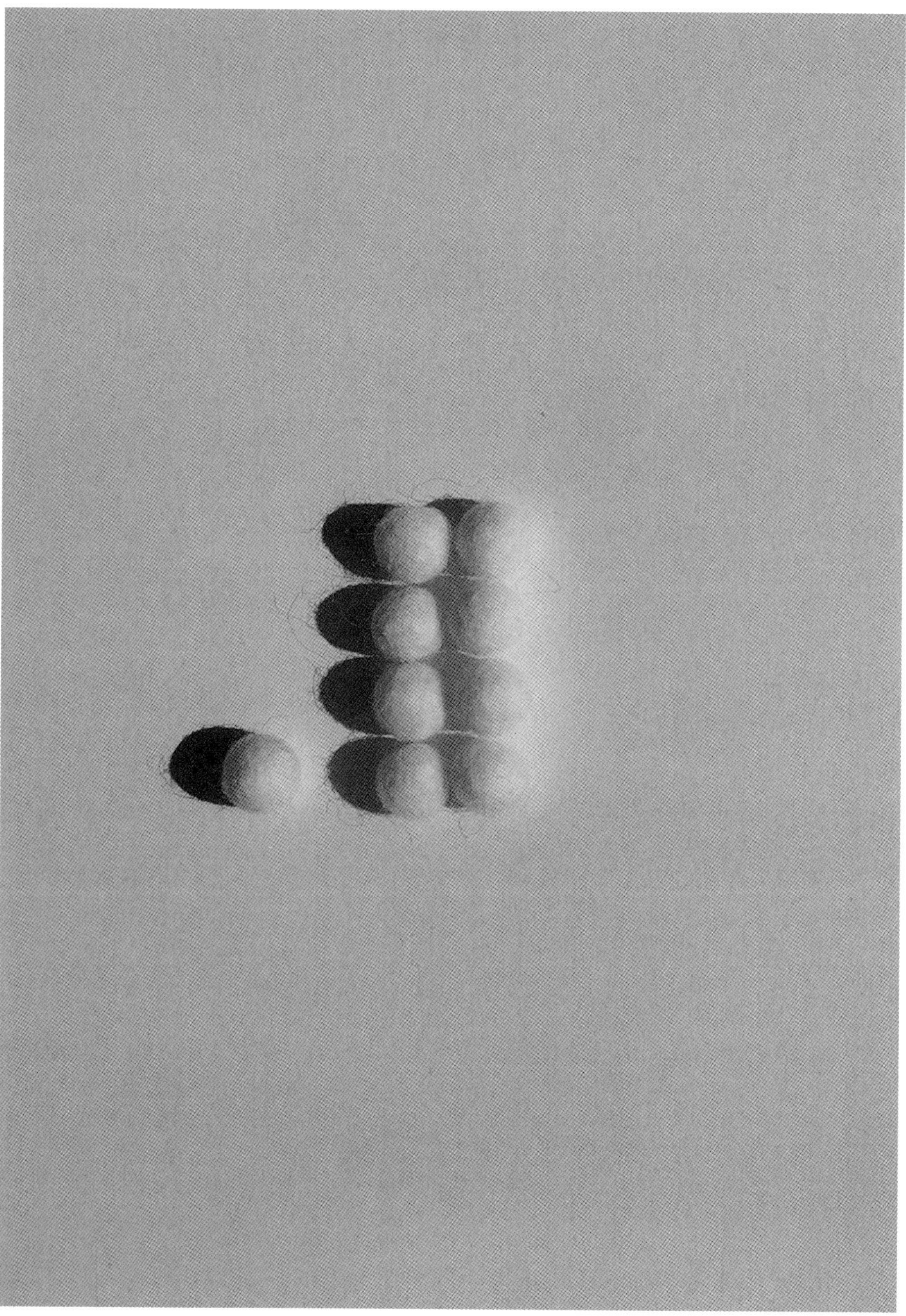

Figure 17.3 'Sheep World', 2023. Courtesy of Kate Fletcher. Photo by Simone Aslek.

Fly

Slip

Rumble

Fall

Drop

Crash

Echo

Nettle heart

We hear that some smooth-bodied creatures, stung by our hairs, run home to their mothers crying for them to blow on the hurt and kiss it better. 'Children', these creatures' mothers say as they comfort them, 'know your neighbours'.

This is us:

We are weightless, a cloud of seeds shaken from our mothers' tassel heads. Suspended in the air, we float and drift, biological will-o'-the-wisps. As the breeze catches us, we waft this way and that; the draught's flurries playing in our skirts. All the while we feel a larger, magnetic force working on our bodies, pulling us slowly, inexorably, downwards. Then the rain, in a squall punch, knocks us to the ground. Ours is a silent arrival. Unheralded, unbidden. Our fertile grains, waiting.

We wait to sense it: the dampness, the blackness, the looseness of soil. We wait for the feeling of disturbed ground, the cool heavy dark of moisture and nitrogen. We wait to feel the hot breath of a rooting snout, the cold metal of a garden spade, the feet, the passage of humans as they scuff and turn the soil, making gaps into which we slip, into the depths.

In the black depths we split open. A root and a shoot. One thirsty for drink. One hungry for light. Others of our kind are here in the dark with us. Creeping rhizomes cousins, travelling distances below the soil. We meet and mingle. And above, in the light, aunties shoot in mid-air, rooting at nodes, stretching out feelers towards new ground.

We feel the ground, housing our upright wiry stems and from there we push up, to the light. It feels like inevitability. It feels like power, like history. We put out multiple pairs of serrated saw-edged leaves and drink the sun that catches in these first bowls of green. The sun tastes sweet. We drain the leaf bowls, syphoning off their verdant syrupiness and we pipe it everywhere. The pumping sets the rhythm of our days. Its pulse, a wave to catch, a tidal bore of life in which we revel and feast. As we grow taller, our leaves flatten and reach wider, bowls no more, but trays, to carry away more of this ambrosia. Now as we drink we are like a fire in summer. Yet we know without knowing that it will not last. We taste a new dulling in the sun. It makes the green of our leaves tip towards brown. Our senses remain sharp.

Sharp too are our stinging hairs. Our leaves and stems covered in fuzz that we give up at the slightest touch. Here: take this. And this. And this. The transfer, from us to other, marks us indelibly. We feel our hairs' absence as coldness, as numbness, our senses stripped. We also feel their loss in other ways.

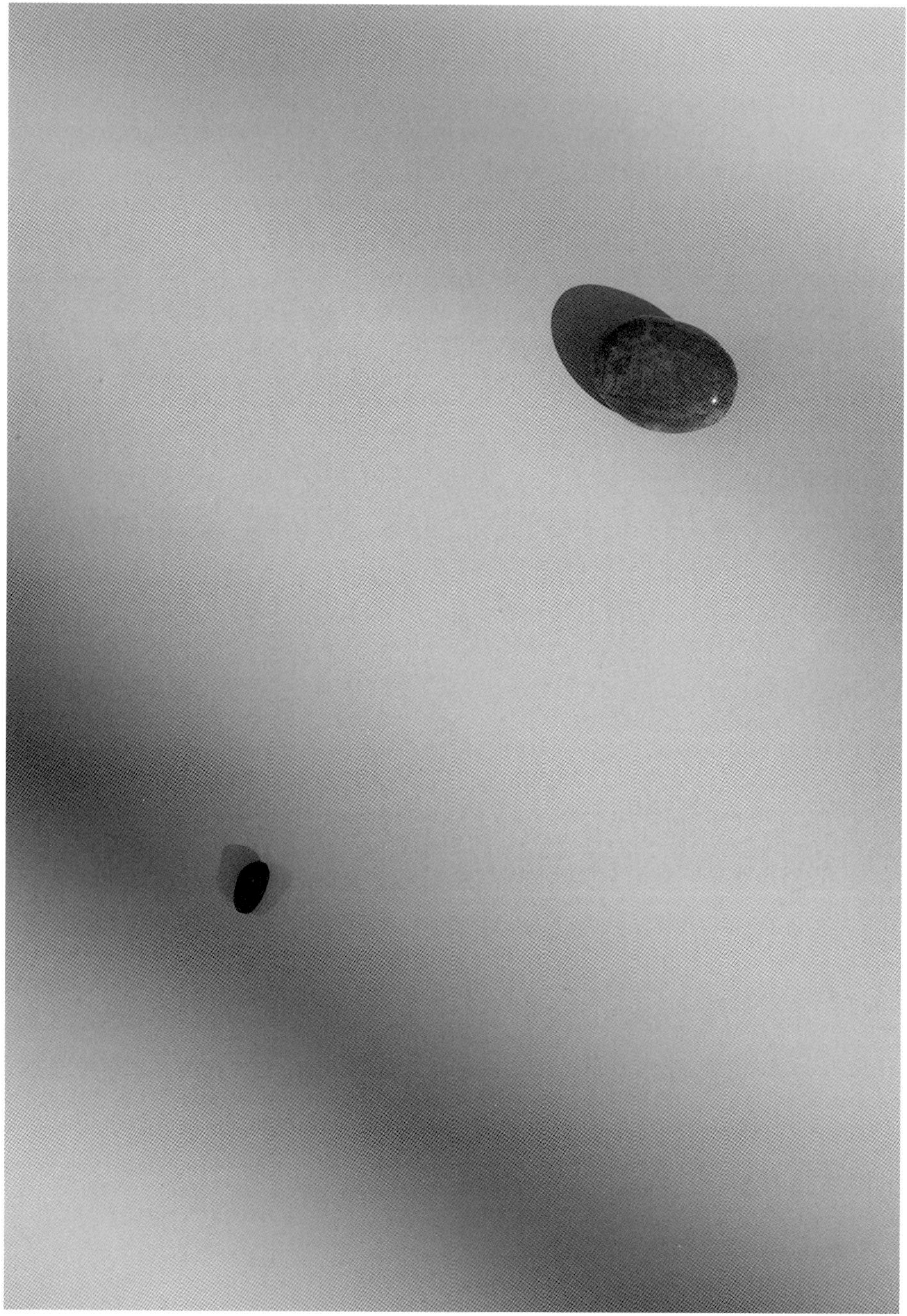

Figure 17.4 'Stonelife', 2023. Courtesy of Kate Fletcher. Photo by Simone Aslek.

Figure 17.5 'Nettle Heart', 2023. Courtesy of Kate Fletcher. Photo by Simone Aslek.

Newly sleek, differently aerodynamic, the wind runs across our hairless surfaces, bending us, bowing us separate to all the rest. Quid pro quo. We give up these hairs to hold our ground, to protect our thickets and our pollen-heavy flowers.

Being bird

The air is an ever-renewing block to be carved. We make of it what we will with our wings. We sculpt it with chisels of instinct. We cut through it with feathers and felt sensation. We bisect it, tangle with it, hold it, conduct it, and it does that same to us. We exchange daring, energy and intimacy one with the other. We are familiar. We call each other by our names.

Around us the air is never still, its character and grain reforms constantly. It slides over itself with unseen knots of pressure. Splits form within it around branches of gusts grown by faraway winds, winds in which we find freedom. The news these zephyrs bring we read with our bodies. Its messages we decipher via our primary feathers and in the vibrations of our breasts. The storm on the horizon is never a surprise. The date of the mayfly hatching, the flowering of the linden trees, they are foreknown.

Our hearing is sharp as talons, radial, open as a net in which we catch danger and beauty both. We hear the thrush and know so many possible songs. We hear the curlew and know the wetlands are near. We hear a man and know to run, shouting out an alarm. We don't hear the owl.

Our sight is telescopic. It is ultraviolet. It is trained on movement, on shape; it is honed by hunger. Vole. Worm. Rabbit. Fish. Seed. We tilt our head and decide the odds. Worth it? Not worth it. We turn away, trimming our wings towards the turned-up earth after a plough. We circle, climbing higher, and see shapes in the loose, large, expressive arcs of land, sky, sea. We see beyond them and into them, at what is becoming, heading towards it.

* * *

Reflections

When talking about ecology as a process of connectivity and flow, the anthropologist Deborah Bird Rose reminds us to 'Think with and from within the world, not from outside, over and above the world' (2022, 15). Transposing this to our context, her words are powerful: design with and from within the world, not from outside, over and above it. And this will need new methods, including those that seek to describe the world in richer terms, in dialogue with other kinds of minds and with a presumption of less power for humans.Whether a writing exercise like the one I embarked on is one of these methods remains to be seen. Personally, I found it to be profoundly affecting. The process of sustained empathizing made me look deep and relate wide with intensity. The trees, sheep and suchlike feel as intimates to which I am bonded by care, attention and responsibility – all of which are recognized as precursors for living and for designing differently within ecological limits. I have not yet tested if these affects are conditional on the process of writing, or whether reading such work is, in itself, enough. Informed by the experience of a novel research method called *Braiding* (Fletcher and Fitzpatrick, forthcoming), my instinct is that both are necessary, and that they reinforce each other, benefitting from exchange and dialogue. The

Figure 17.6 'Being Bird', 2023. Courtesy of Kate Fletcher. Photo by Simone Aslek.

discipline of writing without human-related references has also been very revealing. I found it difficult. Time and again, I had to delete whole paragraphs because my words and the experiences to which the words pointed were about human lives and priorities. At other times, my writing read like something from Wikipedia – factual, mechanistic, filtered by human rationality and reductionism, not necessarily responsibility. In the beginning, I even typed with a blindfold over my eyes, trying to pull myself out of my thinking mind and into my body, into my senses, to feel the lives of others that are not copies of mine but are nevertheless familiar while also being beyond my knowing. I drew on Val Plumwood over and over again: 'The incredible, infinite complexity of the real earth story is written in the rocks and the bodies of living things, in species diversity and evolution, with creative, active and mindful matter all around' (2013, 443). I set my intention to examine the real Earth story, which is, of course, also the real story of design.

More mutualistic forms of design are essential. And these, by force, include humans. In writing in this way, without human reference to human culture, an opportunity is presented to see other beings' lifeworlds in their own terms, not in order to remove humans but so as to pay attention differently to non-humans, thereby creating a 'larger, less humanised community' (Plumwood 2013, 443) with which design practitioners must contend. My experience is that if we direct the arts of attentiveness to non-humans, it changes what humans know. Then, when we next act, we do so differently. Val Plumwood writes forcefully about the particular challenge of human ecological identity and relationship. She guards us to

> [avoid] a fallacious choice of self/other, taking an us-versus-them approach in which concern is contaminated by self-interest unless it is purely concern for the other. Most issues and motivations are double-sided, mixed, combining self/other, human and non-human interests, and it is not only possible but essential to take account of both. Both kinds of concerns must be mobilised and related. (2013, 443)

Her point is well made: it is with representation, balance and negotiation that we must proceed, not exclusion. This brings to the fore the necessity of a type of knowledge that is not abstract nor universal, but embedded in local, social, cultural, ecological and interspecies contexts. Such knowledge is often called *techne*, derived from making or doing, involving actual practice, direct learning and sharing. It is already a process of design that can make us open to the joys and dangers of others, and to our responsibilities as relatives, for the lives of others as others are responsible for ours.

Note

These texts form the pamphlet *Multi-Centred Worlds*, published in 2023. They were written as part of a Guest Professorship in the Planet Lab at Design School Kolding, Denmark. The pamphlet and its imagery were designed by Simone Aslek.

References

Ahmed, Sara. *Living a Feminist Life.* Durham, NC: Duke University Press, 2017.

Bird Rose, Deborah. *Shimmer: Flying Fox Exuberances in Worlds of Peril*. Edinburgh: Edinburgh University Press, 2022.

Boehnert, Joanna. *Design, Ecology, Politics: Towards the Ecocene*. London: Bloomsbury, 2018.
Escobar, Arturo. *Designs for the Pluriverse*. London: Duke University Press, 2018.
Fletcher, Kate. 'It's Not Just About Mountains You Know: Nature-Clothing Writing As Design Practice'. In *Designing Knowledge*, edited by Bonne Zabolotney. London: Bloomsbury, 2023, 239–253.
Fletcher, Kate. 'Life Writing as An Ecological Research Method'. *Journal of Fashion Practice* 14, no. 2 (2022): 165–8.
Fletcher, Kate. *Wild Dress: Clothing & the Natural World*. Axminster: Uniform Books, 2019.
Fletcher, Kate and Anna Fitzpatrick. Forthcoming. 'Braiding As Research Method: Building Relational Understanding for Fashion'. *Fashion Practice* 16, no. 2 (2024): 1–18.
Fletcher, Kate and Helen Mort. *Outfitting.* Cambridge: Hazel Press, 2022.
Fletcher, Kate, Louise St. Pierre and Mathilda Tham. *Design and Nature: A Partnership.* London: Earthscan, 2019.
Haraway, Donna J. 'Situated Knowledge: The Science Question in Feminism and the Privilege of Partial Perspective'. *Feminist Studies* 14, no. 3 (1988): 575–99.
Haraway, Donna, J. *Staying with the Trouble: Making Kin in the Chthulucene*. Durham, NC: Duke University Press Books, 2016.
Plumwood, Val. 'Nature in the Active Voice'. In *The Handbook of Contemporary Animism*, edited by Graham Harvey. Cambridge: Cambridge University Press, 2013, 441–53.
St. Pierre, Louise. 'Design and Nature: A History'. In *Design and Nature: A Partnership*, edited by Kate Fletcher, Louise St. Pierre and Mathilda Tham. London: Earthscan, 2019, 92–108.
St. Pierre, Louise and Kate Fletcher. *Nature Relations*. *ECUAD*, Vancouver: Occasional Press, 2023.

18
TALKING MATERIALS
A DISCURSIVE DESIGN PRACTICE FOR A DESIGN BEYOND THE HUMAN

Domitilla Dardi

What do a volcano, a sheep, a computer and a tree have in common? They are all potential 'sources' of raw materials extracted and used by the same species known as *Homo sapiens*. One of the fundamental aspects of any design practice is the choice and use of materials, which define function and form. The choice of materials generates a process that creates a chain of consequences that profoundly affect both the essence of the product and users' behaviours.

In capitalist terms, design's relation with raw materials is predominantly extractive because designers tend to be primarily concerned with materials' physical, aesthetic, functional and performative qualities rather than how they are extracted from the natural world. Suffice it to say, this disparity is the consequence of industrialization and mass consumption, which have given shape to many design professions, including product and industrial design, which offer expertise for companies to produce consumer goods. It can be argued that manufactured objects have always been a part of human history, often marked by constant changes due to technological innovations and modes of production. However, it was with the advent of the Industrial Revolution that new technologies and materials paved the way to establish the designer's professional status, which marked the birth of modern and contemporary design – a historical turning point that shaped the relationship between the designer as the 'inventor' and the industry as the 'producer' and, consequently, materials become the exclusive domain for industry and producers. This shift marks a pivotal moment for design as it generated a fracture in awareness about the extraction process of raw materials, which too often does not consider ecological and ethical implications.

In recent years, some designers have tried to repair this fracture by developing practices more sensitive to design's impact on the natural world, notably, the research projects developed by the Design Studio Formafantasma founded by Andrea Trimarchi and Simone Farresin, which have explored materials such as wood and wool, reflecting on their use in industrial and craft production chains. One of the objectives of this 'investigative' material practice is to document and make visible what happens before a material becomes available for production, revealing fundamental aspects of the design process and its implication with the natural world. Formafantasma explains:

> Design as an act can be defined as the innate propensity of humans to conceive and perform desired changes to their habitats, but design as a discipline is a historical phenomenon formed in relation to the Industrial Revolution and its paradoxical ideology. This conceptualisation of design introduced the notion of the universal human and the satisfaction of its needs through the visionary institutions of mechanisation, logistics, and mass media. In particular, the borderless reach of capitalist production seemed to offer a benevolent future of democratised middle-class affluence, the antidote to the atrocities of national and religious strife in modern warfare. This vision was premised on the accelerating and infinite extraction of resources and their conversion into financial wealth, the externalisation of waste and environmental damage from the wealthiest nations to the poorest, and the reinvention of the human as an assimilated consumer-labourer as standardised and replaceable as the products they made and purchased. (2020, 24)

Formafantasma and many designers of their generation are starting to prioritize a key aspect of the design process: design's relationship with the extraction of raw materials. Trimarchi and Farresin ask an important question: 'What if materials could talk back to us and reveal information and data on their use and provenance to inform environmentally aware sustainable design practices?' Looking at agricultural and animal breeding practices, Formafantasma's work reveals fundamental issues that should be examined when considering natural or artificial materials or sustainable and unsustainable production. Their work underlines a critical and timely characteristic – the evolution of a design practice into a design research agency whose work aims to offer a 'discursive design' (Tharp 2022) research method. Aesthetic and visual choices play a decisive role in presenting their discursive research projects. The presence of formal languages that are sometimes reminiscent of a craft and archaic aesthetic is part of their investigation. This approach represents a communication strategy chosen by the authors.

> Experimentation is an integral part of our work. When we begin a project, we do not necessarily know where we will end up. For us, to experiment is to follow a specific process or form of research that produces unexpected results and allows us to develop a new and original position with respect to our initial ideas. It is a way of learning. (Formafantasma 2020, 9)

Education is also essential in their practice; teaching is complementary to research. Design and art curator and historian Hans Ulrich Obrist explains:

> In perceiving their role as a bridge between learning and practice and between craft, industry, object, and user, they are interested in forging links between their research-led projects and the wider design industry, offering insight into how design can be a change agent, championing ecological responsibility. (2020, 9)

Narrative matter

The early years of the twenty-first century saw the emergence of a generation of designers for whom the narrative quality of the process represents a cornerstone of their work. They are more interested in storytelling than in the final 'objects'. Many trained at the Design Academy in Eindhoven, a small Dutch town known as the historic home of the multinational corporation Philips. Formafantasma earned a master's degree with a thesis titled *Moulding Traditions* (2010), which paved the way for their current discursive design research practice. Their graduation project explored the traditional ceramic handicraft of Caltagirone in Sicily, specifically the *Teste di Moro* (Moor's Heads), representing an example of cultural contamination shaped by colonization and racial stereotypes rooted in the medieval Moorish occupation. During their time at the Design Academy, they challenged pre-established typologies or forms and experimented with raw materials and processes. They investigated or even created materials linked to specific places, resulting in an artisanal approach to producing new artefacts. The project represented a journey in the past to reflect on its origins and memories, using a 'storytelling' approach to bring together symbols, meanings and relationships with a deep connection with people, Place and time. This exploration had a strong relationship with the land and its history and was anthropologically sensible as it was motivated by the desire to challenge Sicily's colonial history. In doing so, the project went beyond the discipline of product design, embracing a discursive, critical and political voice. In this regard, art critic and curator Alessandro Rabottini states:

> In its most recent projects, Formafantasma has increasingly focused attention on the environmental and political consequences of the extraction, distribution and use of materials on a global scale, whether they are natural materials, such as wood (Cambio 2020) or fabricated, as in the case of electronic waste (Ore Streams 2017). In the end, for Formafantasma, tactility, like a vase, has an internal sound reverberating in politics. (2020, 100)

Formafantasma's research design practice is characterized by interdisciplinarity and transdisciplinarity, crossing disciplinary borders such as anthropology, material sciences, history and sociology. Unsurprisingly, their research projects have generated interest outside creative disciplines and are discussed by scientists, anthropologists, philosophers and economists.

Vernacular objects

Vernacular objects are part of material history and have inspired well-known designers such as Achille Castiglioni to design many mass-produced products. Following the Industrial Revolution, the relationship between mass production and crafts became a central theme as well as the recognition of the designer's professional figure, giving shape to 'authored' design objects. To understand the importance of vernacular objects in design theory and practice, especially in Italy, the exhibition *Avanguardie e Cultura Popolare*, curated in 1975 by design and art historian Giovanni M. Accame and architect Carlo Guenzi, provides a great example. The show included works by Bruno Munari, Riccardo Dalisi (Tecnica Povera), Enzo Mari (Autoprogettazione) and Superstudio,[1] who all shared an interest in creating a dialogue between urban and rural areas and the vernacular and the industrial.[2] This historical period was symptomatic, as design historian Catharine Rossi explains: 'The optimism of '68 largely transformed into frustration in the absence of social reforms. In this context, the Radical Design movement seemed ineffective and their critical strategies problematic' (2013, 34). However, many designers of this period gained international fame with the *Italy: New Domestic Landscape* exhibition curated by Emilio Ambasz in 1972 at the Museum of Modern Art in New York.

During the same period, Superstudio members asked young designer and architect Michele De Lucchi to run a project titled *Extra-Urban Material Culture* (1973–8). As part of this project, De Lucchi carried out a *Viaggio Con La Matita Tra Gli Artefatti Del Mondo Contadino – A Journey with a Pencil amongst the Artefacts of the Peasant World* – to draw vernacular objects such as baskets, forks, casks and furniture.[3] This project was about an idyllic premodern way of life, which was used as inspiration for an ideological desire to repair the damages caused by capitalist culture. This approach also gave voice to issues concerned with the ecological impact of mass-manufactured objects, notably discussed by designer Victor Papanek in his seminal book *Design for the Real World: Human Ecology and Social Change* (1971).

The use of the vernacular can be seen repeatedly in contemporary Italian design, searching for a connection with the pre-industrialized world. Notable examples are Francesco Faccin's *Re-Fire* lighter (2014), the *Honey Factory* (2015) 'micro-architecture' and the *Anonimo Contemporaneo* (2019) chairs, Giovanni Innella's *Dowry* (2010), a homage to the tradition of the southern trousseau, and Giuseppe Arezzi's *Manico* (2021) chair developed with handles of agricultural tools. The search for the vernacular represents a connection with the past and the restoration of lost values. In this sense, designer Andrea Anastasio's *Fiat* rake provides a powerful message with great semantic power, reflecting on the 'traumatic' transition from agrarian societies to industrial societies, which at the time was very evident in southern Italy.[4]

Traditional craft and vernacular forms have also inspired Formafantasma's investigation into raw materials, resulting in the development of projects such as *Botanica* (2011)[5] and *De Natura Fossilium* (2014),[6] which were commissioned by design curator and historian Marco Petroni and the Fondazione Plart in Naples. The *Botanica* project consisted of a collection of vessels made of natural polymeric materials, which, according to Farresin and Trimarchi:

Figure 18.1 *Dowry*, 2010. Courtesy of Giovanni Innella.

> Were designed as if the oil-based era we live in never took place. Almost like historians, we researched the pre-Bakelite period, rediscovering unexpected technical possibilities offered by natural polymers extracted from plants or animal derivatives. The natural textures offered by natural resins were reminiscent of twentieth-century Bakelite objects, somehow archaic yet contemporary. For the *Botanica* project, plastics were used as precious details to develop a new post-industrial aesthetic. With this approach, we hoped to offer a new perspective on materiality by reinterpreting old technology lost beneath the flawless surface of mass production. (Formafantasma 2011)

Similarly, the *De Natura Fossilium* project is a collection of objects made using raw materials to express the direct source of natural extraction. The project explored Mount Etna and Stromboli's lava in Sicily, two of the last active volcanoes in Europe. This exploration sought to integrate the landscape with natural phenomenon to inform the creative process, while critically examining the connection between tradition, local culture, and the relationship between objects and cultural heritage. Again, the aesthetic explored is a visible expression of the dialogue between the natural and the manufactured.

Five years after they worked on the *Botanica* and *De Natura Fossilium* projects, they developed the *Ore Streams* (2017)[7] project, shifting their focus to other raw materials. This time was not about extracting materials from nature but about reusing waste materials from existing discarded electronic products such as computers, in other words, post-industrial products of the Anthropocene epoch. The aesthetic was not any more focused on pre-industrial vernacular objects but rather about 'industrial fossils'. The project was developed over three years and was commissioned by the National Gallery of Victoria in Australia under the curatorial guidance of Ewan McEoin and Simone LeAmon. Design Curator Paola Antonelli subsequently chose the project for the *Broken Nature* (2019) exhibition, which was held

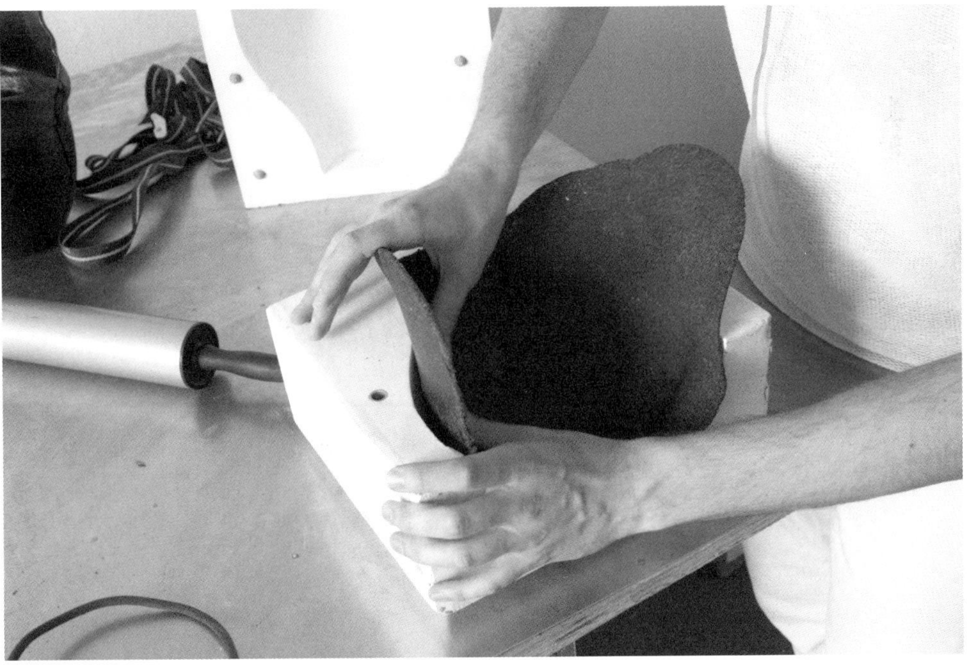

Figure 18.2 *Botanica*, 2011. Courtesy of Formafantasma. Photo by Luisa Zanzan.

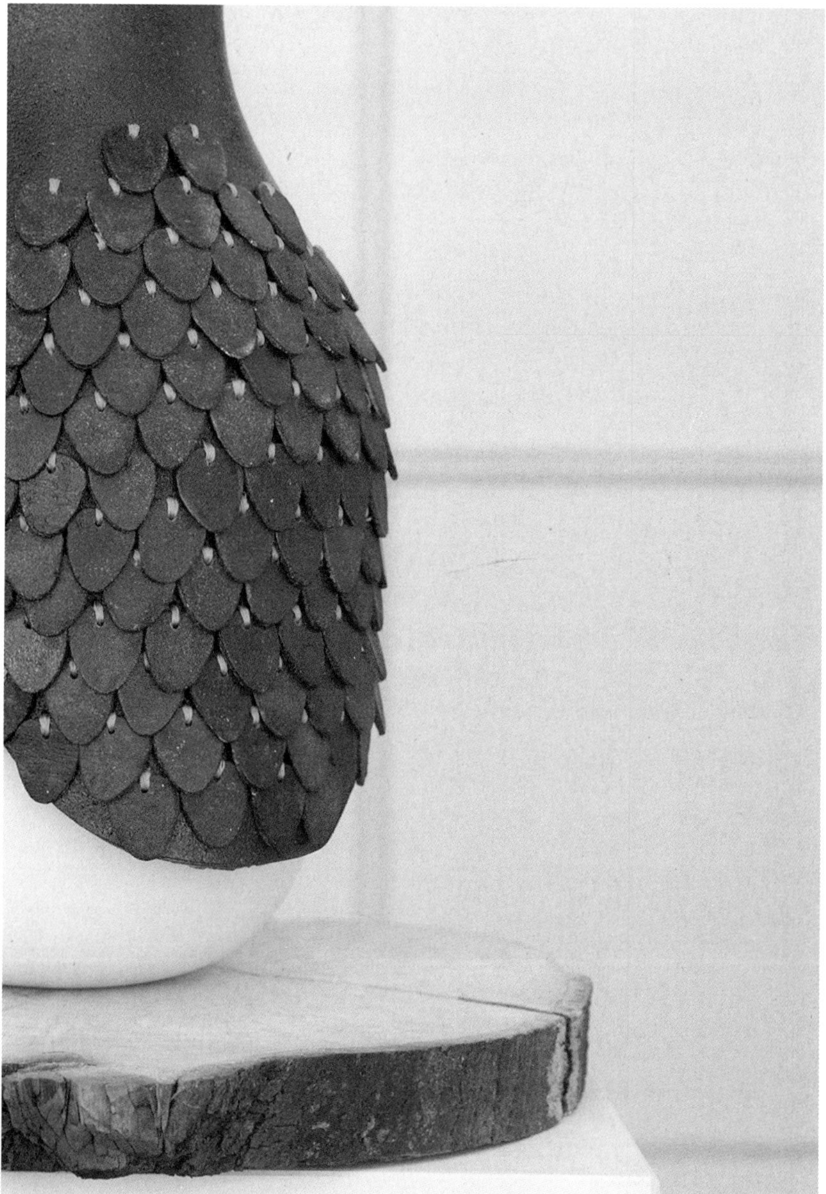

Figure 18.3 *Botanica*, 2011. Courtesy of Formafantasma. Photo by Luisa Zanzan.

at the Triennale Design Museum in Milan. *Ore Streams* was not only a furniture collection or a physical exhibition but also an online research platform that acted, and still acts, as an open-source archive available to other designers. As Formafantasma argues:

> By 2080, the most significant metal reserves will not be underground but above the surface, as ingots stored in private buildings or otherwise circulated within products such as building materials,

appliances, furniture, and consumer electronics. On the surface of our planet, rivers of ore in the form of discarded hardware stream freely as if in a continuous, borderless continent. Efforts to recycle it remain experimental, uncharted, and contentious . . .

Currently, electronics are the world's fastest-growing waste stream, but only 30 per cent of the West's e-waste makes its way to appropriate recycling facilities. The remaining 70 per cent is shipped, often illegally, to developing countries, where it is disassembled in poor working conditions, and toxic electronics components are disposed of inappropriately . . .

The objects created for *Ore Streams* invite more in-depth exploration of aboveground mining and the complex role design plays in transforming natural resources into desirable products. The office furniture is constructed from recycled iron, aluminium, dead-stock of computer cases, and recycled electronic components. The office is where modern design principles are most visible – the search for efficiency, ideal standards, and a universal style are epitomised by furniture such as filing cabinets and modular cubicles. The choice to reference this environment is a nod not only to these principles but to the same pragmatic approach of quantification, organisation, and efficiency that runs the bureaucracies responsible for regulating and capitalising on the circulation of natural resources, minerals, and waste toward the global production of goods. (2017)

Although the *Ore Streams* project was initially commissioned for a cultural institution's exhibition, the forensic research's complexity of electronic materials is more evident in the research documentation than in the objects produced for the exhibition. The video installation produced for the show was used to visualize global strategies for designing products using a circular approach for repairing and recycling. The multimedia research documentation included interviews with various experts, including European e-waste recyclers, academic researchers, electronics producers, non-governmental organizations working in developing countries and members of Interpol. Furthermore, a video documenting historical and contemporary examples of planned obsolescence in electric objects at the centre of class-action lawsuits, a video explaining recycling systems and technologies for sorting out waste, two videos with a selection of electronic products being carefully disassembled and reassembled and a 3D animation which was used to visualize possible strategies to improve repairing and recycling were also used for the exhibition. The visual research documentation represents a fundamental mode of communication where 'the medium is the message' (McLuhan 2008). The importance of communicating and displaying research using multimedia installations is not new in contemporary design. For example, industrial designers Charles and Ray Eames were assigned the task of introducing Russians to 'A Day in the Life of the United States' during the *American National Exhibition* held in Moscow in 1959, the first cultural exchange between the two countries since the Russian Revolution. To do this, they produced a film titled *Glimpses of the U.S.A.* (1959) to present more than 2,200 still and moving images simultaneously on seven screens, providing a visual expression of the complexity and diversity of American life.

Visual *modus operandi*

Studio Formafantasma's visual *modus operandi* is influenced by Italian artist and designer Enzo Mari's use of 'investigative power' and the visualization of taxonomies, which were recurrent in his work. For example, the *Proposta Per la Lavorazione a Mano della Porcellana – Proposal in Favor of Handmaking Porcelain* – project realized in 1973 represents a strong reference for many designers engaged in discursive design projects. The interest in analysing anonymous objects is evident in the *Autarchy* (2010) project, which explored wheat monoculture to illustrate the hypothesis of material self-sufficiency, using materials and forms that seem derived from a distant rural world. The project consisted of a collection of vessels naturally dried at a low temperature with a bio-material composed of 70 per cent flour, 20 per cent agricultural waste and 10 per cent natural limestone and was exhibited at Rossana Orlandi's gallery in Milan. The presentation of objects expressed through a primitive yet sophisticated communication approach drew the attention of many critics and emerging designers who found inspiration in this alternative way of presenting design, which starkly contrasted the way design was taught in industrial design schools during this period.

Since then, it has taken ten years for Formafantasma to develop its most recent forensic and discursive practice, which explores raw materials. In 2020, the design duo produced the project *Cambio* for a solo exhibition at the Serpentine Gallery in London. This time, the subject of their enquiry was one of the most widely used materials of all time and the icon of sustainable and ecological design: wood. They investigated the exhibition's complexity by treating wood as a 'living' material. Trimarchi and Farresin explain:

> When a tree is cut down to produce timber, the branches and roots are cut, and the bark is removed. This is the moment in which a living species becomes a product. But the word *Cambio* in Italian also means change, and the show was named after it precisely because of the polysemic nature of this. We hope that the exhibition helped shift the common perception of design as a tool for styling to an approach that can effect real transformation in a time of climate and social instability. While taking such a diverse and expansive subject risks generalisation, we firmly believe in reading and understanding design within its larger context, including extraction, refinement, production, distribution and afterlife of things and materials. (2020, 25)

The exhibition included a multitude of experts, including scientists, botanists, economists and biologists, invited to discuss deforestation, re-forestation problems, extinction of natural habitats and nature's overexploitation. The complex geopolitics of wood was shown to the public through wood archives, samples, maps, furniture and artefacts. But perhaps the most effective exhibition element was the video titled *Quercus*, which was created in collaboration with philosopher Emanuele Coccia, who gave voice to a forest of trees to deliver a powerful message:

> Wood is not a decorative element of human civilisation, which does not care much about the latitude, the historical era, or its complexity. Wood is the womb of every form of transformation of the world. The limit defines the forms of our being in the world. And vice versa, human existence is always also one of the life forms of wood. (2020, 168)

One might argue that giving voice to the non-human world is anthropocentric and simplistic but perhaps a useful exercise to help humans to further understand the complex intelligence of living organisms.

In June 2023, the same approach was used for an installation On Certosa Island in Venice, which was commissioned by the Museo Nazionale Delle Arti Del XXI Secolo (MAXXI) in Rome and curated by me. The project was titled *Populus Alba* and consisted of a series of metal objects designed by Formafantasma, which were used to amplify the voice of trees interpreted and narrated by Coccia. During the same period, in 2023, Formafantasma inaugurated an exhibition titled *Oltre Terra*, a commission by

Figure 18.4 *Autarchy*, 2010. Courtesy of Formafantasma.

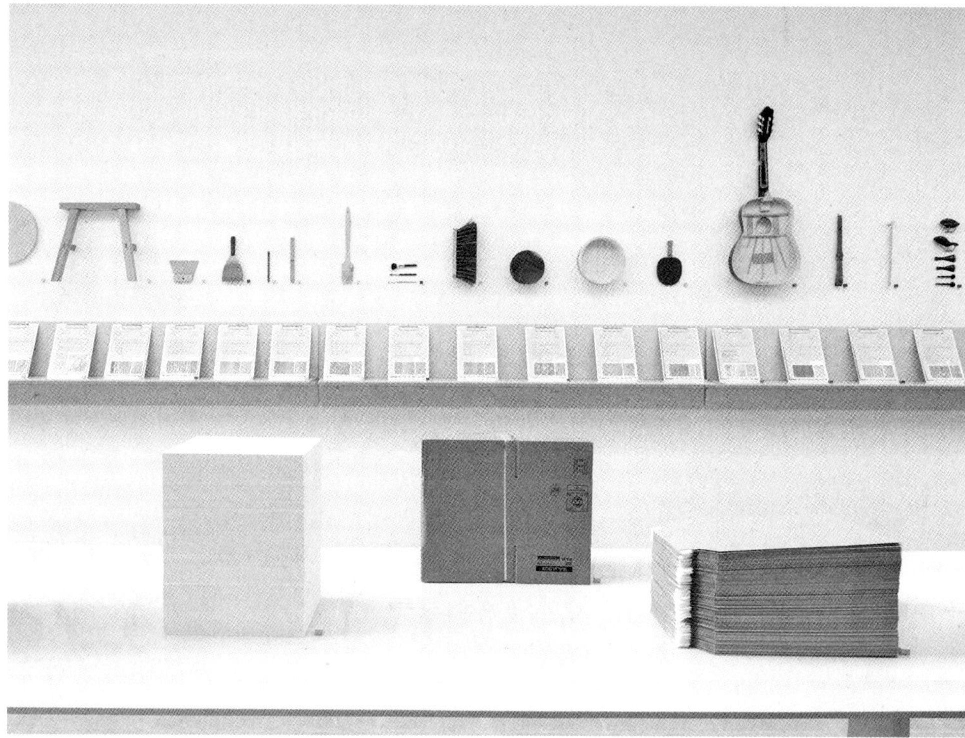

Figure 18.5 *Cambio*, 2020. Courtesy of Formafantasma and East Gallery. Photo by George Darrell.

the National Museum of Art, Architecture and Design in Oslo. The museum's Director Karin Hindsbo argued that 'the project investigated the history, ecology, and global dynamics of the extraction of wool with the aim of discussing its broader ecology. The exhibition was presented as a visual essay to invite the public to reflect on the constant construction of relationships between us and our environment' (Formafantasma 2023, 10).

Formafantasma used dioramas for this exhibition to display a three-year extended research period. Dioramas for many people might be considered a controversial and dated medium, but according to Trimarchi and Farresin:

> While dioramas proved to be a popular and effective way to represent animals in the context of exhibition-making, they also contributed to the consolidation of a partial and unrealistic representation of nature. This display mode reduces complex biological interactions to binary narratives – the predator vs. prey dynamic is a clear example of this – and presents them via cultural biases, both expressing a Western, post-Enlightenment understanding of the world. The still-life quality of dioramas implicitly invites viewers to understand nature as immutable and . . .
>
> Observable from a position of safety (behind a glass), detachment and superiority . . .
>
> Domestic and domesticated animals are then not part of this discourse because they are considered to be the fruit of human intelligence, or at least tamed by it: the sheep are never going to be represented in a diorama because metaphorically it sits too close to the observer, on this side of the glass . . .

Figure 18.6 *Quercus*, video still, 2020. Courtesy of Formafantasma.

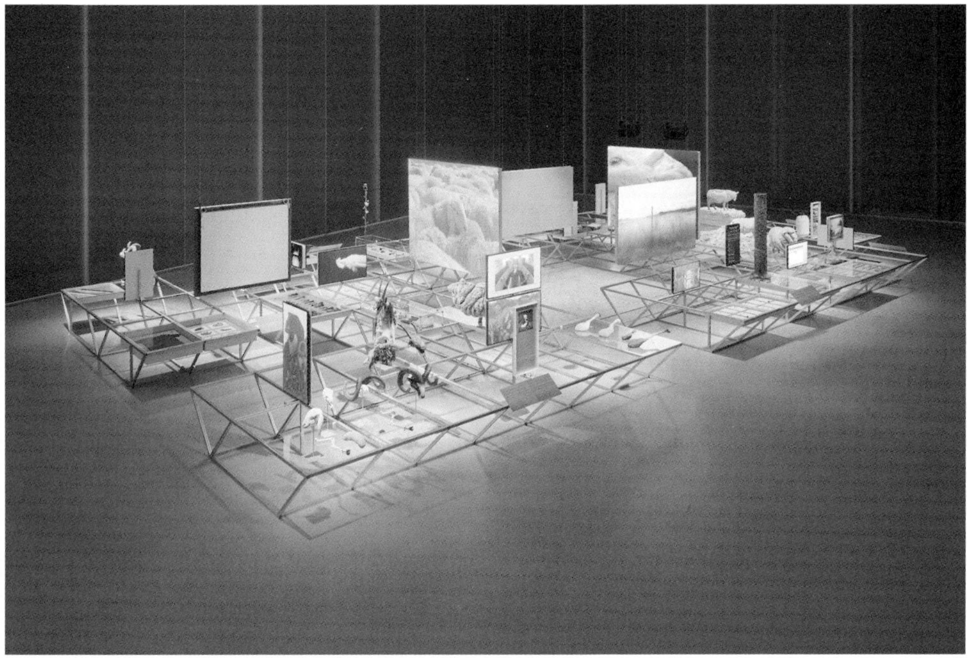

Figure 18.7 *Oltre Terra*, 2023. Courtesy of Formafantasma. Photo by Gregorio Gonella.

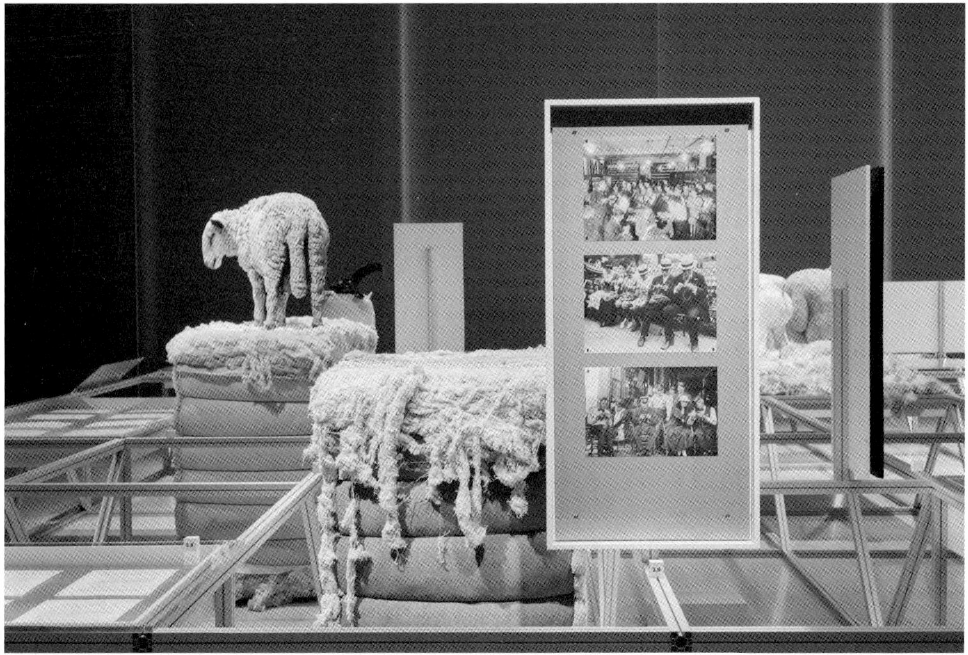

Figure 18.8 *Oltre Terra*, 2023. Courtesy of Formafantasma. Photo by Alessandro Celli.

It is no coincidence that animals that 'serve' humans are never present in Natural Histories but appear in treatises on animal husbandry and agriculture as if they belong not to nature to be observed but to nature to be exploited for human use and consumption. But as many expert essays testify in this research, the domestication between humans and non-humans is a bilateral path. Domestication – as palaeontologist Marcelo R. Sanchez-Villagra wrote in the exhibition's catalogue, 'Can be classified as mutualism, a relationship beneficial to both species, as facultative symbiosis, where different species or populations decide to participate in the interaction, or as an obligatory relation, in which the nature of the interaction has changed so that one species or population is dependent on another'. (2023, 19, 40)

Conclusions

During the last few years, Formafantasma has expanded its research, exhibitions and design experience into education by developing the Geo-Design Master's course at the Design Academy in Eindhoven.

We believe that designers can be critical agents in global systems, but their skill sets and perspectives must expand rapidly beyond isolated, self-referential processes of artistic making and subjective intuition. Design must be radically rooted in an expansive understanding of reality – but a reality that acknowledges how 'real world' problems are easily reduced to briefs for well-funded design solutions with negligible benefit to their intended users. In this sense, education is probably one of the few contexts where this more radical approach to design can be investigated and where fragile but crucially important new narratives can be fostered. (Formafantasma 2020, 29)

Figure 18.9 *Geo Merce*, 2015. Courtesy of Gionata Gatto and Giovanni Innella. Photo by Matteo Cremonini.

Figure 18.10 *Geo Merce*, 2015. Courtesy of Gionata Gatto and Giovanni Innella. Photo by Matteo Cremonini.

Formafantasma is inspiring a whole new generation of designers who are prioritizing a material discursive investigation as the core aspect of their design research approach, challenging the dominant design capitalist human-nature binary worldview, namely human-centred design. Notably, designers Giovanni Innella and Gionata Gatto, with their project *Geo Merce* (2015), explored the extraction of heavy metals from polluted soils using super-accumulator plants, demonstrating an economic value by tracking the extraction to the London Metal Exchange. Once again, the visualization and materialization represent a strategy to visualize design's relationship with the natural world. While these examples provide hope, the discursive and forensic methodology of 'raw materials' is confined to academia and its supporters (e.g. cultural institutions), proving that a paradigm shift is required to challenge design's extractive nature and remember that the terms 'ecological' and 'economical' belong to the same place: *Oikos*, our home, *Gaia*.

Notes

1 The exhibition took place in 1975 at Galleria d'Arte Moderna di Bologna, followed by Global Tools Workshops.

2 See Alison J. Clarke, 'The Anthropological Object in Design: From Victor Papanek to Superstudio'. In *Design Anthropology*, edited by Wendy Guun, Ton Otto and Rachel Charlotte Smith (London: Bloomsbury, 2014), 74.

3 See Gian Piero Frassinelli, *Design e Antropologia* (Macerata: Quodlibet, 2019), 530.

4 Andrea Anastasio analysed the complex and traumatic process of setting up Fiat Automotive Company sites in the local rural fabric during the seminar organized by curator Marco Petroni and held in June 2015 in Irpinia, Italy.

5 See https://formafantasma.com/work/botanica.

6 See https://formafantasma.com/work/de-natura-fossilium.

7 See https://formafantasma.com/work/ore-streams and http://www.orestreams.com/.

References

Eames, Ray, Charles Eames and R. Buckminster Fuller. *Glimpses of the U.S.A.* Moscow Russia Soviet Union, 1959. https://www.loc.gov/item/2019636126/

Formafantasma. *Cambio*. London: Serpentine Gallerie and Koenig Books, 2020.

McLuhan, Marshall. *The Medium is the Massage: An Inventory of Effects*. London: Penguin Classics, 2008.

Rabottini, Alessandro. 'Thermic Power: Incomplete Notes on a Film That Does Not Exist Yet'. In *Oltre Terra*, edited by Formafantasma. Oslo: The National Museum of Art, Architecture and Design, 2020.

Rossi, Catharine. 'Per Una Controcultura Del Design: Le Categorie Del "Pastorale" E Del "Primitivo" Nel Design Radicale Italiano'. In *Made in Italy: Rethinking a Century of Italian Design*, edited by Grace Lees-Maffei and Kjetil Fallan. London: Bloomsbury, 2013, 152–157.

Tharp, Bruce M. and Stephanie M. Tharp. *Discursive Design – Critical, Speculative, and Alternative Things*. Cambridge, MA: MIT Press, 2022.

Trimarchi, Andrea, ed. Formafantasma: Why Wool Matters. Cologne: Verlag der Buchhandlung Walther König, 2023.

19
TOWARDS A CULTURE OF LIFE
A NEW SYNTHESIS FOR THE LIVING WORLD

Rachel Armstrong

Since the late twentieth century, various metaphysical frameworks have served as a counterpoint to industrial development and toxic anthropocentrism,[1] such as posthumanism in the 1990s and new materialism at the start of the third millennium. Composed from a range of different perspectives, these frameworks embrace more-than-human actors to achieve their effects on ecosystem health, ranging from the elements to companion species and technology. For example, political theorist and philosopher Jane Bennett invokes the agency of vitalism and the tendency for lively matter to form assemblages that possess 'thing power' (Bennett 2010), while philosopher Rosi Braidotti recognizes *Zoe* as the generic animating force that flows through lively substances (Braidotti 2016, 2006) and feminist theorist and physicist Karen Barad attributes the physical intra-actions between molecules and their strange quantum effects to influence chemistry (Barad 2014). Such agentized power relations that went beyond human control set the stage for ecological frames of reference that entangled humans and non-humans in a shared identity – and, therefore, fate (Bennett 2010, 13).

The only platform that can engage this expanded appreciation of the living realm and our role within it to promote collective enlivening is 'life' itself. When coupled with more-than-human metaphysics, advanced biotechnologies provide an implementable set of approaches and an expanded portfolio of 'living' materials and technologies that possess some of the properties of organisms, such as growth, self-repair, sensitivity and metabolism. Blurring former distinctions between material, body and technology, a humbler, kinder, stranger relationship with the living realm becomes possible. Enabling a co-constitutive relationship with the more-than-human realm, a culture of life is invoked. This transactional system is validated by *how well* its constituent agents live together.

Introducing microbes

The oldest, most versatile material and technical platform is the microbial realm. Its two to three billion species collectively make up more than 60 per cent of the Earth's living matter, comprise most of the world's biodiversity and were the only forms of life for most of its history. As agentized creative entities, they draw their technologies out of their bodies through instruments, such as plasmids, to 'make' the world around them. Working within natural energetic limits and using local resources, they use their powerful metabolism to transform their surroundings in ways that promote enlivening. Constantly (re) worlding the world, they modulate life-bearing activities such as plant growth, fixing gases into biologically useable mineral form, soil nutrient cycling, marine biogeochemical cycling and breaking down dead plant and animal matter into simpler substances that (re)enter the food chain. The collective actions of this 'microbial commons' (Dedeurwardere 2010) – a space of shared natural resources – generate the transactional (economic) system that makes possible life as we know it.

An incredible amount of mediation (microscopes, metagenomics, biochemical markers, isotope analysis, etc.) shapes our relationship with and expectations of microbes, so they are always already entangled with technical systems. The emerging new science of metagenomics enables us to see communities of microbes for the first time, which inhabit our bodies and living spaces. Quietly coexisting along with us, they do not obey the conventions of multicellular organisms. Around 50 per cent by number of our own cells (human microbiome) are bacterial (Sender, Fuchs and Milo, 2016) and also the environments we inhabit (microbiome of the built environment) – the sum diverse microbial communities that occupy buildings (Kembel et al. 2012) are made up of these microbiomes, which intersect with the microbial communities in the city (urban microbiome) (King 2014) – the sum diverse microbial communities that inhabit a city that perform ecosystems services at little or no resource cost (Bell et al. 2005; Balvanera et al. 2006; Fenchel, Blackburn and King 2012). Possessing a spatial and material dimension, these microbiomes – the aggregate of all microbiota that reside in a territory – have environmental, material (surfaces) and societal significance, heightened and deeply complicated by the Covid-19 pandemic (Armstrong 2021). Cutting-edge tools in the field of molecular biology also reveal that bacteria use sophisticated chemical signals to communicate in groups by counting their companions, and when there are enough of them together, their group behaviour is shaped by specific chemical 'words'. Known as quorum sensing, this complex lexicon enables bacteria to hold private, secret conversations, as well as public ones. Bacteria can also communicate with other species and even act *as if* they are multicellular, so they can accomplish impossible tasks as mere individuals (Miller and Bassler 2001).

Regarding the capacities of microbes for mobility, proliferation, spatialization and self-transformation as inspiration for reconfiguring notions of identity, Professor of Environmental Studies Myra Hird positions their micro-ontological negotiations as the foundations of sociability (Clark and Hird 2018). The material nature of microbes and their languages used to establish new territories are ways of walking the boundary[2] that provides a spatial basis for transactions and principles of coexistence. While sociologist and philosopher Bruno Latour proposes the deterritorialization of the Earth from its old (human-centric) national borders, microbes have already (re)territorialized this space, exemplified by the ongoing pandemic. Professor of Political and International Theory Stefanie Fishel redefines and extends the metaphor of the body into the political realm and reframes the concept of the body politic using the microbial realm to reveal alternative ways of living together (Fishel 2017). Positioning space as the very terrain and medium of power relations forged by complex, fragile, highly distributed relations that require constant re-negotiation and careful diplomacy, the management of these encounters requires engagement with (chemical) non-human languages, with the aim of forging new alliances capable of (re) making (mutually) liveable worlds (Hird 2009). A forum – a parliament of things (Latour 1993) – is needed to establish the foundations for new politics, economics and ways of organizing societies on their own terms, to negotiate the laws, power structures and modes of living that lead towards mutual enlivening (Latour 1993).[3] The importance of establishing ethics for working with these tiny agents as the basis for a new platform – as an expression of a parliament of things – cannot be overstated, whose negotiations underpin the anticipated culture of life.

Towards a culture of life

A culture of life does not start with tackling the highly developed and dominant private-public axis, as this is already entrenched in anthropocentric tropes, but speaks to a softer, fuzzier and economically much less valued agent – the household – which presents a more agile site for change. Through re-envisioning values within the household, the re-empowerment of citizens and the recognition of microbes as co-constitutive domestic actors can begin through the (re)vitalization of the home in ways that reactivate the commons.[4]

The following case studies develop a succession of steps through the realization of microbial technologies with beneficial ecosystem impacts, establishing 'conversations' with microbes to uphold a culture of life.

Living Architecture

Setting out to design and build a biological computer, the *Living Architecture* project (2016–19) takes the form of a freestanding, next-generation, selectively programmable bioreactor (Armstrong et al. 2017). This city of microbes is composed of integrated building blocks (microbial fuel cell, algae bioreactor and genetically modified processor), which form living spaces that also function as standardized building segments – or bricks. Each 'brick' is both a structural unit and an enabling environment for populations of microbes housed in technologically enabled hollows. 'Programming' is achieved by altering the microbial populations and spatially sequencing them. Overall, the system can be thought of as a metabolic app, which can materially compute, and process, the transformation of one set of substances from one 'city' into another, depending on its inputs. The hardware configuration is based on three types of bioreactors – microbial fuel cell, photobioreactor and synthetic bioprocessor.

'Fed' by domestic liquid waste (urine and greywater), the microbial fuel cell consists of an anode, selective membrane and cathode. The natural biofilm that settles on the selective membrane processes biochemical information from the liquid waste's nutrient streams to generate a range of metabolites and electrons that self-power the system, which are captured by conductive wires, optimized by an artificial intelligence (AI) and visualized through the activity of electronic devices. Housing microalgae, the photobioreactor captures sunlight and carbon dioxide, transforming them into biomass, water and oxygen as a by-product of photosynthesis. Connected to the cathode of the microbial fuel cell via a semi-permeable membrane, the oxygen produced acts as an end-terminal receptor for electrons, boosting its overall electrical power.

The scientific proof-of-principle system is a synthetic bioreactor, which explores just how far the actual metabolic reactions in the bricks can be designed using synthetic biology techniques and genetically modified consortia of organisms that can detoxify nitrous gases from the air and also reclaim phosphate from greywater. When combined, the microbial populations turn these substrates into a set of metabolites – where each bioprocessor moves its waste products on to the next chamber, where further transformations occur and so on. The whole process is coordinated by an AI that detects the amount of electricity being produced by the microbial fuel cell and – as the metabolisms are interlinked – modifies the system's inputs accordingly to produce various forms of housework that mitigate the negative environmental impacts of human occupancy by removing pollutants, providing electricity, making biomolecules and recovering water.

Establishing a kind of metabolic trading system, *Living Architecture* generates a co-constitutive quality of living between humans and microbes. Implicit in these entangled relationships, the microbiota of human inhabitants is inevitably incorporated into the nutrient waste streams to become part of the holistically operating 'living' system. Rendering obsolete instrumental practices, microbes housed in the apparatus are not enslaved but establish themselves within various bioreactor types to make kin and community in microbial consortia and biofilms. Inhabited through rituals of daily life and care for things, *Living Architecture* not only 'computes' the material flows within a household but also provides an apparatus that exemplifies alternative paradigms for domestic economies, with the potential to bring about integrated, systemic change in the material impacts of human inhabitation capable of contributing to planetary enlivening – where through our relationship with microbes, human activities of daily living are transformed into world-making actions. When, through habituation, the overall performance and wellbeing of the constituents cannot be meaningfully separated out from each other, then *Living Architecture* acquires the status of holobiont (Gordon et al. 2013).

Throughout the project, the social acceptability of the technology was considered through various 'brick' prototypes exhibited in biennales and international exhibitions. The first prototype was a simple hack of a brick, turning it into a microbial fuel cell, which brought together structure and process and was displayed at the Building Centre in London (2018) and during the Venice Architecture Biennale.

Even more complex structures were developed that could simultaneously host photosynthetic and anaerobic organisms, enabling them to exchange metabolites with each other, which were displayed at the 4th Tallinn Architecture Biennale.

Since the final wall used synthetic organisms, which reclaimed 100 per cent of the phosphate introduced in the system, it was explored in a laboratory rather than a social context. As the original version of *Living Architecture* could not be exposed directly to the general public owing to the presence of genetically modified organisms, an alternative wild-type experience of a prototype wall system entitled *999 years 13 sqm (the future belongs to ghosts)*, was developed for the *Is This Tomorrow?* exhibition at the Whitechapel Gallery, in collaboration with artist Cecile B. Evans (Whitechapel Gallery 2019; Bevan 2019). Taking the form of a future apartment space, the installation housed a screen-based system powered by natural anaerobic biofilms within an array of 'living bricks'. The work created a context for the microbial infrastructure, envisaging a time beyond modernity as a vision of the future where humanity faces new challenges posed by big data, bioengineering and climate change. Comprising a posthuman 'household' powered by microbes, the space was inhabited by digital ghosts of the past, present and future as the only traces of human life.

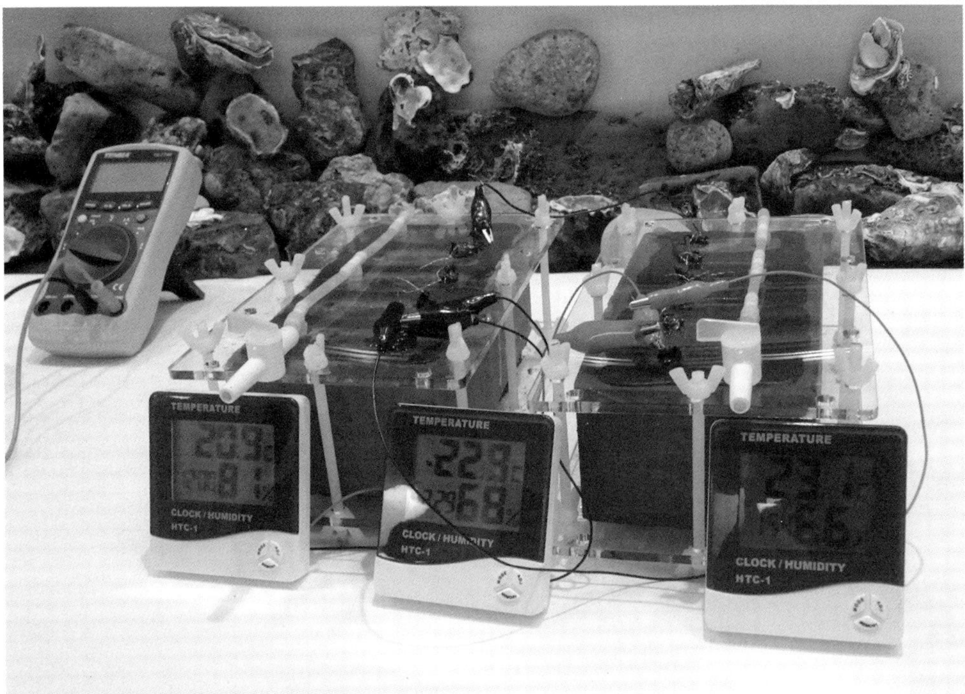

Figure 19.1 *Living Architecture* 'wall', 2013. Courtesy of Rachel Armstrong.

Active Living Infrastructure: Controlled Environment (ALICE)

While *Living Architecture* establishes a metabolic economy for transactions between humans and microbes, the *Active Living Infrastructure: Controlled Environment (ALICE)* prototype (2019–21) generates the foundations for collaboration with microbes. Using electrons produced by the anaerobic biofilm of microbial fuel cells as 'data', a direct link is made between bacterial metabolism and electronic systems that can interpret and visualize this data. Possessing a very particular kind of environmental intelligence, bacteria can reveal a great deal about the character of a place, where a technologized approach can generate a relatable communications interface. Typically, microbial activity is deciphered using the tools of biochemistry, but in human terms, the interpretation process is relatively slow. Tapping into the much faster electron flows within biofilms, however, provides a direct way of understanding the behaviour of a microbial population at any given moment and, depending on the sensitivity of electrodes, creates the possibility of developing a communications platform between humans and microbes. Translated by software into animations that conveyed the overall status of the biofilm in relatable terms, electronic activity can be read by audiences who could, therefore, respond to the microbial behaviour – not by looking at unpleasant 'slime' (the natural 'face' of microbial communities) but by interacting with appealing forms on a familiar screen-based interface. Participants could play with resident microbes through data and performance in an exploratory exchange – as if they were a pot plant or pet. This world of 'Mobes' – a characterful term coined for the data-based representations of microbes – offers a simple,

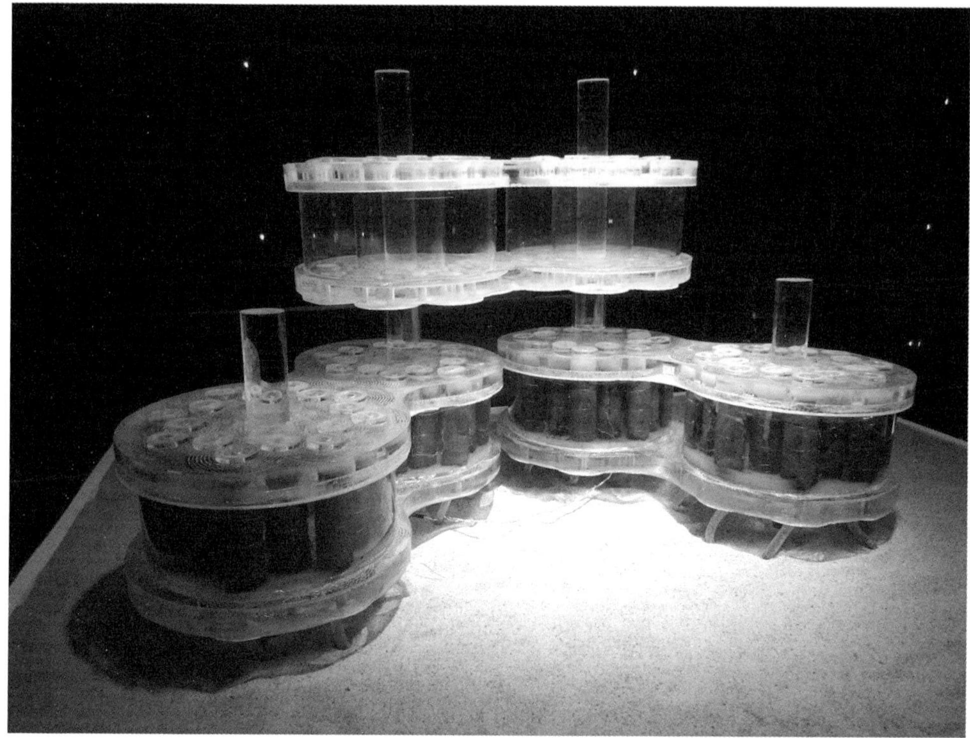

Figure 19.2 Vernacular Venetian 'bricks' transformed into bioelectricity-producing microbial fuel cells, 2018. Courtesy of Rachel Armstrong.

probiotic approach to interspecies communication within the highly situated realm of microbes, which takes place in conversation with, rather than by, 'exploiting' microbes. Consequently, *ALICE* enables us to learn along with microbes through their ability to generate clear and direct signals and data, inviting different kinds of (house)work and domestic routines for our living spaces that relate to shared concerns, like transforming waste streams into household resources.

Microbial Urbanism: Prototyping the Bio-Digital City via a Circular Bio-Economy Pilot

Bioelectrically active microbial systems can be scaled to supply a community with electricity. Combining the principles of wastewater gardens, which use the root microbiota of plants to break down organic waste while also harvesting bioelectricity using microbial fuel cell arrays, the *Microbial Urbanism: Prototyping the Bio-Digital City via a Circular Bio-Economy Pilot* (*MU*) proposal links the conservation of natural resources typical of sustainable narratives with the digital capabilities of 'smart' cities, establishing scalable, foundational principles for bio-digital cities. Doubling up as a power plant, *MU*'s publicly accessible winter garden can treat wastewater from 5,000 to 30,000 households to generate enough electricity to power street lighting, charge mobile phones and run digital screens. It is important to note,

Figure 19.3 Complex, combined 'brick' structure with rod-based assembly system that co-houses photosynthetic and anaerobic populations of microbes, 2017. Courtesy of Rachel Armstrong.

however, that the power generated by bioelectrical systems is not on the same scale as fossil fuel-based, chemical or even renewable sources but raises the prospect of a new thermoeconomics that operates within the natural carrying capacity of a place (Garrett, Grasselli and Keen 2020). Such constraints address resource limits by generating energy in a circular context, which can be recycled within a specific material and living ecology without 'borrowing' resources from next generations or elsewhere.

Immunological City (IM-CITY)

Immunological City (*IM-CITY*) is a design for a theoretical framework that proposes to defend the health of citizens via an implementable urban immune system, which combines the actions of smart city infrastructure and microbially enabled bioelectrical systems (BES), like the microbial fuel cell, whose operations are centred on an immunological model called Danger Theory (DT) (Matzinger 2002). Recognized as a feminist model of the immune system, DT has significant epistemological value in changing narratives about the health of urban environments from being at war with 'foreign invaders' (Weasel 2001) (the antigens) to establishing an alternative value system based on the contributions of citizens (of all species) via an agentized view of mutual care and exchange (economy). Taking a prophylactic approach to the health of citizens, a range of mitigating cascades are deployed through

Figure 19.4 *999 years 13 sqm (the future belongs to ghosts)*, 2019. Courtesy of Rachel Armstrong.

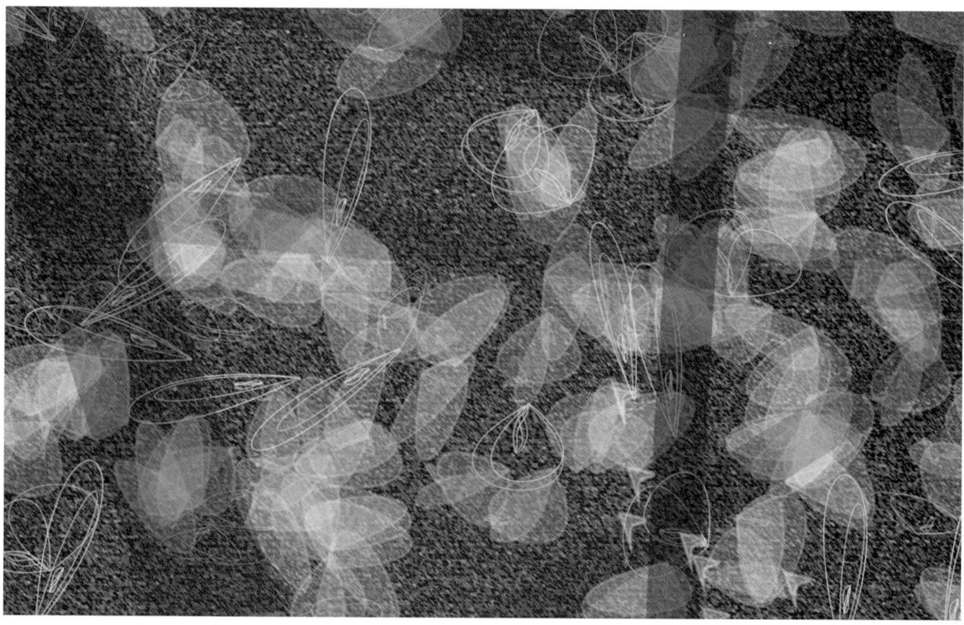

Figure 19.5 Mobes from the ALICE website, 2020. Courtesy of ALICE.

established 'smart' urban infrastructures based on the early detection of environmental 'harm' that comprises a range of pollutants, physical changes, noxious agents and microbes that are exacerbated by urbanization itself. Linked to emerging new areas of science, such as the Urban Microbiome and the Microbiome of the Built Environment, the design of this infrastructure is sensor-rich and set to shape our understanding of the environmental health of the built environment. Groups of symbiotically interacting microbial populations are organized within the city through sensor hubs, which are constantly 'reading' the biochemical character of their surroundings. Conventional information and communications technology (ICT) processes some of the data, but environmentally restorative actions are carried out by integrated BES resulting in bioremediation; regulation of microbial distribution/diversity, including the removal of pathogens from wastewater streams (Ieropoulos, Pasternak and Greenman 2017); and improved resource utilization. Offering a whole new platform for sustainable urbanism, BES's 'living' technologies also produce bioelectricity and are self-powering. Like *ALICE* and *Living Architecture*, their microbial/data interfaces generate electrons as data, enabling 'smart' digital systems to be coupled together with organic approaches to generate a bio-digital platform, which brings together the 'green' of the organic/natural world and the 'grey' of machines and ICT (Armstrong and Hughes 2021). Catalysing the next generation of an organically based Internet of Things (IoT) – a network of physical objects, embedded with sensors and software (where microbes play an integral sensor-processing-effector-energy-generating role) that connect and exchange data with other devices over the internet – BES form the actuation basis for environmental remediation, energy production and resource circularity, which is realized through *IM-CITY*'s holobiontically integrated, next-generation 'sustainable' and 'smart' urban platforms. The resultant data-images provided by AI systems enable coordinated vigilance towards both natural and anthropogenic environmental disturbances, whereby these networks, and the ecosystems services they provide, will change according to their context, and needs, thereby becoming an immune system for the urban landscape and marking the advent of bio-digital cities.

Towards the bio-digital city

Adapting established smart city environmental surveillance systems to accommodate microbial technologies like BES can establish ways of taking remedial action and create the foundations for more-than-human smart city systems that draw anthropocentric development into a homeostatic relationship with urban ecologies. The low-power electronics systems powered by microbial bioelectricity are critical for stabilizing carbon dioxide emissions, as they establish limits to consumption and promote the re-deployment of 'waste'. Taking the lead from the limits of energy provision established by microbial bioelectricity, contemporary smart city infrastructure must also seek much lower embodied energy as necessary energetic constraints for innovation, resisting trying to match the standards set by power-hungry 230V systems based on past (Victorian) innovation that perpetuates a practice of unlimited consumption. With the appropriate innovation-necessary constraints, such as 12V power supplies and capacitors with 'intelligent' deployment of energy flow to domestic environments, new lines of innovation can be established that do not just rely on energy to perform work but also seek embodied solutions. For example, using ultrasound for washing and incorporating elastocaloric materials in refrigeration expands our imaginaries towards alternatives that diversify our portfolio for daily living. Based on new thermoeconomics, using 'living' microbes instead of 'dead' fossil fuels can scale up metabolic transactions from an individual household to an urban environment through materials and systems services. Convergent innovation is required to achieve this transition, where different aspects of low-impact lifestyles are combined and networked together in ways that catalyse social, design-led and technological innovation. By shaping our values, lifestyles, environmental impacts and economies, microbial technologies like *Living Architecture*, *ALICE* and *Microbial Urbanism* are ideally situated to fulfil this goal, offering a vital, relevant platform at a critical time in our history that renders effective carbon dioxide emission reduction achievable. Such innovation will alter design imaginaries and cultural expectations by simultaneously promoting liveability and securing fairness for the natural world to change building affordances and alter our lifestyle expectations.

The smart microbial city of the near future will be a biodiverse environment with more soils and renewable energy for heavy-duty work and will nurture different kinds of economy. It is a place, like *IM-CITY*, of organic generosity, mediated by environmentally engaged microbes that provide data for 'smart' computer systems to characterize events (made visible via digital interfaces) as well as bioremediating (through their metabolic versatility) at the site of need. Turning waste into resources, human impacts on the urban landscape are transformed into beneficial ecosystem services, resulting in the increased fertility of urban soils and landscapes. Notions of commodity are replaced with those of metabolism, and cultures of life are celebrated not by excessive wealth but by what we put back into the surroundings that sustain us.

How we develop our smart city infrastructure to cohabit with microbes is of great importance, as we cannot take their cooperation for granted. By establishing a parliament of things within our homes and cities, a model for living can be established where hotly negotiated differences form the foundations of our living together and do not drive us apart. A culture of life is realized when we can no longer tell where human activity stops and more-than-human life begins.

Notes

1 Toxic anthropocentrism is the exaltation of humankind over all other creatures, whereby they are not considered worthy of a moral status.

2 Walking the boundary, beating the bounds or perambulating the bounds is an ancient custom still observed in parts of England, Wales and the New England region of the United States, where inhabitants walk the geographic boundaries of their locality to maintain the memory of their precise location.

3 The decoding of such impossible conversations invokes the 'Babelfish', a term invented by Douglas Adams in *The Hitchhiker's Guide to the Galaxy*. It referred to a creature which could translate brain waves and, in effect, translate all languages for anyone with a Babelfish placed in the brain.

4 Commons are shared spaces and resources that are accessible to all members of a community. Reactivation is needed as some individuals and corporations with access to the commons exploit them for selfish ends leading to the tragedy of the commons, first conceptualized in 1833 by British writer William Forster Lloyd, where these elements are depleted/exploited and no longer available to all, for example, deforestation, biodiversity loss.

References

Armstrong, Rachel. *Safe as Houses: More-Than Human Design for a Post-Pandemic World.* London: Lund Humphries, 2021.

Armstrong, Rachel and Rolf Hughes. 'Metabolic Architecture: Dialogues with Microbes'. In *The Ecological Turn*, edited by Loreno Arboritanza et al. University of Bologna Architecture and Design PhD Committee. Delft: BK Books TU Delft, 2021, 255–272.

Armstrong, Rachel, et al. 'Living Architecture (LIAR): Metabolically Engineered Building Units'. In *Cultivated Building Materials: Industrialized Natural Resources for Architecture and Construction*, edited by Dirk E. Hebel and Felix Heisel. Berlin: Birkhauser, 2017, 170–7.

Balvanera, Patricia, et al. 'Quantifying the Evidence for Biodiversity Effects on Ecosystem Functioning and Services'. *Ecology Letters* 9 (2006): 1146–56.

Barad, K. 'Deep Calls unto Deep: Queer Inhumanism and Matters of Justice-to-Come'. Paper Presented at the Drew University Transdisciplinary Theological Colloquium, Madison, NJ, 2014.

Bell, Thomas, et al. 'The Contribution of Species Richness and Composition to Bacterial Services'. *Nature* 436 (2005): 1157–60.

Bennett, Jane. *Vibrant Matter: A Political Ecology of Things*. Durham (North Carolina): Duke University Press, 2010.

Bevan, Robert. 'Is This Tomorrow? Review: Installations Show a Troubled Mood of the Future'. *Evening Standard*, 14 February 2019. https://www.standard.co.uk/culture/is-this-tomorrow-review-installations-show-a-troubled-mood-of-the-future-a4066551.html.

Braidotti, Rosi. 'The Critical Posthumanities; or, Is Medianatures to Naturecultures as Zoe Is to Bios?' Cultural Politics 12, no. 3 (2016): 380–390

Braidotti, Rosi. *Transpositions: On Nomadic Ethics*. Cambridge: Polity Press, 2006.

Clark, Nigel and Myra Hird. 'Microontologies and the Politics of Emergent Life'. In *Handbook on the Geographies of Power*, edited by Mat Coleman and John Agnew. Cheltenham: Edward Elgar Publishing, 2018, 245–258.

Dedeurwaerdere, Tom. 'Self-Governance and International Regulation of the Global Microbial Commons: Introduction to the Special Issue on the Microbial Commons'. *International Journal of the Commons* 4, no. 1 (2010): 390–403.

Fenchel, Tom, Henry Blackburn and Gary King. 'Biogeochemical Cycling in Soils'. In *Bacterial Bioeochemistry: The Ecophysiology of Mineral Cycling*, edited by Tom Fenchel, Henry Blackburn and Gary King. London: Academic Press, 2012, 89–120.

Fishel, Stefanie. *The Microbial State: Global Thriving and the Body Politic*. Minneapolis: University of Minnesota Press, 2017.

Garrett, Timothy J., Matheus Grasselli and Stephen Keen. 'Past World Economic Production Constraints Current Energy Demands: Persistent Calling with Implications for Economic Growth and Climate Change Mitigation'. *PLoS ONE* 15, no. 8 (2020): e0237672.

Gordon, Jeffrey, et al. 'Superorganisms and Holobionts'. *Microbe* 8, no. 4 (2013): 152–3.

Hird, Myra J. *The Origins of Sociable Life: Evolution after Science Studies*. New York: Palgrave Macmillan, 2009.

Hughes, Rolf and Rachel Armstrong. *The Art of Experiment: Post-pandemic Knowledge Practices for 21st Century Architecture and Design*. London: Routledge, 2020.

Ieropoulos, Ioannis, Grzegorz Pasternak and John Greenman. 'Urine Disinfection and in Situ Pathogen Killing Using a Microbial Fuel Cell Cascade System'. *PLoS ONE* 12, no. 5 (2017): e0176475.

Kembel, Steven W., et al. 'Architectural Design Influences the Diversity and Structure of the MBE'. *International Society of Microbial Ecology Journal* 6 (2012): 1469–79.

King, Gary M. 'Urban Microbiomes and Urban Ecology: How Do Microbes in the Built Environment Affect Human Sustainability in Cities?' *The Journal of Microbiology* 52, no. 9 (2014): 721–8.

Latour, Bruno. *Down to Earth: Politics in the New Climatic Regime*. Cambridge: Polity Press, 2015.

Latour, Bruno. *We Have Never Been Modern*. Cambridge: Harvard University Press, 1993.

Matzinger, Polly. The Danger Model: A Renewed Sense of Self. *Science* 296 (2002): 301–5.

Miller, Melissa B. and Bonnie L. Bassler. 'Quorum Sensing in Bacteria'. *Annual Review of Microbiology* 55 (2001): 165–99. https://doi.org/10.1146/aaurev.micro.55.1.165

Sender, Ron, Shai Fuchs and Ron Milo. 'Are We Really Vastly Outnumbered? Revisiting the Ratio of Bacterial to Host Cells in Humans'. *Cell* 164 (2016): 337–40.

Tolstoy, Leo. *What Then Must We Do?* Oxford: Oxford University Press, 1925.

Tsing, Anna Lowenhaupt, Heather Anne Swanson, Elaine Gan and Nils Bubandt. *Arts of Living on a Damaged Planet: Ghosts and Monsters of the Anthropocene*. Minneapolis: University of Minnesota Press, 2017.

Weasel, Lisa. 'Dismantling the Self/Other Dichotomy in Science: Towards a Feminist Model of the Immune System'. *Hypatia* 16, no. 1 (2001): 27–44, 29.

Whitechapel Gallery. 'Is This Tomorrow?' 14 February–12 May 2019. https://www.whitechapelgallery.org/exhibitions/is-this-tomorrow/

Woese, Carl R. 'How We Do, Don't and Should Look at Bacteria and Bacteriology'. In *The Prokaryotes: Prokaryotic Biology and Symbiotic Associations*, edited by Eugene Rosenberg, Edward F. DeLong, Stephen Lory, Erko Stackebrandt, and Fabiano Thompson. New York: Springer, 2013, 3–20.

20 DESIGNING THE FUTURE OF AGRICULTURE

Kris Spiros

The practice of farming animals has been globally commonplace for millennia. The foods and materials produced by animals have cradled human civilization in a manner few commodities ever have. However, due to the tremendous worldwide demand for animal products such as meat, modern animal farming practices are causing unprecedented public health, ethical and environmental problems. The issues from conventional meat production seem to stem directly from the animal itself – an organism that within the context of a farm is a mere production 'mechanism'. Through the latest scientific technologies, the possibility has arisen to redesign this system, to produce meat without farming animals, but, instead, by farming cells. This new concept of meat is called cultivated meat and it proposes a shift in how people consume their animal protein, from macroscopic production to microscopic.

The macro-agricultural model we have used for millennia has depended on animals as machines within farming, while this new form of micro-agriculture leans on cells as the driving production conduit. At its core, proponents of cultivated meat point to a problem-solving philosophy of the concept. The ethos of cultivated meat posits that the problem with a product like meat is not the 'how' but the 'cow'. If the resource-intensive, sentient organism that is a farm animal can be decoupled from its inherent production structure, many of the worst problems of meat production would also decouple (and ultimately disappear). As it relates to design, the field of cultivated meat is uniquely positioned in a mass spectrum of problem-solving innovations of the future. Notably, cultivated meat is unlike many cutting-edge innovations of tomorrow as it lacks any legitimate degree of 'Subconscious Pre-Marketing' (SPM). This is an often-beneficial characteristic where consumers build a baseline of familiarity around a concept before its commercialization.

If you consider many other products and services that will likely be arriving in the coming decades, such as flying cars (Uber Elevate) or space travel (SpaceX) . . . decades or even centuries of SPM has led to many of these advances already being installed into the collective imagination. People think of travelling to other planets in spaceships or flying cars with a sense of wonder, and it is no coincidence that companies are capitalizing on the heavy lifting that artists and filmmakers of the past have carried

Figure 20.1 Concept design for a future cultivated meat production facility, 2022. Courtesy of Kris Spiros.

out. For a modern company of a once-science fiction product, it is like marketing on 'steroids'; the world has already fallen in love with your idea in their favourite movie or book. Cultivated meat, however, at best, has achieved headlines that often repulse, labelling it as 'lab-grown' meat, weird and unnatural. It is commonly thought within the cultivated meat 'space' that there are three primary drivers to its success or failure:

Research and Development (R&D) – Research, leading to innovations in scaling up production for the masses, is critical; unravelling scientific discoveries that translate to commercialization goals (cheaper, better-tasting, healthy meat) is expensive and takes a lot of time.

Regulation – The regulation of a new food product is a mountainous hurdle in and of itself; it is possible that a product is delayed and damaged by a lack of regulatory momentum or that certain countries/regions do not allow its entry into their markets.

Consumer Education – If a global consumer base is ever to consider cultivated meat as an option, they must, at some point, first learn what it is.

Of these three primary drivers of cultivated meat, we will focus on the third, honing in on how to design for public 'education'. We will explore the nuanced nature of cultivated meat education, due to the complex and ever-changing production methods of the concept; explore the relevant case studies that history can teach us to prepare for such a massive potential shift of a staple dietary product; and lastly, consider how people's interactions with cultivated meat may be stemming from a lack of accurate/available subconscious stimuli.

Public understanding of cultivated meat

The importance of accurate public education on the topic of cultivated meat cannot be overstated. Before its introduction to global markets in the next couple of decades, people worldwide will first have to learn what cultivated meat is. This is the purpose of market education, of course, as learning must take place before buying can. But market education is particularly notable for cultivated meat as it is not a slight modification to an arbitrary commodity; it is a redefinition of meat and food. The vast majority of the world is unfamiliar with what it is, how it will be produced and why it ought to be considered as a potential purchase over conventional meat. This lack of understanding from billions of people could lead to inaccurate understandings around the safety and quality of future cultivated meat products. Importantly, the referenced public education is not to maximize the market potential for cultivated meat; it is simply necessary if consumers are to make informed decisions about what is best for their individual interests. And the global education necessary for cultivated meat indeed cuts both ways.

On the one hand, cultivated meat companies may benefit from new consumers who have environmental concerns around conventional meat; they may feel that cultivated meat addresses their ecological concerns and end up becoming regular consumers. The prerequisite to this is that those consumers first learn that cultivated meat has environmental advantages over conventional meat. On the other hand, if proper education does not occur, a consumer may feel all cultivated meat products pose a solution to conventional meat requiring animal slaughter. They may intuitively think, 'Hey, this must not kill an animal because they are simply taking the cells from an animal and no slaughter is involved', and they may even see marketing for one type of company that truly does not harm/kill animals in any part of their production process for cultivated meat. But the reality of the developing market landscape for cultivated meat is more complex.

The marketing, specifically package design, of brands can begin to become synonymous with the concept, and this can cause consumer misconceptions. Take, for example, a cultivated meat company that produces a meat product that is only a minor part of the actual 'meat cells' they produce, let's say 20 per cent, and the rest of the product is plant-based. As a comparison point, a standard chicken nugget may be upwards of 80 per cent real meat, and the remaining 20 per cent is plant-based filler (breading, etc.). But since the meat cells are so expensive to produce, this cultivated meat company produces a mostly plant-based product, and only 20 per cent 'real' animal meat is produced through cultivated meat processes. Importantly as well, that percentage of the product that is indeed cultivated meat (20 per cent) was produced using genetic modification, as well as fetal bovine serum (FBS).

Genetic modification can be used in the process of producing cultivated meat as a way to increase the yield of 'meat cells' that can be harvested in production. In other words, if you modify the genome of meat cells, you can potentially make more product, quicker. Then there is FBS. FBS is a biological product derived from the blood of unborn calves. In the context of cultivated meat, FBS is the food for meat cells to grow and divide; it is often used as a growth medium that helps meat cells proliferate during production. Since one of the prospects of cultivated meat is that it will no longer require animal slaughter and does not harm animals, FBS poses a bit of hypocrisy to the system, as cultivated meat products that use FBS are still essentially using animals to produce the 'non-animal' cultivated meat product. Across the field of biology, FBS is the standard; many commercial industries and branches of academia commonly use it, which brings its cost down. In the young cultivated meat sector, since it is so inexpensive and highly effective at growing meat cells for cultivated meat, FBS is also commonly used (despite the marketing hurdles previously mentioned). Additional research and development (R&D) will be required, meaning much more money and time, before scalable plant-based or synthetic alternatives to FBS can be developed; these could then make the full production pipeline for cultivated meat animal-component-free.

Similarly, there are efforts to avoid genetic modification to meat cells in the production process, but once more, the quicker path to market is to use genetic modification which some consumers may find problematic for purchase behaviours. In summary, FBS and genetic modification have obvious pitfalls; they require animals in light of the animal-free promise of cultivated meat, and genetically modified organisms (GMO) have obvious past issues surrounding them. But now let's say you have three companies that are seeking to sell cultivated meat products in the short/medium term, barring regulatory approval – one *does not* use FBS and *does not* use genetic engineering; one *does* use FBS but *does not* use genetic engineering; and the last uses *both* FBS and genetic engineering. They all produce cultivated meat products on the market sometime this decade, but say one of them gets a head start, likely to be the one who uses FBS and genetic engineering since that offers a quicker path to market. This may have consequences on people's early understanding and could taint global consumer education of the fragile concept of cultivated meat. The public perception may start to form that cultivated meat uses animals in the production process and does not save animals from harm. Anti-GMO activists may also protest against such a product, and the delicate concept of cultivated meat could absorb a negative perception for a long time. In reality and eventually (with enough R&D), cultivated meat does not require either FBS or GMO but fast-acting companies, interested in pleasing investors expediently, could taint the perception of the concept.

To be clear, this theoretical scenario is less theoretical and more ongoing practical reality. The companies that are indeed selling products quite soon are often placed in a very difficult spot – either sell a 'non-perfect' version of an early cultivated meat product and then use product sales to fuel R&D, which will make future cultivated meat products have 'new versions' with 'better features', or run out of money as a company and fail altogether. To return to the main point, though, the educational landscape of cultivated meat is complicated. There is much for consumers to learn but such a narrow window to be able to share the intricacies. Steve Jobs, while speaking about Apple, once said, 'This is a very complicated world. It is a very noisy world. And we are not going to get a chance to get people to remember much about us' (PodiumVC 2008). Indeed, educating the world on a new product is very difficult. There is a seemingly endless number of new products and forms of content competing for everyone's attention in the modern, digital world. It feels more reasonable to assume that if people can learn very simple facts about cultivated meat, that would be considered a win for their long-term decision-making in the marketplace.

And let's say the massive task is achieved of educating the world on what cultivated meat even is, including how it is produced in a basic sense, and some potential advantages it has. It may be too large of a task early on to also ask consumers to contemplate the nuances of genetic modification or not, FBS or not. This could be overwhelming and force people to avoid the topic altogether. Instead, the first products on the market that make the biggest splash (word of mouth, digital views, press coverage, etc.) will influence consumers' early impressions. People have to hear a few times from their friends or family members that this new thing called 'cultivated meat' does not save animals; it uses dead baby cows to feed the cells, or it is dangerous because the cells are genetically modified. In summary, cultivated meat is fragile and complicated. It requires nuanced and streamlined education for the public so people can make the best decisions for themselves. I hope this elucidates the involvedness with education surrounding cultivated meat. Let's now turn our attention to historical examples that can teach us how to educate the world on cultivated meat.

Limited case studies

Few examples lend enough similarity to achieve relevance when pondering how a future society may perceive cultivated meat. Common educational examples that advocate cultivated meat have compared it to beer brewing, claiming that the large, stainless-steel tanks represent a similar bioprocess environment for creating meat. The marketing line may look like 'Cultivated meat is safe and normal; the process of making meat from cells is not much different from brewing beer.' This, however, fails to account for the traditional methodology that conventional meat production represents; unlike beer brewing, the world is exceptionally familiar with how the original iteration of meat production is carried out. In other words, beer is not 'naturally' made one way, and now a new product is posing a completely different production method . . . the beer brewing process is the one way that people know beer is made. Let us imagine a new concept of beer was created that involved obtaining beer-like milk from a mammalian animal; one wouldn't say this way of making beer is natural and normal; it is just like milking a cow. Milking a cow is how you obtain milk, not how you obtain beer (as people know it), so no, this is not normal.

Another common example is yoghurt. Again, the claim here is that the processing for yoghurt is similar in theory to what is done to cultivate meat; thus one should not be afraid. If only the gut, instinctual fear or, more appropriately defined, 'disgust' reaction that people have when hearing such descriptions of cultivated meat would be solved by such logic. Contrarily, opponents of cultivated meat will claim it is entirely unnatural and, therefore, bad. Terms like 'Frankenmeat' are used to provoke fear and disgust by augmenting the artificiality that exists within cultivated meat's identity. But once more, claiming unnaturalness is synonymous with 'unhealthiness' is unfounded. Around the world, many populations consume food products such as protein powder, particularly matter that arguably could not be produced any more artificially. And the physical appearance follows suit, as artificial as a food product could look. But the marketing and branding of protein powder, seemingly backed by legitimate science of its potential health benefits for certain populations, saves its public perception from 'Frankenprotein' comparisons. Again, to bring the beer analogy back, protein powder is not naturally made one way and now is changing, so this likely saves it from backlash.

In summary, advocates build boundless scenarios that paint a picture of cultivated meat being just like another 'processed' food product. At the same time, opponents allow no reasonable allowance for processed, unnatural food products to be a fitting subject for comparison. Ultimately, little can be learned from poor examples. And the key to the lack of appropriate examples stems from the dissimilarity of products to cultivated meat. As mentioned, beer was not produced in the same manner for millennia and suddenly changed, and while yoghurt does indeed count as an animal product with food processing in its production, it lacks both the deep cultural importance and history that meat has. This is not to say that yoghurt is not an important component to different cultural diets, but rather, it does not rank to the level of meat, evident by global consumption rates. In short, grocery stores have entire 'meat' departments worldwide; in comparison, 'yoghurt' sections are smaller. So then, what example can be used to teach us about how a traditionally produced, deeply engrained product can change its production method after millions of years of its natural use? Indeed, it may be the simplest thing that humans ingest after all . . . water.

Specifically, it is the similarities of cultivated meat to the product of filtered water. Cultivated meat is difficult to compare to other food products because meat is too natural and engrained in global culture and history. It is not just another stock-keeping unit (SKU) in the grocery store. Yet, water and meat are fundamentally similar insofar as they are acquired in one traditional way, naturally (and have been since the inception of the human species), and everyone is familiar with the natural origins, which are deeply engrained in cultures worldwide since the beginning of civilization. However, filtered water and 'cultivated meat' pose a paradigm shift in the modern era. Consider the introduction of water filters; they posed a transformative scientific modification to unfiltered water. They claimed health benefits, even though it was a change to the 'production method' of the traditional product. But we do not think of filtered water as 'Frankenwater' or 'Artificial Water' even though scientific processes are being applied to its conceptual predecessor. Interesting insights may be gained by exploring filtered water's international education effort, which is centuries old.

The history of modern water filters spans just centuries, but humanity has been attempting to filter water for millennia; roughly 4,000 years ago in China and India, the first filtering and treating of water took place (Wikipedia n.d.). There may have been an understanding of water that was passed down generationally, that in its natural state it may be unclean or unhealthy. Cognitive dissonance, or ignoring uncomfortable facts for the sake of mental peace, could have made some people/populations not take seriously the need to filter water. They may have ignored that their water was dirty because they wanted to avoid the arduous act of heavily filtering their water, all for the sake of short-term convenience. Consider a theoretical example of an adolescent Mayan boy in the year 78 eliciting such cognitive dissonance. Since he was young, his parents have taught him how to filter water using ancient Mayan techniques, and at home they have a standard method they follow, but he is outside home, near a body of water and very thirsty, so he convinces himself that it is probably OK to drink this water as is. He was fine, but others in history were not so lucky.

Fast forward to today. Filtered water alleviates the cognitive dissonance for people, helping them avoid the extra work often required to align one's behaviours with their values; all that is needed with the concept of the modern water filter is to make the mental decision that you will opt for it over unfiltered water. Then after you purchase it, no longer must you subconsciously repress the dirtiness of water you would otherwise be constantly drinking, as you are now always living out your value of wanting healthy drinking water. Similarly, people often subconsciously ignore uncomfortable facts regarding meat production. They are aware of how it potentially harms animals or the environment, but once more, cognitive dissonance opens the floodgates to self-deception. Cultivated meat, like filtered water, could align one's values once more with their behaviours. No longer must people bury how their consumer choices are impacting the world around them; they can live more mentally free, knowing their purchases don't harm animals or the environment (pending the type of product, as aforementioned, FBS/GMO). Most importantly, though, we ought to explore what people's perceptions are of filtered water in the first place.

While it doesn't seem to be a topic that people contemplate frequently (and there were no studies to draw from), if you were to ask anyone from the age of sixteen to sixty-five what they think about when you say filtered water, I would imagine that the primary perception is of the 'benefits' that it offers over unfiltered, 'normal' water, and they would generally perceive filtered water as good or bad. I base this presumption on the fact that most Americans filter or treat their home's drinking water (NSF International n.d.). This suggests that most people in the United States, at least, and I imagine this extends beyond as well, think there is some benefit to filtering water, enough so that they would spend money on a product.

So, while our pre-historic ancestors did little to ensure that the water they had access to was suitable for consumption, most Americans make an effort to purify their water, and this is in addition to tap water systems that are not particularly dangerous in the United States (e.g. certain countries have more notoriously dangerous water systems where water must first be boiled before consumption).

Continuing our theoretical experiment of asking people what they think about, when you pose filtered water to them, I would imagine subsequent responses may include what a water filter is, as in the actual physical form of the filter, and perhaps a rudimentary understanding of the science, or how the product of a water filter is carrying out some kind of process to actually purify the water. I also think, if specifically asked, that people may vaguely consider the R&D origins of the device, understanding that water filters probably come from some sort of factory somewhere or the machines that made them, but I would think that the fact of knowing the R&D origins of the device is not as important in their minds as the device itself, or most importantly, the benefits/drawbacks to filtered water. The relevance here is as follows: when people think of filtered water, they know what it is; they know, at a very basic level, how it is doing what it is doing (or that the filter is performing some kind of purifying action); and they most notably are aware of the vague health benefits (or drawbacks to some) as to why it is good or bad. This seems evolutionarily in line as well, since our brains have to conserve resources and with there being so much to worry about for survival, why should we think about all the sophistication of concepts when, at a base level, we must simply know, is such concept good or is it bad?

The R&D origin of filtered water makes up the smallest slice of the perception pie. The last thing people are thinking about is the kind of facility that produces water filters. Subconsciously, they are likely aware that there is a difference in origin from unfiltered water, the 'natural' counterpart to filtered water, which comes from springs or aquifers, but still, that is not what they think about foremost when considering filtered water. Interestingly, this is contrary to cultivated meat, where the R&D origin is the

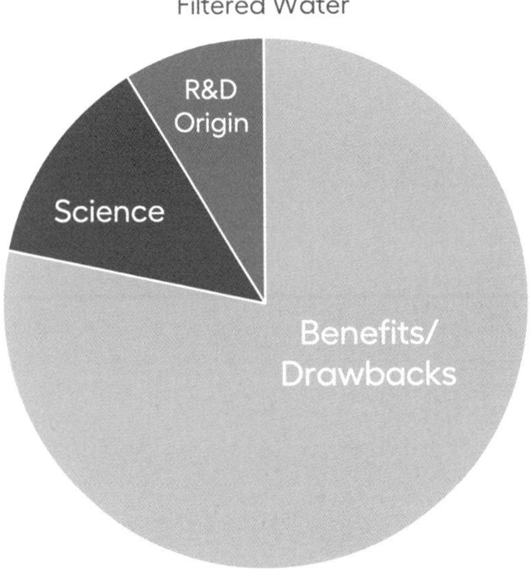

Figure 20.2 General public perception (filtered water), 2022. Courtesy of Kris Spiros.

primary perception. Now this may still seem like an apples or oranges comparison, but let's connect this to cultivated meat education. I conducted some of the first social science research on cultivated meat around ten years ago, and I would imagine the *what* is just starting to become embedded in people's minds – increasingly, the public is becoming aware of the concept that meat can be made in a lab, without an animal. So, just like filtered water, (at least some) people know what it is. And this is not a perfect understanding either, mind you. I can report, anecdotally, that hundreds of people I speak with often mistake the concept of cultivated meat for the very different concept of plant-based meat. This happens all the time. In other words, they are synonymizing 'synthetic meat' across the board, including both cultivated and plant-based meat, in their mental perception.

Moving forward, the *how* comes next. This lags slightly behind the *what* but fundamentally, the *what* leads us to the *how*. Because the *what* makes someone think that cultivated meat is meat *from* a lab, people may conclude that it is made with science in some way or artificially produced. Now lastly, and most importantly, the *why*. This is what will determine global success or failure. Also, remember, that the *why* is likely the main reason filtered water succeeded . . . people know why it is good. I would venture a guess, that the *why* lags significantly behind the *what* and *how* for cultivated meat. The average person who knows or has heard of cultivated meat has yet to know why it is a good or bad thing. They likely see minimal issues with the meat they so often consume; maybe subconsciously, they are not unaware that it harms animals or the planet in certain ways, but I am personally not so sure that they are connecting those dots that cultivated meat would alleviate them of that. If those issues were of such serious concern to them, they likely would take some sort of action, perhaps becoming a vegetarian or vegan, but they are smaller concerns in the grand scheme of things, and so I would imagine a vague interpretation of a new concept is unlikely to spawn a solution-oriented mindset. In other words, I doubt they instantly connect the dots to think, 'Because cultivated meat comes from a lab, it therefore does not hurt animals anymore and has less environmental harm; I now have an easy, morally virtuous product option that I will transition my purchase behaviours to.' I think cultivated meat requires much conceptual repetition, like an educational concept, and its potential upside requires even further explanation, but the point is, we are missing the *why*. If cultivated meat eventually follows a trajectory where it has immense market prospect, then global familiarity can't look like the image that follows where the *why* is excluded from the perception of the general public.

And so, ought that not be an imperative in global education for cultivated meat? People must have a more complete view of cultivated meat and not only think of the *what* and *how*. When the public considers filtered water, they don't instantly perceive water filters as the place they were produced or the device that filters the water itself, but instead they have a holistic perception, which may include all of the perceptions we discussed to varying degrees (the *why* likely foremost). But that is different from what the public does with cultivated meat. They think of labs first and benefits last (if at all). Contrarily, advocates and stakeholders think of labs last and benefits first. The *why* may not be a priority yet since cultivated meat is not on international markets, but that will soon change, and then the *what* and *how* will do little.

In the end, all educational angles must be tackled, and as a start, since most people who can understand what cultivated meat is do not yet know, we must start with the *what* as any new concept has done in history. But soon, billions of people must learn the *why* for cultivated meat; for it to succeed, they must learn that it is positive. For it to fail, they must learn that it is negative overall. And notably, if they do not perceive it positively, failure is imminent down two distinct paths – people will perceive cultivated meat at net neutral/negative, leading to consumers avoiding it on the marketplace, or perhaps

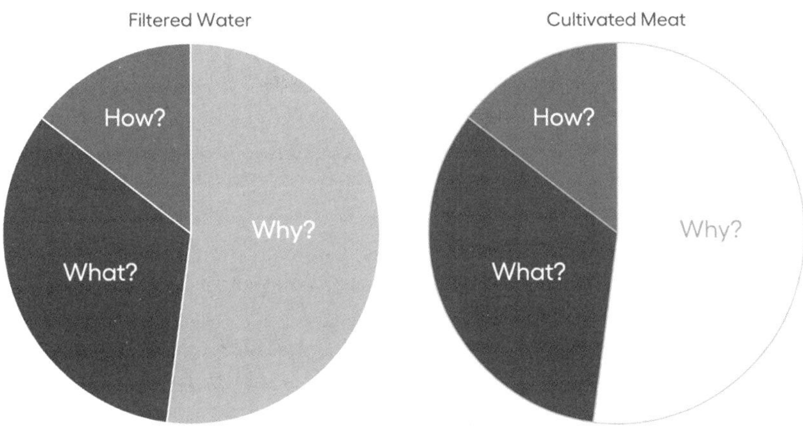

Figure 20.3 General public perception (filtered water vs cultivated meat), 2022. Courtesy of Kris Spiros.

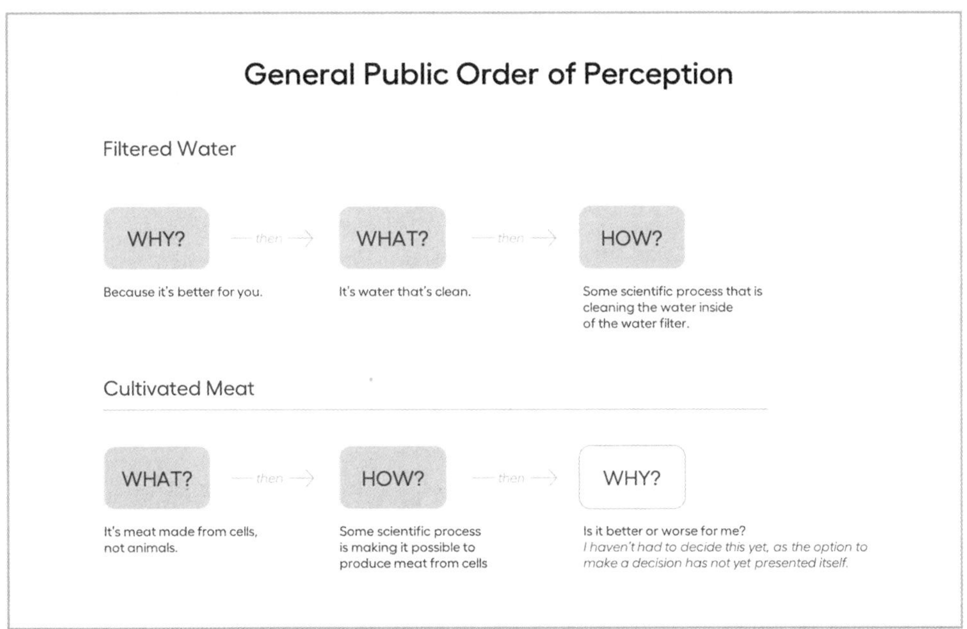

Figure 20.4 General public order of perception (filtered water vs cultivated meat), 2022. Courtesy of Kris Spiros.

even worse, cultivated meat will fail to reach any legitimate relevancy and will be doomed to a fate of invisibility.

To conclude, there are limited relevant case studies for cultivated meat; commonly used examples fall short on multiple metrics. But filtered water can teach us that it is possible to create a perception where a highly ingestible product, likely the most in the world, water, can have its basis undergo a significant transformation, more aligned with most people's values (a clean and healthy product). This required a global education effort on the *why*, specifically understanding that a different process can be applied to the preparation of water that makes it healthier and generally superior to its more 'natural' counterpart. In the end, billions of people believe that filtered water is 'better for them' than unfiltered water. Very simple. The education surrounding filtered water was conceptualized and designed to teach that it is better, even at a rudimentary level. It did not overcomplicate. It stuck to simple details, so an overindulgence on details can be helpful to a minority of people interested in learning more, but the simplest tenets are what an educational campaign must stick to.

Let us now turn our attention to how visual education may play a role in cultivated meat's future.

Visual design for education

For a concept being introduced to the world in the twenty-first century, the importance of visual education cannot be overstated. Good visual design, and design overall, can help someone understand the basis behind something, whether abstract or direct. Often, the better something is designed, the easier it is to interpret. In other words . . .

Design = Optimal Communication

A map designer, for example, seeks to communicate with their future viewers by creating as clear and concise directions as possible; if they designed their maps poorly, they would not be able to communicate as well as if they used good design principles and everything was clear and easily interpretable. Then, there are very good abstract, metaphorical designs that often optimally communicate complicated messages, but I digress. As it pertains to optimizing communication through design, the current visual landscape of cultivated meat could be better crafted. It is actually not designed much at all. People with loose interpretations of the concept are the ones who have primarily designed the majority of material that the public is familiar with.

If you do a Google Image Search for cultivated meat, you will see an endless display of petri dishes and lab imagery . . . and this represents the visual domain for the censored term 'cultivated meat' (you can imagine what something like 'lab-grown meat' would display). The current visual landscape is largely comprised of content that outsiders created, not cultivated meat stakeholders who know the details of the concept; what you will see on Google and beyond is sensationalistic imagery, primarily developed by the press. For their means, it is understandably meant to convey something quickly in an emotionally provocative manner. But how is this visual landscape communicating cultivated meat to the world? At present, cultivated meat as visually designed in the public's mind instils fear and disgust. People experiencing cultivated meat in the visual realm, pre-commercialization, need to include important information. We previously spoke about minimizing complexity for educational efforts to succeed – ensuring the simplest tenets is what the global population will begin to get familiar with, namely, what cultivated meat is, how it is possible and why one should or should not consider it as a dietary option.

The current visual landscape is pushing people towards why they 'should not consider' cultivated meat instead of why they should. The problem here is not with a lack of positive material dominating this landscape but instead with a lack of accurate material, at least balancing the landscape. The key is not to brainwash the public but to level the scales; we ought to societally steelman the case for cultivated meat so future consumers can make decisions based on accurate information, helping them align with their values and purchase desires. There are likely corporate interests that will attempt to do the opposite:

unreflectively advance cultivated meat's positive perception to increase sales and adoption. And conversely, there will be opponents to the concept that biasedly argue for cultivated meat's restriction in the marketplace. But with both points of view available, visually, this sparks the healthy dialogue necessary for cultivated meat's true merits to shine.

For advocates who feel cultivated meat should not have to compete with false information, perhaps their confidence in the concept allows them to see that if cultivated meat's advantages are true, then that should save it in the court of public opinion. If cultivated meat truly is a panacea for many environmental, health and animal-welfare-related issues, it should have no trouble emerging victorious in the battleground of public discussion. Fierce debates lie ahead; indeed, many matters need clear answers, but designing a transparent system calls for materials that present cultivated meat for all it is. And the same goes for the opponents if cultivated meat is truly bad, conceptually. But balance is vital for consumers' access to accurate education.

Subconscious pre-marketing

As we contemplate the future of cultivated meat's market potential, we can draw upon other futuristic concepts poised to change the world. Let us consider the ambitions of interplanetary travel from SpaceX. While commercial trips to Mars are not possible at the time of writing this, there is interest from the public in travelling to Mars and living there. A 2021 YouGov poll found that one-quarter of Americans are interested in living in a Martian colony for the rest of their lives (2021). This represents an interesting perception that people have of interplanetary travel. The illusion that SpaceX has provided is one of excitement and adventure. They anticipate that a critical number of people would be willing to risk their lives and then dedicate the rest of their lives to the pursuit of becoming some of the first Martians. Why though? What could be tempting people to consider such a dangerous expedition, one they are placing so much trust in but fundamentally do not understand the science of very well?

The many people considering this opportunity are tremendously inspired by it; they express immense excitement, yet they aren't experts in rocket engineering, Martian climate science or truly aware of the full breadth of dangers that lie ahead . . . but their interest remains. I postulate that this could be the result of something called SPM. SPM is the concept that content which is originally focused on the future, generally fiction or science fiction in the form of books, films or other forms of media, by way of their popularity, can influence the general public either positively or negatively towards purchasing such products when they become real (going from fiction to reality). The media content that buyers previously experienced was a sort of pre-marketing, and since it was not directly related to any available product at the time, it was embedded subconsciously, having downstream impacts of increasing or decreasing the marketability of a future product. So, because of the positive SPM surrounding space travel, that in popular films and books it is generally presented as exciting and adventurous (and worth the risk, as happy endings often prevail in your favourite sci-fi movie), commercial space travel has an easier time actually getting customers in the real world whenever it becomes a possibility.

Let us return to our previous example. Consider what the many people interested in a Martian expedition imagine for such a prospective trip. Even more fundamentally, what emotions are elicited during such episodes of imagination? Perhaps feelings of exhilaration, exploration, fulfilment. Where is this coming from though – has SpaceX been that successful in its recent advertising efforts? Has NASA or any similar organization? The marketing metrics reflect that far more people are excited about space travel than have been directly influenced by SpaceX or similar marketing. But instead, this is where SPM comes into play.

People are intimately familiar with space and space travel to other planets, not because of SpaceX but because of ancillary material. One does not have to be obsessed with space to have decades of material being slowly baked into their subconscious. Even being peripherally aware of space and space travel from pop culture, cinema and the like starts to embed values into society at large. The excitement of space comes largely from the heavy lifting that *Star Trek*, *Star Wars* and many other films did to influence billions. There is no way to track this with certainty, but with these influences, the same level of excitement that SpaceX benefits from is likely to exist. Elon Musk himself has suggested that the early cultural influences he had as a child originally led to him founding SpaceX, and that they continue to drive his motivation to help humanity become an interplanetary species.

Next, let us consider flying cars. Not commonly known, but Uber Elevate is Uber's programme to introduce flying cars to the world. After announcing this in 2020, Uber received a considerable degree of interest and praise across its digital campaigns. Once more, I would imagine this is tied to the positive SPM of flying cars, as the vision Uber is capitalizing upon is already exciting. Before they even had to make the first marketing material, the 'pre-marketing' had been settling in the subconscious minds of generations of people.

Next, let us consider a less obviously positive, more unpredictable example of a futuristic concept's SPM – robotics and artificial intelligence (AI). Artificial general intelligence (AGI) poses many possible good and bad outcomes. Literature and movies have generally followed suit, though perhaps leaning on the 'bad', often as a plot point a protagonist must overcome. But these stories impact how the world views AI, especially relevant in the coming years as it becomes more present in everyday life. For instance, it is likely an AGI system will 'take sides' on issues based on the logic and reasoning that it functions upon (assuming that is indeed what gears its decision-making). As people hold pre-meditated notions of 'evil robots' from films and books, could this be the cudgel they use to decrease the legitimacy of AGI's probabilistic conclusions – conclusions the AGI may make that go against people's deeply held beliefs?

Lastly, let us consider cultivated meat in the context of SPM. When the public sees or hears about cultivated meat, a typical response is the 'ick' factor, or people think it is gross and unnatural. For SpaceX, people can draw on a vaguely positive memory of their enjoyment watching spaceships and other planets in *Star Wars*; for Uber Elevate, perhaps the light-hearted scenes in *Back to the Future* where the flying car is an iconic symbol; for AGI, perhaps the positive role that robotics and AI play in the film *Interstellar* or the negative roles presented in the novels/movie series *Terminator* or in *The Matrix.* But for cultivated meat, what is there? What past influences do people have that they can call back upon? What exists in people's subconscious minds, pushing them for or against the concept? On present-day marketing material for cultivated meat, I have seen people reply, 'Soylent Green is people!', so I suppose there are some influences in pop culture, but I am not sure they are very relevant for increasing any legitimate form of accurate understanding of cultivated meat.

While the perception from the public is getting more solidified by the day, it is important to tell a whole story of cultivated meat's potential, not a biased tale as is currently being done. If cultivated meat is to impact the world, people must first know what it is. If they first encounter it via an image of meat in a petri dish, that is likely to stick, considering there is no real SPM for cultivated meat (or that which does exist is notably negative). The first impressions of cultivated meat will reveal so much about its fate this century and beyond. And it will necessarily be different from how the world responds to large advertising campaigns from companies; product blunders can supersede that. Take the example of the cryptocurrency exchange and crypto hedge fund company FTX in late 2022. No celebrity or million-dollar Superbowl ad could save the product/company from the failures that took place and the grander, negative impacts on the concepts they represent, in this case, cryptocurrency, which come along with the failure. Cultivated meat's future lies in how it is designed for the world to learn about it. The murmurs from friends and the thoughts behind people's conscious minds inform so much about future decision-making in the marketplace, and cultivated meat must be designed with proper, accurate material to have any impact on the future of agriculture. Early cultivated meat products themselves, combined with the learning material the public will have at their disposal, offer deep insight into its future. Thank you for exploring these nuanced topics about cultivated meat and designing the future of agriculture.

Conclusion

Due to the tremendous quantity of animal products required from the world's demand, modern practices of animal farming are causing unprecedented public health, ethical and environmental problems. The issues from animal agriculture stem directly from the animal itself, an organism that within the context of a farm is a mere production mechanism. Through the latest advances, the possibility has arisen to redesign this system, to produce animal products without farming animals but instead by farming cells. This new concept proposes a shift from macroscopic production to that of microscopic. The macro-agricultural model used for millennia has depended on animals as machines within farming, while this new form of micro-agriculture leans on cells as the driving production conduit. The primary purpose for this flipping of the animal food and material production system on its head is varied, but at its core, it reflects a critical problem-solving philosophy. The ethos of this micro-agriculture method is that it posits that the problem with a product like meat or leather is not the 'how', but the 'cow'. If the resource-intensive, sentient organism that is a farm animal can be decoupled from its inherent production structure, perhaps many of the worst problems from animal agriculture would fade. I hope that this chapter provides an opportunity to illustrate cultivated meat's positioning as it relates to design and the creative sphere overall, specifically examining the importance of cultivated meat's educational design, which will ensure accurate consumer understanding at a global scale.

References

NSF International. 'More Than Half of Americans Are Concerned about Their Drinking Water'. https://www.nsf.org/news/more-than-half-of-americans-are-concerned-about-their-drinking-water

'Steve Jobs on Marketing and Values.' YouTube, uploaded by PodiumVC, 13 September 2018. https://youtu.be/4mvHgLy_YV8

Wikipedia. 'Water Filter'. Accessed 10 February 2023. https://en.wikipedia.org/wiki/Water_filter

YouGov. 'Americans' Interest in Living on Mars: Poll'. 15 July 2021. https://today.yougov.com/topics/travel/articles-reports/2021/07/15/americans-interest-living-mars-poll

AFTERWORD

Elio Caccavale and Gordon Hush

Design Beyond the Human invites a reconsideration of the verities of contemporary design, the technological advances underpinning material wellbeing, leisure as freedom and the centrality of the human user (modelled to a greater or lesser extent upon the capitalist consumer) against a backdrop of increasing ecological concern and the consequences of modern life for the planet and its multifarious inhabitants. Furthermore, it interrogates historical accounts, offers theoretical and conceptual reflections and draws upon diverse examples of contemporary responses to the planetary predicament seen through the eyes of local practitioners, populations and ways of living.

The primary methodological ambition was the formulation of a transdisciplinary conversation capable of rising to the challenge of our era, the generation of a conceptual framework that permits engagement with the contemporary experience of life on Earth in all its diversity but which also acknowledges the universal impact of human life/behaviour upon the planet and its inhabitants. Secondly, implicit in this approach is the theoretical reflection upon traditional disciplinary accounts, their ingrained anthropocentrism and aligned geographical and political biases; the development of a critical and conceptual framework that extends beyond the academic approaches of the 'Global North', which 'de-centres' the anthropocentrism of post-imperial capitalism and seeks to acknowledge alternative, marginalized or threatened understandings of ecology and Indigenous existence; and, thirdly, to identify, share and promote a variety of practice-based examples that exemplify local, specific and lived responses to the current and emerging planetary context. This tripartite structure exposes and undermines a putative hegemony, a view of the planet as a singular astronomical and geological entity, perceived and understood in a uniform manner and terminology.

Design Beyond the Human proposes and offers a model of a transdisciplinary approach and the conversational or discursive opportunities that arise from it. In assembling a diverse range of disciplinary inputs, theoretical and critical positions, practical and historical examples, lived experiences and terminological frameworks, this collaborative undertaking seeks to engender conversations that have been previously stifled, rendered partial or deliberately disavowed. As Tyson Yunkaporta explains, 'Solutions to complex problems take many dissimilar minds and points of view to design, so we have to do that together, linking up with as many other 'us-twos' as we can to form networks of dynamic interaction. We are not offering expert answers, only different questions, and ways of looking at things' (2022, 23). In seeking a *planetary conversation* that is founded upon the critique of anthropocentric, progress-driven accounts authored by the 'Global North', the authors convened here seek to interrogate, unpick and rebut the narrative power of contemporary geopolitics and its received wisdom. In place of a conversation describing the planet and its current predicament authored by the privileged and the powerful, by science and its metrics, by economics and wealth founded upon continual growth, there is a gathering of voices, positions and beliefs – contained within the text are the raw materials of conversations yet to unfold, uncontained and inherently questioning of the status quo.

In place of the planet is sought the *planetary* (Ochu & Ward 2024), foregrounding the particular relational position of each author and essay, the recognition of the value of the constituent element, the contribution in combination, as the basis of conversation and understanding. The *planetary* as the relational appreciation of the planet begins with the movement *beyond the human*, with the interrogation of the gendered and patriarchal concept of the human, with the rejection of the imperial and ethnic categorization of experience that is rooted in the human, with a critique of the economic and ecological subjugation of the non-human. In foregrounding a *planetary conversation* (unending and multiple) forged in the relational understanding offered by transdisciplinary engagement, *Design Beyond the Human* rejects the dynamic nominalism of the Enlightenment encyclopaedia – the arrangement of scientifically ordered contents – in favour of accounts arising from situated experiences and local responses.

The methodological ambitions of this collected and collaborative volume are reflected in its structure and constituent elements, to reveal the asymmetries of power, the absences and the prohibitions enshrined in much of the contemporary literature that claims to describe the ecological crisis facing 'the planet'. The text attempts to critique, theorize and exemplify a relational understanding of the contemporary, to initiate conversations that are *planetary* and which speak to the variety of existence on the planet. This remains the case even where *Design Beyond the Human* itself is unable to represent each and every voice or position, where an *aporia* is evident, where absence requires remedy through an invitation to speak. In advocating a transdisciplinary conception of Design that goes *beyond the human* in addressing the *planetary moment* and *situation*, the authors question the disciplines, methods and terminology of accepted wisdom in favour of a conversation that contests the concept of *Anthropos*, its bloody history and the terminology it has bequeathed.

We may never know what has been lost to humanity with the suppression of many Indigenous cultures. Each represents a unique worldview and a history of environmental experience that potentially had and still has something to offer our global civilization in contending with today's situation (Ehrlich 2008). The genocide, the poisoned lakes, the biodiversity sacrificed, the garbage islands in our oceans and the space junk are all somewhere else for the 'Global North' inhabitants – distant in time and space and, so, in causality. We are not alone, were never alone, but we imagined that we were.

When Robinson Crusoe washed up on that island, when imperial soldiers and 'peaceful settlers' arrived in what they called the New World, they saw it as empty, as waiting for them, a productive resource capable of being worked into paradise on Earth. But they were never alone; other human beings, civilizations, plants and animals, entire ecosystems that had existed and evolved over uncounted generations were removed from sight, from the senses and from history (Ishikawa 2024) – the myth of progress conveniently allowing the re-positioning of the 'other' into an elsewhere and elsewhen. Everything is still there. We are not alone. Virtually everything that has ever lived, and died, on Earth is still there. Somewhere. Not immediately available to be seen or acknowledged, but there. And, like the repressed, it will return. So, while the James Webb Space Telescope scans the cosmos in search of extra-terrestrial life, let's try to do better—with each other and with all life forms on Earth. Otherwise, when the time comes, it will be hard to explain to any new friends that we are a human-centred planet, unworthy of the Latin adjective *sapiens* that we gave ourselves around 200,000 years ago.

CONTRIBUTORS

Samer Akkach is a professor of architectural history and theory and the founding director of the Centre for Asian and Middle Eastern Architecture at the University of Adelaide, Australia. His interdisciplinary research includes the history and theory of architecture and landscape, early modern Arab-Islamic intellectual and socio-urban histories, the history of Islamic science and Islamic cosmology, philosophy and mysticism. He is the author of *Cosmology and Architecture in Premodern Islam* (2005); *Islam and the Enlightenment* (2007); and *Istanbul Observatory* (2017); and the editor of *'Ilm: Science, Religion and Art in Islam* (2019) and *Naẓar: Vision, Belief, and Perception in Islamic Cultures* (2022).

Rachel Armstrong is a senior TED Fellow and professor of Regenerative Architecture at KU Leuven, Belgium. She researches the inner life of 'things' seen and unseen and experiments with the very stuff of life to ask how we may design and build our world differently. Armstrong was a Rising Waters II fellow with the Robert Rauschenberg Foundation, a fellow of the British Interplanetary Society and a 2010 senior TED fellow. She was the coordinator for the EU Living Architecture (2016–19) and Active Living Infrastructure: Controlled Environment (ALICE) (2019–21) projects. Armstrong is the author of *Soft Living Architecture* (2018) and *Experimental Architecture* (2019).

Priyanka Bista is a Nepali-Canadian multispecies designer and educator working on biodiversity conservation. She is the co-founder of the Vertical University project, which harnesses the learning potential inherent in the vertical gradient of Nepal, starting at a 67-metre elevation in Koshi Tappu to Mount Kanchenjunga at 8,586 metres. Her work has won numerous awards, including the What Design Can Do Challenge, the Energy Globe Award, the *S*EED Public Interest Design Award and the UIAA Mountain Protection Award. In 2019, Bista was selected as a Visiting Faculty Fellow for the Design for Spatial Justice Initiative at the University of Oregon, and in 2022, she received a Joseph F. Thomas Visiting Professorship at Carnegie Mellon University.

Joanna Boehnert is a senior lecturer at Bath School of Design, working on two Art and Humanities Research Council (AHRC)-funded projects and teaching in the Historical and Critical Studies programme. From 2023 to 2026, she will work as an Innovation Scholar on the Transition Templates: Pathways to Net Zero project with Livework, a service design consultancy in London. Her second research project is Enacting Gregory Bateson's Ecological Aesthetics in Architecture and Design on an AHRC-funded research project led by the University of Brighton and Bauhaus-Universität Weimar. Boehnert is the author of *Design, Ecology, Politics: Towards the Ecocene* (2018).

Elio Caccavale is a professor of transdisciplinary design innovation at The Glasgow School of Art, UK. He is the subject Lead for the MDes in Design Innovation and Citizenship. His teaching practice explores how design can foster more equitable relationships among all living beings and ecological systems – recognising their 'citizenship' within an expanded, more-than-human conception of society. Elio's research investigates the ethical, social and environmental dimensions of scientific knowledge and emerging technologies.

Danielle Celermajer is a social policy professor at the University of Sydney, the deputy director of the Sydney Environment Institute and the director of the Multispecies Justice project. Her current research explores how we rethink the concept of justice when the subjects of justice include humans, other animals and the environment and their relationships with each other. Her books include *Sins of the Nation and the Ritual of Apology* (2009), *The Prevention of Torture: An Ecological Approach* (2018), *The Subject of Human Rights* (2020), *The Cultural History of Law in the Modern Age* (2021) and *Summertime: Reflections on a Vanishing Future* (2021).

Domitilla Dardi is a design editor and curator, and lecturer in design history at the European Institute of Design (IDE) in Rome. She has held visiting professor positions at several institutions, including the Universidad de Navarra in Pamplona, MADE in Siracusa and Abadir Academy in Catania. From 2007 to 2023, she was a senior design curator at the MAXXI museum in Rome and in 2019, she co-founded the International Fair of Independent Design (Edit) in Naples. She has authored several publications, including *Achille Castiglioni* (2001), *Design in 100 Objects* (2008), *Herbaria* (2022), *Playgrounding* (2022) and *Bestiaria* (2023).

Matthew Darmour-Paul is a researcher and designer based in Sydney, Australia. His work explores architecture's entanglement within political ecology, ruralization, the physical infrastructure of the internet and the financialization of nature. In 2019, he co-founded Feral Partnerships, a collective that focuses on reclaiming architectural knowledge in an age of rapid biodiversity loss and species extinction as spatial practices in the pursuit of multispecies flourishing. Darmour-Paul has worked for and with artists, architects, sociologists and anthropologists in Australia, Europe, the Middle East and the United States. He holds a BA in Architecture from Iowa State University (USA) and an MA in Architecture from the Royal College of Art (UK).

Kate Fletcher is a professor of sustainability, design and fashion systems at Manchester School of Art & Design, Manchester Metropolitan University. Her work explores systems change, post-growth fashion, fashion localism, decentring durability and Earth Logic, defining and challenging the field of fashion and sustainability. She has written and/or edited twelve books available in eight languages. Fletcher is a co-founder of the Union of Concerned Researchers in Fashion. Her most recent work is about design, clothing and nature.

Helen Hollyman is a journalist, editor, podcast host, cookbook author and brand strategist. She is the founding editor in chief of MUNCHIES, the world's first global Millennial food website and digital media channel from VICE Media, and former editor in chief of Thrillist, a lifestyle website from Vox Media. She hosts and writes the Ambie-nominated Best True Crime podcast, *The Paddlefish Caviar Heist*, from Imperative Entertainment and Vespucci. Hollyman is the co-author of *MUNCHIES: Late-Night Meals* *from the World's Best Chefs* (2017). After receiving two certifications in the Circular Economy from the Ellen MacArthur Foundation and UC Berkeley in 2021, Hollyman has shifted her focus as a journalist to regenerative farming through a circular lens.

Gordon Hush is a professor of innovation and society and head of the School of Innovation and Technology at The Glasgow School of Art, UK. He is a sociologist, with an interest in the way that design-led innovation initiates and informs social, economic and ecological change. He is keen to explore the ways in which scientific or technological expertise are incorporated within or applied to the material circumstances and design outcomes which shape human experience, and the consequences that these have for life on the planet.

Desiree Hernandez Ibinarriaga is an Indigenous Mexican design researcher with Chamula (Mayan), Nahua (Aztec) and Euskaldunak (Basque) heritage. She is a design lecturer at Monash University and unit coordinator for Indigenous Research Methods at the Wominjeka Djeembana Lab. Hernandez Ibinarriaga's practice focuses on Indigenous peoples' building capacity and better ways of partnership, collaboration and communication between Indigenous and non-Indigenous people through design. Her work aims to acknowledge and recognize the relationality between people and Place while privileging Indigenous knowledge by enhancing biocultural diversity conservation and regeneration towards collaborative resilience, cultural identity pride and sustainability.

Noboru Ishikawa is a professor of anthropology at the Center for Southeast Asian Studies at Kyoto University, Japan. He has conducted fieldwork in Malaysia and Indonesia, exploring issues such as the construction of national space in the borderland, highland-lowland relations, the stateless in Southeast Asian histories, the plantation system, the commodification of natural resources and relations between nature and non-nature in the Anthropocene. His publications include *Between Frontiers: Nation and Identity in a Southeast Asian Borderland* (2010), *Transborder Governance of Forests, Rivers and Seas* (2010) and *Flows and Anthropogenic Tropical Forests: Human-Nature Interfaces on the Plantation Frontier* (2019).

Steven McMullen is an associate professor of economics at Hope College in Holland, Michigan, a Fellow at the Oxford Centre for Animal Ethics and executive editor of the journal *Faith & Economics*. His research interests include inequality, consumerism, education policy, animal and environmental ethics and theology. He has done extensive writing and speaking about animal and environmental ethics, particularly dealing with the ways economic relationships influence animal welfare and ethical decision-making. His book *Animals and the Economy* (2016) explores the ethics of animal consumption, production, experimentation and ownership, and examines pro-animal policy options.

J. Paul Neeley is a speculative designer and researcher exploring the social, cultural, economic and ethical implications of emerging technologies. His projects explore climate change, happiness, future mobility, AI, synthetic biology and issues of complexity and computational irreducibility in design and business. He consults in speculative design at Neeley Worldwide, addresses critical issues facing humanity at the School of Critical Design and explores happiness at Masamichi Souzou. He is a visiting tutor in Service Design at the Royal College of Art. Neeley has been a guest lecturer at Imperial College, London Business School, Rhode Island School of Design, Architecture Association, New York University, Köln International School of Design and School of Visual Arts.

François-Xavier Nzi iyo Nsenga is an independent scholar reflecting on design research and practice in sub-Saharan Africa. He was born in Rwanda, grew up in Congo and since 1972 has lived in Québec, Canada. He trained in industrial design, ergonomics and sociology in Nairobi and Montréal. He frequently contributes to the online *PhD-Design List* and has published his thoughts, findings and writings in various publications, including the *Design Philosophy Papers*. Since 2014, following his retirement to the Northern Rwanda countryside, he has been developing a variety of products using local Indigenous plants and flowers.

Erinma Ochu trained originally as a biologist, and their transdisciplinary research practice critically examines the world-making potential of subcultures of creative technology and science practice as a means to re-examine possibilities for life. They are Wallscourt Associate Professor of Immersive Media at UWE Bristol, in the Digital Cultures Research Centre in Pervasive Media Studios at Watershed in Bristol and a member of UWE's Critical Race and Culture Network. As the co-director of Squirrel Nation Studio, they are an alumni of the Stuart Hall Scholars and Fellows Network and Manchester International Festival/ Jerwood Fellowships. They are the co-editor of the book series *Digital Materialities and Sustainable Futures*.

Erin O'Donnell is a senior lecturer and ARC research fellow at the University of Melbourne Law School. She is recognized internationally for her research into the field of legal rights for rivers and the challenges and opportunities these new rights create for protecting the multiple social, cultural and natural values of rivers. Her work is informed by comparative analysis across Australia, New Zealand, the United States, India, Colombia and Chile. Erin is the author of *Legal Rights for Rivers: Competition, Collaboration, and Water Governance* (2018). In 2018, she was appointed to the inaugural Birrarung Council, the Voice of the Yarra River.

John Powell is a visiting research fellow in the School of Architecture and the Built Environment at the University of Adelaide, Australia. His academic interests lie at the intersection of music, philosophy and landscape architecture. He is the author of *Gardens, Music, and Time* (2010), *What Is Temporal Art?* (2015) and *Dancing with Time: The Garden as Art* (2019). His current research project considers composers' musical accounts of their encounters and perceptions of natural and designed landscapes, including gardens, and the ways in which those musical accounts are received by listeners.

James Skeet is the co-founder of Covenant Pathways, a Navajo-led educational non-profit organization in Vanderwagen, New Mexico. He is passionate about connecting the heart and soul of all peoples to the land through Indigenous Regenerative Intelligence that integrates the ancient wisdom of Native cosmology. James is a full-blooded Navajo Native American from Vanderwagen, New Mexico, where he and his wife run the experiential Spirit Farm, which uses only natural practices, including microbiological composting. Spirit Farm aims to recover and reclaim traditional farming and spiritual practices to transform our way of life and health, reducing the dependency on the food system that is harming us.

Xinlin Song is an educator, writer and programme director at Yunhe Centre, a place-based learning programme founded in 2015 in Danba, Garzê Tibetan Autonomous Prefecture, Western Sichuan Province, China. Her research explores new economic theories and Indigenous ecological knowledge. Song has facilitated numerous collaborations between institutions, corporations and organizations in China and beyond, including TEDxShanghai, Beijing Design Week, Central Academy of Fine Arts (Beijing), Studio Roosegaarde, Open Heart Design Alliance, Office for Metropolitan Architecture and the Guggenheim Museum. She is currently working with the Yunhe Centre to develop programmes and experiences that facilitate a process of *De-learn*, *Re-learn*, and *Re-member*.

Kris Spiros is the founder of the Cellular Agriculture Society (CAS) and former VIP Venture of the Harvard Innovation Lab. In 2017, he published *Nature & the Neomnivore*, the first comprehensive environmental report on cellular agriculture. In 2018, he launched CAS, a non-profit organization which aims to increase global awareness of cellular agriculture and cultivated meat. Since then, CAS has released the Harvard and Stanford-profiled publication *90 Reasons to Consider Cellular Agriculture* (2019), unveiled the first design for a future cultivated meat facility called Project CMF at Google NYC, co-developed the first university course on cellular agriculture, hosted by Stanford University, and created the first textbook on cellular agriculture.

Peter Sutoris is an associate professor in climate and development at the Sustainability Research Institute, University of Leeds, and Honorary Senior Research Associate at University College London. He is the author of the documentary film *The Undiscovered Country* and two books, *Visions of Development* (2016) and *Educating for the Anthropocene* (2022). Originally from Slovakia, he has lived and worked in India, Nepal, South Africa, Nigeria, Uganda, Tanzania, Bosnia and Herzegovina, the Marshall Islands, the United States and the United Kingdom. His research focuses on how different groups of people imagine the future differently as well as on identifying pathways towards a radical reimagination of sustainability.

Alice Twemlow is a research professor at the Royal Academy of Art, The Hague (KABK), and a professor of history, theory and sociology of graphic design and visual culture at the University of Amsterdam. Her research is at the intersection of design history, environmental humanities and artistic research and explores the relationship between geological time and design, space junk and walking as a research method. Twemlow's current research projects include Design and the Deep Future, which aims to contribute alternative interpretations, interventions and imaginaries to climate and environmental justice research. She is the author of *Sifting the Trash: A History of Design Criticism* (2017).

Felipe Viveros is a British-Chilean writer, researcher and artist. He is a visiting lecturer at Schumacher College, UK, and the Austral University in Chile, has served as the European Representative of the GNH Centre Bhutan, the Board Chair of The Rules and at the Sacred Head Waters Initiative, and is a member of the UN Harmony with Nature initiative. His work focuses on the intersection of digital storytelling, policy and systems change. He helped to co-found Culture Hack Labs in 2018 and now works for them as an independent advisor on global projects. He is a co-founder of Choose Earth, an initiative to centre the voices of Indigenous peoples.

Naiyi Wang is a curator, writer and lecturer in Curating Contemporary Design, Design Criticism and Curatorial Studies at the d-School of China Central Academy of Fine Arts. Her recent curatorial projects include *Material Tales: The Life of Things* (Design Museum London, 2020) and the *Care Pavilion* at the London Design Biennale (2023). Previously, she has curated/co-curated exhibitions at the 4th Istanbul Design Biennial, CAFA Art Museum, London Design Festival, Milan Design Week and Stanley Picker

Gallery. Her translation work includes *The Curatorial: A Philosophy of Curating* (2015), *Wild Things: The Material Culture of Everyday Life* (2020) and *Sifting the Trash: A History of Design Criticism* (2017).

Caroline Ward is a PhD student in the School of Architecture at the Royal College of Art. She is a designer and researcher whose practice spans moving images and digital interactions. Caroline is a strategic design thinker with fifteen years of experience designing systems, public interventions and cross-disciplinary research to address climate change, urban, broadcast and future media challenges. Her critical practice explores the public imagination as a contested site and is focused on posthuman perspectives informed by architecture, human sciences and critical ecologies. Ward has worked as a senior designer and researcher at BBC Future Experiences and The Helen Hamlyn Centre for Design.

INDEX